Robin Eggar worked in the music business for RCA Records and as a punk rock group manager before becoming a writer. He has contributed to *The Times*, *Sunday Times*, *Mail on Sunday*, *Daily Telegraph*, *You* magazine, *Esquire* and *GQ*. The numerous stars he has profiled include Tina Turner, Frank Sinatra, David Bowie, Michael Douglas, Janet Jackson and Mick Jagger. He has written six previous books on a wide variety of subjects. *Tom Jones* is his first biography.

He lives in London.

TOM JONES

THE BIOGRAPHY

ROBIN EGGAR

headline

For my mother Pamela Eggar
As always . . . Jacqui, Jordan and Rowan

First published in 2000
by HEADLINE BOOK PUBLISHING

First published in paperback in 2001
by HEADLINE BOOK PUBLISHING

10 9 8 7 6 5 4

ISBN 0 7472 6247 0

Typeset by Avon Dataset Ltd, Bidford-on-Avon, Warks

Printed and bound in Great Britain by
Mackays of Chatham plc, Chatham, Kent

HEADLINE BOOK PUBLISHING
A division of Hodder Headline
338 Euston Road
London NW1 3BH

www.headline.co.uk
www.hodderheadline.com

CONTENTS

ACKNOWLEDGEMENTS

W hen I first decided to write a biography of Tom Jones
I determined that it must be my take on his
extraordinary career and should not be compromised
by being seen as 'authorised' in any way. However, before I wrote a
word I met with Mark and Donna Woodward and told them my
intentions. Since then we have met and spoken on a number of
occasions. While I am sure they would prefer I had never started,
every time I asked for information or tickets to see Tom perform
they were always courteous and helpful. Without Mark, Tom would
not be the international figure he is today.

At the very core of the book are some four hours of interviews
I conducted with Tom Jones in Melbourne, Australia, in November
1990 and in New York City in October 1994. During those periods
I shadowed him to concerts, TV studios, a boat in Sydney harbour,
and enjoyed a couple of very fine dinners and many more drinks.
Since then we have met and spoken briefly at various parties and
social functions – most recently backstage after the Brit Awards on
3 March 2000.

In the past two years I have conducted over sixty interviews, either face to face or on the telephone. My thanks to all of you and to anyone who I have inadvertently omitted. The mistake is mine.

Extra special thanks must first go to the ladies: Mary Wilson – thanks for lunch; Darlene Love, who still has the voice of an angel; Annie Toomaru – next time I'm in LA, I promise; intrepid Pyramid explorer Brooke Shields; and Nanci Eisner, whose enthusiasm for both Tom and life itself is infectious. Nanci was extremely helpful in pointing out mistakes and misspellings in the first edition of this book.

Chris Ellis, who had previously never talked to anyone, provided hours of entertainment, insight and anecdotes about his years working for Tom. His wife Eva cooked us fine meals and let us talk long into the night. Vernon Hopkins, Mickey Gee, Vic Cooper and Chris Slade remembered their stories about the old days with the Senators and the Squires and in doing so reopened old wounds.

In Pontypridd, Tommy Pitman, Keith Davies, Charlie Ashman and Joan Lister shared their memories of the time before Tom Jones. Ken Evans gave me some excellent background information, and the staff at the Pontypridd library and the *Pontypridd Observer* were extremely helpful. David and Chrissie Evans housed and fed me.

Song writer and musical arranger, Les Reed, lyric writer, Barry Mason, and record producer, Peter Sullivan, told me so much about their business and craft that I hope they will finally be recognised for their essential and often underrated contribution to making Tom Jones an international superstar.

For background on the inner workings of the music business and MAM in the sixties and seventies many thanks are due to: Barry Dickins of ITB; Paul Russell of Sony Music Europe; Jonathan Morrish, Ian Wright, John Giddings, Roger Greenaway at ASCAP; Guy Holmes and Tracey Fox at Gut Records; the effervescent Larry Page; Paul Anka; Rodney Birbeck; David

Hughes; and Johnny Rogan, whose *Starmakers and Svengalis* is essential reading for anybody interested in how the 'biz' used to work. Thanks also to Bill Smith for an illuminating lunch and I hope you're back on the golf course.

My first visit to Las Vegas would have been disastrous without the assistance of: Charles Mather; Gene Kilroy; Ilario Pesco; Chas del Guercio; Joe Delaney; Don Tel; Denny Walker; Myram Borders; Sonny King; and Bob Maheu. And thanks to Charlotte Richards for letting me be the witness to a wedding ceremony in a hot-air balloon at the Little White Wedding Chapel in the Sky.

Scattered around the world are many people to whom I owe much thanks: especially Samantha Eggar and Jeffrey Berkowitz; George Acogni, Versa Manos, Frances Schoenberger, Burt Boyar and Ann Carli in LA; Christa Wenzl, Tine Wittler and Marie Von Waldburg in Germany; Martin Dunn, Steve Lynas, Paul O'Donnell, Mark Hattersley and the other staff at Associated New Media who gave me a home when the builders had devastated mine; and not forgetting Tina Turner, Roger Davies, Troy Dante, Terry O'Neill, Scott Dorsey, Janie Jones, Chris Montgomery, Jonathan Ross, Lenny Henry and Jo Mills who all contributed time and insight; photographer George Bodnar, who first introduced me to Tom in 1990; Tim Ewbank, Margarette Driscoll, Mary Riddell and David Thomas gave me useful advice and assistance on matters of fact; the staff at the News International Library where I did my initial research; Alex Fairtlough sent me some obscure cuttings that I would otherwise have missed; Jon Scoffield shared the experience and knowledge that made *This is Tom Jones* such an integral part of Tom's career, while Frank Chapman gave his view from the floor; producer Graham Smith, whose work on the *Last Resort, The Right Time* and *An Audience with Tom Jones* has introduced Tom to a much younger audience; Suzanne Phillips, who directed the *Green Green Grass of Home* documentary; Bernard Doherty, Claire Singers, Richard Beck and all the staff of LD Publicity; Rob Partridge and the staff of Coalition PR; Caroline Turner at Hyperactive; Niki

Turner, Bernie Kilmartin, Lee Ellen Newman and Lisa Anderson at the Brits. All of them have answered my ceaseless questions.

There have been other books on Tom Jones which proved most helpful. *Tom Jones: The Boy from Nowhere* by Colin MacFarlane (W. H. Allen 1988), *Tom Jones: Biography of a Great Star* by Peter Jones (Barker 1970), *Tom Jones: A Biography* by Stafford Hildred and David Gritten (Sidgwick and Jackson 1990) and *Tom Jones: Close Up* by Lucy Ellis and Bryony Sutherland (Omnibus 2000).

Since the first publication of *Tom Jones: The Biography*, and its accompanying website www.tomjonesbiography.com, I have received e-mails and communications from Tom Jones fans around the world. They have corrected errors of fact, questioned my interpretation of events and related their own experiences with Tom. Some of their input can be found in this edition of the book. Special thanks to Keith Cooper at Jones The Voice (www.jonesthevoice.com).

Sadly Burk Zanft, Dai Perry and Lord Grade have all died since I started researching the book. They are all missed by their family and friends.

Thanks also to: Stuart Millar at Travel Centre who knows how to stretch a travel budget; Clare Webber of Wordware who transcribed most of the interviews – four letter words and all; Doug Young, Lorraine Jerram, Jo Roberts-Miller and Heather Holden-Brown at Headline Book Publishing.

Special thanks are due to longstanding Tom Jones fan Julian Alexander of Lucas Alexander Whitley. As my agent, not only did he keep on at me to write the book but without him I would never have been able to finish it.

My family and friends have had to live with Tom and me for the past two years. Special thanks are due to fellow writers Simon Kinnersley, Barry Miles, Rosemary Bailey and Alexandra Campbell for the loan of source material, rare books and interview transcripts. But more than that . . . their support, advice and encouragement kept me going when I wanted to give it all up.

Diane Bonham looked after the children through thick and thin. Martin and Sue (who will now have to endure further gibes about her 'boyfriend Tom') Sinnatt.

Most of all I could never have done it without the constant love and encouragement of my wife, Jacqui, and my children, Jordan and Rowan.

So it is with great relief that I write these words: 'Yes, Rowan. I really have finished Tom Jones.'

THE BRIT AWARDS
1998

The Brit Awards show, held on 9 February 1998, was the usual meet and greet, wine and dine, let's pat ourselves on the back and remember how cool Britannia is, music business awards show. The entertainment, provided by the Spice Girls, All Saints and others, proved a most acceptable background cabaret to drinking and bragging. Even the Docklands Arena, the most acoustically inept venue in Britain, began to acquire a rosy glow. No one took any risks, just sang their hits, shook their butts, or imported a gospel choir for background vocals. The usual awards stuff – all good for business – until the duet from the *Full Monty* soundtrack.

A twelve-piece band took the stage, complete with get-on-down bass and funky horns. Robbie Williams, once of Take That and a million bedroom posters, bounded on stage in a skintight, black leather catsuit, cut so tight in the crotch that several teenage girls considered fainting. Gyrating, vibrating, using every ounce of stage craft and vocal nuance he knew, Robbie belted into *You Can Leave Your Hat On*. The girls screamed, how they screamed. Then they stopped. They stopped to hear Tom Jones sing.

No one saw Tom walk on stage. He just materialised there, microphone in hand and opened his mouth. He hardly moved a muscle, just used the Voice. Every line he sang pushed Robbie on to sing better, to writhe harder. Robbie had never given a better performance in his life, but the end result was not so much a duet as a one-sided demonstration of how forty years of experience can leave no room for anyone else on the stage. The audience was mesmerised. When it was over they were on their feet cheering and whooping.

That was the night Robbie Williams grew up ... and Tom Jones became the epitome of cool.

Surprising considering that he was fifty-eight years old and had never been cool before. In fact for years Tom Jones had been the antithesis of cool, a living, breathing example of Jurassic showbiz naffness.

Yet in the soundtrack to my life, to the Baby Boomer generation's life, Tom has always been there. His early hits *It's Not Unusual, Green Green Grass of Home, Delilah* all resonated through my childhood. Unlike today when if a single doesn't debut in the Top 10 it's a flop, in the sixties singles took weeks, sometimes months, to get to number one. Most big hits seemed to be around for ever. Tom Jones's hits were around for forever. And a day. I didn't actually like them very much. Compared to the rawness of the Rolling Stones or Eric Burdon the arrangements were too overblown, altogether – that most damning of indictments – too middle-of-the-road.

But I can sing every word of them.

Tom Jones had the voice, he had the presence, the raw get down and dirty sex appeal. He had the black leather trousers and the grinding crotch. He could have become the greatest white soul singer of his generation, he could have been Joe Cocker with sex appeal – but he was out of sync with his times. The Beatles had turned the music industry into the record business. Before them the songwriter was king, the singer an interchangeable voice. Now the cool and the clever wrote their own songs – they earned more money too.

Tom Jones has never written his own hits. He can scarcely manage three chords on a guitar. The fact that at his peak he could sing better than anyone alive, sorry Frank, sorry Elvis, has never been considered relevant. We had Janis, Jimi and Jim, Jagger and Plant, Lennon and McCartney. They had attitude. Tom Jones wore a dinner jacket, for chrissake. He sang in front of an orchestra.

Thirty years ago Tom Jones abandoned his opportunity to become a rock icon, without a backward glance. Instead he became a Las Vegas superstar. He does not see that as unfulfilled potential for his cup still brims over with vintage champagne, and cognacs almost as old as he is.

Three decades later Tom Jones's time had finally come. Duetting with Robbie Williams made perfect sense to Tom. And everybody else present. Watching him at the Brits giving his all so damn effortlessly reminded me that Tom Jones is literally the last of a dying breed. The true working-class, rags to riches superstar, hewn from the same stuff as Frank Sinatra and Elvis Presley. Like Frank and Elvis he was born to perform and when he burst onto the scene there was something pure yet raw about that voice, about that feral appeal. Musical credibility? Who needed it?

Tom Jones made his choice a long time ago.

• CHAPTER ONE •

THE BOY IN
THE ATTIC

T here's no rain like Valleys rain.

It did not have to rain much before there were waterfalls falling off the mountains and the river was in full flood. In Treforest, between the rows of terraced houses that cling to the hillside like an afterthought, the water charged down the steps, turning short cuts into water slides. All the lads hated it when the rains came and stayed, but when the sun shone again they would be back outside.

Tommy Woodward hated the rain more than anyone else because he was imprisoned in his attic bedroom, confined by that black spot on his lungs. For two years Tommy Woodward sat in his attic room, two years that felt like twenty, staring at the mountains beyond Pentre-Bach across the Taff valley. A boy with coal-black bags beneath his eyes, too weak to go to school, slumped by the window, his face scrunched up against the glass pane. His tiny attic bedroom was strewn with paintings, drawings in charcoal and crayon. All pictures of girls.

He was trapped by his body. It changed and grew as he lay there, too feeble to run. A boy too weak to sing but not too frail to dream. He dreamt of a girl playing marbles on a cobbled street corner, a blonde girl in a pale blue dress, little gold rings glinting on white earlobes, bare legs in white ankle socks running up a green hill.

'The worst thing . . .' whispered Tom, the scene still etched deep in his memory four decades later, 'the worst thing was that I couldn't sing. I used to sing all the time. I remember thinking, "If I could only walk to the bottom of the street I would be better". We lived in the end house and I would look down on the railings and see the lampposts which we would play around as kids – when the gas lights came on in winter we would gather around them. It's still vivid in my mind, seeing kids come back from the swimming pool and thinking "Jesus, I wish I was with them." '

Tommy Woodward was twelve years old when they diagnosed him with tuberculosis. At eleven he was a mischievous lad, short and pencil thin with a shock of brown curls and a winning smile. He needed it. He got bored easily and school was not the answer, the words and symbols on the blackboard never made the same sense inside his head as they did for other kids. At school he was only happy when he sang. The teachers told him he was good and every time he let go, powerful notes clear as a bell, he knew he was.

He knocked around with a gang from Laura Street and a small stretch of Wood Road that backed onto his house. Inside the gang they called him Woodsey. He was an in between kid, well dressed without looking like Little Lord Fauntleroy. His mother saw to it that he was decently turned out and the kitchen floor was always spotless when he tracked his muddy boots across it. All the boys were in gangs. They had to be, in case they ever ran into any kids from the Graig. Graig kids were notorious, hard cases and scruffy with it. Then they would fight.

That was what boys did when they were not getting into mischief. One favourite trick was to cut down clotheslines on Fridays. Wash day. The clothes fell in the mud and the boys were chased away by angry housewives. In the autumn the gang ranged further afield. They bunked off school and went out into the country to pinch apples where irate farmers set dogs on them.

On Saturday mornings they were straight down to the New Cecil cinema on Broadway for the children's matinée, in time for the newsreel, the serials (Tommy loved *The Phantom* and *The Lone Ranger*) and the main feature. They did not want to miss a thing. Bad boys — and he was one often enough — would pay for one of the gang to go in. Once inside, he would slip the fire exit door open and then they all sneaked in. Some days old Wood, the manager, or one of the usherettes would catch them in mid-furtive sneak. Another chase. Another slap from his mother. Normal stuff for Laura Street.

Tommy was always getting into fights. 'Often,' he said, 'it was over a girl.' Eleven-year-olds were not supposed to care about that sort of thing, but Tommy did. He first spotted ten-year-old Melinda Trenchard playing marbles when he walked past her. He was out begging pennies for the guy for bonfire night. The gangs all got very competitive around Guy Fawkes night, so Tommy was seriously neglecting his duties paying attention to a girl.

'She lived just around the corner in Cliff Terrace,' he recalled. But there were problems. 'She went to a Catholic school, I was Chapel and went to a Protestant school, so we didn't mix that much — but I always liked those Catholic schoolgirls because they wore little gold earrings. Little Catholic girls always had their ears pierced. Very sexy. So I saw her playing marbles and she had great legs. That was it. We would play kiss chase.'

Tommy started playing with girls and suddenly he had lost his appetite for mischief. Who knows what his pals thought? His get up and go had vanished and he started losing even more ground at school. Every morning his mum had to force him out of bed to go to school. He moaned, 'Mum, I feel tired,' and like mothers have always done she said, 'You don't want to go to school.' Eventually they took him to the doctor. The diagnosis was devastating. The dreaded black spot. So many of Tommy's cousins had TB, the family thought it was hereditary.

In 1952 tuberculosis was a killer. Antibiotics were not yet widely available. The only effective cure was bed-rest in an environment where the air was clear and clean. 'The authorities wanted to send me to some bloody convalescent place in Scotland because that was the only TB hospital in Great Britain that had a school,' recalled Tom. 'But little Tommy didn't want to leave his family. I'd never even been out of Wales, so my mother asked if she could keep me in the house, in a room to myself. Fortunately we lived on a hill and the authorities came to see and said, "Fine, if he can have this room at the top of the house, get plenty of fresh air and have a tutor that's all he needs." '

Treforest Central Secondary School arranged for a tutor, Mrs Warren, to visit every day. Basking in the individual attention he started to enjoy lessons for the first time. Unable to sing, he spent most of his time painting, or drawing with charcoal and crayons. The boys in the gang were allowed to come and chat to him for a while after school . . . but no girls.

'In those days girls wouldn't dare go into boys' houses, and they wouldn't come to mine even though I was bedridden,' Tom said, 'so I got my creative urges and went through puberty simultaneously. I had just fallen in love and there I was locked away for two years. I would look out of my window and see Linda in the street, see her going to play up the hills above town. I'd see her with other boys and that pissed me off more than anything else. I was very aware of her, very jealous. It was the first time I'd felt anything like that for a female. But it came from the heart more than the groin. I wanted to talk to Linda. I didn't know it but I was pining.'

Pining or not, for eighteen months Tommy ruled the household as only an invalid child can. His demands took precedence over those of his father. Whenever he wanted something, a book, something to eat or drink, however trivial, Tommy banged on the floor with a stick and up his mother would come. He had always been the apple of her eye, but this was special control. He loved it.

The second year he managed to get up for an hour a day, but still could not go outside. 'The doctors didn't know how long I was going to be ill. I had to have an x-ray every few months until the shadow on the lung went away.' So he sat downstairs – but only if he felt strong enough to negotiate the stairs – and watched his mother rake the coals before baking Welsh cakes on the hot stones. Tommy liked to eat and throughout his illness his mother encouraged him to eat to get his strength back up.

'When they finally set me free, the doctors told me not to get too active because my muscles hadn't been used,' he said. 'I forgot, of course, and was running around with the other boys, until suddenly my legs seized up. The pain was unbelievable.'

Within a few weeks Tommy's behaviour was pretty well back to normal. Soon he was climbing over the wall in his secondary school to 'frighten' the girls. His illness had changed him.

It was arguably the most formative experience of his childhood, perhaps of his life.

Sigmund Freud observed that, 'Subconsciously you remain the same age throughout your life.' The Tom Jones who would mesmerise the world, and particularly its women, with the power and sexual vigour of his singing, has in many ways remained at heart the chubby fourteen-year-old who emerged from the ashes of his illness and convalescence a strutting, randy phoenix.

What Tom had missed lying in his bed were two things: girls and singing. During those two years he had gone through puberty and to the frustration of sexual longing was added the inability to do anything about it. During those months of exile he had focused on two women. One, his mother, who was at his beck and call, who he could have with the bang of a stick, had made him the centre of her universe. The other, the object of his desire, he had scarcely seen and never touched.

Since then he has always demanded and sought both things. Domestic contentment through being master of the house. He possessed the weapon to achieve his ambitions. He had the Voice.

Tommy Woodward had stared out of his window for months without end. As he watched but could not feel he had made himself a solemn vow, 'Once I get up from this bed and can function properly, I'll never mourn anything else again.'

And he never has.

CHAPTER TWO

THE BIRTH OF
THE VOICE

———————

On his father's side Tom Jones is only second generation Welsh. The Woodward family moved to Pontypridd from Cornwall in the late nineteenth century. The tin and slate mines of Crantock were fading, but the coalfaces of South Wales promised employment for life and for generations to come. They settled in Treforest, which had lost its mighty oaks almost a century earlier, felled to build the ships that allowed the British Navy to rule half the world. Thomas John Woodward was born there on 31 March 1910. He had two older brothers Edwin and George, generally known as Snowy.

'My father's side is English, my mother's side is Jones, pure Welsh,' said Tom Jones. 'My dad loved being Welsh, even though his parents were both English. He was born in Wales, he was a coal miner, and that's the way he was.'

One of the most intriguing facts about the coal society and traditions in the Valleys of South Wales is that it was an artificial construct – created to fulfil economic demands by immigrants – which lasted little more than a century.

In 1851 the Rhondda was a sleepy rural area with a population of 1,998 and a handful of small collieries. After the 1870s businessmen with flair and money started to invest the necessary sums to get at the rich coal seams deep beneath the valley floor. By 1911 the Valleys had a population of 152,781 and there were fifty-three large collieries, twenty-one of which employed over 1,000 miners. The population of the county of Glamorgan stood at 1,130,668. It had multiplied five times in just sixty years. Between 1901 and 1911, when 129,000 people moved into the area, South Wales was absorbing immigrants at a faster rate than anywhere in the world except the USA.

The Valleys became a melting pot. The coal rush attracted immigrants from North Wales, South West England, Scotland, London, Yorkshire and Ireland. Where houses could be built they were flung up, with little regard for the niceties of either town-planning or the aesthetics of the landscape. Two or three streets of terraced houses wriggled like demented snakes along ridges, or beside the river banks mimicking every kink and bend of the Rhondda and the Taff. Because of its unique geography the Rhondda was incredibly densely populated, with 23,680 people crammed into each habitable square mile (the national average was 618).

Although he did not know it, by 1924 when Tom Woodward turned fourteen and started working at Cwm Colliery in Beddau, the coal boom was over. During the First World War the demand for coal to keep the Navy at sea had been so vital that the coalfields had been taken over by the state. In 1921 they had been handed back to the owners, who promptly locked out one million miners who refused to accept wage cuts of nearly fifty per cent. Tom was scarcely seventeen when the owners demanded that miners accept further wage cuts plus an extra hour's work a day. The dispute expanded to become the General Strike of 1926. The strike lasted nine days, but the miners, angry at what they considered was a betrayal by the TUC, stayed out until the end of the year.

Following so soon after the lockout, few families had enough money put by to survive for long. As the weather turned cold, and there was no fuel to heat the homes and nothing to plug the black holes in children's stomachs, men who prided themselves on always providing stood helpless and hopeless. The queue for the soup kitchen was six deep and stretched all the way from Calvary Church down Wood Road, beyond the intersection with Tower Street. Tommy, his stomach growling, watched the wives and children queuing, and helped the men as they scoured the slag heaps for a few scraps of small coal. He picketed the mines, abused and sometimes attacked the scabs. Eventually, the strikers too joined the soup line before starvation drove them back to work, defeated.

The miners felt betrayed. The bitterness endured for years. No one who lived through it ever forgot.

The Great Depression devastated the Rhondda still further. It was more expensive to mine coal there than elsewhere, and by 1929, having once supplied thirty-three per cent of the world's coal exports, it supplied only three per cent. In fifteen years 241 mines were closed and the number of working miners halved. By 1932 36.5 per cent of the working population was unemployed. Half a million people – a third of the population – left the Valleys. Pontypridd was less hard hit: only a fifth of the population left. To cap it all the mortality rate was fifty per cent above the national average.

The Woodward family were relatively lucky. Tom remained in work throughout the Depression. But an employed miner was only thirteen shillings (65p) a week better off than an unemployed one. Charlie Ashman, who was later to give Tom Jones his first paid gig, recalled how his family survived, 'We were all always hungry. My grandmother'd have a big fire, and we had a big boiler and we would go down the shop and get a shilling's worth of bacon pieces, about 2lb [0.9kg] worth, and that would be there nearly all the week to feed us. I had six sisters and two brothers, and my mother died when I was eighteen months old, in childbirth. The tenth child she had at thirty-three. I was the ninth and she died with the tenth, and the first one died, so eight lived on. It was a tough time.'

The Second World War meant coal was once again a national priority. After it ended oil was in short supply. The nationalisation of the coal industry in 1947 ended the perennial cycle of lockout and strike. Money was thrown at the pits by the National Coal Board. Relative to the general populace miners were well paid. A structured training and apprentice scheme was instituted claiming 'a job for life'.

In Treforest everybody celebrated. The good times were back. For ever. Or so they thought. Now miners would no longer have to worry about being laid off or thrown out of their houses by the bailiffs.

Tom Senior had learnt several lessons from the Depression years: he did not want his son to follow him down the pits. He had discovered that community spirit was fine when everybody was on strike, because that was the only way to survive. But the General Strike and the first Labour government had shown what workers' solidarity was really worth – nothing. The bosses worked on a divide and rule basis. When some pits were working and others closed it was more basic. In the end it was every man for himself and his family. Shared blood was thicker than shared beer.

The Woodwards have held to that ever since. Tom Jones's loyalties are specific. Family, family, family. They are the only ones who matter, because ultimately they are the only ones who can be relied on.

Tom Woodward met eighteen-year-old Freda Jones in a local dance hall in 1933. At the weekends, scrubbed clean of coal dust, he turned into a dapper young man, a sharp rather than an elegant dresser, turned out in a double-breasted suit, wide trousers properly pressed. He wore suede shoes, with both the soles and edges polished, coloured shirts and he selected different coloured ties to go with them. He sported a narrow, immaculately trimmed moustache. He was unfailingly polite and never seemed to be in a hurry, even when he was heading down to the Wood Road Non-Political Club on a Saturday night. He greeted everyone by name, 'Hello, Charlie. Nice now, innit.'

Tom wore a trilby, which he never took off. His hair thinned as he grew older and he never liked that. 'He'd never take his hat off in the club either,' recalled Ashman, 'that was his excuse. He had no hair.'

Freda was a feisty girl who loved to dance and would sing whenever the occasion arose. They were married on 9 September 1933 and moved into the Jones's home at 57 Kingsland Terrace. Sheila was born on 11 March 1934 – too soon for the neighbourhood gossips.

'I know it wasn't nine months from the time my mother and father got married to when my sister was born,' said Tom Jones. There was a twinkle in Tom Senior's eye for the ladies. 'My father was a good-looking man and women would open their doors and call "Good morning, Thomas." I liked it. I thought, "Ooh hoo my father's a cool guy."'

Their second child was born at home on 7 June 1940 (which in astrological terms makes him a Gemini with Aquarius rising). He was named Thomas John Woodward, after his father. The birth was registered at Pontypridd Register Office on 1 July and witnessed by registrar Gwilym James. His father's occupation was listed as 'Assistant Colliery Repairer (below ground)'.

'There was only my sister and myself,' said Tom, 'but my mother came from a family of six and so did my father. All their brothers and sisters lived in Pontypridd, there were loads of cousins and we were all together. So if I came home from school and Mother wasn't there, I could go to my auntie's house or my grandma's house. You were never alone, I knew everybody around, they knew me.'

Treforest was an insular, safe community where everybody knew each other's business but kept quiet counsel. A mining village overlooking Pontypridd, which it all but touches, it is categorically not part of the town. Ponty itself is only twelve miles from Cardiff but its world view is more parochial. It looks inland and underground rather than out to sea. The Valleys had their own social scene and as long as the coal kept coming what need was there of anything else? Life was hard but because everyone else was in the same position it did not matter so much.

'We were no worse off than anyone else around us,' recalled Tom Jones. 'We were working-class coal miners, we lived in a terraced house on a street built for coal miners, with a tin bath hanging on the nail outside. I never felt we were poor because everyone was in the same boat. I always thought I would be a miner like Dad. It's a Welsh tradition – or it was when I was eighteen – that a lad would follow his father down the pits.'

What was good enough for Da was good enough for his son. The community was fiercely protective of its own but it lacked ambition. When Frank Sinatra was growing up in Hoboken, his dream was always visible: the lights and towers of Manhattan over the Hudson River. All Tom could see on the other side of the Taff was an elongated railway platform, a few pubs, sets of rugby goalposts and the far side of the valley.

Not that talent was discouraged, it was just expected to be

incorporated into normal life. Men sang in choirs, played rugby and drank beer with their 'butties'.

Woodward family legend has it that little Tommy was always a singer. At six months he was making sounds 'like musical notes', which quickly turned to screams if anyone tried to shut him up. A chubby, sedentary baby, he was persuaded to walk by being encouraged to chase his elder sister round the kitchen table brandishing a stick.

'My mother says I could sing before I could walk and that I would crawl about the floor giving voice for all I was worth. She used to treat it as a joke until one day I was singing a song I had picked up from the radio, and she stopped what she was doing. "Sing that again," she said. It was called *Mairzy Doats and Dozy Doats*. I sang it and she said, "You know, you've got a lovely voice." I was five and after that there was no stopping me.'

Music was in the family genes. Saturday nights often ended with a singsong in Laura Street (Tom's family had moved there after his grandfather died) after the Non-Political Club had closed. George, who was the club entertainment secretary, and Edwin both had fine voices and were regulars in the local male voice choirs. Tom Senior had a strong voice, but he was shy and would sing only after a few pints. Freda, however, was a natural performer who enjoyed letting rip.

'I got the combination,' said Tom. 'When my mother got up to sing, she would incorporate some movements. I remember her singing *Silver Dollar*. She'd give it all that business. My father had a better voice than my mother, but he was inhibited. My Uncle George, his brother, had more of a way with a lyric, he would sell a song better. My father would sing sitting down, but my Uncle George, he'd have to get up. I was taking notice of all that.'

Sometimes George would drag the sleepy boy out of his bed and make him sing. The first time the dopey lad mumbled into his feet, head down, but George soon put him right. 'No,' he said. 'Sing to people's faces, let them see what you were singing about.' Once woken up there was no stopping the boy.

'All of my cousins are singers, some are in male voice choirs. We'd all sing, but when we were kids they'd be shy, stand in the corner, but I always had to get on the table.'

While his ma was busy cleaning the house Tommy would get up on the windowsill, pull the curtains across and demand to be introduced. Freda would claim she was too busy but Tommy would nag her until finally she relented and cried out, 'Ladies and gentlemen . . . Tommy Woodward'.

'I'd throw back the curtains, leap off the windowsill and start singing. Even though there was nobody there but my mother.'

His first public performance was at Tom Marney's post office and village store on Wood Road. Marney had heard stories about Tommy, and one day demanded he get up on an upturned orange box and serenade the shoppers. Impressed by his singing the shopkeeper insisted over Freda's protests, 'Come on, give the boy a few coppers then. You can't have talent like that for nothing.' Tommy discovered early that his singing would bring him money for sweets or cakes.

'He always had ability and bags of confidence,' said Freda. 'When we went on a family outing he'd be dead keen to get up and sing. He knew most of the popular songs of the day off by heart. I remember taking him to Women's Guild meetings. He used to make his own beat on a table and sing to the members.' Soon he was regularly attending meetings of the Guild, which met five minutes' walk from the family home in a small hall at the top of Stow Hill. His star turns were *Ghost Riders in the Sky*, *Lucky Old Sun* and *Mule Train*. In return he was given cakes by the women. Women have always liked his voice.

Tommy's Uncle Edwin also loved to take the boy out and

show him off. Edwin was an altogether wilder character than his brothers. 'A proper rough diamond,' recalled Charlie Ashman, 'a mountain fighter. He never boxed, but he was a rough-and-tumbler.' Doubtless reckoning that it would be worth a good few pints Edwin took Tommy into a pub down Llantrisant way and stood him on a chair. 'He just had to sing to all the patrons. He'd get up and give a song anywhere.'

At home Tom was for ever listening to the radio. He liked what in America they called 'race music' — rhythm and blues, boogie woogie, and he also loved gospel. His family preferred sweeter songs, white bread show tunes and crooners, but Tommy always liked edgier expressive performers, like Billy Daniels's version of *That Old Black Magic* which is all drama and excitement. 'When other people did *That Old Black Magic*, it was a cool song, but when Billy Daniels did it, he put life into it. The exaggeration. The drama. There's a natural freedom in Negro voices that you don't find in white voices. I liked music that stirs you up.' He loved Big Bill Broonzy's country blues holler on *John Henry* and *Glory of Love*.

While he loved black voices it was seeing *The Al Jolson Story* at the pictures that got Tom practising his moves in the mirror. He said, 'They showed him on the screen building a ramp down the middle of this theatre because he wanted to get close to the people. I was doing that at school when I was ten.'

When rock and roll came he embraced it with the fervour of the convert. The only BBC radio show playing the music was Jack Jackson's *Off The Record*, while Radio Luxembourg offered the occasional gem through the crackling ether. He hung around in Ponty's record shop with a bunch of fellow fans 'listening to Jerry Lee Lewis, Elvis, of course, and Bill Haley's *Rock Around the Clock* and, before that in the early fifties, Tennessee Ernie Ford doing boogie woogie — which was black music anyway, created in a whorehouse.'

He started at Treforest Primary School just as the Second World War came to an end. During free periods on Friday afternoons Tom would get up and give everyone a song. It kept everyone quiet and put him centre stage. Tommy was in the choirs, but he preferred to do the solos. Even aged nine his style was too distinctive, too egotistical, to blend in with others.

'I was singing the Lord's Prayer in the junior school,' he said, 'and the teacher asked me why I was singing it like a Negro spiritual. I didn't know what she was talking about. I told her I just thought it should be sung that way. Apparently I was bending the melody. So they got the whole school together in the assembly hall, I sang it and all the kids applauded. No one could understand why I sang it like a spiritual, and I had no answer for it either.

'Even by Welsh standards I was outstanding, I was different. Most Welsh voices are all-male voice choirs, all very serious stuff, very strict and stilted. They are taught that way, that's the way they liked it. I love the sound of a Welsh choir, but it sounds very strict to me, I never wanted to be in one. When I sang it was in a transatlantic accent.'

In those days gender roles were fixed. Men had their jobs and women had their place. That was the way it was, and most of them were glad of it. The men seldom talked of what their job entailed, but everybody knew. Eight hours down the pits. Eight hours asleep. Two thirds of their lives spent in darkness. One of the facts of life.

Whatever the seasons brought for Tommy's dad and mum, the routine was always the same. For forty years she was always up before him, before dawn, stumbling across the dark bedroom and downstairs to the kitchen to make sure the fire was lit and to lay his clothes round it to warm them through. If she slept through the alarm he missed a shift. Tom Senior came downstairs, pulled on his moleskins, flannel shirt and his hobnails and ate his breakfast. He took a last sip of tea, slipped on his worn waistcoat and jacket, put a tea jack in one pocket and a food tin in the other, wrapped an old scarf round his neck and tugged on his cap.

Sometimes Tommy would watch his dad go to work. To keep the memory fresh. Every so often a miner's luck ran out and there would be an accident down the pit. Anyway, it was hard to sleep through the clatter and the crash. The noise was terrible all up and down Laura Street, echoing up and down the Almas, the length of Wood Road and Rickards Street. All the way to the Graig and beyond, the sparks of hobnail boots on cobblestones, the good mornings and the wavings goodbye. Out in the dark he went and back he came in the light: white face moonshining in the dark before dawn, black face returning in the afternoon. The reverse of what went before.

It was a long walk to the Cwm in Beddau: three miles over the mountain in the dark, three miles back at shift end. The face workers had to be in the cage by 7 a.m. and it was a quarter of a mile down the shaft. Once down by the cage, which dropped fast enough to push the collywobbles up, it could be another mile to the seam. Always walking downhill, three yards forward one yard down. And as the boots crunched downhill so the water followed, a constant stream, a sinister black rivulet. Water was an enemy, lapping over the lip of the boots, perishing the leather and chilling the toes.

It was always damp inside the mine, the chill, the smell permeated everywhere. The timbers that supported the tunnels were dry, though the mist that surrounded them was clammy and the air was stale, lingering and so fetid it could be cut with a mandril. When the fresh air came it came in cold, chill but fresh.

Underground light was the miner's constant need. Without it he was lost. On the surface, even when the moon blots out the sun, we think we know what dark is, but in truth we have no idea. Deep underground without light there is literally nothing, just blackness without end. For ever. Sense of direction disappears, leaving nothing except touch and the sound of breathing.

Cutting coal in a seam a yard high was an art form. Tom Woodward lay on his side, swung his elbows and twisted his wrists without moving his shoulders. He chipped the solid coal away fraction by fraction until there was a groove a foot deep. Then he threw water in the groove to soften it for later. He moved fourteen tons of coal every day, getting paid for every square yard instead of a labourer's money. Every day for forty years he breathed coal dust deep into his lungs.

He broke for lunch by lamplight. The food had to be kept in tins otherwise the mice or rats nibbled away at it. There were huge spiders called jaspers that could make a man jump.

Sometimes in winter Tom Senior arrived back in Treforest after the lamplighter had lit the gas street lights. On Fridays he'd walk back, pay held tight in his left trousers pocket, right arm swinging free. There were no pithead baths in those days, so his face was as black as the coal seam save for the whites of his eyes and the gleaming of his teeth. Unless it had rained hard and long, when the water would wash away the black dust, streaks of white meandering down his cheeks like the fading of his mother's hair.

Freda knew when he was coming. All the wives had a sixth sense about it. Everything was waiting on that click of the back-door latch. Tom walked in the door and there was his tea waiting, steaming on the table, with Freda and the children standing there all spick and span. He washed his hands and got stuck into the food, his clothes still full of coal.

The tin bath had already been taken off its nail outside the kitchen door and filled with hot water. (There was only one house in Laura Street, Tom remembered, that had its own bathroom. It belonged to the local builder.) It was only a small bathtub, so he would kneel down on the floor and wash his top half first and then stand in the tub and wash his bottom half. When he was doing his top half he called for Freda to wash the pit grime from between his shoulder blades. There was a tradition that miners should never wash their backs, for they believed it made your back weak. But Freda did not hold with that. She was not sending her husband out to work in a dirty vest. That was how traditions died.

Tommy loved watching his dad in the bath. 'I always thought what a good physique he had and I wanted to be like him. Sometimes if Mum wasn't talking to him she would send me in there, which he didn't like at all. I'd start rubbing his back and he'd say, "Where's your mother?" And I'd say, "She's not talking to you. So I've got to do it."

'When I was little I yearned to be a man, to be the best I could. I have a memory of being a small boy hearing a noise in the night and my father getting up to see what it was. I remember thinking, "When I grow up will I be as brave as that?" '

Freda's domain was the house. For ever cleaning and polishing, washing the front step, buffing the door with furniture wax until it glowed, cheating the greyness of life outside with cheerful, shiny perfection inside. They lived in the kitchen. There was the best room at the front, but no one went into it. That was where visitors were entertained, where the family celebrated Christmas and when a woman was having a baby she had a bed brought down. The living room was a bright sparkling cave of horse brasses and copper ornaments. Freda loved her brasses, polished them so regularly that a fingerprint would have stood out like a boil on a supermodel's nose.

On their summer holiday Tom Senior used to install Freda, Sheila and Tom on the beach and go off on a beer-drinking session on his own. 'My dad just refused to be henpecked,' recalled Tom.

Although Tom Senior was always in work, money was tight.

Once, when the kids were both at school, Freda got a part-time job at a factory down on Treforest industrial estate. Her husband did not approve at all. The family were in the queue for the pictures one day when a young boy came up to them. 'Hello, Freda,' he said. Tom Senior was livid and demanded to know who the boy was. She told him it was just a kid who worked in the factory. 'You're not going to the factory any more,' came the command. 'If they can't call you Mrs Woodward then you don't work there.'

'My father was right,' said Tom years later. 'You see, a woman needs respect, she needs caring for.' That was the attitude in the Valleys. A man never swore in front of a lady, he never took advantage. Sometimes on Saturday night Tom Senior might come home after a few pints too many and let fly with a few 'bastards' or 'bloodys' to show he was really angry. When that happened Freda told the children they had deaf ears, that they never heard those words and that was as far as it went. Women, Tom told his son, were fragile, sacred things. A lesson his boy holds hard to this day.

'I don't swear in front of ladies, I don't think it's right. It's the way I was brought up. We'd go to the club and every other word was a swearword, but as soon as a woman stepped into the room, I cut it off. Years ago, when I was a teenager drinking in the pubs in Pontypridd, women were not allowed in the public bars. It wasn't because we were macho but because we respected women, so we didn't want to be swearing, breaking wind and telling filthy jokes in front of them. There were other rooms to take your girlfriend to protect her from the nastiness of men. It is our duty as men to do that no matter what women say. When a woman walks into a room I automatically watch my language. For me a woman is a very different creature. And I love the difference.'

The difference – that was the thing. Tommy Woodward was always fascinated by women. He liked being fussed and mussed over by his mum's friends, but when he was young he did not have them sussed. When he was ten or so he learnt about real power.

During the week women and men had separate social lives. Sunday lunch was family time. There would always be a joint of meat on the table. Turkey (unless they were strapped, when chicken had to do) and ham at Christmas. Saturday night was the night when the men took their wives out for a drink. For years Tom and Freda went out with her sister Violet and her husband. Then Violet refused to go down the Non-Political any more, so Freda stayed at home with her.

Tom had already noticed how all the womenfolk, young and old alike, Sheila, his cousins, aunts, all their friends, were going on about this revivalist preacher. He had come down from up north in England, Burton or somewhere like that, to preach hellfire and damnation for a month or so, and boy had he struck a chord with the ladies. Attendance at Chapel went sky high, as he railed against the demon alcohol and about the Kingdom of Heaven, and they lapped it up. The women prattled on about him non-stop rather than watching Tommy sing.

Tom decided to check out the competition. He waited outside the chapel one Sunday. The preacher was a good-looking fellow. Smart, too, with a tailored pinstripe suit, his wingtips shone mirror bright, clean manicured hands, tidy black hair going grey at the edges. He carried himself straight, tall and confident – exuding class as though he were a boss. So different, Tommy thought, from his dad with his coloured shirts and his coloured ties and his hat, and from all the other miners in their wide-legged suits from the Fifty Shilling Tailors on Taff Street, with fingernails that no matter how hard you scrubbed were always a fraction black. The preacher didn't talk to the women as if they had to have dinner on the table when the back door creaked. They came to see him dressed in their finery and he made them feel that each one of them was important. And when he got on a roll full of passion and fury each of them felt it was directed only at them. It was personal. Of course, it helped that he was good-looking.

Tommy took it all in. The next Saturday Violet was round Laura Street again sitting with Freda while the men went to the club. 'Go on, Violet, have a glass of stout, that won't hurt you,' insisted Freda. Violet struggled for a bit about how she had seen the light and how a drop of alcohol would never sully her lips again but then, as she reckoned the preacher would never know she had broken the pledge, consented to have just the one.

'Aha', thought Tommy as his mum poured the glass of stout, 'this could make a good joke.' So he leapt up waving his arms and shouting, 'Get thee behind me!' Poor Violet froze like some poor bunny trapped in a searchlight by the angel of abstinence, and she did not touch another drop for months. One clip round the ear later Tommy had learnt a crucial lesson. That preacher had some real power over women. They'd do anything for him. Tommy wanted some of it.

CHAPTER THREE

TEDDY BOY
WITH A PRAM

———————

Following his bout of TB, the Tommy Woodward who emerged from the front door of number 44 was a very different physical specimen. He was now fourteen, six inches taller, a great deal plumper and his head was covered with thick black curly hair. Puberty had turned his voice into a pleasing light baritone with which he could still hit and hold the high notes. Tommy went to bed a boy and got up a man. He could not wait to be a man.

Tom and his closest friend Dai Perry started going to pubs regularly, anywhere that would serve them, but The Bridge and The Otley Arms soon became favourites. It was a drinking culture. 'When I was a boy my father and uncles would go into the pub and I wanted to stand alongside them,' recalled Tom. The idea was to consume a lot of beer and not show it.

'I only had one year left at school, we all finished at fifteen unless you were at grammar. It wasn't dropping out, it was being pushed out, unless you'd passed your 11-plus – and we didn't really know what that meant – it was just another test you took. I didn't like school. I can't spell that well even today.'

For Tom school was a case of going through the motions. Reading and writing were to be a problem all his life. He now claims he is dyslexic, a condition that was scarcely understood and certainly not recognised in the fifties. A child was considered plain stupid, bone idle or both. Not that it mattered if he was going down the pits or to the Broom Lennox chain works, but it ruled out working in a shop. Nor was Tom a particularly good sportsman. He played rugby for the school team, but lacked the skill of Dai Perry, and he occasionally turned out for soccer matches. He was not a natural team player. He enjoyed a workout at a local boxing club, for boxing was a practical and necessary survival skill, but he lacked the dedication to emulate the exploits of local legend Tommy Farr.

Tommy was not interested in learning a skill. Instead he took a job at the Polyglove factory down on the Broadway 'because the factory closest to my house was a glove cutter'. He had too much living to catch up with to worry about the future. And rock and roll had arrived.

In many ways fifties teenage culture scarcely touched the Valleys. It did not change the course of their lives, or their core values, though it did change the way they looked. The nationalisation of the mines had given an economic stability to pit workers with a knock-on effect on the rest of the local economy. Most school-leavers went straight into a manual job as they had always done. They stayed at home and made a contribution to the family budget.

They had cash to spend and something concrete to spend it on, which marked them out from and infuriated the pre-war generation. The neighbourhood gangs that had played 'Tarzan' or

'Cowboys and Indians' up on the mountains had another alternative to choirs and rugby teams. Tommy Woodward embraced the Teddy Boy look and its music.

'When I left school in 1955 rock and roll came in for real,' said Tom. 'Dancing was the thing. It was all Elvis, Jerry Lee Lewis, Carl Perkins, Little Richard, Tommy Steele, Marty Wilde and even Terry Dene. I was a Teddy Boy and proud of it.'

Each community – Rhydfellin, Ponty, Beddau, the Graig – had their own gang of Teds, each with a slightly different uniform. The common enemies were the City Boys and the City Slickers – gangs from Cardiff who never dared venture any further up into the Valleys than Ponty.

'They wouldn't go up yonder. They'd be beaten to hell up there,' said Tom Pitman, a Rhydfellin Ted and occasional bouncer at the Legion, known locally as the 'Bucket of Blood'. 'We'd wait for them to come out of the dance hall down by the station, and then have them before they got on the train. They were always outnumbered, of course. But if the City Boys didn't show the local boys fought each other.'

Knives broke the unwritten code – though some of the Cardiff gangs started to bring bike chains to even up the odds. Battles were fought with head, foot and fist.

'Kids in our town used their heads when we fought in the streets,' recalled Tom in the sixties. 'That's why I hate my horrible nose – it's been worked over, bent sideways and patched up more than any other part of me. And always hit by a head – we liked to keep our hands nice and smooth, like! My nose has been broken so many times in punch-ups that I can't remember which particular one made it this shape. Drinking was part of my trouble.'

Friday night punch-ups might have been part of growing up, but Tommy soon acquired a reputation as a hard man. If Tom was late getting to the pub his mates would dissuade anybody from chatting Linda up with a hissed 'She's Tommy's girl'. Not that that stopped him getting into fights over other girls as well. His temper was so short that he used to fly at people ridiculing him for pushing a pram dressed in his Ted finery.

Tom was always self-aware. He had the miner's payday walk, learnt from his dad but turned into a strut, one hand swinging at his side, the left placed on his thigh as if he were guarding the change in his pocket. Waiting for the pub to open he stood with his legs well apart, arms folded across his chest. He was never without his comb, sliding it through his slicked-back hair.

In one scrap, fellow Treforest resident Alan Barratt gave Tom a good hiding and broke his nose. For years afterwards Tom was wary of him. Barratt was a small wiry man who after one drink too many could turn vicious. Even after Tom became a star Barratt was always allowed into his dressing room, although Tom insisted that his cousin Alan Woodward was there, just in case. People wondered why Tom let him in at all, but the singer was adamant, saying, 'It's better to let him in, it's better the devil you know, and know where he is.'

'I was always in trouble with the cops for fighting,' said Tom. 'Most parents in Ponty wouldn't let their lads talk to me. When I got drunk I'd fight anybody, even my best mates.'

Tommy Woodward fought the way Tom Jones performs. Full on, no holding back. On one occasion he and some mates had been to an Indian restaurant after a few drinks in the pub. A taxi pulled up and these Graig boys starting mouthing off. Tom and one lad exchanged insults. Tom hit him. Hard. The boy scrambled back into the cab and Tom, deep into the red mist, tried to leap in after him, swinging fists and insults, as the driver headed off at top speed. A few nights later the word went round that Dai Hunt was out looking for payback.

'I was with Dai [Perry],' he said, 'and he kept saying, "He's looking for you, so be careful." I knew who this guy was and thought, "He's got no chance, who gives a shit?" Dai and I came out of the pub one night and had fish and chips. We were standing in this doorway and the guy came up, he was with his dad, and said, "You remember the time you hit that friend of mine?" I said, "Yeah." He said, "I couldn't get out of the cab. If I'd got out it would have been different." I said, "Why don't you run along, you've got no chance," and I was so confident I kept on eating my chips. Dai whispered, "Keep an eye on him." But I didn't care. I said, "Where do you want to fight? Let's go up on the Graig," and while I was talking he suddenly let me have it – wham – and I was smashed right through the door into the fish and chip shop. I jumped up and was just about to let him have it when two policemen arrived and told us to stop it.'

But, covered in broken glass, blood streaming from his nose, Tom was not going to let it go at that. Despite Dai's warnings he followed his assailant and his father up to the Graig, and without even bothering to take off his overcoat or tie threw himself on top of both screaming, 'I'm going to get both of you.' For a moment it seemed he might get away with it as he had Dai Hunt spread-eagled beneath him.

'But his father jumped on my back and he had his arms round my throat and I screamed at Dai to get him off. Then this guy's mother came flying into the action and his brother ran out of the house and together they beat the shit out of me. I've still got the scar where the guy bit my finger.' Because of the honour code Dai felt he could not hit an older man and certainly not a woman, so he stood by and let the fight come to its natural conclusion.

As he admitted, Tom was no stranger to the local police. But it was not just because of his fighting. Like many young men he got involved in petty theft. The mistake he made was trying to sell the evidence down the Wood Road Non-Political. 'The truth is that Tom Woodward was a young thug,' said his second cousin Billy Russell. 'He was a lout. People round here like to forget it nowadays, but Tom and a cousin broke into a tobacconist's shop just near the end of his street. The poor old woman who ran the shop was absolutely devastated by the break in. Tom tried to lie his way out of it, of course, but they found the cigarettes under the sofa in his mother's house. His parents thought the world of him but he made their lives a misery tear-arsing around.'

At a time when riding a bicycle without lights could merit a whopping 10 shilling (50p) fine, Tom was lucky to get away without a record. He had his family to thank for that. 'The police were always on the look-out for me but I got away with most things like getting into the cinema without paying,' he told showbusiness reporter Donald Zec in 1965. 'I got into trouble, but when the officials came to see my mother with the brass nicely polished in the front room, picture of Grandad with his medals on, they went away saying, "No ruffian could live here."'

'My mates and I once nicked some records from the local record shop,' he admitted. 'We had a specially adapted sort of greatcoat with big pockets sewn inside, and one of us would distract the guy running the shop while the one in the coat would drop LPs into the pockets.'

Saturday nights had their own rituals. A casual promise to see the local girls at the Coronation Hall or the Ranch. The Ranch was Tom and Linda's favourite dance hangout, an old wartime Nissen hut up on Graigwen that doubled as an old folks' club. It was popular with the younger teens and a lot less dangerous than the Legion down in Rhydfellin. In the afternoon a visit to the rugby, or even a game. Then it was back home and change out of the T-shirt, black leather jacket, turned up jeans and winkle-pickers into the finery of the Treforest Teds – sky blue Edwardian suit with a velvet collar and black suede, crepe-soled shoes. Strut down

Rickards Street, smoking a Woodbine, down the Tumble, keeping a wary eye out for any passing Graig psychopaths, and then a sit-down on the red wall opposite the station. By five to six the wall was lined with Teddy suits all sitting waiting for the doors of the White Hart, the Dog or the Clarence to open. That left nearly three hours' drinking. The boys had to be at the dance hall by 9 o'clock, because nobody was allowed in after that.

The girls, meanwhile, had gathered half a dozen at a time at someone's house to chat, play records and get ready. It did not matter if the hop was a two-hour walk, through piles of cow dung, over the mountain in Caerphilly, which in perm-free days messed their hair something awful. Twenty girls might go and they would have an hour left before it was *God Save the Queen* and back home to Treforest.

Teenage girls drank pop and ate crisps. Any girl who liked to drink alcohol was shunned by her peers while the boys called her a slag and bragged about her. Boys, however, drank as much as possible all the time. However some of the girls were quite capable of fighting their own corner as Tom recalled: 'I remember saying to a girl at a dance, "Do you want to jive?" She said, "I will if you wait a minute." Then she turned around and – thump – sent another girl flying across the floor before matter of factly saying to me, "OK, let's dance." I said, "You sure you want to dance, or do you want to fight?" '

Boys without a girl sought solace in fighting. 'The dance halls were rough,' recalled Keith Davies, one of the original guitarists in the Senators. 'You couldn't say much in the Jive Club in Ponty or the Judges Hall in Tonypandy, before you had a chair over your head. When we were playing in the Memorial Hall up the Valleys suddenly the police were in there and the gangs were on each other's shoulders hitting their helmets off and trying to jump up on stage to drag us off, while Mike Roberts was hitting them with the heel of his shoe to get them down. It wasn't so much the drink as somebody dancing with somebody else's girl.'

In contrast Sundays were long empty days. Church or Chapel in the morning then a family lunch. Sundays everything was closed, closed dead. No rugby, no cinemas, no pubs. The only places open were the Bracchi Shops, two Italian cafés at opposite ends of Taff Street, Rabaiotti's up by the old bridge and Sarvini's, which had a jukebox, down by the Tumble.

The Monkey Parade was the Sunday evening ritual. It drew dirty looks from the good folks coming out of Chapel. Gaggles of girls strolled in their finery: hoop skirts, stockings and a flash of scarlet across the lips; gangs of boys marched by in their Vaseline-sculpted Tony Curtis hair – big DA at the back and quiff in the front. All evening they criss-crossed, exchanging glances and giggles, sometimes pairing off for a sneaked coffee, but more often relying on flirting and safety in numbers.

Getting married at seventeen or eighteen was not uncommon in the Valleys. Having sex underage was. Dances finished at 10 p.m. and the pubs shut half an hour later. That left an hour to walk a girl home slowly. Their mam wanted to know 'exactly where do you think you've been' after eleven. Courting was slow and leisurely, a kiss and a cuddle the best a fella could aspire to. Nice girls didn't go any further.

The first time Melinda Trenchard saw Tommy after he came out of his TB cell she did not recognise him. But he was looking for her. 'We got together at dances at the youth club,' Linda said, 'and though at this time we were too young to say we were going out together we always seemed to end up with each other. Tom's mother and mine knew each other well so it was quite natural that when his sister got engaged he should invite me to the party. It was at the party that I first really heard him sing. Tom was the star. He sang *Ghost Riders in the Sky* and accompanied himself by tapping his fingers on the table.'

Tommy, however, was a lad in a hurry. Before long he had convinced Linda to join him walking on the hills. Passionate kisses turned into embraces. 'When we made love,' he said, 'it was the first time for both of us. In a field in the long grass.' He was fifteen, she fourteen. A year later they discovered she was pregnant.

'There was a gang of about twenty of us girls from Treforest,' recalled Vimmie Pitman. 'Only one member of the gang was considered a bit promiscuous and none of us ever really knew whether to believe her stories or not. So Linda getting pregnant did come as a shock. Linda was besotted with Tom. She was a lovely looking girl, she developed very quickly, and she was as pretty inside as she was out. I've never heard her say a bad word about anybody. And we all knew it could only be Tom anyhow, because they were always together. They were bonkers about each other. He was always talking about Linda.'

The options were limited. The Trenchards were Catholic, so an abortion was out of the question. The time-honoured solution was for Melinda to go away for the last months 'visiting relatives', have the child adopted and then return home and pretend that nothing had happened. The couple could get married but both families thought they were much too young and the Trenchards did not think much of Tom as a prospect.

'It took bloody ages to convince the family that I wanted to marry this girl,' said Tom remembering the final confrontation that took place in Laura Street in November 1956. 'They were arguing as only families can, and time was running out. It could have been straightened out by my wife's auntie adopting the baby – she had no children. While they were busy making plans for the baby that did not include me, my father looked at us sitting in the corner holding hands and said, "We're discussing their futures, don't you think we should ask them what they want to do?"

'I said I wanted to get married to Linda and she wanted to get married to me. Many in the family were against the marriage, but my dad stood up to them all. I was underage, so I had to have permission. Linda was only just sixteen, on 14 January, so it could have been nasty – but we just scraped through.'

They were married at Pontypridd registry office on 2 March 1957. The couple moved into the basement of the Trenchard house at 2 Cliff Terrace, overlooking the railway siding. Mark was born on 11 April in Cardiff Maternity Hospital. He never knew his maternal grandfather, Bill Trenchard, who died from tuberculosis a month after his birth. Two weeks from his seventeenth birthday with an infant son, a grieving wife and a widowed mother-in-law, Tom found himself beset by responsibilities.

A year later he was a seriously disaffected young man. His future stretched before him offering nothing but more of the same dead-end jobs. His job as a trainee glove cutter at the Polyglove factory paid only thirty-eight shillings (£1.90) a week, poor when some of his friends were getting twice that, and certainly not enough for a married man with a baby, so he moved to the British Coated Board Paper Mills on the Treforest industrial estate.

'When Mark was born I didn't have two halfpennies to rub together,' he said. 'I was excited but the first thing I thought was, "God, how can I support him?" I was working night shifts at the paper mill and I couldn't even afford to take a shift off when Linda went into hospital. I set off for work on a push-bike as the ambulance was taking her to hospital. I had to work longer hours because I wasn't getting a man's wage. I was working five twelve-hour shifts for about £10.

'I remember going to the hospital and seeing Linda with my baby, and it was like, "Nobody can touch me now I'm a man". It gave me more drive, more determination. I had to take care of my wife and child. I don't know if I'd stayed single whether I would have pushed on. Maybe.'

Within a year Tom was promoted to running his own machine at the paper mill, which alleviated some of their money worries. The local trade union representative (who was also a relative) complained he should not be paid a full wage because he was underage. Although such petty politicking was common in post-war Britain, Tom was incensed when a couple of the older workers tried to sabotage his machine. Because he needed the job he kept his temper. Not a natural grafter he loathed having to do shift work.

Tom never neglected his responsibilities to his family. All his life Tommy had been indulged, told he was the greatest singer in town. But now he was caught in a job which made a singing career all but impossible. He was trapped and miserable. Small wonder he sought relief in drinking and fighting.

'I always knew I had talent. As a youngster I had a terribly strong belief that I would make it big. I couldn't see myself living in Pontypridd all my life. But not being able to get a break affected me. The ambition was all bottled up. I'd work all week, then get a skinful of beer at the weekend and that would lead to fights.'

While married life did calm Tom, he felt trapped and for the first and only time in his life he lost the unshakeable confidence in his vocal abilities. He gave up his singing. 'I had one really bad patch when I lost confidence,' he said. 'It was soon after my marriage. We were only sixteen. I knew the biggest problem with my married life at the beginning was getting to know each other and I wanted my marriage to last. I never went out without her. Never saw my mates. Linda never stopped believing in me, like my mother.'

Determined to stop her young husband brooding, Linda made him sing all the time, in pubs, clubs and family gatherings. The

Voice returned. She said, 'I wanted Tom to sing again. It meant so much to him. So I encouraged him. But never in my wildest dreams did I guess what would happen.'

Linda was strongly supported by Freda and her mother Vi, a bouncy waitress, who remained one of her son-in-law's most ardent fans until her death. Tom eventually quit the paper mill 'and went into construction. I wanted a day job so I could sing at night.'

Others remember it slightly differently. He did work for Wallis, a local building contractors, but for much of the time he was on the dole.

'He was always chasing stardom,' said Tommy Pitman. 'If anybody could be dedicated at anything, he really was. I've never known such determination. The man deserved all his success. He was prepared to lose everything for it.'

CHAPTER FOUR

THE SENATORS

Tommy Woodward's first professional gig was at the Wood Road Non-Political Club in early 1957. Charlie Ashman, entertainment secretary and vice-chairman at the time, recalled it well: 'It was a small club, no more than sixty, and we used to have guest nights for members on Sundays. If they sang a song we would give them one pint, and if they sang two songs we would give them two pints.

'I was working one Sunday, and I goes to the club about 1.30 in the afternoon, and the steward says to me, "Charlie, that banjo trio from Gwynedd can't come tonight." "Oh Christ," I said, "that's buggered it then!" I spotted Tommy Woodward out of the corner of my eye, and he was sitting around the table with a couple of lads, so I went over and said, "Tom, sing us a couple of songs tonight, the show we booked can't turn up."

'So I came home, I had my dinner, my bath, I went back there at 6.45, and about 7.45 Tom comes through the door. "All right,

Charlie?" he said. So we went upstairs, and the concert started. Then we called Tom out and he sang *Blue Suede Shoes*, I forget the other songs now, but he sang three songs and we had a bit of an interval, then he did another three. Everybody had to be out at 10.30. No pubs open then, mind.

'We couldn't give him a drink because he wasn't eighteen, so I said to Ernie Selby, who was in the chair at the time, "What do you think we should give him?" "Half a quid," he said. "Oh Christ," I said, "I know the beer's only 8d [3p], but half a quid? He kept the bloody crowd here and we were paying £4 for the show that didn't turn up. I'll tell you what I'll do, I'll give him a quid because we enjoyed him." I signed for the £1, went upstairs and said, "Here you are, Tom, here is a quid for you." "A quid?" he said. "Aye," I said, "you were bloody great!" And he was chuffed.'

Encouraged by the reaction and the fact that singing in public substantially increased his beer money, Tom looked around for other venues. 'I enjoyed singing, it was about getting attention from everybody,' said Tom. 'I would go into the singing room of the Wheatsheaf, get up there and sing. I'd hear songs on the radio and prove I could do it better.'

The Wheatsheaf, on Rickards Street, had three bars with a singing room on the top floor. Its Saturday night singsongs, accompanied by local piano player, Blind Johnny, proved ideal. 'If Tommy was singing, and this is the honest truth, there'd be silence,' recalled landlady Joan Lister. 'If anybody else was singing they would all be talking, they used to be terrible. If you weren't good they were the worst audience in the world. But if you were good they'd sit and listen. Tom was always the favourite. We all thought he was wonderful. When Tom was singing they wouldn't even get up for a pint. They'd all just sit there.'

Often in the audience in those early days was Vernon Hopkins, a piano tuner's son from Rhydfellin. Vernon had been captivated by rock and roll since he had first heard Elvis, and he had started playing the guitar. A friend had told him about this singer up in Treforest.

'I went upstairs at the Wheatsheaf and saw a lot of girls all up there to see this guy, Tommy Woodward. Another guy was singing like Frankie Laine, but when Tom got to sing he would come out with something else. He was going, "Here's your momma" and all of that rock and roll. The others were good, but he was using better phrasing because he'd been listening to Jerry Lee Lewis. I spoke to him, told him I was forming a band. But he wasn't very interested, he just wished me luck.'

Within two years beat and skiffle groups were all the rage, and Vernon's band the Senators – formed with his neighbour, fourteen-year-old Keith Davies – had become a major local attraction. They also made their debut at the Non-Political Club as a guitar trio, playing the Shadows' *Apache* on which Vernon muted the strings to give the effect of the drums. Tommy Pitman, who had started his singing career as a National Serviceman on the air bases in Cyprus, was recruited as their lead singer and rechristened Tommy Redman. Pitman had a very good voice, especially on the sweeter ballads. Their repertoire, full of Presley, Buddy Holly, Cliff Richard, Frankie Laine songs and Shadows instrumentals, went down a storm.

Tommy Woodward, however, had not fared so well. He had flirted with joining local beat group the De Avalons and even taken up the drums. Although he had an excellent sense of rhythm, drumming and his singing style were incompatible. His success at the Wheatsheaf led to his being asked to join two other acts in a concert party called the Misfits. Concert party groups had always been popular in the Valleys' working men's clubs for weekends and he could earn £2, and occasionally £5, a night. It was a harsh apprenticeship and taught him a great deal about performance and control, but it was not an unending series of triumphs. Not every club audience appreciated his talents.

'I saw Tom a couple of years later, he was dying a death and he wasn't very happy,' recalled Vernon. 'He knew just two chords on the guitar, bang bang, and he was singing on his own, stuff like Ray Charles's *I Can't Stop Loving You*. He got paid off from a number of places because he wasn't what they wanted and there were just as many good singers there who would sing for a free pint. He was singing with phrasing, but to them it was a bloody noise. "Sing bloody straight, man, what's the matter with you? Pay him off!" they'd say. He was fed up.'

Individually the Senators earned less than Tom did as a Misfit. They might split £6 or £8 a night, but money had to be pumped back into equipment and for out-of-town gigs they had to carry their gear, drums, amplifiers and all, on the local bus. The difference was that they were playing the rock and roll songs Tom loved, and the girls liked them. Over a period of months Tom and Vernon became more than nodding acquaintances. Passing in the street Tom always asked, 'How's the band going?' Little asides like, 'Got a singer, then?' when he knew perfectly well it was Tommy Pitman, who now lived in Treforest and was an occasional drinking buddy of his, and 'I wish I had a band' made sure Vernon knew he was interested.

Tom's chance came on a Friday night in September 1961. The Senators had landed a residency at the YMCA on the corner of Taff Street and Crossbrook Street, but Tommy Pitman was bored with the routine. The Senators were Vernon's baby. 'Vernon was the main man, he kept it going,' said Pitman. 'Whenever there was a problem, Vernon solved it. If anyone squabbled, Vernon would calm it all down. All Vernon wanted was for the band to be successful.

'We were in the YMCA every Friday for weeks, I was a bit fed up with that. One night I never turned up for a booking, I was playing three-card brag. I said, "I can't be bothered, I'm not going up tonight." I knew they could have carried on and Vernon could sing a song. Tom was never far away, funnily enough . . . he was probably waiting for a chance.'

For Vernon cards over chords was the last straw. The Senators played their first set that night as instrumentals. In the break Vernon sprinted down Taff Street, up the High Street and into the White Hart. Tommy Woodward was in his usual position at the bar with a pint of bitter in his hand. Initially he did not seem too keen. 'Vernon,' he said, 'it's Friday night. It's beer night. They don't sell beer at the Y.'

'What if we put a crate of light ale in the back behind the curtain?'

'OK, I'll give it a go.'

Following that casual exchange Tom sauntered up the street and bounded on to the stage at the Y. He turned his head to Keith Davies and said, 'Do you know *Great Balls of Fire* in C?' The reply came, 'You sing it . . . we'll play it.'

And then he was off. 'Before, I'd always just stood there and sung,' said Tom. 'But that night I started to move in a suggestive way. I can't tell you to this day why I did it. It just happened, something inspired me. People stopped dancing to watch me and I began to move even more with a lot of sexy gyrations. The chicks were really excited. It worked then and it's worked ever since. In between songs my friend Roy Nicholls would hand me a bottle of beer from behind the curtain.'

Vernon remembered it slightly differently. 'He was a bit heavy for the audience, and they didn't quite know what to make of him, but I knew from that moment I wanted Tom to sing with us.'

The Senators rehearsed in the front room of Vernon's house at 2 Glyndwr Avenue, Rhydfellin. His sister kept them fuelled with sandwiches and his father with shillings to feed the electricity meter. Tom was invited to rehearse with them the following week. 'Tom was different from what we had been doing, more raw,' said Keith. 'I thought, "Who the hell is this?" He had this powerful voice and he was Jerry Lee Lewis mad. Then suddenly he sang this hymn – *Thora*. He beat it up, a bit, clicked his fingers and then left. I said to Vernon, "I'm not having no bugger in the band that sings hymns." '

Pitman was having second thoughts and wanted back in. Other members of the band shared Keith's reservations and there was even a suggestion they have two singers. 'Two of them didn't like the idea of me being out. So I said, "How about having two singers?" But Tom said, "No, I don't want no part of that. It's either me or Tom, or we'll leave it there." And they voted for Tom.'

Pitman soon joined another local group, the Strollers. To this day he remains sanguine about his ousting from the band. The real difference between the two Toms he reckons was, 'the want. He wanted it bad, so bad that nothing else mattered. Tom would stand up and sing anywhere for anyone. There were a lot of people in the Valleys who could sing as well as Tom, but they didn't have his aggression on stage. Even then, before he was big, he was always thrusting himself. It wasn't the done thing. But Tom would do it. He had this gyrating voice and hips and everything that went with it.'

With Tom rechristened 'Twisting' Tommy Scott, the Senators became one of the top attractions in the Valleys. Tommy's hips were part of the appeal. The advert for their 23 June 1962 gig at the Empress Ballroom in Abercynon reads, 'The Fabulous Senators featuring Tommy Scott (TV Vocalist). Girls you will swoon when you see and hear Tommy dancing, 7.30 to 9.30. Admission 2 shillings [10p].' Regular gigs included the Regent Ballroom in Hopkinstown, the Green Fly in Bedwas on Thursdays, Friday nights down at the Y in Ponty, the Welfare Hall in Newbridge, the Memorial Hall in Tredegar, the Cwm Welfare in Beddau and the Wood Road Non-Political. Soon they were commanding £12 to £15 a night, which meant Tom could work even less during the day.

'Basically we played ninety-five per cent of the Valleys,' said Keith Davies, 'This was where the social clubs were. Down in Cardiff you went to see a band in a dance hall. By the end we'd have 300 people at the shows. We'd play a couple of hours in two spots. We played the ballroom on the end of Penarth Pier, we played in the Connaught Rooms. Our Cardiff equivalent were the Raiders, they all had blond hair. First time I'd ever seen anybody play the guitar with a tremolo arm – that was Dave Edmunds.'

The difficulty for the Senators was keeping both types of audience – working men's clubs and dance halls – happy. The set was a mixture of styles and material: *Great Balls of Fire*, *Breathless*, *Spanish Harlem*. *The Young Ones* stayed in the set, despite Tom's hatred of Cliff Richard, because Keith liked playing the instrumental solo. 'They didn't like rock and roll music in working men's clubs,' said Tom. 'They wanted to hear big voices or a funny comedian. When they saw the amplifiers coming in they'd go, "Jesus Christ, rock and roll, pay them off." I'd built up a bit of a reputation in the clubs, so I said, "Just listen." I'd do a lot of ballads and then smack 'em with *Great Balls of Fire*.'

Vernon's street was a veritable musical hothouse. Another neighbour was a classically trained soprano. After being introduced to Tom she reckoned he had the basic ability to become an opera singer and perhaps emulate Sir Geraint Evans, one of Pontypridd's most famous sons. Tom preferred to stay singing pop – the disciplines of tenor training would have curtailed his drinking – but he took a few lessons from her which taught him how to control his breathing and how to project his already powerful voice with less effort. It was to prove a few shillings well spent.

Compared to what was happening in London the Senators looked like old-fashioned, retro Teds. In Wales they always looked smart. Tom had a suit with a Beatles jacket without any lapels, while the band went into Foster's and had matching black trousers and wine-coloured jackets run up. Tom spent hours practising his new signature — a big T, a big S and two more Ts. Their act was increasingly slick. They did one song where at the end for the last 30/40 bars they all put guitars behind their heads. Tom made an appearance on the TV talent show *Donald Peers Presents* . . .

The Senators might have been pretty slick and sexy for South Wales, but they were stuck in South Wales. While in 2000 the slightest sniff of something exciting can lead to a gridlock of record company A&R men *en route* to a cow shed in the Brecon Beacons, in 1963 the record business was much smaller, more insular and only interested in what was coming out of Liverpool and a hairy bunch of louts out in Richmond called the Rolling Stones. The infrastructure was simply not there. If the Senators were to break out of Ponty they needed external help.

The frustrations inherent in being a big pike in a narrow pond came out in the occasional fight. Trivial incidents could escalate into major rows. Rows were settled by blows not words. 'Tom and I had a barney one New Year's Eve,' said Keith. 'We'd had a few drinks in the afternoon and we were in the dressing room at Treharris Legion Club. Vernon was messing around on the piano playing the *Moonlight Sonata* then Tom tried to pick it up. I said, "It's Christmas, for Christ's sake. Play something like *Jingle Bells*, sounds like a dirge in here." I pushed the piano lid on Tom's fingers and he grabbed hold of me by the shirt and pushed me around a little bit, until all the boys said, "Hang on." I was still the youngest in the band.

'Later I was in the car park putting the gear in the van. Tom came out and said, "I'm sorry about what happened in there. We've all had too much to drink." He held out his hand to shake and I said, "Fuck off, Woodward," and turned to put the gear back in the van. Next thing I know he'd yanked me out of the back of the van into the car park and kicked me. For the next few weeks it was hairy on stage. If Mike Roberts was playing the intro he'd turn round and say, "Great," if I was playing it he was very off.'

The coldness continued for months. On the way to gigs the band parked the van at the Blue Star Garage on the Broadway and took it in turns to run up the steps and bang on the grille of Cliff Terrace. That meant that it was a caller for the Woodwards. A knock on the door was for Vi Trenchard. Keith sat in the van and grunted, 'It ain't my turn.' Silence greeted him. Finally Keith knew what he had to do. He went up, banged on the grate and shouted down, 'Hi Linda, it's Keith.' He went in, had a cup of tea and chatted to Linda, who seldom went to gigs. Tom was shaving in the mirror.

'You all right?' offered Keith.

'Yeah,' came the reply. 'You?' That was it. It broke the ice, the incident was forgotten. Later the band used to laugh about it.

Tom and Vernon became particularly close friends. One evening, Tom, who had not passed his driving test, arrived at Vernon's house behind the wheel of a gleaming red Ford Corsair. The car belonged to Tony Thorn, who was married to Linda's sister Rosalind. Bought on the strength of a football pools win, it was Tony's pride and joy. The duo drove around for a while and eventually fetched up on Barry Island. Tom dropped Vernon off, but was stopped by the police on the way home.

Unfortunately, Tom had borrowed the car without permission and Tony had reported his car stolen. Although he tried to get his brother-in-law off the hook, Tom ended up in court and was fined. Tom was furious that Vernon did not offer to pay half the fine. 'He didn't ask, so I didn't offer,' said Vernon. 'By the time the case went to court I was out of work, sacked for sleeping on the job too often.'

The Green Fly in Bedwas was a crucial venue for the Senators. One Thursday night, Vernon and Keith started chatting to Chris Ellis, a young TV and radio engineer from Nantgarw. Ellis had a slight stutter but was full of energy and thought the band was great. That night he gave the boys a lift home, and soon found himself the Senators' driver and roadie. He sold his car and bought a cream-coloured Morris J van.

'The back of the van was great,' said Ellis. 'There was carpet on the floor, carpet on the wall, there were a couple of sofas that somebody had thrown out in the back. It was like a real passion wagon. It was who could get a girl and get her in the back of the van. It wasn't a sexual orgy every night we were out, somebody pulled maybe every five or six weeks, but Tom was the most successful. I was getting paid £1 a night for petrol. That van got smashed up skidding on ice coming back from Cwmtillery and hitting a wall. So I bought a Standard Eight.'

If there were no girls around after a Saturday night show, the band would pile into the van and head into Cardiff to grab a curry. Then they would go into a local nightclub for a drink. One evening they were sitting in the back of a club while Danny Williams was performing his biggest hit *Moon River*. 'I can sing better than this,' grunted Tom, standing at the bar. The band egged him on. Halfway through the song he joined in. His powerful voice soon drowned out Williams's delicate tenor, even with a microphone. The crowd applauded loudly so a mortified Williams murmured, 'I knew you had some good voices in Wales,' while Tom was being patted on the back and bragging, 'I knew I could sing him under the table.'

The Senators had a succession of managers – Horace Turner,

the father of drummer Alva booked shows even after his son was replaced by 17-year-old Chris Rees. The first sniff of interest came from two local grammar school boys and aspiring songwriters, Ray Godfrey and John Glastonbury, who chanced upon the Senators in the Green Fly. It was not a relationship forged on mutual respect. They found the band to be lackadaisical and unreliable; in return the band called them Myron and Byron. (Godfrey, who now runs a music publishing business in Arizona, calls himself Byron to this day.)

'Myron had slitty eyes,' recalled Ellis without much charity, 'that was Raymond Godfrey, and the tall one was Byron. They looked like a couple of used-car salesmen.'

A few demo tracks were recorded in the gents' toilets of the Pontypridd YMCA because, said Keith, 'It was like a big football changing room and the acoustics were great.' But at least they had something to play to companies in London. In 1963, the capital was swarming with wannabe beat combos, but eventually the managers secured a one-year production deal with record producer Joe Meek.

So off they went to London. It was the first time the band had ever left Wales. Guitarist Dave Cooper (a disillusioned Keith Davies had left the band a few months earlier), who had been born in London, managed to get them as far as Shepherd's Bush Tube station. 'Beyond that it was a jungle to us, we were terrified to go further,' said Ellis. 'So we carted everything across London, changing trains twice, and eventually got to Holloway Road. We did the session then lugged everything back on the Tube in rush hour. We stuck everything back in the van, then Dai took us into the West End. We wandered around Oxford Street and Trafalgar Square like a bunch of Welsh hillbillies, absolutely mesmerised by the whole thing. Tom too.'

On the surface Meek was definitely the big time. At only

thirty-three he was the country's leading independent record producer at a time when everybody else was on a salary. His use of echo and atmospheric sound effects had turned the Tornados' *Telstar* into a chart-topper on both sides of the Atlantic. While instrumental effects were his forte, he had also had a big hit with John Leyton's *Johnny Remember Me*.

The problem was that Meek was a self-loathing homosexual, mentally unstable, and prone to violent outbreaks. (On 3 February 1967 he shot his landlady dead before committing suicide.) He recorded in a Dickensian three-storey house with steep stairs situated above a shop at 304 Holloway Road. Vernon, who had to do the session on crutches because he had broken his leg, remembers it as being like 'Dr Who's TARDIS, full of tapes and all his little inventions, all his sounds and all, limiters and things like that which are common now, but which we'd never seen before.'

The studio was in the front room. Joe used to put the drums in the fireplace because he got a great sound in there. There was a window knocked in the wall which overlooked a bedroom. Lying naked in his bed was Heinz, who had just been in the Top 10 with his tribute to Eddie Cochran, *Just Like Eddie*. The Senators did not know where to look.

The session produced seven songs, one of which, *Little Lonely One* – all about Meek – was supposed to be released as a single. The B-side, *I Was a Fool*, was written by Glastonbury and Godfrey. They also laid down two Jerry Lee Lewis songs, *Great Balls of Fire* and *Chills and Fever*.

Despite Meek's prompting, Decca did not seem very interested. They postponed the release date for month after month, telling Joe that P.J. Proby was taking priority. The band tired of the long treks up to London, one of which had seen them arrive at Holloway Road at 10 a.m. to find Joe had forgotten all about the session and was recording a band in Cheltenham.

Meek treated them all with contempt. He despised Myron and Byron, and dismissed the Senators out of hand, rating their musical attributes on a par with Kenny Lord's Statesmen. Tom he liked as much for his tight trousers as for his vocal range, though he showed his affection in increasingly bizarre ways. 'He certainly had his eye on Tom,' said Vernon. 'Being the singer he probably stood out more than the rest of us and Joe was around him a lot. He'd got a big reputation, so we were all going, "Watch him, backs against the wall, lads". One day he made a physical approach to Tom who stomped out of the room steaming.'

'We cut about five songs,' said Tom, 'and he said to the boys, "Pack up the instruments and load the van, I want to talk to Tom". He said, "You sound great but I haven't seen you perform. Give me a demonstration of how you move on stage." And I said, "I can't do that now. Come see a gig – we'll do a pub or something in London." He was giving me the come-on – only I wasn't getting it. To me he was Joe Meek, Mr Telstar. He was eyeing me from head to toe and said, "Those jeans fit you well, don't they?" '

Tom got it when Meek added, 'You've got a nice set in there, haven't you?' and stroked his crotch. Down on the street the band heard the yells, the sound of equipment flying down the stairs, followed by Tom incandescent with fury yelling, 'The bastard, he just grabbed my balls.'

At the next session Meek stormed into the studio right in the middle of a take, pulled out a gun, levelled it at Tom and fired. It was only a starting pistol, but Joe walked out, 'laughing his balls off', leaving a room full of shivering wrecks. It looked like the only way Meek was ever going to play a company their tapes was if Tommy Scott submitted to his advances, but as far as Tom was concerned that was never ever going to happen.

To the Senators it seemed that Myron and Byron were close to useless. Ray Godfrey has claimed that they put money into the band by buying them a van and a PA and that they played Jimmy Savile a tape and he put them in touch with Decca. At the time Savile was one of the top disc jockeys in the country. He had clout. If he liked an artist it opened doors. The managers had discovered that Savile often stayed in a bed and breakfast hotel somewhere near King's Cross. Chris Ellis brought Tom up to London in his white mini van. There was only enough money for one room so, while their managers were in the hotel, Chris and Tom slept in the van. They woke up at six and breakfasted off milk stolen from local doorsteps.

Tom recalled the incident: 'Myron and Byron? They might as well have been called Pinky and Perky for all the good they did me. One of them had been up in London for a week and we hadn't heard a word from him. I went to London and tracked him down to his hotel room to find out what was going on. I was banging on the door and Jimmy Savile came out of the room next door. We had a chat and he gave me some really helpful advice.'

After a fruitless discussion with his manager Tom again knocked on Savile's door. 'I was a bit drunk and banged hard on the bedroom door. Jimmy popped his head out and I explained that I had been let down badly. He told me to come and see him the next day. So I did, and gave him a tape. He gave the demo tape to Decca and that was it.'

Savile's own autobiography, *As It Happens*, though written in elliptical terms, bears out Tom's version of events. The net result was that a tape ended up in Peter Sullivan's hands at Decca. 'His voice was very distinctive, that was the thing that turned me on,' said Sullivan. 'The guy sounded great. Tom had a very hip sound and he has got this quality, a soully voice, but very distinctive. His voice stood way out there.

'I went to see him in Pontypridd in one of those working men's clubs there. He was a real hard rocker, not the balladeer he turned into. As soon as I saw the guy I thought, he's got it, he's unique. The band was adequate. I wasn't signing them, I was signing the singer.'

Myron and Byron then went up to see Joe Meek and told him they had met Dick Rowe at Decca who had denied all knowledge of Tom and any release date. There was a row and Joe duly terminated their contract by tearing it up and slinging it in the bin. Tom insisted he himself went back to Meek's studio and grabbed him. 'He thought I was going to kill him, ran around the desk and flew up onto the mantelpiece! It was like Peter Pan! He said, "That's it, leave me alone, don't touch me." So off I went and thought that was it. But Joe still had the tapes – which we found out when we released *It's Not Unusual*.' The upshot, though, was that Tom was now free to sign with Decca.

In the career of every artist chance, happenstance and plain luck have their parts to play. Tommy Woodward knew he was a great singer. People had been telling him that for twenty years. Yet, whether through fear of failure or loyalty to his family, he never took the initiative. 'In the days before the motorways and the Severn Bridge, South Wales was a long, long way away,' he said. 'It took a long time to get to London and I didn't know anybody there. If I went to London on my own, what was I going to do? Walk around the streets singing?'

Hundreds of stars have done just that. But not Tom. He was reactive not proactive. To fulfil his dreams he needed somebody to believe in him absolutely. Someone who had drive, determination and who knew what he was doing.

In early April 1964 a struggling songwriter and minor pop star living in London was sent a very small royalty cheque by his accountant. There was just enough money for Gordon Mills to take his pregnant wife Jo on a week's holiday down to see his mother in Tonypandy. Gordon was on the lookout for an act to manage. Both his former singing colleague Johnny Bennett and his old school friend Gordon 'Gog' Jones were singing the praises of a certain Tommy Scott.

On the morning of 10 May 1964 Johnny Bennett picked up Tom, Vernon and rhythm guitarist Dave Cooper and took them to the Lewis Merthyr Club in Porth. Tom, dressed in his usual leather jacket, did not impress Gordon, who described him as 'a scruffy bastard'. At the club a comedian was running through his Sunday morning routine. Gordon did not like it. At one point he just pointed his finger at the comedian and stared at him as if he were some lower lifeform. Eventually Gordon agreed to come along to see Tom and the band play at the Top Hat Club up in Cwmtillery that evening.

The evening did not get off to a good start when Bryn the Fish's van broke down. Bryn Phillips was a comedian who often appeared on the bill with the Senators. His day job was a fishmonger and they often used his van to transport gear and friends to gigs. Keith Davies, who still helped out even though he no longer played in the band, hitched a lift up with Gordon and Jo in their plum-coloured Ford Zephyr.

Up at the Top Hat Club there was a problem because the hall was packed out and it was a members only club. Eventually, with Tom pleading to the committee members, 'That's Gordon Mills from London, he's come to see me,' the Mills party was let in provided they stood at the bar and did not upset any of the members.

Stories about what actually happened that evening vary in detail, depending on who is doing the telling. Keith Davies recalled Gordon saying, 'I'd like to have that boy under my belt for a time.' 'In the interval I got a round of drinks in, like I always did for the band, and I happened to tell Tom what he'd said. Tom wasn't interested and just said, "He'd better go talk to the boys" — meaning Myron and Byron.'

Just as he had with Vernon at the White Hart, Tom's laid-back manner hid his real nerves. He had been so wound up by the prospect of playing in front of Gordon that Linda, then 22, had agreed to come along, which she seldom did. Her intended moral support backfired. 'She got so bloody drunk that I had to go into the ladies' room to get her out once the whole thing was over,' said Tom. 'She'd bloody collapsed in there, because she'd got too excited. That's the way she's always felt. If I go for a high note, she's worried I'm not going to make it.'

To Bennett, Gordon pretended he thought Bryn the Fish had a better voice. Jo Mills put him out of his misery. 'Do you want to know the truth?' she said. 'I don't know what this boy is doing in a club like this. He's too bloody good.' Johnny said, 'Gordon didn't seem to think so.' Jo laughed and replied, 'If Gordon didn't think so he would have gone after the first half.'

'I was absolutely stunned by Tom's performance,' said Jo later. 'I'll never forget it, it was an amazing experience. I came away just overcome, it was as strong as that, he was fantastic. He wiggles nowadays, but then, wow! He was just a remarkable raw talent. Gordon felt the same. I don't think at first that Gordon even thought of managing Tom. But on the long drive back to London we were both shattered by what we'd seen. At one point Gordon suddenly pulled the car over to the side of the road and said, "I've just got to do something with that guy, I've just got to do something." '

Gordon had been captured by Tom's performance from the opening bars of *Spanish Harlem*, but knew he had to play it cool. 'As soon as I saw Tom I knew he had what it takes to go all the way to the top,' he said later. 'He was sensational. That night at the Top Hat he had the audience in a frenzy. The first few bars were all I needed to hear. They convinced me that here was a voice which could make him the greatest singer in the world.'

Having told Johnny what he really thought, Gordon asked, 'Can you get hold of Tom for me?' Myron and Byron promptly told him to 'piss off'. Bennett remonstrated, pointing out that Gordon had already written hit songs and had the contacts with record companies they so obviously lacked. That night the Senators played for nearly three hours and in one of their ten-minute breaks Gordon and Tom had their first serious conversation.

It was what Tom had been waiting for. Here was the missing piece of the jigsaw. He had heard the bullshit before but this was a local boy who had actually done what he dare not, left the Rhondda and made it in London.

'Gordon was so important for me; I needed someone to recognise my talent, handle all the agents and producers and all the rest of it. Gordon was in showbusiness. I knew he knew what he was talking about because he had done something and I liked the way he talked. He was telling me what I felt about myself. That I could sing all these songs. That I was versatile. I had a powerful voice. That I had a great range. He said, "If I can't write you a hit record I'll do my damnedest to get you one." '

Gordon went back to London for seven weeks. During his absence Tom and Vernon discussed the options over and over, with Vernon pushing Tom to take that great leap. He did not realise that Gordon's long-term plans did not include him.

'This is our chance,' reasoned the bass player. 'We've got to get in there. This guy Gordon Mills, perhaps he can do something. He's living in London, he knows the ropes. Myron and Byron haven't done anything.

'So we told Gordon Mills about our problems and he said, "Forget it, I'll sort it out." I was relieved. We just dumped them. We all wanted to go with Gordon. We were very impressed with him and drawn to him. The only thing I didn't like about him was when he pointed his finger at the comedian which made me feel a little uneasy. But that was soon forgotten.'

According to Tom, the band's contract with Myron and Byron was due to run out within a few months. In late June 1964, up at the Hibs Club in Ferndale, Gordon made a side deal with the duo. 'Gordon said, "Look, fellas, I'm not trying to steal him from you. I'll have a separate contract with Tom and you can have five per cent." But we couldn't put any dates on the contract because I hadn't then got anywhere, so we left the dates open. It just said Myron and Byron will be paid five per cent from blank to blank.'

Five years later that document was to prove expensive for Tom and Gordon. At the time it did not worry Gordon, five per cent of nothing is nothing. And he had a more serious problem. He had just convinced Tommy Scott and the Senators (who had agreed to a very high fifty-fifty split with their new manager) to move up to London, where the streets were paved with record contracts and he had instant access to the most important movers and shakers in the record business.

The reality was rather different. He lived in a small rented flat. His wife was pregnant. He had £250 in the bank and a beaten-up old Zephyr. But he had found an artist who he knew was a world beater.

CHAPTER FIVE

THE MULE

—————

Most nights Troy, though he was still plain Noel Fredericks in those days, could push the Mule into believing that he held a winning hand. The Mule was a good poker player, had all the right gambler's instincts – except for that single fatal weakness that gave him his nickname. Even as he saw the pot keep climbing and the bets still coming, even though he knew that the odds were stacked against him, Troy could get him going and he'd bet more and more and more. The Mule knew someone else had a perfect hand and he couldn't beat it, but he still wouldn't give in. The Mule was a bad loser.

That Friday night in late May 1964, the Mule was most distracted. He couldn't settle into his usual routine. Usually he would hide behind a cloud of Woodbine smoke, step back inside his midnight, anti-matter, eyes. He never talked much, but the others in the gang knew he was always listening, always calculating. That night, something was bursting to get out, but nobody asked what it was. The Mule played his life, like his cards, close to his chest.

Most of the usual crew were there: the Mule, Barry Mason, Mitch Murray, Troy Dante, Andy Ray. Barry had christened them the Collection, Notting Hill's answer to the Rat Pack. Everyone who came to play poker in Uxbridge Street, just behind the Gaumont Cinema, dreamt of making it in 'the business'. A couple of them had enjoyed its taste for a moment. The rest just inhaled the smell of frying fish and chips wafting out of Geale's, and dreamt on.

Barry Mason was a careful player, always waiting for the big hand. He had fetched up in London in 1959, out of Wigan via America, and determined to become an actor. Down in his basement lived Tommy Bruce, who worked as a driver's mate at the Covent Garden fruit market. Tommy Bruce possessed an extraordinary voice, memorably described as 'a subtle blending of corncrake, steam hammer and gravel polisher'. Barry loaned Tommy the money to record the demo tape which landed him a record deal with Norrie Paramor at Columbia and Barry, despite knowing nothing about the business, found himself as a manager.

Tommy Bruce and the Bruisers had a massive hit with their first single, a cover version of Fats Waller's *Ain't Misbehavin'*, but after that the hits had dried up. One night Barry lay in bed and thought up a little song in his head. The next day, he got the guitarist to put the music down, and found he'd written his first song. That night in Uxbridge Street Barry was still pretty high with success as *Don't Turn Around* had been a Top 20 hit for the Merseybeats a month earlier.

Mitch Murray had cracked the big one a year earlier when Gerry and the Pacemakers took *How Do You Do It?* to number one — even though The Beatles had turned it down first. The Mule had notched up more hits than anyone, both as a singer and as a writer, but he wanted more. To make the rent, he'd worked for a while as an assistant recording manager, and he was always talking about finding the right artist to manage. He'd been married to Jo Waring, a stunning, successful model who was earning much more than he was, for a couple of years. Men from South Wales are not brought up to be supported by their women. And now she was pregnant. Perhaps that was what was bothering him. Certainly something was affecting his game.

Eventually even the Mule couldn't keep quiet any longer. He shuffled the cards in front of him, put them face down on the table and announced, in his soft Rhondda way, 'I've found him.'

'Found who?'

'The one.'

'What one?'

'I've seen this singer in Wales and I'm going to manage him. He's going to be bigger than Elvis, bigger than Sinatra.'

'Shut up and deal.'

But, of course, the game could not go on after that. This was the dream they all had, the one that would change all of their lives. If one of them happened, they'd all benefit. If only at the poker table. So one of them, nobody remembers who, asked the question that had to be asked if they were ever to play another hand.

'So who is he?'

'His name,' said Gordon Mills, 'is Tommy Woodward. But I'm going to change that.'

From the moment he signed with Gordon Mills, Tommy Woodward never had to worry which direction he was heading in. What Tommy had finally found in Mills was the missing chunk of the puzzle, someone who knew the answers, someone who held the key to escape the Valleys.

Gordon Mills was born in Madras, Southern India on 15

May 1935. His father Bill was born in the Valleys and trained as a carpenter, but when times got tough in the twenties he joined the Army. Posted to India, he soon rose to the rank of sergeant, and married Lorna, a pretty, dark-haired Anglo-Indian girl several years his junior. Just before the war the family returned to settle in Tonypandy.

His father might have returned to his roots, but for all his talk of being a Rhondda boy, there was always something restless about Gordon. In South Wales, the communities were tight, interwoven by loyalties not just of blood but by the simple intangible presence of being there, down the pub, down the shaft, down the pitch, sitting in the Bracchi Shops. Gordon lacked that basic grounding in the ways of the Valleys because they were not bred into his bones. As an only child of exotic parentage – even when he never knew it – he was always different. Something never commented on, but a constant given when the gossip chattered up the cobbles.

Boys generally settled any disputes with their fists, but Gordon used his mouth to far greater effect. He failed his 11-plus because the rote and fixed patterns of school never absorbed him. Music did. Bill had cut quite a dash playing the clarinet back in India; Gordon could not afford one, so he picked up a harmonica. At the time the harmonica was very popular and Larry Adler, Tommy Reilly and Ronald Chesney were big stars.

Terry Blinkhorn, his best friend at Trealaw Secondary School, told Gordon that his older brother Albert gave classes in his Tonypandy home. Soon he was in a harmonica band playing for a few bob a night. 'He had a strong character and certainly stood out,' recalled Albert Blinkhorn. 'There was no way you could take him off his path if he thought something was right. He had a lot of talent musically and played the harmonica very well. He always had that go-ahead thing. He was a good organiser, and with other kids of his age he was usually the chief. He always said that he would come back one day with a couple of Rolls-Royces parked outside. He could tell you a thing was black and even if you knew damn well it was white, Gordon would convince you it was black. He would gamble on any damn thing and he and his friends would have all-night sessions with cards.'

From the age of fifteen, Mills saw the harmonica as his way to another life. After playing a few concerts with the harmonica group he determined to join the Spades, the pseudonym adopted by the Bennett family who lived in Western Terrace, Edmunstown. After charming and impressing the Bennetts with his ability they broke the family-only rule and voted him into the group. Soon he was earning 15 shillings (75p) playing local pubs and clubs at the weekends. The youngest member of the family, Johnny Bennett, can remember Gordon coming to their house brimming with confidence and new numbers to rehearse.

'I left school at fifteen to go to work as a motor mechanic,' Gordon Mills told Ray Connolly in a rare interview in 1970. 'But I packed it in after a week because they had me breaking stones to make a yard for them. Then I went underground for a while in the mines and worked in the steel mills. Everything like that. I wanted to join the Army when I was sixteen and filled in the forms to sign on for twelve years, but I got an answer saying they didn't have any vacancies at that moment. Just imagine, I would have had to do fifteen years in all if I'd been accepted.'

At seventeen he was called up for National Service and served in Germany and Malaya. He hated his time in the Army, though he did later confess it taught him 'self-discipline, personal hygiene and self-respect'. His fellow soldiers had been impressed by his harp playing, but returning home to more of the same was very depressing. He constantly told friends, 'I'm going to get somewhere in life, you just wait and see'. He took a job as a bus conductor with Rhondda Transport, and continued to daydream about breaking into the music business and becoming famous. For ages they were only fantasies, but one day he read in a music paper that Hohner were staging a British harmonica championship at the Albert Hall in London.

Pawning his prized tape recorder to pay his fare, he went up to London. He came second in the championship, though later on he claimed he'd won and had been sounded out by various agents. Gordon hated to be anything other than the best. He came back to the Rhondda boasting that he would soon be off to London for ever. For some weeks he hesitated, torn between security and the fear of failure. Eventually his old teacher and fellow conductor Albert Blinkhorn told him, 'You've got to take a chance. If you don't do it now you're never going to do anything.'

For such an innate chancer there was little choice. It was a time when austerity still ruled. Even with rationing over, its hoarding principles lingered in the national psyche. When Harold Macmillan was announcing to the people of Britain, 'you've never had it so good', he was chiding the voters as much as inviting them to celebrate their good fortune. The mantra was, 'Be cautious; save for the future; study hard, get to grammar school and there might be a job in the bank at the end of it all.' In a couple of generations a family could drag itself by its bootstraps up into the lower-middle class. For a working-class boy who'd blown out of his secondary modern school at fifteen, a job was for life, and back then there were jobs aplenty in the Valleys – down the mines, on the buses, or standing behind the assembly line until the gold watch chimed retirement.

There were escapes out of the rut. Sport was an option, but boxing and rugby offered only local glory and little financial reward. Footballers were still tied by the minimum wage, £20 a week, whether you were Stanley Matthews, Bobby Charlton or a journeyman hacking through the mud at Grimsby Town. Show-business offered the best chance, whatever the skills. Lenny Davies became Larry Page, the 'Teenage Rage' and never had to go back to packing records for EMI in Hayes. Ronnie Wycherley, a Liverpudlian tugboat man with a weak heart, was reinvented as Billy Fury. The money was pretty good, but never a pension fund. A good middle of the bill performer could take home £50 a week clear.

Of course they all dreamt of stardom, what young man doesn't, but their intentions were to buy a nice place in the suburbs rather than a mansion on the hill. The first purchase a new star inevitably made was a house for mum and dad. A symbol of escaping the terrace – and a fall back if things went wrong. Life on the variety tours gave everybody a taste of the probable and a glimpse of the possible. Most settled for the former and so eventually the strong and the ambitious became songwriters, arrangers, producers, backing singers, booking agents and artist managers.

The money was not in record sales. Not when an artist was earning a halfpenny (½d) for every single sold. Sell half a million copies and he earned just over £1,000, before the manager took his cut. A quarter if he was lucky, half if he wasn't. The living wage was in performance. 'If you were a Columbia recording artist, hits or no hits, you could fill venues,' said Larry Page. 'If the bill said, "Star of 6.5 Special or Ready Steady Go, you could pack the theatres.' Although Larry Parnes, and later Evie Taylor and Colin Berlin, had started packaging rock and roll tours in the late fifties, those were short, sharp twenty one-nighters back-to-back. The regular work was on variety bills.

The old-style acts, the ventriloquists, the jugglers and the magicians were uncomfortable with these rock and roll upstarts. They had spent their lives in variety, often born into it, and all they could see was the onrush of progress, the twin onslaught of television and pop music, swallowing them up and spitting them out toothless and unemployable. 'The variety people hated that,' said Larry Page. 'You could go into your dressing room and find all your clothes down on the floor in a heap, or find someone had sabotaged you, pulled one of the mikes out of the socket.'

Gordon took Albert Blinkhorn's advice and, along with Ronnie Wells, whom he'd met at the harmonica championships, landed a job with the Morton Fraser Harmonica Gang. For two years Mills worked 200 dates a year. He started off playing in pantomime at the London Palladium, but was earning only £14 in a good week and £10 in a bad one. He was so broke, according to flatmate Ronnie Wells, 'he used to borrow my shoes'.

He learnt his trade, absorbed the techniques of stage craft. That was the thing about variety: learning how to work the room, how to play to the gods, while not losing the floor. Hecklers came with the gig, so Gordon had to learn to cope with them and not miss a beat. He discovered how he could do a show in London and the next night in Manchester do exactly the same thing to a different reaction. He saw comedians telling exactly the same joke, how some would survive and others die. He also saw how the times were changing and how rock and roll was affecting the kids. Morton Fraser did not like the way Mills, Wells and singer Don Paul were letting an *Oh Boy!* attitude creep into the act. Eventually Fraser fired Paul for moodiness and petulance, attitudes learnt from watching too many James Dean movies. His friends resigned in sympathy and together they formed the Viscounts.

The Viscounts were very slick, a good close harmony vocal group who could churn out the hits of the day coupled with an engaging patter. When the Coasters hit the charts with *Charlie Brown* the Viscounts sang it that night . . . unless the bill-topper had first dibs on the song. The Viscounts were a good solid support act, capable of a twenty- or thirty-minute slot, perfect to close the first half of the show, or kick up the pace in the second half if the talking dog had swallowed his tongue. For a while they were managed by Larry Parnes, who gave them work on packages like *The Rock 'n' Roll Trad Show*, and paid them properly for it.

Gordon had a wild streak that rebelled against such demands and often appeared on stage in odd-coloured socks. He could make a fool of himself with aplomb. 'Every night,' said Don Paul, 'one of the artists sang *The Madison* and the whole cast had to come and dance across the stage. You'd done your act so you might be playing cards and this was the finale. As the tour went on the amount of people turning up for the routine dropped until one day the words "Madison discontinued" appeared on the notice board. Gordon hadn't seen the notice and he ended up going out dancing on his own. He thought he'd be the hero. We all fell about. Professional to the end was Gordon.'

Working on the road gave Mills a practical grounding in the music business that was to prove essential. It was his further education. The circuit was small, an endless slog of one-nighters broken by week-long seasons in the seaside variety theatres. The same faces kept on popping up, just as they were to keep popping up in the career of Tom Jones. The choices and styles of the people Gordon had met on the variety circuit became reflected in Tom Jones. Some, like songwriter Roger Greenaway and his colleague Tony Burrows (both in the Kestrels), would have a peripheral influence. Others would be much more important.

Late in 1959, in a working men's club in Coventry, the Viscounts discovered that Gerry Dorsey, a struggling crooner below them on the bill, was planning to sing one of their numbers, a Top 10 hit earlier in the year for both Tony Newley and its American original Lloyd Price. Gordon, who because he was never afraid to ask for anything had become the Viscounts' enforcer, was dispatched to deal with this unknown upstart. Wisely, Dorsey caved in and let the Viscounts showcase their version of *Personality*.

Mills and Dorsey hit it off. Both had been born in Madras and had Anglo-Indian mothers. They were physically similar, with a dark look that attracted the girls, and a burning ambition. For both it was like looking in a smoked mirror and seeing this hazy reflection of themselves, everything they desired and wanted in life laid bare in another pair of eyes. Gordon had confidence where Gerry had insecurity; Gerry had a three and a half octave range while Gordon had never sung before the Viscounts.

Arnold George Dorsey was born on 2 May 1936, the second youngest of ten children. His father, Mervyn, was an engineering consultant who left the Midlands to work in India on a government project. His dark-skinned mother, Olive, was a singer. In 1947, following Indian independence, Melvyn retired and the family returned home to Leicester, swapping the vibrant chaos, the stifling heat and the relatively comfortable expatriate life style of Madras for a grey semi-detached house in Stroughton Street and a country depressed by rationing and perpetual drizzle.

Arnold went to the Melbourne Road Secondary Modern School. Depressed and culture shocked, he plummeted straight to the bottom of the class. He retreated into a shell which gave him little respite from angry teachers. Bucktoothed and overweight, he was beaten up by local bullies simply for 'being ugly'. One school report when he was twelve described him as a 'very shy boy suffering from innumerable complexes'. That basic insecurity has dogged him all his life.

He did have one talent. Music. His father bought him a saxophone and in that he found his escape. He took lessons, practised hard, and when he blew his horn he dreamt of emulating his namesake, Jimmy Dorsey, the great British saxophone player of the day. His family were more concerned with his finding a proper job when he left school. He attended college for a while and then joined a local engineering firm as an apprentice. Arnold had no intention of following in his father's footsteps, so he quit to work in a semiskilled job in a local boot and shoe factory earning £4 a week.

In his spare time he practised hard on his sax and with his older brother Eddie began getting small gigs at working men's clubs. One night the audience took to heckling, 'Give us a song', so he put down his saxophone and sang. Once Gerry revealed his three-and-a-half octave range, they stopped throwing beer mugs. From then on his horn took second place to his singing. Reinventing himself as Gerry Dorsey, part homage part shrewd move, the bookings began to come in from social clubs all over the Midlands. Called up to do two years' National Service, he was promoted to lance corporal in the Royal Corps of Transport stationed in Germany. His stint in the army helped him develop both his singing talent and his confidence as he was regularly asked to sing and play in the NAAFI and at camp concerts.

Back in civvy street, he found that music had moved on and the bookers had forgotten his name. He took another job at a shoe factory but soon infuriated the management because he was continually late. Determined to attend a talent contest in the Isle of Man he bunked off work. He won the first prize of £75, but came home to the sack. With his prize money and a small suitcase he made the big step and headed towards London.

To the showbiz agents in the West End, Gerry was just another hopeful tramping from door to door diffidently begging for an audition. Hymie Zahl – ever on the lookout for a fresh young face – took a shine to Gerry's exotic look and signed him up to Foster's. They set about grooming him for stardom and arranged a contract with Decca. The only impression his first single, *Mr Music Man*, made was when it was dropped on the floor. A cover version of

Johnny Ray's *I'll Never Fall in Love Again* did marginally better. It failed to dent the charts, earning a total royalty cheque of 5s 4d (26p), but made enough of an impression to land him several guest spots on the TV show *Oh Boy!* It was enough to get him a tour with Marty Wilde, but that was as far as he went. By the turn of the decade the business had dismissed Gerry as yet another poor man's Frankie Vaughan. But he never gave up. Gerry Dorsey has always refused to give up.

Gordon and Gerry became close mates. Too close some people hissed. They paid £4 a week for a flat in Bayswater, so damp the wallpaper was hanging off the walls like strands of rancid pasta. There was hardly any furniture, while cooking was done on a solitary gas ring and the pots fell off the sideboard when the trains clattered by outside. When money was good, the pair would celebrate at a cheap café behind Paddington Station, but when times got bad Gerry was reduced to pawning his saxophone. Eventually they did a moonlight flit. Mills found them alternative accommodation in a house in Cleveland Square, known as Rock and Roll House, full of aspiring artists trying to make the big time.

At Terry Dene's 21st birthday party in Rock and Roll House, Gordon met Rhodesian Jo Waring, who had originally come to Europe to work as a Bluebell girl in Paris. After a six-month stint in the clubs of Las Vegas, where she enhanced her wages by modelling nude for a set of playing cards, she fetched up in London and was making a splash as a fashion model. When they married, Gerry Dorsey was the best man. A few months later, on 18 April 1963, Dorsey decided he wanted to marry his fiancée of long standing. Pat Healy was a secretary from Leicester whom he had met at a Midlands dance hall. Gordon was the best man, and Jo designed Pat's wedding dress. The newlyweds lived in a room in the Mills's flat in Campden Hill Towers, but, seeking independence, moved a mile to a shabby flat in King Street, Hammersmith.

During his first flirtation with stardom, Gerry had struck up a friendship with Les Reed, the pianist with the John Barry Seven. As well as playing their own set, the John Barry Seven accompanied other artists. Gerry had to open the second half, a tough slot at the best of times. Broke and shy, he was dying on his feet. Les, however, was drawn to something in his performance.

'He was a great singer and a good, good man,' he said. 'He had so much *simpatico* towards people, he would cry his eyes out if something upset him. I got friendly with him, and I did him these arrangements for nothing, so that he could continue to do the tour with us.

'Gerry brought me home from Sheffield one night. I lived in Woking, and he said, "I've got a place for you, I share with a friend of mine in Bayswater. Why don't you come and kip there for the night? He's on tour with the Viscounts so you can have his bed."

'That was great. I got into bed but at about 4 o'clock in the morning, I was rooted out from a deep sleep by this livid Welshman yelling, "What are you doing here, you bastard? What are you doing in my bed?" Gordon had come home unexpectedly. He was completely pissed off, so he rooted me out, got into his bed and I slept on the floor. The nice thing was that about 9 o'clock in the morning he got up and made me breakfast. He obviously felt a bit guilty.'

Gordon Mills always had a beguiling manner. Even cooking breakfast over a solitary gas ring in a soggy flat where the cockroaches wore flippers, he exuded a confidence and charisma that impressed Reed. Les could not help but notice his fingernails. They were bitten, savaged down to the quick. 'He did it right up until the last, he always bit his nails,' noted Les. The pair got talking and before long the Viscounts found themselves sharing the bill with the John Barry Seven. Reed and Mills became friends.

There was never much of the showman or rebel about Les Reed. Born and brought up in Woking, he has always preferred the suburbs to city life. His musical interests were encouraged by his father Ralph from the age of seven (his genes helped as his maternal great-grandmother played piano with Johann Strauss's orchestra) and his uncle, who turned up at the house with a piano of dubious provenance. By the age of fourteen he had passed his London College of Music examinations and spent the next four years touring with his own jazz band. After two years' National Service and two years playing cocktail jazz in the West End and at Butlin's, he landed up behind the piano in the John Barry Seven, which was formed in early 1959 to provide the music for the TV series *Drumbeat*.

Ever flexible, Reed switched his allegiance from jazz to pop and soon found himself backing major league rock and rollers like Gene Vincent, Eddie Cochran, Roy Orbison, Jerry Lee Lewis and Adam Faith, who was best man at his wedding. In 1962 Reed left the John Barry Seven to work as a freelance arranger and musical director, scoring a big hit with Joe Brown's *A Picture of You*.

'Early in 1963 I was up in town,' he recalled, 'and Gordon came up and told me he'd got a new artist, a girl called Dodi West, and he said, "Do you fancy doing a bit of writing?" So we did. I went to his place, he had a little flat in Notting Hill Gate. His wife, Jo, was there and we wrote *In the Deep of Night* for Dodi. We struck up a good relationship, we knew musically and lyrically we could work together.'

Although the Viscounts had managed two minor hits — *Short'nin' Bread* and *Who Put the Bomp* in 1960 and 1961, it was obvious to Mills that they weren't going anywhere. Cute striped shirts, distinctive harmonies and a gruelling work schedule aside, he knew that however much he worked on arranging their songs, it would not make any difference. He was looking for some other route to making it.

'Larry Parnes once said that the Viscounts were too good,' Mills told Ray Connolly, 'and in a way we were. Everything we did had to be perfect and it took all the earthiness out of us. We were too polished. I never enjoyed it.'

Gordon needed to take risks, just as he had when he left Wales with nothing more than his mouth organ. 'When we did cabaret clubs up north,' Ronnie Wells remembered, 'there were these card schools, and Gordon could hold his own with good players. We didn't realise this until one morning when he said he'd won £50, big money then. I wouldn't have thought of Gordon as a manager then, but he was single-minded and ambitious and he had that all-important lucky streak.'

The cards fell Gordon's way when Johnny Kidd and the Pirates covered *I'll Never Get Over You*, which hit number four in July 1963. Originally written as the B-side of a Viscounts flop, it had been touted round Tin Pan Alley by his publisher Lionel Conway of Leeds Music. Although he could not read or write music, Mills proved he was no one-hit-wonder. In the space of a year he wrote three more hits: *Hungry For Love* for Kidd, *The Lonely One* for Cliff Richard and the Applejacks' *Three Little Words*.

Life on the road began to pall for Gordon soon after he married Jo. Don Paul recalled, 'We travelled to Newcastle and Manchester to do television and Gordon kept saying, "Do we have to go there?" I'd say, "It's all right for you, Gordon." He could more or less not go anywhere because Jo was earning a fortune. She was against him touring because she couldn't bear him to be out of her sight.'

The reality was rather different. There was a piano shop on the ground floor of the Mills's block of flats. Every day he would stop and look in the window wishing he had a piano. 'I used to sit up until four in the morning trying to write and Jo would be out all day working,' Mills told Ray Connolly. 'Sometimes when she got home at night after a day's work I'd still be in bed. But one day there was knock at the door and these fellas started bringing a piano in. She'd saved up for me out of her own earnings. We used to write a bit together in those days.'

Songwriting royalties take a minimum of six months to come through, and due to the intricate accounting practices of most publishers often much longer. Mills was to earn £3,000 from *I'll Never Get Over You*. It arrived just in time to finance his first venture into management. Mills was uncomfortable about being supported by his wife and he decided to quit the Viscounts to try his hand at songwriting.

Mills was a fast learner, he knew about touring and how to put on a show. But now there were publishers, record companies and managers to study. Notting Hill was a good base for a young man aspiring to make it in the music business. Three stops on the Central Line to Marble Arch with EMI Records just round the corner; six to Tottenham Court Road, a stone's throw from Tin Pan Alley. The British music industry congregated in Denmark Street, a road so short that after 100 paces a man would be swallowed back into Soho.

The supplicants used to sit in the Giaconda sipping on a cup of coffee for hours while they planned their pitches, punted their songs and spun their dreams. If the money ran out the Gate was close enough to walk home. It took an hour. The aspirants rented a poky office for £3 a week. Everyone hassled the publishers. Pretty boys, with stage names their talent would seldom match, were ten a penny; songs were the key.

'The whole world of music was in Tin Pan Alley,' recalled Larry Page. 'If you wanted to do something in music then there was only one place you could go, Denmark Street. Every time I went into Julie's for lunch, the whole place was full of either well-known singers, established writers or up-and-coming artists. I was in there one day in 1963 when Gordon came up and started talking to me. We'd met years before on the package tours and got on pretty well, probably because my family was originally from the Mumbles.'

Despite being described by Bruce Welch of the Shadows as 'the worst singer I ever heard in my life' and never troubling the charts, Larry Page had enjoyed a modestly successful singing career. He showed a natural penchant for headline grabbing, by marrying a fan after an eight-day courtship, and having his hair tinted blue. For a while he retired to run a pub in Wales, but the lure of the limelight refused to dim, so he resurfaced as a booker for a Mecca Ballroom in Coventry. Then Page moved back to London and teamed up with Eddie Kassner to form a management company, Denmark Productions.

'Gordon was always asking advice as he knew I had never found a manager who did the job for me. All the television I got myself, recording contracts, everything. I think managers were of the opinion that artists were the enemy and that's how they should be treated. You could be sent out to buy a dozen suits and straightaway you'd have a hefty bill against your account. As long as you were in debt you were under the thumb.'

Gordon had already learnt how jealously an original song would be guarded. In the Viscounts he had seen how careers were made or lost on the choice of song. If a song was a big hit in America, the British record companies rushed to get it covered by their hot artist of the moment. Including the American original there might be five recordings of the same song available in the shops. Several could make the charts. Marty Wilde on Phillips and Anthony Newley on Decca were particularly successful at covering American classic songs. Newley took *Why* to number one at the expense of Frankie Avalon, Marty hit the Top 10 with *A Teenager in Love*, while Dion and Craig Douglas only made it into the Top 30. Douglas did far better, hitting the top with *Only Sixteen*, leaving Sam Cooke's sublime original fighting it out with the third rate version by Al Saxon.

'I'd write a song with Peter Lee Stirling,' said Barry Mason, 'then we'd take a bit of paper with the lyric written on it, the music in our heads, and go down to Denmark Street. I would go in to Leeds Music, chat up the secretary and beg for just five minutes of Lionel's time and then they'd let us in. If he liked it, he gave us £5 to make the demo. We kept a quid each and then we would spend £3 to make the demo in Regent Street Sound, just over the road. We'd bring it back to the publisher and then he'd sign it up, then try to get covers on it. The publisher would give you a little acetate to plug your own records.

'There were only three major record companies and maybe ten A&R men who mattered in London. They would play your song, sit back and say, "I'll have that," and that's where you'd get your songs placed. If a record company liked the song they might cut it within a few weeks.'

The myth of Swinging London has refocused the way people think and write about the pop music business in the sixties. The Beatles, the Mersey Sound, the international explosion of groups dominating the charts on both sides of the Atlantic (nowhere else mattered that much – where English and American pop stars led, other countries followed – though sales were relatively small), flower power, the rise of independent labels, all happened in five short years. At the beginning of the decade groups were good for dashing out the odd instrumental hit – as the Tornados did with *Telstar* – but their real job was to back a proper singer like Cliff Richard. By the time Neil Armstrong walked on the moon two-hour live shows and twenty-minute drum solos were *de rigueur*. Groups ruled, the artist was supreme. The tail was wagging Nipper's head.

Or so it seemed. The reality is that until 1967 the British music business remained very small. It was tightly controlled by the three big companies – EMI, Decca and Phillips (the American companies CBS, RCA – despite having Elvis Presley – Warner Brothers and Reprise had no serious presence until the late sixties) – and intrinsically corrupt. Everybody knew everybody else who mattered, and it was in their interest to keep it that way.

In 1960 television was still in its infancy, reaching less than half the country. The Independent Television Companies were learning to flex their muscles, and ATV, owned by Lew Grade and based in Manchester, was not scared of televising variety shows. The Grades owned showbusiness: West End theatres, theatres around Britain, and a major booking agency. If an artist offended them there was nowhere to go.

From the late fifties the single most forceful personality in British rock television was Jack Good, Oxford University graduate and would-be actor, who saw Bill Haley sing *Rock Around the Clock* and understood what he had to do. Almost single-handedly he forced great rock shows onto British TV, beginning with the quaint *6.5 Special*, fronted by a strange mixture of boxer Freddie Mills, blazered wide-boy DJ Pete Murray and the frightful Don Lang and his Frantic Five. It was there the country caught its first glimpse of Gene Vincent and Eddie Cochran, as well as home-grown talent such as Adam Faith, Cliff Richard and Billy Fury. When the BBC tried to tame *6.5 Special*, he launched *Oh Boy!* on ATV, as well as other total music shows like *Boy Meets Girl* and *Wham!*

The explosion of groups in 1963 demanded new TV formats. *Ready Steady Go*, fronted by Keith Fordyce and Cathy McGowan, first aired in August 1963. The BBC, frightened of missing a trick, followed suit with *Top of the Pops*. The show first aired on 1 January

1964. It quickly outstripped its rivals and the initial run of six episodes was extended indefinitely. Throughout the sixties *Top of the Pops* regularly pulled an audience of seventeen million and became the one TV show that could guarantee a hit record.

If seeing was important, hearing was even more so. Radio in the early sixties was a wasteland, which the pirate stations and then Radio 1 were to plough and reap fully. The BBC Light Programme offered the long-running and hugely influential *Saturday Club*, fronted by Brian Matthew. But as the BBC only gave a few hours a week to pop records, the station that really mattered was Radio Luxembourg. Transmitting from the Royal Duchy in Europe on 208 Medium Wave, up until the arrival of pirate radio ships in 1964, it was a record company's dream.

On the surface Fab 208 appeared cool because it did not follow BBC regulations and played new releases six hours a night. From the mid-fifties it became the show that every teenager, Tommy Woodward included, listened to under their bed covers late into the night. The signal used to cut in and out adding to the drama. 'You had a bloody hard job to get on it,' remembered Larry Page, 'but that was the station everybody listened to.'

It was also a commercial operation. From 1946 to 1968 record companies could buy their own fifteen-minute show and pay a top Luxembourg DJ to present it. So *The Decca Chart Show* would be pre-recorded in London by Jimmy Savile, Alan Freeman or Jimmy Young. The music might be very varied, but there was always one unifying factor: the dark blue label in the middle of the 45.

To turn a radio hit into sales, vinyl-pressing capacity and distribution were crucial, and the majors controlled the only means of production. So a small licensed label, like Chris Blackwell's Island Records, were at the mercy of the majors when they had a song bubbling under. If EMI had a big hit on their hands the presses at Hayes would be busy stamping that out first – as the profits were higher.

Until January 1963 the charts were not independently audited and so were open to abuse. After that it got a name – chart hyping. Chart hyping was the norm. Inside the industry any savvy manager knew which were the chart shops and would recruit family members, roadies and Uncle Tom Cobley and all to buy up enough singles to scrape into the Top 50. After that the public would make up their own mind.

The rewards were high. The life of a record was a long one, it could take ten weeks to creep up to number one and as many to fall down again. Engelbert Humperdinck's *Release Me* entered the charts on 26 January 1967, reached number one five weeks later and spent six weeks at the top. In all it spent fifty-six weeks on the charts. Conversely a drop of more than two places signified chart death, even a stall could be a major catastrophe.

Because the industry was so small only a few people mattered. There were the managers: Larry Parnes, a legend of his own making; Evie Taylor, the Queen Bee of Showbusiness, who used Colin Berlin to book her tours; Phil Solomon, the upstart Irishman. There were the booking agents headed by the Grade Organisation and Foster's.

The focus of attention was the record company A&R men. 'It was simple,' said Page. 'If you got the opportunity of a deal then you grabbed it with both hands. By the early sixties the standard royalty rate was two per cent, and it was take it or leave it. If you've been turned down by every record company, then any deal is a good deal, and they had the power. Norrie Paramor, and Norman Newell at Columbia, George Martin and Ron Richards at Parlophone, Johnny France at Phillips, Jack Baverstock at Fontana, Dick Rowe at Decca.'

It was Dick Rowe who turned down the Beatles early in 1962.

The reason was more practical than prophetic. His assistant, Mike Smith, was a young lad who knew what was happening. He told Dick he had found two groups — the Beatles and Brian Poole and the Tremeloes — and that Decca ought to sign them both. Dick told him to choose one. Mike came from Dagenham, Brian Poole's home town, and the local boys were a much neater, tighter, more together, more professional band. It was a business decision and not a bad one. Brian Poole and the Tremeloes enjoyed tremendous success in their own right. They had nine Top 10s and two number ones in Britain and a series of hits in America. They just weren't the Beatles.

At EMI George Martin was given the Beatles, not despite but because of his work with Peter Sellers, Sophia Loren, Bernard Cribbins, and *The Goon Show*. He was in charge of novelty acts. In 1962 groups were viewed as novelty acts. The groups that mattered were the Shadows, and then the Tornados. In 1962 the pop scene was dominated by pretty boy singers with manufactured surnames like Fury, Wilde, Eager and plain old Joe Brown, or traditional balladeers. A year later it had changed beyond recognition.

The first of the new groups to hit the top was not the Beatles, whose *Please Please Me* had stalled at number two in January 1963, but their Mersey rivals Gerry and the Pacemakers. Between 11 April 1963 and 11 March 1965 there were forty-one different number one records, of those forty-one acts thirty-five were groups. Of the remaining six the sixth was Tom Jones.

Once groups were in, it made Gordon's job much harder. Male singers — unless you were Frank Ifield, Elvis or Roy Orbison — were out. In that respect the music business has not changed a jot. The suits made their decisions as they have always done. The difference was that the influx of groups brought outsiders into Tin Pan Alley. Groups were less easy to manipulate; they possessed an internal dynamic, a camaraderie, an arrogance, a self-sufficiency.

They would still sign the same two per cent deals, but they didn't want to end up topping a variety bill. More importantly many of them wrote their own songs, thereby taking a whole slab of control away from the record companies.

This upset the cosy gay mafia who controlled a substantial slab of the pop music business. It wasn't just the managers, notably Larry Parnes, who displayed the innate tastes of a teenage girl, and the desire to discover a pretty working-class boy and rechristen him with a name imbued with rough trade promise. It spread across the industry. A new boy singer was discovered and then passed around from record company chum to agent. Boy singers were always told not to get married because it would upset their female fans. But was it really because it upset their agents?

'If you went to an opening night at the Edgware Road or the Shepherd's Bush Empire and went into the bar you saw everyone,' said Larry Page. 'You had record companies, you had producers within the record companies, you had agents, who were there to represent artists. It was all a gay situation. If you were not used to that it was scary. I never played the game, but I was careful. You knew where the control was. We all did.'

In early 1964 Gordon Mills was ready to make his move on the business. He knew how to perform, how to arrange and how to write songs. He had the contacts, he knew who was the right agent, the right arranger and the right publisher. He knew where the power was. He was ready to manage. He had found the right artist. Someone he could believe in. Someone he could take all the way.

There was just one small problem. Groups were in. Male singers were OUT.

CHAPTER SIX

IT WAS UNUSUAL

———

Gordon Mills had convinced Tommy Scott and the Senators that he was their key to unlocking the bright lights of London. In the Rhondda Valley he was a hot shot, but in Tin Pan Alley he was just another youngster with everything to prove.

His first step was to show off this new talent to his mates. Barry Mason went to see Tommy at the White Horse in East Grinstead. 'I was knocked out,' recalled Mason. 'I just thought he was unbelievable, a voice like you've never heard before. They were doing rock and roll, *Good Golly Miss Molly*, mixed with standards, all dressed in leather. But I told Gordon, "I don't think he's commercial, his voice is too good and he's not pretty enough." He wasn't what was in vogue. In vogue were groups and these little, soft, pretty voices. Here was this bull of a man with a broken nose, big shoulders and a huge voice. Tom looked and sang like a bricklayer.'

Les Reed was more encouraging, though he too had his doubts. 'Gordon and I went to the Top Rank Cinema in Slough one Sunday night. I couldn't believe this kid, he was just an incredible singer. I was into blues music, and he was so black in his delivery. The drummer was going nineteen to the dozen with his drums while Tom stomped about the stage.

'I was impressed with his voice, but not the way he looked. He had this rabbit's foot on his trousers, which kept swinging from side to side, he had medallions on and his shirt well open. It was far too sexy for that time. The girls weren't ready for this kind of explosion on stage. They'd be almost shying away from him. There was an earthiness that I couldn't get over. I said to Gordon, we've got to do some blues stuff with this guy, but let's dress him up first.'

In their earlier recording forays with Joe Meek, Tommy Scott and the Senators had hurriedly returned across the Severn. When they moved up to London in June 1964 it was for good. Lead guitarist Mike Roberts had just taken a job as a TV cameraman and chose to stay in Wales. After auditions held at the Thorn Hotel in Abercynon (owned by Dave Cooper's parents) he was replaced by Cardiff boy, Mickey Gee, who preferred strumming to delivering beer for Brains Brewery. Vernon Hopkins quit his job as a printer with the *Pontypridd Observer*. Drummer Chris Rees was only seventeen and had upset his parents doubly when he simultaneously dropped out of the local grammar school and changed his last name to Slade. Tommy Woodward signed off from the dole office, and kissed Linda and Mark goodbye.

The dreams that Gordon had spun before them were rudely quashed on arrival. After a couple of nights in a grotty hotel, 'a real dosser's paradise' according to Vernon Hopkins, the band were moved into a two-room basement flat at 6 Clydesdale Road. In 1964 Notting Hill Gate, where Gordon lived, was floundering on the edges of Bohemian respectability. At the wrong end of Ladbroke Grove, a riot brick's throw from Portobello Market, Clydesdale Road teetered on the cusp between the black ghettos around All Saints Road and the hookers and Irish bars on the fringes of the Grove. Seventy per cent of the population were West Indians, the rest were Greeks, Portuguese and a smattering of other races.

Poverty was the uniform all the inhabitants wore. Gordon gave the whole band an allowance of £1 per day to live on, a drastic cut in income for each man in a town where the prices were higher and there was no family support, and no mam to cook the evening meal. There were three beds in one room, two in the other and when it rained it got very wet and uncomfortable.

The band would sleep until midday and then stagger down to Pete's Café, the cheapest eating place in the Grove. There the Greek owner would feed the boys for a shilling a head. The rest of the day was spent ekeing out the budget, splitting a packet of ten Woodbines five ways while they played cards and watched the paint peel off the walls. In the evening the choice was between a couple of pints of beer or a sausage sandwich. The beer usually won.

'We were young, aching with hunger, and there was no food,' recalled Vernon Hopkins. 'We were so hungry that twice we went into an Indian restaurant and did a runner. When we went past it the smells would drive us up the wall. It was a case of, "Right, here we are, lads, what are we going to do? We can't eat, and that smell, let's get in there and . . ." Then we did a runner, sprinted down Ladbroke Grove, and hid behind the bins, with the waiters shouting and screaming behind us. We shared everything then. All the emotions under the sun, and all the intensity, all the disappointment, all the aggravation, all the starvation, the pain and the hunger.'

The band were too proud to admit to anyone back home how

badly things were going. Chris Ellis heard that things were not going so well in London. He drove up from South Wales with food parcels (tins of beans and loaves of bread) as well as girlfriends. They left Wales just before midnight and arrived at Clydesdale Road early in the morning.

'Linda thought it was great that she could actually go to London and see Tom,' said Ellis. They would spend the weekend at Gordon's flat up in Notting Hill Gate, so Linda never had to go through that humiliation of sharing a room with the boys.

'There was no telephone at the flat, so sometimes they never knew we were coming up. We'd knock on the door and wake them up and there was always a danger some girl was there.'

Most nights they never slept until after three in the morning as the local prostitutes would drop by between tricks. When the weather turned foul and the punters dried up the girls would stay for hours, handing out cigarettes, in exchange for tea or coffee.

'In the end we got to know everybody in the community,' said Hopkins. 'The van was outside, with all the gear, and it never got touched.'

The Senators had arrived in London to find their identity had been stripped away as there was another band of the same name. So from then on Tommy Woodward was Tom Jones, and they were the Playboys. Larry Page remembers Gordon ruminating for weeks over what to call his protégé. Woodward was obviously a no-no, but there was nothing intrinsically wrong with Tommy Scott as a stage name. However, renaming an artist was part of a manager's prerogative. An effective means of showing exactly where the power lay.

The genesis of the name came about by accident – though Gordon always took the credit. The Irish entrepreneur Phil Solomon, who was Mills' business partner and agent for a few months (they fell out because Solomon's house producer Bert Berns considered Tom little more than a Welsh Elvis impersonator), misread his signature Thomas John and suggested he call himself 'Jones'.

The choice of Tom Jones was inspired. Gordon did not settle on Jones because it was Freda Woodward's maiden name — he probably did not know about that coincidence for years, though the inherent Welshness certainly helped. He was named Tom Jones after a hit movie. Tony Richardson's liberal adaptation of Henry Fielding's racy eighteenth-century bodice ripper had dazzled cinema goers in 1963 and won three Oscars including Best Picture. John Osborne's spicy sharp scripting of the picaresque tale of a young foundling's adventures amidst the hypocrisy of the ruling classes had given it a telling relevance in the last days of a crumbling Tory government. Albert Finney, as the hero, managed to achieve the perfect balance between good-natured innocence, and sexy, horny little devil.

Over the next few years Tommy Woodward was to grow into that roistering hellion. First he had to prove to a sceptical world that he had more to brag about than a swinging rabbit's foot. Out of town gigs earned less money than playing the socials in the Valleys. But they did get a regular support slot at Beat City in Oxford Street in London where their first date was as support to the Rolling Stones.

'On 18 July hundreds of fans jammed the streets around the West End and there were police everywhere when we played the Beat City Club in Oxford Street,' recalled Bill Wyman in his autobiography *Stone Alone*. 'Inside, the heat was terrible. Tom Jones and his band, relatively unknown at that time, were our support group; he later reminded me that the temperature was so high that stewards were throwing buckets of water over him and us during our respective performances. We played a forty-five-minute spot to an audience of six hundred, sixty fainting girls had to be carried out – ten per cent of the audience.'

Tom wore thin white trousers and a white T-shirt. He sweated so much the trousers turned see-through and the young girls in the front started covering their eyes. 'I loved that so much I was giving it even more,' said Jones. 'They were looking a bit frightened at me, I could feel it. Afterwards we were all sharing a dressing room, and Mick Jagger said, "God, it must be hot out there; look at him and he's only the compere."'

Otherwise the Playboys only did a couple of gigs a month and a session or two up in Tin Pan Alley if Gordon needed a demo of any of the songs he'd written. They did one for Max Bygraves. One night they backed Gerry Dorsey at a nightclub in Barnes and Tom came along for the ride. They shared the dressing room with a belly dancer and her python, which was asleep in its basket. Outside the door were parked the food trolleys. Eventually the half-starved Tom could resist the tantalising smells no longer. He lifted the cover off a plate, snaffled a large T-bone steak and replaced the lid. The meat was wolfed down in huge chunks by the ravenous band. After the theft was discovered the dressing room was invaded by jabbering Portuguese waiters and a furious manager. 'It was the snake that did it,' said Tom, pointing at the sleeping python, while all the Playboys nodded their agreement.

The record companies did not share Gordon's faith in his new discovery. 'People gave me all sorts of stories,' he recalled. 'They said Tom shouted and screamed. They said he was too old-fashioned. They said he moved too much like Elvis Presley.' Finally Gordon convinced Decca to let Tom Jones and the Playboys record their first single. *Chills and Fever* was produced by Peter Sullivan, long a champion of Tom's voice, and released in August 1964. It died everywhere apart from the Fountain Record and Music Shop at 11 Taff Street, Pontypridd, where it actually made the local Top 10 – for one week.

Gordon was fast running out of money. His songwriting royalties were coming through in dribs and drabs and the band – who were rechristened the Squires in November – were not doing enough gigs to support themselves. Jo Mills remembered, 'We just didn't have the money. My modelling money was drying up and I even did a few jobs after Tracey was born but it broke my heart to be away from her. Gordon's money soon went and our overdraft kept growing and growing. Sometimes Tom and the Squires did get a gig and they would be paid about £30 which we thought was fantastic.'

Initially Gordon solved his cash flow problems by walking into a bank in Leicester Square and asking for a loan to support the band until they found work. His belief and certainty were such that the manager agreed to give Mills overdraft facilities before discovering that he had not yet opened a bank account. The loan was not enough, and the situation soon required desperate measures.

Jo was totally supportive. Larry Page recalled, 'Gordon and Jo idolised each other, and between the two of them they had this total belief in Tom. Whatever they earned, whatever they worked for was invested in Tom Jones. He sold his car to pay for some demo recordings.'

'He sold his wristwatch to my old publisher Bert Curry for £50 to keep the group eating,' said Les Reed, 'and he also brought people like Mike Bradley and Phil Solomon in on ten or fifteen per cent of Tom Jones ownership. Tom probably had five or six managers he didn't know about. You know what I mean. And Gordon used to do deals like this. Just to keep it going.

'I got to like the guy simply because of the way he was handling Tom, and I asked him, "How are we going to get him to the public?" He said, "We need a blues song." He was still into this blues thing with Tom. So I said, "OK, but in the meantime what do we do, shall we write a few songs for him?" Gordon said, "No, we need to earn some money, so let's write a song for somebody who's at the top of the charts." '

Reed went over to 97 Campden Hill Towers where Mills announced he had a great idea for a song for Sandie Shaw, who was then at number one with *(There's) Always Something There to Remind Me*. He started to play very badly and slowly on the piano. 'I've only got two bars,' Gordon explained and started singing, 'It's not unusual to go out with anyone . . . it's not unusual to have fun with anyone . . .'

That was as far as it went. Gordon was lost and had no idea where to go next. For the next three days the pair worked on the song. 'It was the hardest thing to write that song,' said Reed. 'Gordon knew what he wanted but he couldn't put it down. I'm not a lyricist, but I came up with a few ideas. Between the two of us we finally finished the song.

'Right at the end Gordon asked the million-dollar question, "Is it right for Sandie Shaw?" I replied, "Probably," then I played the rhythm, which is what you hear today, and suddenly the whole song came alive. It was just an ordinary song up until then.'

Gordon insisted that the song be signed to Leeds Music (a fact which Reed has regretted to this day), and after extracting a £10 advance and rousting the Squires from their damp pit, they went to record a demo at Regent Sound. Les Reed was waiting behind the piano.

'We used to cut a record in about twenty minutes in those days,' said guitarist Mickey Gee, though Vernon insists it was because Gordon could not afford to pay for the full hour. 'Gordon played it for me and straight away I smelt some interesting chords. I thought, "Yeah that's for us, that's nice but different." Dave Cooper and Vernon couldn't get it at all, they couldn't learn it. They were great blokes but not great musicians, so we went in and recorded it with no bass or rhythm guitar. Tom sang, Chris Slade played tambourine, I played lead and we dubbed some rhythm on.'

Everybody at the demo session knew that this was something special. Sitting in the George, one of Tin Pan Alley's favoured watering holes, the Squires decided this was their last chance.

Mickey and Vernon let rip at Gordon. 'Look, we're here living in a pigsty,' said Gee. 'What's it all for? So we can be famous. And here you are, Gordon, our manager, and you've written a hit. Of course, Sandie Shaw is a guaranteed hit and Tom isn't, but bloody hell, give us a break. That's a great song.'

'We were all saying like, "We've got to do it or we're going home," said Hopkins. 'Although he wanted the song, Tom didn't say a lot, he let us do it. Gordon Mills left the George saying, "My hands are tied, I'll do my best." '

Tom, who knew he wanted that song and was already closer to their manager than the band knew, tried a different approach. 'It's funny,' he said 'with this particular song something was telling me all the time, "Don't let it go, this is it." '

'That was the only time Tom has ever played me up,' Mills said. 'He wanted that song so badly that he hardly spoke to me for a week.' All weekend he hassled Gordon to give him the song until finally his manager agreed he could have it — if Sandie turned it down.

Early the following week Gordon and Les Reed determined to play Evie Taylor, Sandie Shaw's manager, the acetate of the demo. Tom insisted on coming too, not prepared to give the song up without a fight. The three waited outside Evie's office for half an hour while she chatted to one of her regular acts — Des Layne, the penny whistle man. Eventually Les went and rapped on the door.

'Evie, it's Les,' he said.

'Don't you realise I'm busy?' she said.

'I've got something here which I think you should hear.'

'I'll give you three minutes,' snapped Evie. 'Put the song on the record player,' she commanded. After hearing eight bars she took it off. 'Who's it for?' she demanded.

'Sandie Shaw.'

That was it. Eve Taylor decreed the record would never be a hit, and kicked them all out. 'We were dumbfounded,' remembered Les. 'Gordon was in such a state financially, he would have signed with Evie, he'd have signed Tom to Evie. I'd have signed to Evie as a writer. We needed someone to help us out. And so she turned down a trillion dollars – for Des Layne, the penny whistle man!

'We just had enough money to get back on the Tube. We were waiting on the platform when Tom announced, "If I don't do that bloody song, I'm going to give up the business; in fact I might throw myself under this train." I think he was half joking but you never know with the Welsh, do you?'

It was not the first time Tom had threatened to use the London Underground to terminate his life. Skint, half-starved, with holes in their shoes and no way to get home except by hitchhiking, all the band had got depressed, but Tom worst of all. Never a deep thinker, after six months of going nowhere slowly, he was getting very depressed.

'I asked Gordon if he could send Linda £5,' Tom said. 'She was working in a factory to keep herself and Mark while I was in London. We needed the extra money badly. When I asked Gordon he said, "I can't really afford it. I've spent all my own money trying to keep you together. Now I'm existing on a loan from the bank."

'I felt so depressed. I waited at Notting Hill station wondering what to do with myself. A train was coming and I stood on the platform thinking, "Shall I jump off and end it all?" '

Later that day Vernon came into the room they shared to find the singer sitting on the bed, tears in his eyes, sunk in despair. These Welshmen might have shared their beer but they had not shared their souls. For months Tom had kept everything bottled inside him, but family pressure, no money and a career sinking into indifferent London's gutters had cracked the mask.

'I nearly chucked myself under a train,' he wept. 'I can't go on, I can't carry on any more, nothing's happening. Linda's on about going back home, I've got my family, I've got my son . . . I can't go on . . . I've got to go back.'

Vernon was quick to reassure the distraught Tom. He knew that if Tom went home they would all follow. He was prepared to give anything, do anything to make him stay. 'We're all in this together,' he said. 'If you stop now you've got to go back home. Remember that send-off you had. You're going to go back and lose everything that you've done. Give it a bit longer.'

Eventually Tom was persuaded to give it one last crack. Having made the decision he stuck with it. He and Vernon never discussed their heart to heart again.

Fortunately for Tom, Decca loved the idea of his doing *It's Not Unusual*. Unimpressed by their performance on the demo and exasperated by their attitude, Gordon decided to cut the record without using the Squires.

'Gordon told us it had a big-band sound and that we weren't going to be used,' said Hopkins. 'We were totally disappointed, but then we were thinking, "If Tom does this, we're still all together." We started looking on the bright side, "OK, we're not on the record, but we're still going to make it, we'll still be able to go home with our heads up high and a few bob in the bank." We didn't know it, but things were changing. That's when we became just a backing band.'

Instead Mills employed the cream of professional session players. The lead guitar break was supplied by Joe Moretti and rhythm by little Jimmy Page. John Carter, Ken Lewis and Perry

Ford of the Ivy League provided backing vocals as singing harmonies have never been a Jones strong point. The first recording session was a disaster. It did not help that the studios were booked solid and the only space producer Peter Sullivan could get was in the large orchestral room at Decca number two studio in Broadhurst Gardens, West Hampstead starting at 10 o'clock on the morning of 11 November. Reed had arranged the song with a very laid-back Motown feel, like an early Marvin Gaye number, all rhythm section, vibraphones and bells.

'They had a bass hook on the demo which sounded quite sophisticated,' said Peter Sullivan. 'I had this idea of a Hammond organ and a vibraphone going "ching ka ching". After I finished it, it sounded like a jazz record. It was too slick, it didn't gel – his voice and the arrangement just didn't marry, they conflicted. I hoped to set it right with his vocal – his voice was outsinging the backing – it was the backing which wasn't happening.'

'It didn't sound right,' said Tom. 'We recorded it with a few different instruments. We were looking for a sound and we weren't getting it. I felt like death.'

Sullivan finally put his finger on the problem. 'I thought about brass mixed with a guitar to give it a punch. It would sound like a groovier, funkier sound. Les didn't like the idea. He said, "It'll sound like a dance band."

'I said, "Not if we mix the guitar in with the brass playing the same lines, it'll be a hip sound." '

'I told them we've got to give it some balls. Reluctantly everyone agreed, so we cut it. As soon as I heard this arrangement going against the vocal, you could hear it was working. At that time it was very original.'

For the second recording they decided to use the trumpet section, the sax section and a brace of trombones from the Ted Heath Band. That time it worked. The 'shh shh' sound effect was an extremely simple idea of Gordon's, created by a musician rubbing sandpaper on a rough stool. Tom recorded his lead vocal standing in the cupboard where they stored all the tapes. He nailed it in one take.

However, as the recording was completed in early November, Decca wisely refused to release it before Christmas. Clutching their demos, Tom and the band returned home for the holidays. It was a great relief for the Mills family, who were now completely strapped for cash.

'We suggested the boys stayed at home for Christmas because we simply had no more money to pay them,' said Jo Mills. 'They had virtually nothing to go home with, they stopped down there because it was cheaper that way. But secretly Gordon and I wondered whether they would ever come back. Christmas 1964 was our worst time ever. Decca kept putting back the release date; we were £1,000 in debt at the bank and I was having problems with my second pregnancy and was laid up in hospital.'

Soon after Christmas Les Reed held a party. 'I invited Liberace, Russ Conway, many heavy guys from the business. Gordon was away and Jo came with a friend. She brought the final cut of *It's Not Unusual*, and I asked her if we could play it. And she said, "In front of all these people? No Les, you can't." She had a few more drinks and she said, "Oh, go on then." So we played it, and everybody loved it. Jo was crying. I asked her, "Why are you crying, Jo?" She said, "It's because Gordon told me never to play that record to anybody."

'I said, "These are all my friends, it's not going to go past this room." She grabbed the record and went home. She was terrified of Gordon finding out that she'd played that record.'

It's Not Unusual, with Burt Bacharach's *To Wait for Love* on the flip side, was finally released at the end of January 1965. Its first supporter was Alan Freeman on Radio Luxembourg. Appearances on TV shows *Top Gear*, *Ready Steady Go* and *Juke Box Jury* followed in rapid succession.

Perhaps because it broke all the rules, there was something compelling about *It's Not Unusual*. It was a song in conflict with itself. A teasing, questioning lyric written for a woman but sung by a very masculine man; the Motown rhythm opposed by the pumping pounding brass. But most of all there was that voice, fighting off the trumpets, giving a sexual urgency to the words. The antithesis of everything pretty and fluffy, managing to be raw and sophisticated at the same time.

And there was Tom himself. Even with his hair pulled back and tied in a rakish bow, it could not hide his broken nose, crooked teeth and jiving pelvis. For his first appearance on *Top of the Pops*, Gordon dressed him in a white sweater and white trousers to soften the edges. Soon he was back in black leather trousers bumping and grinding away. Now he had a hit, the girls were not so put off. The song entered the charts at number twenty-two and hit the top spot on 1 March, St David's Day. It sold 800,000 copies in four weeks.

Although it was his first hit, *It's Not Unusual* remains the ultimate Tom Jones song. *Delilah* and *Green Green Grass of Home* may be the songs beloved by imitators but *It's Not Unusual* has proved too difficult for anyone else to do really well. It has been a hit for Tom several times over and featured in some 190 films including *Mars Attacks*, *Play Misty for Me*, and *Edward Scissorhands* as well as a classic episode of *The Simpsons*.

In March 1965 *It's Not Unusual* delivered Gordon Mills what he craved more than anything else. A number one meant more than an end to his debts. It meant power.

And he knew just how to use it.

CHAPTER SEVEN

A NEW STAR
IS BORN

At 4 o'clock on the morning of Sunday 21 February 1965, a battered blue Morris J4 van with failing brakes stopped at a transport café on the A1. Six men, all smoking Woodbines, hurried into the café, where they huddled around the wood-burning stove in the centre of the grim room. A truck driver, heading north, put down his early edition of the *Sunday Mirror*. In a strong Welsh accent the van driver asked if he could look at it. Suddenly he gave a whoop and showed the paper to the other men.

'*It's Not Unusual* had gone up to number seven,' said Chris Ellis. 'We were sitting in this grotty transport café in the middle of nowhere with just enough money for a sausage sandwich, a cup of tea each and some petrol to get us back into London ... and there's a hit record.'

The immediate effect of *It's Not Unusual* was to get the Squires out of their grotty basement and onto the road. Gordon was in such financial straits that any gig was a good one. Fortune smiled when P.J. Proby split his trousers once too often.

Perhaps it was coincidence in that both were the top male singers (with a penchant for crotch enhancing trousers) in an era dominated by groups, but the careers of Jones and Proby were to intersect frequently over the next three years. In January 1965 Proby was the man in possession, cruising on the back of three Top 10 hits. On 29 January he began a major package tour with Cilla Black, the Fourmost and Tommy Roe. Proby wore skintight velvet trousers which had a habit of splitting whenever he dropped to his knees. Such behaviour was not acceptable to the ABC Theatre chain. On 1 February his trousers split during the first number and the curtain was pulled. After two more incidents he was fired from the tour.

Colin Berlin was on the phone to showbusiness promoter Joe Collins (father of Joan and Jackie) before P.J. had left the building. Tom was added to the bottom of the bill for £600 a week. On 4 February all five of the band were packed off in the Morris. Ellis had been summoned up from Ponty to be their driver. He got the call late one night, quit his job on the spot and hitched up to London. When he arrived the band had left for Plymouth. Gordon gave him a bollocking for being late.

As *It's Not Unusual* leapt up the charts the reaction of the Proby fans softened. While a feud between the two singers was invented by the press at the shows, the hisses and boos turned to cheers and tears and then frenzy.

'I was sitting in a pub at Southampton having a drink with the boys, when I heard a noisy crowd outside,' Jones said. 'I thought, "What the hell are they waiting for? It can't be me, I'm just a nobody on the bill." So I walked out of that pub eating a pork pie. I was also wearing a new black mac, very proud of it too, with my collar turned up against the cold. Suddenly, the girls saw me and I walked straight into them like an idiot and they threw me to the ground. They were pulling and shouting and trying to strip me, pulling my lovely mac away in shreds. I was frightened out of my life, I thought I was going to be killed.

'My drummer started punching people to save me. Then two policemen grabbed me and literally threw me into the road. "Run like hell for it, son," they yelled. I picked myself up and ran straight into another crowd at the stage door. In the safety of the dressing room I looked at what was left of my clothes and said to myself, "This is it, boy. This is the start of something big for you." '

The singing star's first press handout described him as 'twenty-two, a miner and single'. At the time it was inconceivable for a pop star to be married, so Tom was told to deny the existence of his family. The secret did not last long. The week before *It's Not Unusual* hit the top the truth was revealed. He was 24 and married with a son who was about to turn eight.

'I was told by everyone to say I was single,' he told the *Daily Mirror*. 'I was not happy about it because it's not true. I am married. It's never been a secret at home in Wales that I was married. When I came to London, it was felt it was best if my wife and son were dispensed with. I should never have agreed to say I was single in the first place. You can't fool teenagers.'

After a year in which Tom had been sinking into despair, it was if he had been picked up by an enormous tidal wave. His life was turned upside down and there were constant demands on his time. Gordon quickly moved Tom into his flat, until he could find a place with Linda, and started to lay down the rules. Les Reed was sitting with Tom and Gordon in Campden Hill Towers the day the song hit number one. 'The phone rang all the time,' Reed said. 'It was *Disc* or the *NME*, they all wanted to talk to Tom, and I'll never forget Gordon almost pinned him against the wall, and said, "You talk to no one. I do all the talking, you don't even talk to Les." That went right in there with Tom. And it's still stuck to this day, he's never picked the phone up to me once, in all these years. I doubt whether he's lifted the phone to anybody.'

Gordon was in his element. When Tom was due to record a *Worker's Playtime* for the BBC, he told the producer, 'Tom has to go on last.' The producer bridled because the Rolling Stones were also on the bill. 'But look who else is here,' said the producer.

'Who's got the number one record now?' snapped Gordon. 'Tom has.'

The producer insisted, 'Somebody has to come on after him.'

'Look,' snarled Mills, narrowing his eyes and pointing that finger as if it were a gun barrel, 'there is only one person who goes on after him and he's up there. So if you can't get him down here to do it, that's it. Tom either closes the show or we walk.'

Tom tried to make the peace, 'I don't mind when I go on.'

'Shut up and smoke another Woody,' commanded his manager. He did. Tom closed the show.

Tom had gone from zero to hero in four weeks. He shared the billing with the Beatles, the Rolling Stones and the Animals at the *NME* Poll Winners' Concert at the Empire Pool Wembley on 11 April. Later that night he shot across town to appear on *Sunday Night at the London Palladium*. The Beatles were everywhere in those days, the Sun Kings in the Versailles of Pop. Tom was not overawed.

'When I first went on *Thank Your Lucky Stars* with *It's Not Unusual*, The Beatles were on there,' Tom said. 'You had to do a camera rehearsal in the afternoon, and I'm sitting there waiting for the Beatles to come out just to see them close up. John Lennon came up, gives me a look and sings, "It's not a unicorn it's an elephant," taking the piss. He says, "How are you doing, you Welsh poof?" I said, "You Scouse bastard, come up here and I'll show you . . . " Gordon said, "It's his sense of humour." I said, "I'll give him a sense of fucking humour." '

Gordon had taken Burt Bacharach down to All Saints Church

Hall to watch Tom and the Squires rehearse three numbers. On 26 April Tom recorded Burt's theme song for a new Peter Sellers movie, written by New York Jewish comedian Woody Allen. Tom disliked *What's New Pussycat?*, complaining it sounded like 'a Humpty Dumpty song'. Gordon told him such a contrasting song would be good for his career and forced him down to the studio. Bacharach helped Peter Sullivan produce the song and Tom did admit 'he had me singing better than I've ever done before'.

He was to be very grateful as his follow-up single, *Once Upon a Time*, was a flop. The situation was not helped by Joe Meek deciding to capitalise on his tapes. *Little Lonely One* was rush-released by Columbia just in time to split sales. Later in the year the Meek record actually made it to number forty-two in America. 'I have four other tapes of his which I would like to release,' threatened Meek. 'Tom auditioned for me and nobody wanted to know about him because it was the time when the group scene was very "in" and everybody said he sang too well.'

'This *Little Lonely One* is something I could well do without,' Tom complained to the press. 'I made it a long time ago . . . and tastes have changed a lot since then. They were tough days when the group and I made *Little Lonely One*. Joe said it was great and he was going to get it released, but we didn't hear any more after that. We had a big row about it and in the end got our contract back. It was two years before a chance came again – and now they bring out this relic from the past. I think it's dated and I'd like to dissociate myself from it.'

Joe Meek was annoying but hardly a major worry as *It's Not Unusual* reached number ten in the US. On 2 May Tom made his first appearance on the *Ed Sullivan Show*, who, convinced he could repeat the success he'd had with the Beatles the previous year, had offered £10,000 for five exclusive appearances. Like Elvis nine years earlier, Tom was shot only from the waist up as his hip gyrations were considered too suggestive. His fellow guests included the Rolling Stones and comedians Morecambe and Wise.

It's Not Unusual was also an r&b hit, and many programmers on black radio stations assumed Tom was black. They soon learnt the difference. While doing a *Top of the Pops* Tom had met Dionne Warwick. He phoned her and told her he wanted to go to the Apollo Theatre up in Harlem. As white folks did not survive long up there Dionne agreed to escort him.

Said Jones, 'When we got out of the car at the stage door it was, "Dionne, hey baby, what's going on?" Then, "Who's this honky motherfucker?" And she said, "This is Tom Jones." So I was in. I was thrilled to bits. There I was, backstage at the Apollo with Dionne and The Shirelles and a bunch of people.

'Chuck Jackson was closing the show and he said, 'You've got to come on." He said, "Now, ladies and gentlemen, we've got a soul brother from England," and they all start screaming, and I walked on and all these black faces went . . . huh?

'I belted into *What'd I Say* and brought the bloody place down. I did fifteen minutes and got a fantastic reception. A white Welsh guy on stage at the Apollo! It was great.'

Back in England Tom embarked on a four-week tour, followed by his second appearance on the *Ed Sullivan Show* on 13 June, and then a week's residency at New York's Paramount Theatre. His first album, punningly titled *Along Came Jones* (but only in Britain), was released in June and sold steadily.

Tom returned to America in July to promote *What's New Pussycat?*, which eventually reached number three (a much bigger hit than in England). On 14 July he topped the DJ Murray the K's Brooklyn Fox stage show bill over Ben E. King and Gary Lewis and the Playboys. Then on 1 August he joined one of Dick Clark's Caravan Tours with Sonny and Cher, the Turtles, Jackie de Shannon, the Shirelles, Mel Carter and the Jive Five. The only other Brits were the public school duo Peter and Gordon — not exactly soulmates for Tom. The principle was the same as the tours Tom had done in Britain, but the distances were huge and the bus only had hard seats. Tom slept in the luggage rack. Worse still, he had to use a pick-up band.

'It was murder, the tour from hell,' he said. 'The best part of it was when people would get out guitars and start singing songs. The country is so big that after so many hours in a bus, arriving just in time to do a show, then back on the bus all through the night, I thought, "God, if this is showbusiness in America, you can keep it."

'Going through the Southern states, every time you stopped you had to make sure that a white person got off to go into the truck stop. If one of the black people went in there, they'd shoot them. You had to be careful who you were talking to. Shirley, the lead singer of the Shirelles, and I were talking away in this hotel and all of a sudden she marched off. Later I said, "What's up with you?" and she said, "Didn't you see those people in the lobby? They were staring at us. We were touching. You can't do that in the South. They wouldn't only hang me, they'd hang you as well. Nigger-lover they would call you." '

On another occasion, in an Alabama truck stop, the local rednecks started to bait the singers with abuse and cries of "Who let niggers eat in here?" Eventually Mel Carter, a former gospel singer who had just enjoyed his first pop crossover hit, lost his temper and retaliated. Within minutes bottles and chairs were flying everywhere and the local law turned up.

'The cops just ran in, grabbed Mel and flung him in a paddy-wagon,' said Jones. 'I said to this cop, "You can't come in here and just grab somebody and throw him in there. You didn't even ask any questions." And he said, "You gonna stay out of this, boy?" I said, "No, I'm not going to stay out of this, I'm British." And the cop put his left hand on my chest and his right hand on his gun, and I started seeing it come out in slow motion, and he said, "I'm gonna ask you one more time, you gonna stay out of this?" And I said, "Yessir." My legs were shaking. There was nothing I could do. He would have shot me. I thought, "Jesus, these people are mad." '

But there were some good times before the tour ended on 6 September. Dick Clark still has a picture of Tom in drag. 'We used to do these parties. Dick would sort of pop in and see us. When he would show up we would have a bit of a ding-dong. One night we all changed parts. I was Shirley, and Shirley Alston was me. I put on her make up, dress and wig, and she put on my suit. We all mimed to each other's records in some hotel.'

The highlight of Tom's trip was meeting Elvis. Presley was filming *Paradise Hawaiian Style* in LA. Both artists were told that the other wanted to meet him. On the pretext that Tom should be getting into the movies, Lloyd Greenfield, Mills's management representative in the States, took him on a visit to Paramount Studios.

Presley certainly liked *It's Not Unusual*, so when Marty Lacker, the unofficial foreman of the Memphis Mafia, got a call from the Colonel's office saying that Tom Jones was going to be on the lot and wanted to come by and say hello, he passed the message on. Elvis gave it the OK.

'They told me Elvis was there and wanted to meet me,' said Jones. 'It was my first big year, I didn't think he'd even heard of me. They took me to a closed set where he was filming in a mock helicopter, singing to a little girl. He looks out of the helicopter at me and sort of moves his hand. Joe Esposito says to me, "Elvis is waving at you. Why don't you wave back to him?" So I sheepishly wave back. Then he starts walking over to me. I had a single out at the time, *With These Hands*, and as he was walking over to me he was singing it. I mean he was doing it – the hands, everything. As he gets nearer he is singing the song and pointing at me and he said, "It's a great song." And I mumble, "Oh thanks." He said, "Oh man, how'd you learn to sing like that?" And I said, "It's your fault – I was influenced by you." '

'Tom came over to the set with a guy who was, I think, his agent,' said Marty Lacker. 'He was a bald-headed guy with a big mouth. We came outside and as they started talking, I got up on the first or second rung of a big ladder that was leaning there and just held on, listening. Jones was telling Elvis how much he'd been influenced by his music, how much he loved what he did and what it meant to meet him. He had this look of awe on his face like he was talking to God. He was literally shaking. And Elvis surprised him, I think, when he told him how much he liked his record. Which was the truth.

'Then all of a sudden this agent guy popped up and said, "Listen Elvis, I can book you in England's Wembley Stadium with a guarantee of $1 million for one show. What do you say?" Well Elvis kind of ignored him, but the guy kept on. Finally I turned to him and I said, "Hey look, why don't you just let 'em talk? If you've got some offer to make go call Colonel Parker. Elvis doesn't discuss business with anybody."

'It still didn't deter him, he wouldn't quit. So I got a little testy and said, "Look sport, don't bring this up again." And then Tom told him, "You'd better stop." Because Elvis was getting agitated. He felt like he'd been used.'

Tom was embarrassed by Greenfield's transparent attempts to use him to snare Presley. From that day he never trusted him fully. He returned home, jaded by his experiences, saying to an American interviewer that 'my long-term career will be in Britain'.

On 17 November Tom starred in his first ITV Special, *Call in on Tom*. Perhaps because of his own variety background Mills believed that Tom's future lay as an all-round entertainer. When

John Barry and Don Black approached him to do the theme for the fourth James Bond movie *Thunderball*, Gordon jumped at the chance. Tom was less convinced, and when he arrived at Cadogan Square to start rehearsals the first question he asked Barry was, 'What does Thunderball mean?' The answer was difficult because it didn't mean anything.

'Tom, just sing it, OK?' said Barry, 'Don't let's get deep. Deep's not what we're looking for here. Take a leaf out of Shirley [Bassey]'s book and don't worry what it means. Just sing and act like you mean it.'

'I can't do that,' Tom objected.

'You've got to,' said John, 'Just sing like hell.'

Tom did just that. By the Wednesday he'd got it taped. In the studio he recorded the whole song in one take. But when he hit the final note he was giving it so much power he blacked out and fell off the podium. John Barry rerecorded other bits of the song, but Tom could never hit that grand finale again.

As Bond themes go *Thunderball* was not successful, but it kept the momentum going. On 15 March 1966 Tom won his first (and only) Grammy Award as Best New Artist. A month later he had his tonsils out. Because of the way he pushed his voice they had been giving him trouble for months. During one season at the Palladium the doctor was called out so often that the promoter Leslie Grade was having palpitations over cancelled shows. There was the possibility that taking out his tonsils might damage Tom's voice, which terrified him. However, the operation at the London Clinic on 11 April was a total success.

Following the operation Tom gave up smoking Woodbines and took up cigars – not inhaling, which caused less damage to the vocal cords. At the same time he started to take more care of his body. The Woodwards have a propensity to put on weight unless they keep fit. By 1966 Tom weighed over fifteen stone (210 pounds) and was showing signs of a double chin and bulging belly. Years of stodgy food and drinking way too much beer meant he had to cram himself into his stage outfits. He cut out drinking pints in favour of champagne.

In 1966 pop stars were hedonists; they did not exercise no matter how tough their schedule. Tom was way ahead of his time. His adoption of an exercise regime so early in his career has certainly contributed to its longevity. It was hard to stop overeating, but he changed his diet radically. To this day he never eats a pudding and chips are a no-no. His weight eventually reduced to eleven stone five (159 pounds) – the lightest he had been since he was twelve years old – and has not fluctuated more than ten pounds since.

He was still a party animal. Late on the night of 21 June 1966 he crashed his brand-new red Jaguar XJS on Park Lane. 'I was in the Cromwellian with a couple of members of the Squires,' he said, 'and these girl stewardesses wanted a lift home. It was two in the morning. They asked, "You're not going up Park Lane, are you?" It was in the wrong direction. But I said, "Look at this, I've got a red Jag, pile in," and off we went. Going up Park Lane this girl yells, "Turn right here," and I bloody did, doing 50 mph, into a barrier by the Dorchester.

'Everything came to a stop. I woke up in hospital and I had fourteen stitches, a headache and my mother looking at me saying, "Who do you think you are? You don't really think you're Tom Jones do you, all that publicity hasn't gone to your head?" My head was thumping, and she said, "You'd bloody better pull yourself together." So I did.'

What that meant was that Chris Ellis drove Tom around in his first Rolls-Royce. One night Tom and Chris were going into the Bag o' Nails in Kingly Street. (The Bag, owned by the Gunnell brothers, had started its career in Victorian times as a high class brothel. In 1966 the ladies wore miniskirts and did not charge.) The *maître d'* warned them that P.J. Proby was in the club. There was still bad blood between the two stars, and Tom, having had a few drinks, was in a belligerent mood and kept saying, 'Let's have the bastard.'

Proby came over, stuck out his hand and said, 'Hi, Tom. Let's sit down and talk about all this'. By three in the morning they were still chatting away and had become good friends. Tom offered P.J. a lift home to the King's Road. The Rolls was a silver-grey S3 with blacked-out windows. Smoking the windows had made them very brittle, so as Proby was getting out of the car Tom said to him, 'Please don't shut the door very hard, because the window will break.' Proby jumped out of the car and slammed the door as hard as he could. Sure enough the window split right down the middle. Chris drove off with Tom swearing in the back seat and Proby laughing fit to bust. Although the two never met again, Tom was to have the last laugh. There was this song called *Delilah*, which Proby had the first crack at.

Convinced of his own genius Gordon had not given up his own grandiose plans. While Tom was in America in 1965 he had started his own album. On *Do It Yourself* Mills wrote or co-wrote, produced and sang all the songs. Les Reed did the musical arrangements and conducted the orchestra. Tom was drafted in to sing backing vocals on *The Rose*, which, while it might have been a commercial decision, only served to emphasise the vocal gulf. Mills's voice is pleasant enough, but it's thin and lacks any real power or personality.

The failure of the album confirmed what Gordon subconsciously understood but had not accepted. As an artist he was competent, professional ... but ultimately uninspiring. In Tom he had the perfect vessel for his talents. Tom had a voice from God and the sex appeal of Bacchus, but he was lacking in ambition and malleable. It was a perfect fit.

One can see Tom nodding agreement in the background when Gordon told *Life* magazine, 'Most performers sing what they want. That's a mistake. You've got to know what that person sitting in the audience wants you to sing. When he wants to hear a ballad. When he wants some pathos. When he wants a dose of rhythm. The artist is too much within himself to do it. He needs a mirror.'

Mills always saw himself as Tom's mirror. But inside Gordon's hall of mirrors was glass that distorted the true picture, so that it was the manager who appeared the bigger star. He had dreams enough for both of them . . . and more. Aware of the fickle nature of the business, Gordon needed an outlet for his energy when Tom was out touring. He was always looking for other artists to manage . . . a safety net.

For a year Gerry Dorsey had been pestering his old friend and best man to manage him. Gordon was not sure if he wanted to because Gerry was already a two-time loser. The years had not been good to him. In 1961 he contracted tuberculosis and spent seven months recuperating. Everyone except Gerry thought he would never sing again. After he married Pat the two moved into a small flat above a furniture shop in King Street, Hammersmith. The pair lived on five shillings (25p) a day, sleeping late, living off porridge and mince and bags of groceries provided by his parents, 'usually with a few pound notes hidden among the tins'.

'Even when we were starving, Pat would never let me surrender,' he said. 'We had no friends . . . we couldn't entertain a soul. The only regular caller was the local tax collector. He was always dropping by to discuss some scheme so we could pay our overdue taxes. What really kept me going was that I'd have all these terrific fantasies about success. Even when I felt a failure most my ambition never stopped. It never let go of me.'

By early 1966 Gordon was prepared to take on Gerry's

career . . . but only on his terms. The first was a new name. Mills was leafing through a pile of classical albums when the name of the nineteenth-century German composer of *Hansel and Gretel* caught his eye. He phoned up Dorsey, who was doing a club season up in Newcastle, and said, 'Your name is no longer Gerry Dorsey. You are now Engelbert Humperdinck. It's a name no one will ever forget.' It took Gerry weeks to learn how to pronounce, let alone spell his new name.

Engelbert was to become Mr Romance, to Jones's Mr Sex, a sophisticated cool balladeer for the mature market. Les Reed was drafted in to handle the music. Enge's first outing was at a European song festival in Knokke Le Zoutte in Belgium. An English team of unknowns won, but as Gordon had surmised, it was the bloke with the funny name who engaged the media interest. Intrigued, Decca signed him up and handed him over to Peter Sullivan. His first single, the self-composed *Stay*, made few waves, while *Dommage Dommage* sold well in Europe. But what he needed now was the right song to go with his unforgettable name.

One of Mills's greatest gifts was his ability to see how a song could move across genre boundaries. While out driving he heard Esther Phillips singing *Release Me*, a powerful r&b interpretation of an old country hit that had made the US Top 10 in 1962. As he often did, Gordon made a tape of the song which he played to everyone while gauging reactions.

'We were doing a gig outside London with Tom,' said Vernon Hopkins, 'and Gordon came down. In the break he played a tape of this song and asked us what we thought of it. I said it was all right, a good country number. The next thing Enge was singing it on the Palladium.'

The former Gerry Dorsey was due a slice of luck. It came in January 1967. Mills heard that Dickie Valentine had flu and was unable to appear on *Sunday Night at the London Palladium*. Musical director Val Parnell was persuaded to let Engelbert on the show (the fact that *Green Green Grass of Home* was still at number one probably helped). The next day the record started to sell. It made number one for six weeks and sold over five million copies worldwide.

Gordon Mills now managed the two most successful male stars in Britain. Some turnaround. For years afterwards Enge refused to acknowledge he had once been Gerry Dorsey, the other name was bad luck. Over the Christmas holidays of 1966 everyone was having drinks at Gordon's, and Tom's brother-in-law, Ken Davies, asked innocently, 'Can I get you another drink, Gerry?'

'My name's not Gerry, it's Engelbert,' snapped Humperdinck. Ken said, 'Well, to me you always have been Gerry and you always will be.'

The once affable Enge appeared to become increasingly precious. All the resentment that had built up inside him as he struggled to become a star now sometimes manifested itself in tantrums, when he had to be cajoled on stage. Even though he had achieved his life's ambition, Gerry Dorsey was still second to Tom Jones. To Gordon, Tom always came first. Both were reflections of Mills's own personality, but where Engelbert was closer to what he actually was, Tom was what he aspired to be.

Despite all the press coverage saying what good friends they were, the pair never got on. But it never worried Tom when Humperdinck was selling more records than him. Tom Jones has always been secure in who and what he is. He is a true original.

CHAPTER EIGHT

IN THE STUDIO

By August 1966 Tom Jones's hits were getting decidedly thin on the ground. He had released six singles since *It's Not Unusual*, and not a single one had cracked the Top 10. *Once Upon a Time* had stalled at number thirty-two, *With These Hands* had done better and got to number thirteen, *What's New Pussycat?* had disappointed in the UK. Gordon's plans to have Tom sing film soundtracks foundered still further when *Thunderball* failed to reach the Top 30 – one of the poorest ever showings for the theme from a Bond movie. The double A-side, *Once There Was a Time/Not Responsible* did make it to number eighteen, but *This and That* stuck at number forty-four. He might have been voted top male singer in the *Melody Maker* poll at the end of the year, but Tom's career as a pop star was starting to wobble.

He was worried, 'not because I think my own little world is coming to an end,' he said, 'but just because something must be wrong if people don't bother to buy a record. The fault could simply lie in the material; lord knows it's hard enough to find the right song at the right time.'

Salvation came from Tom's rock and roll hero Jerry Lee Lewis. 'I could listen to him all night. Just curl up in a big chair and lose myself in his music,' he said, when complaining his touring schedule left him no time to listen to his Jerry Lee albums.

'I was in New York in 1966,' said Tom, 'and one of the first things I did was to find a record store where I could buy Jerry Lee's album *Country Songs for City Folks*. That's when I first heard *Green Green Grass of Home*, and I wanted to record it straight away. When I went back to England I met Jerry and we became friends. I joined him on stage at Bradford where we sang *Green Green Grass of Home* together. I wanted Jerry to play piano on my recording but he'd already returned to the States.'

Claude Curly Putman's song was inspired by John Huston's classic film noir *The Asphalt Jungle* in which Marilyn Monroe had a memorable cameo role. Sterling Hayden's character, Dix Handley, a dumb but stand-up gangster, dreams of making a big score and buying back the family horse farm in Kentucky. Everything unravels and eventually he collapses and dies on the green grass of home.

'It was the right song,' said Tom. 'Some numbers are so personal that they can hardly fail. Immediately there is a bond between the singer and the lyrics and the audience. What makes me specially proud is that it was chosen by me alone. I knew instinctively it was right for me.'

Tom was determined to record the song. He was confident that it would be a hit for him − which he had not been since he first heard *It's Not Unusual* − and convinced Gordon. It represented such a big change in style that the record company were very nervous. All the executives could hear was corn pone country.

'*Green Green Grass of Home* was a different bag,' said Peter Sullivan. 'We were very nervous about it because it was so different to what Tom had been recording. We all knew it was a potential hit, but it was so different. I told him he needed to try the song out in his act to see what it was like.'

Gordon Mills played the song to Les Reed. 'This isn't a hit that way,' said Les. 'I'll have to rearrange it.' Reed returned to Woking and spent three days turning a country song, which he hated, into a ballad. When he was first played the new arrangement in Decca number two studio, Tom did not like it at all. It was nothing like the Jerry Lee Lewis version.

'It's too big, you've got choirs, you've got strings,' he complained.

'This is the way I see it, Tom,' replied Reed. 'This is *Green Green Grass of Home* the way I see it.'

'OK boyo,' came the answer.

That was it. It took an hour to record the biggest hit of Jones's career. 'Les did a great arrangement,' remembered Sullivan, 'fairly simple, nothing too complicated, everything fitted and it just worked.

'In the recording studio Tom was very confident, but he didn't often impose himself. Tom is very self opinionated about what he likes and what he doesn't like. He's not a pushover. He analyses it and if he doesn't like it, he'll tell you. He had an opinion but he was always willing to try something, he wasn't ever adamant.'

Green Green Grass of Home went to number one in three weeks, very fast for the sixties, when only the Beatles could jump that fast that quickly. It stayed at the top for seven weeks over Christmas, remained in the charts for twenty-two weeks and became Decca's first ever million-seller. The song had a universal appeal. It meant something different to everybody. Many inhabitants of Treforest believe it was written about the Valleys, and it made Vietnam veterans cry.

Another tragic but important contributory factor to its

success in Britain was the Aberfan disaster. On 21 October 1966 a giant slag heap above the mid-Glamorgan mining village, just six miles north of Pontypridd, collapsed and slid down the hillside, engulfing much of the village, including the school. In all 144 people died, of whom 116 were children.

'The Aberfan disaster affected everybody,' said Peter Sullivan, 'so that song, sung by a Welshman, made people feel a togetherness.'

Overnight Tom Jones had changed his market position. Instead of being just another rock and roller he was the only big balladeer in town. But not for long. Within weeks his stablemate Engelbert Humperdinck was at the top with *Release Me*. The two singers unleashed an extraordinary run of hits; everything they touched turned to gold, and neither of them were out of the charts for the next two years. In 1967 Humperdinck spent ninety-seven weeks in the charts (*There Goes My Everything*, which got to number two and *The Last Waltz*, which went all the way to the top, made him the UK's biggest selling artist of 1967). Jones was second to him with sixty-eight weeks. The following year the positions were reversed, Tom with fifty-eight, Engelbert with fifty-seven.

While the summer of love was actually dominated by Engelbert, Tom unleashed a steady stream of Top 10 hits. On the 'if it ain't broke' principle, the follow-up to *Green Green Grass of Home* was the rockier *Detroit City*, also on a Jerry Lee album. Then came Mickey Newbury's country lament, *Funny Familiar Forgotten Feelings*, a remake of Lonnie Donegan's *I'll Never Fall in Love Again*, and in November, Reed and Mason's *I'm Coming Home*.

When it came time to write the arrangement for *I'm Coming Home*, Les Reed decided to give it the Sammy Davis Jr treatment. Sammy always insisted on singing among the string section, which caused problems of separation with the microphones, but created such 'a close, beautiful sound I knew I had to try it with somebody else. So I arranged it with Tom standing in the studio amongst the strings.

'Tom's first take was so beautiful. He put such a performance into that song, hard-bitten string players had tears in their eyes, the drummer had his mouth open. I thought, "I will never make another recording like that."

'Then the bloody button went down in the control room. "OK we're ready when you are!" They hadn't recorded it! Tom did the song once more, but he never sang it like that again. The creative magic of that five minutes was something you could never ever repeat.'

Now Mills was too busy playing the big-time manager to write lyrics, Les Reed had hooked up with his poker buddy Barry Mason. Gordon, who knew and cultivated both men, had never introduced them. 'Barry came into my office one day,' recalled Les, 'and said, "I'm a lyric writer, can we write together?" We wrote a song called *Here It Comes Again* for the Fortunes.' It was one of those rare symbiotic writing partnerships. The pair had little in common. Les preferred a suburban existence while Barry enjoyed more of the fruits swinging London had to offer. But when they got together, the hits started flowing.

One Sunday in November 1966 Barry headed down to Surrey to play golf with Les. It was raining so they scrapped the game and sat down to write songs in Les's chalet bungalow, just off Evelyn Close in Woking. The first number was an idea Les had had for ages called *The Last Waltz*. They moved on to other songs. By 10 p.m. they had basically written seven songs and started one other. Five were Top 10 hits. In addition to *The Last Waltz*, they wrote *Love is All* for Malcolm Roberts, *I Pretend* for Des O'Connor, *Les Bicyclettes de Belsize* for Enge and *24 Sycamore* for Gene Pitney. The unfinished number was *Winter World of Love*, a Top 10 for Enge in 1969.

Despite his long association with both Les and Barry, Gordon never asked them for songs. When he called up to 'chat', it was down to them to pitch 'sexy songs for Tom, romantic songs for Enge'. If he liked one, the inevitable call would come from his publisher, Cyril Simons, saying, 'Gordon likes the song, but he won't record it unless we publish it.'

After the first couple of hits Gordon had started his own publishing company, Valley Music. Inside the music business he was famous for trying to get the publishing rights for songs covered by Tom or Engelbert.

'He would do his damnedest,' said Roger Greenaway, who with his partner, Roger Cook, was a prolific hit-maker, performer and writer, 'if the song was free for publishing he would want to publish it. If it wasn't free, he'd try and do some deal with the publisher to get a piece of the action. Roger Cook and I had songs that might have been selected for singles, but weren't because we would not agree.'

The standard business practice of the day was for the publisher to pay fifty-fifty of money received (not money earned at source). An international hit meant more money for the publisher. If a song was a hit in Australia and the UK publishing company had no office out there, they struck a sub-publishing deal and gave twenty-five per cent to a local company to administer and collect money due. Of the remaining seventy-five per cent, twenty-five per cent remained abroad (thus avoiding UK taxes) and the writer was paid fifty per cent of the fifty per cent that came home. In some cases there would be sub-sub-publishing deals bouncing the income around, which could mean that the writer received only about six per cent of the original income received.

A piece of the action might only apply to a particular recording by Tom or Engelbert, not if the song was recorded by someone else. The deal might be for twenty-five per cent of mechanicals (royalties earned on record sales) or on mechanicals and PRS income (the writer of a song gets a set fee each time his song is played on radio or TV. On a big hit this can be thousands of pounds a year).

'I never saw one of those contracts,' said Greenaway, who now works for ASCAP (American Society of Composers, Authors and Publishers) in the UK, 'but they were fairly notorious. Major artists still do it these days. You hear lines like, "He was in the room", which means they walked through the room while the song was being written. Elvis Presley didn't write at all, but that's not to say he didn't get a lot of the publishing.'

When Reed offered *To Make a Big Man Cry* to Adam Faith and P.J. Proby, Mills took the song off the album *A-Tom-Ic Jones* when it was released in America. *Love Me Tonight* – and *A Man Without Love*, which was recorded by Engelbert – were Italian songs for which Barry Mason wrote English lyrics. Both of them are still published by Valley Music.

'After *I'm Coming Home* when I called Gordon he said, "How do we top that?" ' Les Reed recalled. 'So I brought him *Delilah.*'

For a singer who does not write his own material, finding the right songs can be a slice of luck. Just as *It's Not Unusual* could have been covered by Sandie Shaw, *Green Green Grass of Home* could have been Presley's, *Delilah* could have become a standard for Tom's old rival P.J. Proby. Instead it is the first song Tom Jones imitators cover, a melodramatic tale of infidelity and murder, with a suitably overblown arrangement.

Les Reed had been approached to produce and write P.J.'s album *Believe It or Not*. 'When I had to do the album with Proby, I went to Barry and said I needed twelve songs. Out of the twelve we wrote eight; I wrote the other four with different lyricists. We gave him nine hits on that album. Amongst those songs were *I'm Coming Home*, *Delilah* and a song called *It's Your Day Today*, which was a very banal song, and that's the one P.J. picked for his single. So I took the P.J. recording of *Delilah* to Tom and Gordon who thought it was a smash.'

Delilah came easily. Les fooled around on the piano until he came up with an introduction. As he picked out the theme Barry burst out, 'That's great, what is it?' Les started to sing a melody against it, as Barry said, 'Oh, we need a hook, what can we call it?'

'I don't know,' said Reed. 'But it needs to go . . . "my, my . . . "' Barry just came out with . . . "Delilah . . . that's it." '

'The first pop song I remember hearing as a little kid was *Jezebel* by Frankie Laine,' said Mason. 'That stuck in my mind. Jezebel was a bad girl, "If ever the devil was born without a pair of horns, it was you, Jezebel, it was you. When an angel fell, Jezebel, it was you." Suddenly I thought of the name Delilah.

'I'm a very emotional person. Jealousy is such a terribly strong emotion and love and jealousy combined is just lethal. You can kill someone over jealousy and almost get away with it because you are insane. That fascinated me, and the lyric just grew from that. It's a lyric I'm really proud of. Thank God Proby didn't like it. If he'd released it as a single it could have really buggered us up.'

'I heard *Delilah* when there was just a chorus to it and it had such a commercial hook,' said Peter Sullivan. 'It was a hard-hitting 3/4 song. A lot of people thought it was a joke song, but when you analyse the vocal and the power it was really a very commercial package. Any singer other than Tom trying to get into that song and sell it would have had a hell of a job because of its range, and the musical drama created by Les's arrangement.'

Recording sessions were hectic affairs. In the days of four- and eight-track studios there was no time to record a single instrument and develop the song from there part by part. Sullivan aimed to cut three songs a day and finish recording an album in a week. The average album budget varied from £10,000 to £20,000, of which the main cost was the musicians. Decca were notoriously tight. 'If I started running overtime,' said Sullivan, 'I'd get hit up by the label. I used to have to get it down in one session. We'd work from two to six in the afternoon and seven to ten in the evening, with thirty minutes' overtime. Further overtime was another half-session for the musicians for the next hour. If you had a forty-piece orchestra that was a lot of money.

'We'd cut three songs at a time. Most tracks were recorded live and mixing was much simpler than now, when everything is spread across thirty-two or forty-eight channels. The sweat was in the tracking as you couldn't do too much repair work after the track was cut. I couldn't mess around too much with a brass section, so I had to get it right on the day.'

The amount of time spent on each track depended on how the song sounded on the run-through. During the first session, Sullivan heard the whole arrangement before attempting to record it. Then he would break the band and the orchestra up into different units. The trickier parts were sent out while he got the main track down. Then the guitar solos and the horn breaks would be overdubbed separately.

Tom seldom came to the afternoon sessions. He liked recording in the evenings, partly because he had usually been gigging the night before, partly because he hated getting up in the morning. He arrived prepared, the lyric learnt, ready to start right away. Because he liked to be amongst the musicians and to do his vocals live, he recorded not in his own isolated glass booth, but in a separate baffled room built on the studio floor. A singer with a weaker, thinner voice might have had problems with other instruments bleeding into the vocal mike.

'His vocal,' said Sullivan, 'was so powerful it would knock out any leakage. I never had any problems with him. The only time he couldn't sing was if his voice was blown out. He'd give everything he'd got, there was no temperament.

'I never had any other artist of that standard or calibre. It was a pleasure to record with him. Normally you have to work like crazy to make a hit, but he'd make everything seem so good, Tom could make something insignificant sound better than it was.

'We did a session of a Burt Bacharach song called *Promise Her Anything* [released only on the US version of *A-Tom-ic Jones*]. Burt was very hot at the time and Tom made it sound incredibly good, but the song itself was really very mediocre.'

To Tom live performance was more important than recording. He would inject such a lot of excitement into the vocals live it was hard to ignore that in the studio. Most singers are more subdued when recording a song live in the studio, saving their best for the vocal overdub. 'Tom would go out and give it everything on the live session, so if the quality was there, I'd think, "What is the point in tracking anything?" It was only if there was a lack of performance within a certain phrase that we would overdub.'

In the late sixties, as Tom's commitments to TV and demands for live performance increased, so his energy for recording sessions was sapped. 'The more success he had the more the stress came on the physical side, so he didn't have the energy to give the attack he normally did, and on those occasions we would give a full vocal overdub. During a recording session the voice will lose its effectiveness after a while because of fatigue, but he had enormous endurance,' said Sullivan.

Gordon Mills was all but omnipresent at his artist's recording sessions. In the early days he would act out Tom's role and then literally coach his protégé. Many of Tom's nuances and phrases came from Gordon, who showed him how to bend certain notes and to project the lyric more.

'Tom would literally sing the song on a piece of paper that

was put in front of him,' explained Les Reed. 'He would put his own interpretation on it, but Sinatra would have learnt that song backwards before he went into the studio. He wouldn't have a piece of paper in front of him, because that would affect his flow. Frank would say, "I don't like that, I can't sing it, it's not musical." Tom always had a piece of paper in front him so he couldn't think 100 per cent about how he was going to present that lyric, because it was written down in front of him. That's the difference between the two. But when it comes to styling a musical phrase there ain't no one like Tom.'

As Tom and Engelbert became more successful, Mills grew more dogmatic in the studio. One song he never liked was *Help Yourself*, but Sullivan insisted it be put in a session. Even though it came out as the follow-up to *Delilah* and reached number five in the charts, Gordon was still angry. According to Barry Mason, he told Sullivan, 'Don't you ever make me put a fucking record like that in my session again! Even though it was a Top 10 hit, he still insisted it was shit and told Peter off for making him record it, you know, persuading him. Gordon was very unpleasant sometimes, very suspicious, very hard.'

Sullivan, who often had a rough time, was more discreet, saying, 'We had a lot of disagreements on a professional level, and it got pretty verbal at times. He would definitely not sit back, he'd say if he didn't like something. He and I used to have our moments of disagreement – particularly on arrangements.'

When Engelbert was recording, Gordon was even more in control. In a cover story for *Life* magazine it was reported:

Mills picks every song, supervises every arrangement. He personally produces every TV show and every record for both. He approves every booking. He makes all the business decisions and his is always the last word. He'll decide on something and say, 'That's it,' Jones says with a shrug. 'It's open and shut.'

Mills was in the US recently with Jones, while Engelbert Humperdinck was in London recording *My Marie*. The first tape of the song was immediately sent to Mills and the next recording session was interrupted by the phone. Orchestra, conductor, engineers – everyone stopped short.

'Engelbert,' said Mills on the transatlantic line, 'I don't like the way you're doing *My Marie*. Put more guts into it.' Click. Engelbert put more guts into it.

Sullivan, who was producing that session, shrugged the anecdote off as, 'It makes a good story. I don't want to go into that more deeply because a lot of things with Engelbert Humperdinck were dealt with so differently from Tom. Tom was very much the senior partner, Gordon absolutely gave Tom more time and energy than he gave to Engelbert.'

In the sixties the unions held much of the country to ransom with sheer bloody-minded application of the precise letter of the law. A full orchestra running into time and a half could whack the recording budget into the red. One night in 1969, recording in Decca number two studio, there were ten minutes left to finish the last song, *Daughter of Darkness*. At precisely 10 o'clock, with thirty seconds of the take still to play and the tape running, trumpeter Freddy Clayton put down his instrument.

As a Musicians' Union official he would not play a second over. Most of the orchestra shrugged their shoulders. What was half a minute on the end of a session? One of the backing singers was furious. Young Reggie Dwight stomped over to the trumpeter and said, 'You were bloody late today, you were five minutes late coming in, but Les didn't kick you out did he? So why did you put your trumpet down?'

That was the start of a shouting match. Eventually the fixer, Charlie Katz, came in, pushed Clayton against the wall and said, 'Tom's given you a lot of work over the years, don't ever do this again.' Eventually the musicians all stayed to finish the song.

Despite his help, that was Reg Dwight's last session as a back-up singer for Tom Jones. Within two years, as Elton John, he had become one of the biggest superstars in the world. Peter Sullivan and Les Reed booked the cream of London's studio musicians for Jones's sessions. Guitarist Joe Moretti was the featured player on *It's Not Unusual*, but most of the guitar work was performed by Big Jim Sullivan (who later joined Tom's live band) and Jimmy Page. John Paul Jones played bass on a few sessions, but he and Page became unavailable when they formed another successful band – Led Zeppelin. Regular drummers included Kenny Clare and Ronnie Verrell from the Ted Heath band, and the rockier Tony Newman.

Generally at recording sessions Tom was a model professional, but occasionally it slipped. On 23 February 1970, during the sessions for the *She's a Lady* album, Chris Ellis arrived at Tor Point to pick up Tom, who was due at Decca in West Hampstead at 3 p.m.

'I got up to the house, and the house was stone dead,' said Ellis. 'There was nobody there. I got the car out of the garage, where I saw that Tom's red convertible Corniche was missing. So I waited. And then flashing down the drive came Tom and Mark in the Rolls-Royce. He slammed on the brakes, but because the drive was all pebbles the car wouldn't stop, and he went straight through the privet hedge and landed up on the lawn.

'Tom and Mark had gone to the Seven Hills restaurant up near Cobham and they got through God knows how much wine and champagne. Tom jumped in the back of the car with his cigar going and we get to Hampstead two hours late.

'There was a studio full of musicians, and Gordon started shouting at Tom and there was a big argument, "The session's almost over, and the guys are going to go home."

'Tom said, "I can do this in one take." Gordon said, "No fucking way," and bet him £5 that he couldn't do it. Tom did it, drunk, stone drunk, and he did it in one take. That was *She's a Lady.*'

Daughter of Darkness, written by Les Reed and Geoff Stephens, was the last record on which the hit-making partnership of Sullivan, Reed and Mills all worked. Mills, by now a control freak who owned the two biggest singers in the world, believed the other two had got too demanding.

Although Gordon never solicited songs from Les, he could not stand it when he gave his material to other artists. Sullivan had left Decca and joined Beatles' producer George Martin at AIR Studios. MAM were interested in acquiring AIR, but when the deal fell through, according to Sullivan, 'it severed our relationship. The business side got in the way of a lot of decisions.'

After MAM went public and renegotiated their contract with Decca, they assumed complete control of all recording budgets, took on all the costs and could dictate exactly what was going on. Decca could no longer impose their choice of producer. It became 'Gordon Mills Productions for MAM', and he saw no need to pay an outsider. Gordon's insistence on total control was to prove the downfall of his artist's recording career.

It worked to begin with. Gordon's production on Gilbert O'Sullivan's first three albums made them international bestsellers. Tom's rendition of Paul Anka's *She's a Lady* was a massive hit, followed by *Till* and the ridiculous *Young New Mexican Puppeteer*. But after that Tom Jones did not have another hit in his native country for fifteen years.

'It is very hard to put your finger on why it didn't make it,' said Sullivan. 'The artist was still there, the songs were available, but the magic didn't happen on the recordings. It was a tight unit, unique in my career. When I split and everyone went their different ways that is when it all went wrong.'

'When we became very successful Gordon was affected by it,' reminisced Tom in 1994. 'I'm not having a go at Gordon, but when Peter Sullivan left Decca and formed a company with George Martin, he became very expensive. Decca said, "We can't afford that." I said, "Just pay him, what's the difference?" Gordon said, "We don't need him," and started producing my albums, and it didn't really happen. We'd make these continuous albums, but meanwhile the hits had stopped.'

CHAPTER NINE

THE SUPREME

L ate on the afternoon of 19 January 1968 Tom Jones knocked on the door of a dressing room in a Munich TV studio. American booking agent, Norman Weiss, had promised him a blind date with one of the hottest black singers of the moment. Although Mary Wilson was only one third of the Supremes, she was a far bigger international star than Tom.

Berry Gordy, an ambitious R&B songwriter, had formed Motown records in 1959 (named after his home town of Detroit – MotorTown). After enjoying some local success, the Marvelettes' *Please Mr Postman* gave the fledgling company its first national number one. Refusing to be stuck in the old ghetto for 'race music' Gordy marketed Motown as a brand, 'The Sound of Young America', and aimed it four square at the white audience. Because it was more than a series of independent acts, Motown matched the Beatles and the British beat invasion hit for hit.

The Motown sound was a vibrant blend of soul and pop,

marked by a pounding bass rhythm, while complex, angelic harmonies added a light commercial touch. Its influence was huge. When writing *It's Not Unusual*, Les Reed and Gordon Mills were inspired by some of Marvin Gaye's early recordings, while Tom has always loved r&b music (though he prefers purer singers, like Brook Benton and Jackie Wilson).

Mary Wilson, Florence Ballard, Diane Ross and Betty McGlown were schoolgirls in the Detroit projects when they started a singing group, the Primettes, in 1959. Three years later they were down to a trio and rechristened the Supremes. Despite having Smokey Robinson writing their singles, the Motown magic eluded them until 1964, when the songwriting duties were taken over by Holland, Dozier and Holland. They went from bottom of the package tour bills to the top and became the most successful female vocal group of all time. In 1968 they were at the crest of a phenomenal run of eighteen consecutive American hits, including ten number ones. (In the UK, which fell in love with them before the States, they had enjoyed twelve Top 40 hits, including seven Top 10s. In 1964 *Baby Love* was the only song by an American group to reach number one.)

Early on Berry Gordy had seen that the Supremes' long-term future lay in the middle-of-the-road market. As early as 1965 they played the Copacabana and the Flamingo in Las Vegas, then the Deauville in Miami followed a year later. They recorded an album *Live at the Copa* and another covering Rodgers and Hart Broadway standards. 'We had gone from poverty to becoming international stars, from being Negroes to being princesses,' said Wilson.

Mary, at twenty-three, was rich, successful, pampered and – since the end of her relationship with the Temptations' Duke Fakir – unattached. Although on the surface her group reigned supreme, underneath it was floundering. Florence Ballard had quit, to be replaced by Cindy Birdsong, and Diane, now Diana, Ross was the undisputed lead singer and spokesperson. 'When Florence had to leave that devastated me. My mirror was cracked. I was lonely.'

Throughout 1967 Norman Weiss had been teasing Mary about 'this guy who is a huge smash in England and wants to meet you.' Mary demanded, 'Who is the guy?' to be told, 'Tom Jones.' Then she asked him in all innocence, 'Who's that? Isn't that a book?'

She was not impressed, as there were dozens of minor celebrities all trying to bag a Supreme. She heard his records, then when she saw him on the *Ed Sullivan Show* and got over the shock of discovering he was white, she liked what she saw. 'I thought, "He's kind of cool." ' The badinage with Norman went on for months as their schedules criss-crossed. Eventually he arranged a meeting at the Bambi Awards ceremony in Munich – the European equivalent of the Academy Awards – at which both artists were booked to perform.

Tom Jones knocked on the door of Mary's dressing room while Diana was still only half-dressed. ' "Who is it?" I asked, my heart pounding,' wrote Mary in her autobiography, *Dream Girl*. ' "It's Tom Jones," he replied in his beautiful Welsh accent. Diane screamed, jumped up, and ran into another room. I had been waiting for this moment for weeks and wasn't going to blow it. I opened the door and there he was, dressed in a ruffled white shirt, black tuxedo, and – of course – skintight pants. Sparks flew; he was gorgeous. Why had I waited so long!

'We spoke for a few moments, making plans to meet after the show at a dinner party. When he left, I was speechless.'

That night they chased each other across Munich, from party to party, until finally they were back at her hotel.

'Within moments we were throwing back glasses of champagne and having a wonderful time. I could see instantly that Tom was like no man I had ever met. He was extremely down-to-earth and passionate. We talked, then we cuddled, then we kissed, and by the time the evening had ended I knew I was in love.'

Tom was equally smitten. He told Chris Ellis the next day, 'She's fantastic.' Unfortunately, Tom had omitted to tell Mary one small but essential fact. He was married. The affair had been going on for several weeks before Mary found out. 'I couldn't believe it. Maybe Tom figured that since every other woman in the Western world knew that he was "unavailable", I should have known too. At first I felt like a fool, then I felt betrayed, as if I had been the one cheated on. After my experience with Duke I had vowed never to get involved with a married man again. I resolved to break it off the next time I saw him, but when that time came, I realised that I couldn't. It was too late then. I was already madly in love. I felt bad, but not bad enough to stop. I was so young. That's my excuse, Tom is a man, he has that double standard.'

Years later, when travelling between shows, he'd ask his backing singer Darlene Love to sit with him at the front of his private plane and reminisce. Said Love, 'I'd say, "Man, you really like black women," and he would go, "Yes," and then he'd tell me about Mary Wilson, about how much he loved her. He really was in love with her.'

'Tom always liked black girls, he always said their skin was like velvet, but his thing with Mary was special,' laughed Squires' keyboard player Vic Cooper.

Later in the year Tom returned to the Bayerischer Hof in Munich for a TV appearance. As he and Chris were checking in at reception, Tom was greeted with, 'Come up here and have a drink with me, you fucking Welshman.' Richard Burton, who was still filming *Where Eagles Dare*, was sitting in the bar with Elizabeth Taylor. Both had been drinking heavily and Burton was in full flow, swearing, cursing and wandering off into long rambling rants.

'We are both fucking Welsh,' he said, force-feeding Tom

Buck-skinned, bronzed and beautiful in the mid-seventies (*Terry O'Neill*)

Enjoying a pint in Pontypridd in
November 1966
(*Syndication International*)

Recuperating in a London clinic after
having his tonsils out in April 1966
(*Western Mail*)

Showing off his new Jaguar to fans in May 1966. Only three weeks later he pranged the car and ended up in hospital! (*Western Mail*)

On tour in Australia in 1966 (*Chris Ellis*)

Playing snooker with Gordon Mills after routining songs for his 1970 tour (*Terry O'Neill*)

Tom, Gordon Mills (on Tom's car) and Engelbert Humperdinck with their matching Rolls-Royces in 1969. At the time of the launch of MAM, the cars were the company's only physical assets (*David Farrell/Redferns*)

With Engelbert in Barbados in the mid-seventies (*Terry O'Neill*)

Backstage at the Flamingo Hotel with Priscilla and Elvis Presley in 1968
(*Syndication International*)

At home in Bel Air (*Terry O'Neill*)

Tom and Linda in Wales for Christmas in 1967 (*Syndication International*)

With mum and dad, Freda and Tom senior, in 1969 (*J. Barry/Scope Features*)

At Pinewood Studios with Kirk Douglas on the set of *London Bridge* in March 1972 (*David Steen/Scope Features*)

Filming stunts at Lake Havasu, Arizona (*Chris Ellis*)

champagne, 'and when you come from Wales you're a fucking man, and we take pit ponies and we put a piece of rubber fucking hose pipe in their mouth and drag them into the sea, to wash the grime off them, we're tough in Wales.' Elizabeth Taylor tried to calm him down, 'Oh Richard, please don't swear so much,' to which he snapped, 'Oh you shut up, just because you've got fucking big tits, who the fucking hell do you think you are?' Tom was visibly shocked by Burton's bad language.

Everyone went out and got almost as drunk as Burton. Tom and Chris finally got to check in at four in the morning. Staggering along the black oak corridors to their suite on the second floor, Tom noticed a pair of black shoes, polished to a shine by the night porter, outside a room. He grabbed a fire axe from the wall, picked up the shoes and put them in the middle of the corridor. Then he took up the axe and slammed it right through the toe of the shoe, embedding the metal deep into the wood floor; so deep neither could move it. Giggling they lurched off to bed.

Because of the pressures of their twin careers Tom and Mary did not meet that often. Whenever she could get four or five days off she'd fly to London; Tom would send his Rolls to meet her and take her to the Mayfair Hotel. To begin with they were both discreet, Mary would take off her fur jackets and put on sunglasses. It was a stolen romance full of coded phone messages. 'If one of us missed the other's call, we would leave a coded message saying that "Jimi Hendrix" had called, which must have kept people in our entourages buzzing,' said Mary. The Hendrix code was inspired by Mary's Afro hairstyle and made safe by the knowledge that the real Hendrix was never going to call up. Emboldened, they started visiting Tom's favourite pubs and eating out in restaurants. Inevitably they were spotted one night in Mr Chow's.

It got worse during the summer when Tom was doing a summer season with Roy Castle at the Winter Gardens in

Bournemouth and had rented a split-level house in exclusive Canford Cliffs. Mary flew over from the States, had a chauffeur drive her down and moved in to Tom's upstairs bedroom.

'They were like teenagers in love,' said Chris Ellis, who was living in the bottom half of the house with his girlfriend Eva Lundahl. 'Mostly they talked about silly stuff but they would get into deep stuff as well, arguing about music. Mary was a good arguer, but she was a very sweet kid, she was streetwise, she was sharp. I can really see why he fell for her.

'One night Mary said, "I'll make dinner tonight, soul food, a real southern recipe." So we went out and bought a chicken, and one of the tricks with this chicken was to make a sauce by pouring a tin of mushroom soup over it. It was a great dinner, and everybody enjoyed it. Tom and Mary were laughing, cuddling, lots of private jokes and long looks over the dinner table. Some of the chicken wasn't finished, so it was left in the oven, and we just forgot about it.'

Unfortunately this idyll was not to last. Local reporters had spotted Tom and Mary together and the story made the gossip column in the *NME*. Back home in Shepperton, Linda read the item early in the morning. Something snapped in her.

The phone rang in Tom's bedroom around 9 a.m. – horrendously early. Mary picked up the receiver and passed it over to Tom. 'Hello,' he grunted.

'You get that cow out of there now,' shouted Linda.

'What are you talking about?'

'I know that Mary Wilson is in that room with you, now you get her out,' she yelled. 'I'm going to be in that house in five minutes.'

'What do you mean? Where are you?' stammered Tom.

'I'm in the phone box at the end of the road.' Then she hung up. Tom was out of the bedroom in seconds flat. Wearing only a dressing gown, he sprinted down the stairs and started banging on Chris's door shouting, 'We're in trouble, we're in trouble.' There *was* a phone box at the end of the road, and Tom believed Linda was going to come up there and give him hell.

While Chris threw on his clothes, Tom ran back upstairs and told Mary she had to, 'Get out. Now. Pack everything and go.' As a Supreme did not travel with less than five suitcases, this was not the easiest thing to do. But within fifteen minutes, while Tom paced the floor like a cornered lion, Mary was bundled out of the house into the Rolls-Royce clutching a small tape recorder in her hands. Mary sat in the back crying her heart out, while the tape recorder played *Green Green Grass of Home* over and over all the way to London. Aside from the shock and the degrading circumstances – a superstar thrown out as if she was some tart – Mary now understood the status of their relationship. Even though he loved her she would always be second to his wife. No wonder she cried all the way to London.

After Chris left her at the Mayfair Hotel, he turned straight back for Bournemouth. Just after 1 p.m. he was driving back up the unmade road, 200 metres from the house, when he saw Tom wandering about in the road.

'He was dressed, but looked in a total daze. He was in shock, no doubt about it. He'd walked up the road, probably to face Linda, gone into somebody's house, and had been drinking tea with them.'

Linda, who did not drive, eventually turned up later in the day, accompanied by their black Labrador Blackie, still furious with Tom and looking for clues to see if Mary had been in the house. Linda knew she'd been there because she had talked to a local paper reporter who confirmed he had seen the couple together. She went into the bathroom and found some black hairs in the bath. 'What are these?' she shouted, accusingly.

'I don't know,' Tom said, and then pointed at Blackie. 'It's the dog, he's been in the bath.' Unconvinced, Linda then went into the kitchen and eventually she opened the oven to find the remains of the chicken.

'That looks nice, Tommy, did you cook it?' she asked Tom, knowing full well he could not lift a frying pan. 'Chris cooked it,' said Tom desperately. 'He's been taking cookery lessons.'

'Don't give me that,' she snapped, 'he couldn't even boil an egg.'

Having suffered such a narrow escape, the affair continued to burn as hot as ever. On July 20, 1969 – the night the Apollo 11 astronauts landed on the moon – Mary and her friend, Margie Haber, were in Tom's dressing room at Westbury Music Fair in Long Island waiting for him to change so that they could go out to eat. 'When he emerged from his shower, barely covered by a towel, he cried, "Oh, Mary" and started hugging and kissing me. I was so engrossed watching the moon walk that I shooed him away. Margie later told me that the whole time I stared at the screen, Tom stood there staring at me.'

At Tom's shows he would sing songs directly to Mary. One night at the Flamingo in Las Vegas he sang *Green Green Grass of Home*, then segued straight into *That Old Black Magic* while looking straight at Mary. When she was on tour and her relationship with Diana Ross was disintegrating by the day, she would telephone his home in England, only to put the receiver down when Linda answered the phone.

Such public displays of private affection had seriously begun to worry Gordon Mills. Tom's career was on the fast track, he had a new TV series and the Vegas contracts and a major scandal could destroy everything. His audience was middle America which would not countenance a married man having an affair with a black girl, whoever she was.

'Gordon saw dollar signs flying away,' said Chris Ellis. 'He didn't like it at all, he tried to break it up many times. He'd talk to Tom and say, "You can't go on with this, you've got to think of your marriage."'

'We were still in the sixties. If anyone, especially in the States, heard that Tom, a married man, was dating a black girl, that was not considered nice,' admitted Mary. 'Gordon was a great guy, and I think personally he liked me very much, but if you are a manager you don't want anyone coming in and messing up your money. Gordon tried to break it up and rightfully so. Gordon wanted something that was a fling but not real caring or real friendship. Tom and I were very good friends, we really liked each other as human beings.'

Tom's relationship with Mary Wilson was a relationship between equals. Both were superstars, used to being in the public eye and the acclaim that went with it. Both were natural conservatives at a time when it was *de rigueur* to consume drugs. The dippier, the hippier, the better.

'Tom is square, totally square,' she laughed. 'Like me. That's what was great about it, because this is what people don't understand: you could be a square, a good person, a nice person and have fun. Tom was a real man. There are people who are just earthy people, not necessarily pretty or handsome, but they are just there. Tom was like that, he's a man's man, no frills.

'I am a performer, but some men can't accept that. Tom understands what the performer has to do. All he ever wanted was music. We both enjoyed being an entertainer . . . and being together. Whereas most times his girlfriends were the type where it was just sex, we were friends which was different. I could go out with the guys too where he could be himself; he didn't have to be romantic, just be.

'Tom never really talked a lot, and I never did either, so that's what was really great about our relationship. I would put him amongst my best friends in life. We should have been friends instead of lovers. But men don't know how to separate it. Men have to have sex, right?'

Mary started to dispense Tom career advice. With her experience in the supper clubs of America she knew what she was talking about . . . but it was not her role. She said enough to worry Gordon.

'I think that's part of what put me out of the picture, kind of sealed my fate with Gordon,' she said. 'I always told Tom, "It's great that you're a sexy guy and that the women throw their panties and all that stuff, but it cheapens what you really are. You're a great singer, you have one of the most beautiful voices I have ever heard; you're a great performer, you can aspire to be that." '

When Tom was recording his TV show in LA, a Hollywood magazine published a picture of him and Mary together. Members of the crew were dispatched to buy every copy on sale in Hollywood Boulevard to stop Linda seeing it. Such protection proved unnecessary for Tom had bought his own copy of the magazine and taken it home. In November 1969, soon after Diana Ross had announced she was leaving the Supremes, Mary and Tom split for the final time. She threw a party at her house in the Hollywood hills, but she and Tom took shelter in her bedroom. 'Mary,' he said, 'I don't think this is fair to you. There is no future for us, and I think we should break away from this affair now.'

'Maybe he got tired of me, I don't know,' said Mary. 'Maybe Gordon did get to him; certainly all the other forces around him were telling him to break off the affair.

'He finally understood it was the time that he had to make a decision. Tom was a very good boy you see, and when he was told that this wasn't something good, it took a while to sink in. He loves his wife, he's always loved his wife. He's always been with her, he wasn't about to leave her, and it was getting out of hand. I think it was the right thing to do, I really do . . . of course I cried like a baby for months and months afterwards.'

Mary and Tom kept in sporadic touch. Whenever he could, Tom attended her Hollywood parties. Part of Mary always hoped that there might be a final hand in their love affair still unplayed.

Tom thought differently. As he has always done when a close relationship ended, he moved on, thinking of her fondly. Mary knew there was no chance of any rekindling or romance when Tom brought Linda backstage after a Supremes show and introduced the two of them. 'Linda,' Mary wrote sadly, 'was very nice.'

Linda played the meeting like a champion. 'It's very nice to meet you,' she said graciously.

Tom, who for all his womanising ways, seldom kisses and tells, appeared rather surprised and a little aggrieved when *Dream Girl* was first published in 1986. 'I've had my flings,' he said, 'Linda knows that. When she finds out I've had a fling, she gives me a right rollicking. When I went with Mary Wilson, Linda gave me hell. Now Mary's got a bloody book going on about it and Linda's given me a second rollicking.' He considered it disloyal and not a little inconvenient. Tom has never liked to be inconvenienced by his women.

To this day Tom Jones remains one of the great loves of Mary Wilson's life, as she is the other great love of his life. Unlike nearly all of his affairs, it was about more than sex. Just like Linda, Mary was also his friend. It is not something he has experienced much.

'Tom was going down a dead end. He was in love and love was blind,' said Chris Ellis. 'He realised that the actual crunch had come, that it was either leave Linda and marry Mary, or leave Mary, and he had a hell of a tough time trying to decide which of those it was going to be. It's probably the closest he ever got to leaving Linda. When he chose Linda over Mary Wilson, I think it broke his heart to do it.'

CHAPTER TEN

VIVA LAS VEGAS

O n 18 March 1966 Tom and the Squires began an Australian tour, co-headlining with Herman's Hermits. Ironically, Tom's biggest hit in Australia had been with Joe Meek's pre-Decca version of *Chills and Fever*. From the beginning there were arguments over who should top the bill.

'At the time,' recalled Vic Cooper, 'Herman's Hermits were a major group. They were very, very big in America. Peter Noone, the lead singer, had that cute little boy-next-door look. If you're big in America, that's it, so they went to the top of the bill, but Tom had had a more recent chart success in Australia, so we swapped. To be fair a lot of the time Herman's Hermits blew Tom away.

'We played at Darwin to a horde of fifteen-year-old girls screaming, "We want Peter." They weren't calling for Tom. To them he was this guy of twenty-six who looked thirty-five. We never died, but Tom was a little bit dismayed that it wasn't the great success that he thought it was going to be.'

To add insult to injury, in both Brisbane and Sydney, the Australian police decided to warn Tom against his lewd and lascivious behaviour on stage. The police threatened to close the Sydney show because Jones took his shirt off on stage and began to move in 'a suggestive way'. When asked why he had done that, Jones's glib reply was, 'Because it was too hot.'

That did not endear him to the Australian police. In Brisbane, where the cops had necks as red as their colleagues below the Mason-Dixon Line and similar Neanderthal attitudes to enforcing their laws, one officer walked into Jones's dressing room, prodded him in the chest and shouted, 'Listen, you. This is a clean town and it's gonna stay clean. Any trouble from you and we'll shove you inside. OK?'

'I felt like butting him with my nut,' said Tom later. 'But my hair had just been combed ready for the act.'

From the outset Gordon Mills realised that for Tom to have any long-term future he had to establish himself internationally. The British pop scene has always been ephemeral, fast moving and fad conscious. In the sixties album sales had only just begun to establish themselves as major money earners and the hit parade moved at a breakneck pace. Today's teen hero was tomorrow's P.J. Proby.

There were no carefully co-ordinated international marketing campaigns backed by promotional videos. The stream of hits Tom enjoyed between November 1966 and July 1968 could not support indefinitely the lavish lifestyle Gordon and his protégés espoused. Hits across Europe helped fill their wine cellars with vintage Dom Perignon, but the market was not developed enough to sustain regular live work.

Tom had to break North America. For a rock act, the established method of breaking in the States has long been to go out there and work every inch of the forty-eight mainland states.

The media key has always been to crack the big coastal cities, but the longevity and the money reside in the heartland, in white bread, middle America. Any halfway decent live act prepared to devote a minimum of three years to slogging up and down the freeways will get its reward, but ever since the Dick Clark Roadshow Tom was not keen to repeat the experience. As a live performer he has always thrived on applause that was his and his alone, singing to the converted, not the doubters.

Fortunately for Tom his return from America in 1965 coincided with the opening of the Baileys circuit in the North of England. A series of old theatres and cinemas were converted into nightclubs. With a gambling licence, serving food and alcohol until two in the morning, they were prepared to pay good money for the right entertainment. It was a godsend to Tom, because the screaming teenagers, who would have wet themselves over a performing chipmunk if it reached number one, had moved on to new younger meat.

The Baileys audience was one he and the band knew from back home. 'It was exactly the same as playing South Wales working men's clubs,' said Chris Ellis, 'exactly the same, except everybody dressed a bit nicer, and instead of getting £16 we were getting £2,000 a night.' The Squires played the same set they had done in the Valleys, with the hits thrown in. They were bloody good at it.

There was one other major difference. Women loved the new Tom, particularly mature women. Gordon Mills began to wonder whether, if Tom was a hit on this pseudo-Vegas circuit, he couldn't crack the real thing.

For Gordon Mills, Las Vegas provided the perfect solution. The money was very, very good. Vegas was just starting to become the place of pilgrimage for middle America, enticed by the neon, the gambling and the frontier image. Because of his variety background Gordon understood what the punters required: high quality entertainment, titillation, not aggressive sexuality. They wanted a new Sinatra, a younger Dean Martin, a straight Liberace, somebody who could sing better than Wayne Newton. In 1966 Tom Jones was too rough for Vegas.

The first step was simple. Fix that broken nose and straighten those teeth. The band came back from Spain to discover Tom had mysteriously acquired two black eyes. 'My nose had been broken a few times in fights and it was twisted. I had the bone broken and reset in 1966 and it didn't turn out very well, the right nostril was still collapsed,' confirmed Jones. 'I had operations on my teeth to make them look better. One was twisted, others were decayed and I needed them to look right.'

The massive worldwide success of *Green Green Grass of Home* enabled Mills to set the second part of his plan into operation. He booked Tom into a month's residency at The Talk of the Town in London, and set about remodelling his act as radically as the surgeons had remodelled his broken nose. It cost a small fortune.

Playing The Talk of the Town was a calculated move. The venue was famous for not paying high prices – £2,000, take it or leave it. For the run, not a single gig. Everybody played for that: Frank Sinatra, Judy Garland, Louis Armstrong. The Grade Organisation, who ran it, knew they could get away with those fees because playing The Talk of the Town meant literally that. A star had arrived.

With the gigs coming up, Mills began to impose his views on the stage show. 'Gordon had a good eye, he made sure that he got the best out of Tom, so he could progress,' said Vernon. 'He would say, "No, you're not doing that right . . . take that number out." He knew his music, had a good ear too.'

'That's when it changed musically, The Talk of the Town,' said Vic Cooper. 'Before then the live arrangements were kind of hit and miss. Session guys did the record, I had to learn the string parts on the Vox organ and play the rhythm on the piano. Now we were doing proper music, orchestrated straight away. Our four-piece band joined the Ted Heath orchestra, so there were thirty or forty musicians, and Johnny Harris as the musical conductor.

'The music had to change, Tom had to sing different songs to show off his voice. It was a different audience at The Talk of the Town and the response was fantastic. Suddenly here was this pop singer doing all this beautiful music. The rock and roll went out of the window. We might do a couple of Sam Cooke numbers and *Land of a 1000 Dances* to close, but most of the set was swing stuff. *I Can't Stop Loving You, That Old Black Magic, In the Rain*. We were playing to please the people that control all the music, to the music establishment, and Jewish songs like *My Yiddishe Momma* went down well.'

After the opening night on 1 March Lew Grade brought along Marty Starger, vice president of programming at ABC TV in America. He was knocked out. Tom's jeans and black leather jacket had already been discarded on the Baileys circuit in favour of a blue dinner jacket worn over a low-cut double-breasted waistcoat, white shirt and a clip-on black velvet bow tie. His trousers were still cut tight. The subsequent album *Live at The Talk of the Town* was a big success in England, staying in the charts for ninety weeks.

Now Tom was ready for Vegas. And Vegas, though it did not know it yet, was ready for him.

In 1968 Las Vegas was on the cusp of an enormous change. In 1967 the state of Nevada passed a Corporate Gaming Act, and after it was revised in 1969 it became not only possible but beneficial for a publicly traded company to own a casino. Until then the state's arcane structure for regulating casino gaming had effectively made dirty money the only capital available. Under Nevada law every casino owner had to be certified by a Gaming

Board Investigation. Fine for a private individual 'with interests in the olive oil business', but impossible for a public company with three million shareholders.

Once gambling became legal in Nevada in 1931, it became a magnet for gangsters. They already ran all the illegal gambling operations in the States, and they knew how to keep books and how to discourage cheating. 'There was no such thing as blackjack card counters,' recalled performer Sonny King, who first played Vegas in 1953, 'because they would cheat one time and you would never hear from them again.'

Technological advances in the late fifties altered Vegas, direct flights from major cities put it on the map, and the Carrier Air Conditioning Company worked out how to air-condition the casinos. Castro took over Cuba and closed Havana's casinos. With Frank Sinatra and the Rat Pack in seemingly perpetual residence, Vegas suddenly became a year-round city, no longer a place to escape the spouse, but a glamorous vacation destination. To cope with the tourist influx the city needed more 2,000-room hotels, and there were not many gangsters with that much money stashed away.

However, the boys knew a man who did. The connections between Jimmy Hoffa, the Teamsters union and the Mafia had been stand-up since the Teamsters had hired the Mob to protect them from strike breakers during the Depression. Between the late fifties and mid-seventies the Teamsters Central States pension fund provided $250 million in loans or mortgages to, among others, the Desert Inn, the Stardust, the Fremont, the Tropicana, the Dunes and Circus Circus. Jay Sarno, who started building Caesars Palace in 1964, could not have broken ground without a loan from the Teamsters. Despite his successful track record across the country, the banks would not, could not, help him.

The largest sea change in Vegas ownership began in the early hours of Thanksgiving Day 1966 when a private train brought

Howard Hughes to town. The billionaire was transported to the penthouse suite at the Desert Inn and did not leave the top floor for the next four years. Just as legend erroneously credits Ben Siegel with inventing the casino resort hotel, so Hughes is seen as the man who brought corporate culture to Vegas. Because he did not want to leave his rooms, Hughes bought the Desert Inn for $13.2 million, and then set about buying up a further five casinos. After he promised to build a medical school for the University of Nevada he was given a gaming licence. (He never built it.) The business community realised that Hughes was an opportunity to remove Vegas underworld influence.

Hughes's money created waves in town, stirring things up enough for the corporations to start coming in. Hughes did not chase the Mob out of town, nor usher in the era of the corporation. He brought the image of legitimacy to town, but while he was stuck atop his tower, petty corruption and skimming continued unabated on the casino floor.

While the shadowy goings-on in the count rooms did not impinge directly on the performers, nobody was in any doubt as to how the business was run. 'Entertainers in the late sixties and early seventies were very important,' recalled Bob Maheu, a former FBI agent who was Hughes's right-hand man in Vegas. 'There was tremendous competition among the casinos to get the big names like Sinatra, Elvis Presley, Barbra Streisand, Bill Cosby, Dinah Shore, Jimmy Durante, and [comedian] Shecky Greene. In the early days Tom Jones was a hell of a draw. Presley could break all records, but he didn't leave too much of a drop (a performer's success was measured not by sell-out crowds but by how much the casino takings went up when they were playing – this was known as the 'drop'). After his show half his audience would walk out the casino and the other half would stand in line for the second show. Whereas Sinatra gambled, and customers would flock around him.'

Frank was always, indeed still is, the undisputed king of the Strip. Consistently he had the best 'drop'. For years Frank had gambled with abandon, regularly losing $100,000 a night on the tables. The punters loved it when, fresh from his midnight show, Frank took over the dealer's spot at blackjack, even more so when Dean Martin, multiple bourbons to the good, would rewrite the rules. 'Take another card,' he would tell a player sitting on 20. 'Don't worry, 30 wins on this table.' Then he'd force the dealer to keep flipping cards until they were bust.

Punters loved seeing the stars round the tables. Telly Savalas, with stacks of one-dollar chips in front of him because he liked to push big piles onto the roulette table, Jimmy Durante and Sonny King would fill the crap tables four deep, because Jimmy would place a two-buck bet and holler like he was rolling for $10,000.

This was the world Tom Jones entered when he opened at the Flamingo on 17 March 1968, a world where the rules were different, where performance counted far less than dollars lost at the tables. But he had to be careful at the Flamingo, where he was a rising talent harnessed to a fading star. 'You had to be wary in Vegas, because if you died there once, it was goodnight Irene,' recalled Vic Cooper. 'We all knew we had to go down well, had to.'

In Las Vegas there were two types of singers. Lounge singers and showroom singers. The money paid to a lounge singer was high – excellent by British standards – but a lounge singer was background entertainment not the main attraction.

'I advised Gordon not to let Tom become a lounge act in Vegas,' said Jo Mills. 'I had worked Vegas as a Bluebell girl, and I said to him, "Whatever you do, say no to him becoming a lounge act, because it's very difficult to cross over to be a major showroom star." The lounges were offering wonderful money, but I was able to help Gordon there because I'd been to Vegas and he hadn't. We held out and eventually signed him at the Flamingo as a headliner.'

Tom's first proper American tour in 1968 was Gordon's biggest gamble to date. All they had was a guaranteed three nights at the Deauville Hotel in Miami, while the Copa in New York would only agree to a 'heavy pencil' deal. He was provisionally booked for two weeks, but if the Copa did not like him, or he didn't pull in the punters, he could be fired at any time. When Tom, the Squires and MD Johnny Harris left Britain, there was nothing confirmed for Vegas.

'All we were told was that we were going to Miami, and from then on touring America,' said Vernon Hopkins. 'We never knew where we were going next.'

At that point the tour figures simply didn't add up. Musicians were relatively cheap as the house orchestra was part of the package. The Squires were only earning £80 a week each (and having to pay for their own accommodation). Johnny, as musical director was on a more reasonable £250, while road manager Chris Ellis earned only £100. However, the cost of airfares, transportation and hotels was relatively much higher in 1968. With no guarantees of a Vegas pay day, Gordon prepared to go for broke, putting his reputation – and his house – on the line.

Gordon never did things on a shoestring. The royalties from *Green Green Grass of Home* were coming in, but according to the company accounts submitted at the time of the MAM flotation in 1969, Tom's profit, from 31 July 1967 to 5 February 1968, was £28,075 before tax. Tom was not prepared to risk his money. Gordon, who in the year up to 31 July 1967 had showed a profit of £35,239 with a tax bill of £12,000 to pay, hardly had enough ready cash to invest in an American tour. But he prepared to gamble everything he had worked for to break Tom in Vegas.

'Gordon virtually sold his soul to people in Vegas to get Tom to work there,' said Les Reed. 'He went over there and literally put everything he had on the line – his house, his family, the lot – to get Tom into Vegas. If it had been a failure, he would have lost everything.'

Gordon had first negotiated with Davy Victorson, the entertainment director at Caesars Palace, for a month's residency at a fee of $12,500. Jay Sarno, Caesars' maverick owner, had never heard of Jones and refused to sign the deal. The Flamingo, with its smaller, less prestigious room, was interested, but entertainment director Bill Miller wanted to see before he bought.

The Flamingo Hotel had fallen a long way from its glory days, when Ben 'Bugsy' Siegel had put his and plenty of the Mob's money on the line to create a glamorous casino hotel in the desert. Siegel was gunned down on the order of his irate partners before he saw the success he had created. In 1967 the Flamingo went out of business after its owners were arrested for skimming the profits and for gangster involvement. Financier Kirk Kerkorian bought it for a song and opened it up again primarily in order to train up an efficient management team for his extravagant new casino, the International.

They needed a decent headlining act. Charles Mather, a British-born former Royal Marine turned nightclub bouncer and impresario who had moved to Vegas in 1959, suggested they check out Tom Jones. Miller, already an anglophile (his son Jimmy had moved to England in the early sixties and made his name producing the Spencer Davis Group, Traffic and the Rolling Stones), had shown a more radical policy by booking British stars such as Anthony Newley and Tommy Steele into the Sahara. Miller flew to New York to see Jones at the Copacabana, accompanied by the wife of Alex Shoufy, the Flamingo's general manager and president.

Success at the Copacabana was a direct conduit into Las Vegas, partly due to its Mob connections. The Copa had been a favoured Mafia hangout since its inception. In the early fifties, Jack Entratter, who had fronted the club for Mafia bosses Frank

Costello and Joey Adonis, moved to Las Vegas to run the Sands Hotel. In Vegas the Mob's presence was understated. At the Copa it was blindingly obvious.

The Copa was a tiny venue, a glorified supper club with a sky-high reputation and a postage stamp-sized stage. Everybody who was anybody – Sinatra, Ray Charles, Dean Martin and Jerry Lewis – had played there. 'It was when we headlined the Copa that I knew we'd really made it,' recalled Supreme Mary Wilson.

At the Copacabana the rules were different. The club was managed by Jules Bodell (in return, so legend had it, for taking a prison rap for a Mob capo). All night, every night, he sat by the cash register in the kitchen. He never left it, never saw a show. Whenever he wanted a drink he would rap the huge gold ring on his left hand on the counter and a fresh glass would materialise beside him. Every night, when Tom entered the club, he would go up to him and say, 'Good evening, Mr Bodell.' That was one of the unwritten rules: Frank did it, Sammy did it, everyone did it.

The Copa held a maximum of 150 seats, and the position of your table depended on how much you tipped the *maître d'*, and whether your last name ended with a vowel. It was hard to get in unless you were connected, impossible for women or men on their own. The stage was tiny, raised barely a foot above the dance floor. The tables were scarcely big enough to take a pair of plates and a brace of glasses, but food and drink had to be purchased. Tom quickly became a favourite with the Mob's wives and girlfriends (who would be brought on alternate nights) and the club was soon packed for all three shows.

'If the police had raided that place they'd have cleaned up New York in about three seconds flat,' said Ellis. 'The *maître d'*s were making thousands and thousands of dollars a night. One night I was standing by the lighting booth when this guy refused to leave his table when the *maître d'* wanted it back. All of a sudden three extremely large Italian guys, who were supposed to be waiters, came flashing by me. This guy, his girlfriend, the table, and the food and everything, were thrown straight out of the back door into an alley. The door was shut, the table came back in, it was put back down, the tablecloth was dusted off, and this other obviously higher ranking gentleman and his girlfriend were seated there. Other times we'd come in for the last set and find tables on the stage itself.'

Entertainers at the Copa got no break on food and drink. They paid the same restaurant price as the punters. Chris Ellis used to buy beers for the band at a nearby liquor store and smuggle them in. When he was seen drinking a different brand from those sold in the club his beer was taken away by a bouncer. No arguments. It was the same rule for Tom. 'One night Tom had a really bad cold,' sais Ellis, 'and his throat was really bad. He could hardly speak let alone sing, and we were doing three shows. So I called down and said I wanted some lemons and honey. They sent up four lemons and a jar of honey and a bill came with it. It was $1 for each lemon and $10 for a jar of honey, and we had to pay it.'

The dressing room was small and cramped, up three flights of stairs so steep that it was almost like scaling a ladder. He refused people entry at his peril. 'You never knew who you were dealing with. Tom played along with it. He was excited by it but clever enough to build these guys' egos up, not so stupid as to put them down. It was very strange because the guys were egging their girlfriends on. "Go on, go up and give him a kiss." Tom couldn't refuse.'

After a while it became pretty obvious that every Italian ice cream seller in the four boroughs had cottoned on that he could bring his girlfriend up and have a drink with Tom Jones. Ellis had a chat with one of the *maître d*'s downstairs, who promised to fix the problem.

'The next night as I got up to the top of the stairs, I saw this huge pair of shoes standing outside the dressing room. There was this man mountain standing there. Lenny Montana was terrific, he knew who everybody was. It was nothing for him to pick up people and throw them bodily back down the stairs again – he was a huge man. After that it was only the real guys who got in.'

'One regular was Sonny Fransici. He was a real gentleman. Except he was a hit man and he had the blackest eyes you'd ever seen in your life. There was no feeling in those eyes, his eyes were actually stone dead. Gordon Mills had the same look, could have been his brother. Suddenly Sonny wasn't there any more and we were told, "Oh, he's gone away for a little while." We never saw him again.

Three years later, when watching *The Godfather*, Tom and Chris were mesmerised by one particular scene when Don Corleone's hatchetman, Luca Brasi, was garrotted. Brasi was played by none other than Lenny Montana.

For the first few nights Tom's act at the Copacabana was not a huge success. What changed everything was the singer's spontaneous reaction when a woman handed him her underwear.

'I was perspiring heavily and the women were handing me table napkins,' said Jones in 1991. 'I was wiping myself and handing them back. They were getting excited. Suddenly this woman got up in front of me, lifted her dress up and pulled her knickers down. She gave them to me so I made a whole thing of it – if you're going to go, go the whole way. I said, "Watch you don't catch cold." '

'Then the audience changed,' said Vic Cooper, 'and by the end it was forty made men in dark suits surrounded by eighty screaming women. I saw women throwing knickers to him. Then he picked them up and started wiping his brow. That was way, way out for those days.'

Earl Wilson, the most influential entertainment columnist in America, saw the incident, and wrote about it. 'So women started to make a thing of it and would bring underwear in their handbags, sometimes they'd actually remove it,' said Jones. 'It just became my thing.'

After seeing him at the Copa, Bill Miller and Joan Shoufy were convinced. The deal that was struck between Miller and CMA (Tom's American agents) was no fortune, $25,000 (approximately £10,000) for the month. Las Vegas has never been notoriously open-handed with first-time entertainers, untested at the box office. The Flamingo showroom only had 500 seats and, as insurance, the nominal headliner was American singer/comedienne and Vegas veteran Kaye Ballard.

What the Flamingo promised to do was give a huge publicity push; in promoting Tom they were promoting themselves. Nick Naff, the casino's publicity director, coined the phrase 'Tom Jones fever'. A bottle of Tom Jones fever pills were placed on each table, 'guaranteed not to cure you but to make the fever more tolerable'. A series of commercials aired on local radio stated what the Tom Jones fever temperature was that day. They even put an ambulance at the back of the showroom, just in case it all proved too much.

The week before he opened in Vegas, Tom was rehearsing for the *Jonathan Winters Show* in LA. He told Lawrence DeVine of the *Hollywood Reporter* that he was pinning his hopes for American success on his nightclub efforts. 'It's not just the money, it's to get me known. I want to do films, I've got to have audiences who recognise me. I can't be sitting back and waiting for a number one record.'

It was one hell of a gamble. Gordon was biting his over-mortgaged nails below the quick, but Tom was immune to pressure. Pre-show nerves have never bothered him.

By the time Tom Jones reached the Flamingo, the word was

out. The shows were sold out, standing room only. The women —
including the wives of the casino's senior management — were
waiting with their underwear and room keys poised.

The wife of one of the casino executives had been mesmerised
by Tom's performance both on and off stage and she determined
to get to know him better.

'When we got out to Las Vegas they jumped on each other,'
said Chris Ellis. 'Tom told me that when he was making love to
her, she used to back him off the bed up against the wall, and he
said she was as strong as a horse. She was a great looking woman,
but she frightened him a bit because she was so strong. She had a
vibrator, some sort of metal thing, and she left it in his room. I
had to get it back to her at 2 o'clock one morning in the car park
of the Flamingo Hotel. I wasn't very happy about it, I didn't want
to be seen with a boss's wife at the back of the car park in the
dark.

'I don't think it went on very long. I don't know if her husband
found out and she was warned off. This was Las Vegas, remember,
you don't go messing around with people there. There's a very big
desert out there. You could disappear quite easily. But Tom didn't
appear to care.'

Within a week Tom Jones was the talk of the town. The
gamble had paid off. Big time. Every entertainment director in
Vegas wanted to book him. Soon after Tom opened, Charles Mather
was over at Davy Victorson's office in Caesars Palace early one
morning. Suddenly the familiar, short, plump silhouette of Jay
Sarno appeared at the door.

'All right, Mr Entertainment Director,' he snapped, 'who the
hell is the greatest singer in the world today?' Davy sat back looking
a bit quizzical and replied, 'Sinatra?'

'No, who's the biggest, the most exciting singer?'

'Barbra Streisand?'

'No, for Christ's sake,' snarled Sarno, a compulsive gambler, always at his worst after a heavy night at the tables. 'You don't know a damn thing. The guy across the street in the Flamingo, that Welsh kid, Tom Jones. I saw him last night, sensational.'

Davy jumped up, 'You fucking bastard, just stay there.' He sent his secretary to get the file. He opened it up. 'See this? That's the contract for $12,500 a week, half of what he's getting over there. Who wouldn't sign it? You! You'd never heard of him. That's a year ago. We could have had him, but no, you know better.'

Sarno told him to get Tom Jones for Caesars. 'Whatever anybody offers him give him a thousand bucks a week more.' It was three years before they got their man. After another season at the Flamingo, when the queues went round the block, Vegas columnist Bernard Barry reported, 'Tom Jones has become the hottest showbusiness property in America, and that is not forgetting Frank Sinatra or Elvis.' Once the International was complete, with the largest showroom in town – and a golf course on the third floor – Kerkorian wanted Tom's contract transferred to the International.

As the International showroom was three times the size of the Flamingo, Gordon wanted a commensurate hike in pay – closer to Elvis's fee of $150,000 a week. According to Charles Mather, Alex Shoufy, who had moved to become the general manager of the International, didn't care much for Tom, and subsequently Bill Miller, who was the entertainment director, kept going to Alex and saying, 'I need a decision, are we going to renew this boy, how much are we going to give him?' Shoufy refused to up the money. Gordon promptly went over to see Davy Victorson at Caesars. Tom Jones played at Caesars Palace from 1971 to 1984.

Tom and Gordon had both arrived in a neon heaven under the desert sun. They were blissfully happy there – for very different reasons.

CHAPTER ELEVEN

STARDOM CHANGES EVERYTHING

Stardom changes everything. People, relationships, previous certainties dissolve in its glare. Every star says the same thing: 'It won't change me.' And they believe it. But while a star may not change, his circumstances do. In the presence of power, people defer, an offhand suggestion becomes a royal command. Protection becomes sequestration. Access equals power. A star is, by definition, the centre of his own solar system. At best, preternaturally self-centred. At worst, self-obsessed.

Tommy Woodward was always the centre of his mother's solar system. TB made him more self-centred. During his days with the Senators, when the musicians bought equipment, he did not cough up for a microphone. It was easy to lose such signs inside a Valleys culture, where groups of men bonded together over pints, and women knew their place was in the lounge bar and the kitchen. Starving, half-freezing in Clydesdale Road, all dreaming of stardom to come, it was easiest to believe that mates stuck together through thick and thin. Comforting. One for all, all for one.

Back on stage, pumping out the riffs, while Tom ground his hips and sang, it was just like the old days in Wales. Five mates going to the top. Together.

Except that with the release of *It's Not Unusual* the balance of power had shifted forever. Tom Jones was the star. The Squires were his backing band, not his equals.

Stardom changes everything.

Gordon Mills always treated anybody who went back with Tom further than he did with contempt. Bryn the Fish stopped opening for him because Gordon heard him call Tom 'Woodsy'. Bryn refused to apologise, so he was out. Gordon was fearful that they had a prior call on him, that no matter how far he took Tom out of the Valleys, some of those brotherhood values would remain. As his success mounted, Gordon brought Tom into his orbit, introduced him to the finer things of life: beautiful clothes, vintage wines, the best steaks. The band were left behind economically and socially, constant reminders of what Tom might have been. When there was no further need for them, they were dispatched without ceremony.

It started well enough. Suddenly Vernon, Mickey, Chris and Dave were earning £30 a week. Each. Pretty good in the days when the average weekly wage was £20. It left a bit of a sour taste when Gordon informed them that they had to pay back the four bob (20p) a day he had given them to live on in Notting Hill, and they had to pay for their own digs when they were on the road. Nor did he tell them until much later, that they had to pay their own tax and stamps. But what the hell . . . they were all going to be rich. Tom had promised them. Gordon hadn't. His philosophy was to keep the band underfoot and squeeze them dry.

That first tour with Cilla Black everyone was together, crammed into the J4 with no brakes, and all the equipment. Not that they had much gear — a pair of Marshall column speakers, three Vox amplifiers, a couple of microphones — nobody miked the drums in those days — a basic PA system, drums and guitars. Nobody stayed at hotels unless the gigs were back-to-back. It was cheaper to drive back to town. The back of the J4 was thick with cigarette smoke, empty beer bottles crashed about. When there was no time to stop for a piss, they used a milk bottle and slung the contents onto the road. Everybody did it. Like everybody stopped at Gobblers Gulch, the Blue Boy Service Station on the M1. On any given night the Rolling Stones, the Beatles, Manfred Mann, Gerry and the Pacemakers and the Searchers would be eating breakfast at 4 a.m., smoking and swapping stories.

The J4 was replaced by a brand-new Thames Commer van. Within three weeks it was a wreck. The fans took everything they could, mirrors, hubcaps, wipers, and covered the body in lipstick love letters. But the gigs continued.

In the beginning it was chaos. Gordon needed to pay his debts, so Colin Berlin grabbed every gig that came his way. Seven nights a week, two shows a night, if the gig was there; £500 for a dance hall in Leeds one night, £350 in Exeter the next. At one club the stage was so small that Mickey Gee had to stand behind the glass panelling in the DJ's booth.

Chris Ellis never minded. Gordon gave him bags of big yellow pills. Dexedrine. He chucked the bag on the dashboard of the Commer and every time he felt tired he popped another one. Chris wasn't scared of anybody. He wore a black mohair suit, white shirt, black tie and when a bowler hat mysteriously turned up in the van he wore that too.

One of Chris's favourite tricks was driving down the M1 in the middle of the night with everybody else crashed out, Tom leaning on his shoulder. Doing seventy miles an hour, he'd suddenly slam on the brakes and start screaming his head off. Everybody woke up. One night, after the fourth incident, Tom picked his face out of the windscreen and announced, 'You do that one more time and I'm going to fucking kill you.' He meant it too. Instead, soon after that when he bought his first car, he had Vic Cooper drive him to the gigs.

After the success of *It's Not Unusual* the Squires were temporarily augmented by a brass section, but when they were let go, Mills told Dave Cooper, 'We don't need a rhythm guitar now.' Vernon was in their shared digs when Cooper came back and told him, 'I'm going.' 'And I didn't know what to say to him. He just left, slung out.'

Dave's replacement was Vic Cooper (no relation), a chirpy Londoner, who had played schoolboy football for Chelsea, and was a veteran of Johnny Kidd and the Pirates at twenty-two. 'Tom was a Jerry Lee Lewis fanatic, boogie woogie, and that's my thing,' said Cooper. 'They wanted a guy who could play the piano and organ, fill out the sound. I was cheaper than three brass players. They also wanted somebody who could sing a little bit, because the Squires would do a half hour before Tom came on.'

Vic never bought into the dream, at the time it just was a good gig. He was a dope smoker in a band of boozers, a practical joker who scared the superstitious Chris Slade half to death by tying cotton to objects in their room and pretending to be asleep when he pulled the cotton and they crashed to the floor. On the morning of a gig Vic, a time-keeping freak, would turn up at Rose Bank, Manny Gate Lane, around ten. Linda greeted him cheerily and made a cup of tea. Tom stumbled into the kitchen half an hour later to grunt, 'Linda, iron my trousers.' He always wore a particular French bath oil, Zebaline by Wella. Gordon had introduced him to it, an expensive affectation at £8 a bottle. Soon Vic wore it too. In the mornings, Tom usually slept in the car. Otherwise Vic entertained him.

'I made him laugh. I used to wind him up about his suits not fitting him. He was a little bit careful with his money – after he got the Rolls-Royce he moaned about it using so much juice. We'd talk about music, general chitchat about women, the usual sort of stuff. Tom told my girlfriend that his grandmother was haunting him. He often had a nightmare about his dead grandmother coming to get him.'

Vic knew he was replaceable, but he retained a tremendous admiration for Tom's ability. 'Once I went over with Georgie Fame and Tom to Johnny Kidd's house in Harrow. I played the piano and Tom was singing a blues number. It sounded better than great. That was Tom, a great singer. He was never nervous, it was quite freaky really. When he sings this internal switch just goes on. I've never heard him make a mistake. I don't think he's made a mistake ever. Just brilliant. He was born with a beautiful voice, a stunningly good rich voice. It's just amazing, his vibrato is perfect. A flat, nobody sings an A flat, I mean top tenors get at C, but to sing an A flat, to hit those notes . . .

'He's such a beautiful singer I thought he would be a different person. I thought he would be the warmest person you could meet.

'I never got close to him. I never saw Tom Jones smile with his eyes. Tom was for Tom. I always knew how it was going to end. With the boys it was different. They grew up with Tom. He and Vernon were like brothers.'

Vernon was never the greatest musician, but adept enough, a competent bass player and a pretty good songwriter. Most of all he loved music, lived and breathed rock and roll. Tom did too. In Wales Tom and Vernon were tight. Gordon did not like that. On the road they were always together, downing a few pints, on the pull for the birds.

Tight as brothers they were. Tom had said so the night he had slagged off Vernon's brother, who was a policeman. 'All policemen are bastards,' he'd snarled in his beer. 'Hang on. What about my brother, Norman, he's OK.'

'Your brother?' snapped Tom. 'I'm more your brother than he'll ever be.' Vernon has never forgotten that.

Naturally there were girls on offer, though not as many as came later. The teenagers wanted to scream, not to have sex, and as the band would almost always travel back to town there was little chance for serious romantic encounters. 'There was no time,' said Chris. 'We literally threw everything in the van, and just headed off home again. If somebody did pull a girl, it was a quickie against the back wall of the dance hall.'

The best times were when the Squires were doing the clubs up Newcastle way. They stayed in digs for a week, though it was almost impossible to smuggle a girl back into the boarding house. The girls who worked in the casinos were the best bet as they worked the same hours and had their own flats. In the early days Tom, Vernon and Dave, the best-looking in the band, were the most successful pullers. Tom, who was always scared of catching the clap (not without reason) liked to get straight to the point. Once he had his own car it got easier.

One night Vic Cooper was driving Tom's Volvo P40 from Stockton-on-Tees to the second show in Sunderland. 'Tom had pulled this girl in the back and was doing the business. The boys were in the van behind, it was foggy. I clocked him at it in the mirror and he shouted at me to stop looking. Then I hit a roundabout and drove straight over it. Tom screamed at me, "Stop the car. You were looking." I replied, "I'm driving, what can I do?" He made me get out the car and go wait with the van until he'd finished.

'It's no secret that Tom liked women. He was pretty indiscriminate, a horny so-and-so, and he knew he could have anybody he wanted. He was always on the pull. He was a user of women:

next one please, go, next one, that was it.

'All the band got spin-offs. Wherever we went there were loads of women who wanted Tom. So we all took advantage. Sometimes I think we had more girls than he did. Tom didn't like it if someone pulled a girl he fancied.'

Said Vernon Hopkins, 'A couple of times I pulled a girl from Tom and he got furious because I'd copped for a girl he fancied.'

Tom stayed in hotels, the Squires in digs. Tom had the star dressing room, and some time in 1966, after the Australian tour, soon after champagne replaced bitter as his drink of choice, the boys started to knock on the door instead of crashing in. While they all drank together on the road back home, the boys waited to be asked instead of calling up. Tom, Vernon, Vic and Chris would meet down the Magpie. Everyone stood their rounds, though Tom always seemed to be the last to pay. 'He was a little bit careful with his money,' said Vic wryly.

In concert Tom never introduced the band individually. He'd say stuff like 'those hooligans at the back are my backing band, the Squires'. It was always greeted with a laugh. But it showed the gap widening. Once they were augmented by the Ted Heath Orchestra they slipped further into the background.

For The Talk of the Town Johnny Harris came in as musical director. The Squires called him Johnny the Boot, because he wore an iron on one leg, the legacy of childhood polio. Johnny was a wild man. During the show he would jump in the air, spinning round, his shoulder-length hair whirling and land on his good leg. Johnny brought the house down, which Gordon hated, so his days were numbered.

Gordon made it quite clear to the band, 'You can't be late, if you're late once you are out of a job.' Once, between shows at the Palladium, Vernon and Mickey stayed on having a pint. Suddenly Vernon realised his watch had stopped. They sprinted over to the stage door and on to the stage where Mike and Bernie Winters had been forced to stretch their opening act by an extra five minutes. After the show Gordon stormed into the dressing room and shouted, 'You are all fired.' He did not carry out his threat. That time.

Then there was the time when Vic smoked a joint with Vernon and Chris Slade just before a gig up north. The opening number was *What's New Pussycat?* It turned into a shambles. Vernon recalls coming in on the background vocals half a bar late and getting a glare from Tom that would melt an iceberg.

Tom was livid. It is a story he still uses as an example of why he has always despised drugs. 'I did take pep pills for a week,' he has admitted. 'Speed, I suppose. But I didn't like the effect and ditched them. Sick of staring at the bloody ceiling.'

By late 1967 time was running out for the Squires. After playing with Tom for years and knowing he was earning two grand a gig, the Squires thought they deserved more than £40 a week. Musicians always complain, but they had only squeezed out that extra tenner after learning how much the session musicians were getting.

'Tom knew what our lifestyle was, the wages we were getting,' said Vernon. 'He was there in the dressing room when Chris Ellis came round giving us our wage packets. He knew what we were driving at, we were saying, "What's going on, Tom, what's happening?" All he'd say was, "Go and see Gordon." He just wiped his hands of it.'

Tom did try to get them a raise once. Keith Davies was walking past the dressing room in the Capital Theatre in Cardiff and he heard Tom arguing with Gordon. 'I heard Tom say, "They have been with me a long time, Gordon." Gordon said, "You give them bugger all." Tom, as usual, demurred to his manager. From then on it was always, "Ask Gordon." '

Even when *Green Green Grass of Home* had reached number one and Tom was playing a season at the London Palladium, there was no pay increase. Instead the band all admired the singer's new gold bracelet. '£180 it cost,' he told them. They did not even get a Christmas bonus. Vernon gave Tom an album for Christmas, but got nothing in return.

Mickey Gee got really hung up about it. 'I was a gnat's bollock better than the other musicians, and I could read music, so they made me musical director,' he said, 'which meant I had to write out the chords for the other lads.' In the autumn of 1967 Mickey decided to confront Gordon and Tom with an ultimatum. The rest of the band waited outside.

'I had a meeting with Tom and Gordon in a dressing room in Southampton,' he said. 'It was 6.30 in the evening and they were both wearing dark glasses. We just wanted them to pay the hotel bills and give us a raise to £50 with tax paid, or £60 a week and we'd pay our own tax. Gordon said, "I was in a band once and I didn't like it and I left. You're not getting any more money, and if you don't like it you can leave." '

Mickey quit on the spot, expecting the rest of the band to follow suit. 'Gordon said to me, "I hope you're going to do the show tonight." I said, "Don't insult me." A week later I got a letter saying, "Thank you for your contribution to Tom" and enclosing my last week's wages — a measly £40.'

Confronted by Gordon's refusal to compromise at all, Vernon's resolve crumbled. So did the others'. He justified it to himself, 'I'm not going to leave because they're not going to cheat me out of seeing America.' It was his life's ambition to go there. Mickey was replaced by Bill Parkinson.

Vic was the next to depart. During the Copacabana season he was approached by Don Kirshner, creator of the Monkees and the cartoon group the Archies, and Harry Saltzman, producer of the

Bond films, to audition for a group called Toomorrow. (This 'supergroup for the seventies', which also included Olivia Newton-John, petered out in 1970 after making a science fiction comedy film and one album.) Following the Flamingo season Tom had to return to England for a TV appearance and Vic was summoned to auditions in London. Swearing the band to secrecy he flew back first class to be met by a white Rolls-Royce. Vic won the part of 'the lovable Tommy Steele Cockney', and was immediately offered £500 a week – ten times his Squires wage. He sent Mills a telegram resigning immediately.

'I got the usual bunch of threats – you'll never work again sort of thing,' he said. 'Yes, I dumped him, but a side man only rarely gets opportunities. They could have got on the phone and got 3,000 piano players in New York that could sight-read and play better than me with one hand tied behind their back. It was the fact that I left that upset them.'

Chris Slade discovered that too, when he was approached to join Elvis Presley's band. When they first started out on the road Slade was, in the words of Mickey Gee, 'dreadful', but he had always had the ability to accentuate Tom's movements with his playing. Mills paid for him to have a series of lessons with Kenny Clare, and almost overnight he became a great drummer. Like any good drummer should, he acquired a few eccentricities – while flirting with Buddhism his diet swung between plain boiled rice and raw beef.

Presley saw Slade with Tom at the Flamingo and offered him a job, playing with James Burton and Glen Hardin. 'You're under contract,' snapped Gordon, and refused to let him go. Vic had never signed a contract, but Slade stayed on. Gordon's contracts with the Squires appeared to only work one way. His way.

The friendship between Tom and Vernon was now just a memory, the gap between their position, too vast to be bridged.

Occasionally Tom and Chris Ellis would stop by at the Magpie, a pub in Shepperton where Vernon had his digs, but their relationship had changed. Tom's old Dougie Millings and Robbie Stanford suits fitted Vernon, but instead of giving them to him he would charge him £6, the equivalent of a week's rent, for each one.

'I paid for one suit at a time over months,' he said bitterly, 'collecting them out of his own hands on the doorstep at Tor Point, handing the money over to him. He would smile as he put every last penny in his pocket.'

After the American tour Tom and the Squires, augmented by the Ted Heath Band, did a German tour. It was a series of disasters. Tom's voice was shot and he cancelled several shows which almost led to riots. Ronnie Verrell, Ted Heath's drummer, was nearly killed as he tried to cross a road in Hamburg. Vernon and Bill Parkinson witnessed a fatal car crash. To cap it all, in one of the shows Vernon's bass lead was defective and crackled during the show. He replaced it, but that too was defective and crackled, barely audible over the screams of 10,000 fans.

After the show one of Tom's agents came into the band's dressing room. 'Tom wants to see you. He's furious about that lead crackling,' he announced, pointing his finger at the guitarist. 'You're in trouble, young man.' Outside Tom's dressing room he knocked respectfully and waited for the signal.

Tom, wearing a white towelling dressing gown, champagne flute in one hand, Monte Cristo cigar in the other, sat in his chair and said nothing as his acolytes bollocked Vernon. Eventually he made a single pronouncement, 'Yeah, you want to get that fucking lead sorted out for the next show.'

Once Tom started work on the pilot for his new TV series, the Squires' future was sealed. Although the band had coped at The Talk of the Town, Jack Parnell, leader of the TV orchestra, was concerned about the band's inability to read music. He doubted whether they would be capable of learning new numbers in a short time and play for other acts at short notice.

'Tom had to agree with him,' said Chris Ellis. 'There were a number of discussions in the band room over at ATV. Tom's main objection was the fact that Chris Slade knew all his movements very well. He said, "Nobody else can follow me like he can." The whole seed of the Squires' demise was sown there. Big Jim Sullivan came in, and Tom never lifted a finger to stop it.'

Gordon refused to countenance the idea of keeping the Squires on for touring. He claimed it was a waste of money to keep the band on, even though all together they only cost half the £1,000 a week he ended up paying trumpeter Derek Watkins.

Vernon had one last service to perform. Ray Godfrey and John Glastonbury had been following the inexorable rise of Tom Jones with great interest. They had a piece of paper which said they owned five per cent of him 'in perpetuity'. Once *It's Not Unusual* hit, Mills told them, 'your contract's not worth a light'. The duo took the legal route and, assisted by Legal Aid, their case reached the High Court in January 1969. The case was eventually settled with Myron and Byron being paid £100,000.

The night before the settlement was reached Tom's lawyers, concerned that the case was not going that well, decided to call Vernon as a witness, as he had been present when the original contract was signed.

The next morning the case was settled without Vernon having to speak. The party, led by Tom's lawyer, Michael Balin, went for a celebration drink at the Wig and Pen in the Strand. After a quick pint Tom announced he had to go on the town. 'Gordon will take you home, he wants a word with you,' he said to Vernon. 'See you around.'

In the car Gordon told Vernon that he had a song for the Squires to record and that Tom was going to be working on the TV show and in the States. 'It means you're going to split,' he told the stunned bass player.

The next day the headline in the *Daily Mirror* read, 'Tom Jones and the Squires in amicable split'. So amicable the Squires knew absolutely nothing about it. The song Gordon had selected for the band was *Games People Play*. The band recorded it, but it came out with zero promotion, and to compound their helplessness Joe South's original version went Top 10. They did play one more gig with Tom Jones, at the Prince of Wales's Investiture in June. 'We got the biggest amount of money we'd ever earned – £100 each for doing that gig,' said Vernon. Chris Slade played with Tom for one more tour before he discovered how much more the other musicians were being paid.

Some months later, Vernon received a bill from his accountant for £4,000. The tax man wanted to be paid for all the TV appearances Vernon had done. Every time the Squires had done a TV show each member had been paid a set fee which had been pocketed by the management. Nor did they receive any royalties or recording fees for a live EP and the *Live at The Talk of the Town* album. The maths is simple. In four years Vernon, a backing musician, actually earned Gordon Mills more than he paid him. The tax bill was sent to the MAM accountants and nothing more was heard of it.

Gordon could be vicious, but his treatment of the Squires was not simply shabby. It was premeditated, vindictive, despicable . . . and totally unnecessary. Certainly they were naive, but Mills exploited this ruthlessly. As for Tom, he must have seen what was happening, and while he made some token protests, he chose to look out for his own interests.

How difficult would it have been to sit Vernon down and tell him face to face? Tell him that he did not fit anymore. Yes, they had grown apart, but Vernon, despite all the warning signals, still believed they were friends, that the Valley bond held firm. Tom had somebody else fire the man who had once been his best friend.

Tom did not face his responsibilities or do the deed himself. Stardom does that. Nor did he even offer to sugar the pill. Give Vernon a lump sum – say £10,000 – as a thank you, enough to buy a house or start a small business. Small change for a millionaire.

Without the Senators there is a strong possibility that Tom Woodward, like his predecessor Tommy Pitman, would still be in the Valleys, singing in the pubs and wondering about what might have been. Myron and Byron pocketed £100,000 for less than a year's work stumbling round the fringes of the music business and the hassles of fighting a court case.

All Vernon got for eight years' work, friendship and emotional support was three weeks' wages, £120.

CHAPTER TWELVE

THE MAM EMPIRE

aving disposed of the baggage from Tom Jones's past, Gordon Mills set about making him even richer. The genesis of Management Agency and Music, came about because Tom, who was always careful with his cash, had been complaining to his manager about how much tax he had to pay. 'Find a way of paying less tax or you're out of a job,' snapped Gordon to his accountant Bill Smith.

The tax system was particularly inequitable towards pop stars. A musician might earn no money for years and then suddenly it came pouring in. They had to pay income tax at the full rate after expenses. At the time the top tax rate was 19/6d (97p) in the £1, 85 per cent income tax plus thirteen per cent surtax. Taking all the allowances into account, an artist earning £100,000 might end up with £25,000 in his or her pocket. Smith realised that if the artist were to form a public company, the allowable expenses would be much greater. Tom could then run cars, employ staff, and pay the bills out of company funds rather than from his own pocket. As the top tax rate on company dividends was lower, it could leave the performer with up to half of his £100,000.

The Beatles had been the first pop stars to enter the financial world when they floated Northern Songs. It was a sure-fire bet. There was little chance of Beatles' classics like *Yesterday* or *Paperback Writer* losing popularity. A catalogue of songs is a solid, if indefinable, financial asset. Tom Jones and Engelbert Humperdinck were huge million-selling artists, but they did not write any of their own material. There was no guarantee that their popularity would not wane as fast as it had waxed. If that were to happen, public confidence would be damaged and the share price would fall.

(In the UK that is exactly what did happen. After MAM was floated Tom Jones had only five Top 10 hits in the next three years. He had had seven in the previous three. Humperdinck had just the one hit after and seven before.)

The financial analysts of the day were worlds away from the pop scene. Seeking a common ground, City men asked Smith if his singers had ever played at La Scala Opera House in Florence. Journalist Robert Head pointed out that for the 13s 3d (66p) being asked per share, the investor got only one penny of tangible assets, and that MAM only owned seventy per cent of the stars for ten years.

They also had the right to keep part of their overseas earnings abroad. On 6 February 1968 and 26 February 1969 both Tom Jones and Engelbert Humperdinck had signed contracts with Ebostrail granting the company 'exclusive rights to his services outside the United Kingdom and Republic of Ireland until 31 July 1979'. In return Ebostrail paid each artist and Gordon Mills a salary of £5,000 plus a commission on profits not exceeding a further £10,000.

The MAM flotation prospectus explained, 'Ebostrail is a private trust company incorporated in England of which Mr W.L.L. Smith and Mr D.A. Landau are directors and in the net profits of which they are interested. Ninety per cent of the profits arising in respect of services rendered to Ebostrail by Tom Jones, Engelbert Humperdinck and Gordon Mills, as stated above, are paid to such three persons by way of remuneration except where in the circumstances stated above 100 per cent of the profits are paid to the Group.' Exactly what Ebostrail did was never disclosed. The company was registered in the Caribbean and there were always strong rumours that a lot of the money that Tom and Enge made abroad never made it all the way back to MAM.

The management contracts between Gordon and both his artists were to last for a further ten years, until 31 July 1979. Gordon was paid a net commission rate of fifteen per cent of their earnings, and twenty per cent on record royalties from Decca prior to 1 April 1967 and none after that. (This does appear to contradict the still prevailing belief that Tom paid Gordon fifty per cent but if all the money from Ebostrail never made it back to the UK one cannot be too sure.) Aside from the fixed assets — three Rolls-Royces worth £22,879 — all of the other current assets (royalties and fees) owed to the Group were offset by a tax liability of £87,700 and £108,156 owed to creditors. The flotation documents stated, 'Creditors include an amount subsequently agreed to be payable in settlement of claims against Tom Jones and Gordon Mills including legal costs.' This confirms that Myron and Byron were paid a settlement of £100,000 for their efforts on behalf of Tommy Scott and the Senators. And the new company — not Tom and Gordon — paid for it.

The public realised MAM's intangibles were worth a great deal more than three Rolls-Royces. MAM owned the talent and this was a chance for anybody to buy into the romance and myths of stardom by association. The shares in March 1969 were seventeen times oversubscribed. They quadrupled in value within the year – making Tom's holding alone worth nearly £2.5 million. Within three years MAM was the most important non-American music conglomerate – outside of record companies – in the world.

The initial perception was that Tom Jones, Engelbert Humperdinck and Gordon Mills were MAM. In fact they were just the management side (and the principal shareholders). AMA, the agency and concert promotion side, was headed up by Colin Berlin and Barry Clayman, supported by Alan Field. Berlin had been Gordon's agent back in the days of the Viscounts, just as Bill Smith had been his accountant and Michael Balin his lawyer. The year before flotation they had contributed £116,280 of a gross income of £466,187.

Bill Smith understood that MAM would have to expand its activities outside the core artists if it was to continue showing the necessary growth and profits. In its first year MAM made some spectacular leaps. The first step was to bring the Harold Davison agency, AMA's biggest rivals, into the fold, merging two serious powerhouses into one super agency.

Davison had started off in jazz, promoting the big bands, Frank Sinatra, Tony Bennett and Judy Garland, before he moved into rock music with the Dave Clark Five and the Animals. When Chas Chandler, former bass player with the Animals, discovered Jimi Hendrix he brought him to Davison and his eager young protégés Barry Dickins and Dick Katz. The artists represented by Harold Davison in 1969 represented the cream of British talent: Barry Mason, Terry Reid, Susan Maughan, Eric Burdon and the Animals, Lulu, Jimmy James, Jimi Hendrix, Cleo Laine, Marianne Faithfull, Fat Mattress, Tony Christie, Tony Blackburn, Kenny Lynch, the Alan Price Set, Cat Stevens, the Small Faces, the Searchers, Scott Walker, Procol Harum, Amen Corner, Julie Felix,

Neil Young, Joni Mitchell, the Kinks and Dusty Springfield.

'Harold had just bought his company back from the Grade organisation,' recalled Barry Dickins. 'Then MAM made Harold an offer he couldn't refuse. Rather than fight each other to steal acts and cut each other's throats, they got together to make one gigantic company.'

The price was a salary of £7,500 a year plus 225,000 shares for Harold, his three boys (Lawrence, Ron and Gary) and his wife, the singer, Marion Ryan. Nobody can guarantee a chart hit, but Davison helped load the dice in MAM's favour. He had invaluable contacts. 'It's all about power. Who you represent, who you know,' said Barry Dickins. 'When you phoned up and said you were from MAM, the doors opened. Harold was very friendly with Bill Cotton Jr, who was the boss of the BBC. Harold pretty much went to the head and got people on *Top of the Pops*. He also represented lots of Radio One DJs like Tony Blackburn, Ed "Stewpot" Stewart and Dave Lee Travis.'

In the early seventies the BBC held a *de facto* monopoly over the pop charts. The BBC chart was the only one that mattered, and with weekly viewing figures of over eighteen million, an appearance on *Top of the Pops* could treble sales. Radio One was the only game in Britain, the pirates and Radio Luxembourg having long gone or been marginalised, while commercial radio did not start until 1973. If a single made it on to the Radio One playlist, it was almost guaranteed to be a hit.

There was an arcane exchange system still operating. If an American musician – regardless of stature – worked in Britain for one day, a British musician could work in the States for one day, and vice versa. Because Harold Davison promoted a lot of jazz big bands, he always had days in the bank. Bringing the twenty-five-piece Buddy Rich Big Band to Britain for one date could be swapped for the five-strong Deep Purple working for five days in America.

Record companies, desperate to promote an American artist, would ring up MAM begging for an exchange. Said Dickins, 'We'd say, "OK, but we want the band." '

In December 1970 the agency represented ten of the artists in the Top 30. In 1972 and 1973 artists represented by MAM were at number one in the singles charts for thirty-two weeks.

The agency used their connections and clout with Tom Jones and Engelbert Humperdinck to get agency and promotion of touring US artists. MAM had reciprocal deals with heavy-hitter American managers like Jerry Weintraub. It worked both ways. 'Barry Clayman virtually gave Weintraub the Moody Blues,' recalled MAM agent Ian Wright. While there were other agencies – such as Chrysalis – doing very well with younger, hipper acts, as promoters MAM were pre-eminent. It took nearly ten years for any other promoter to seriously challenge their position.

The long-term big money in the record business is in copyrights. MAM had strong publishing interests. A record label was the next logical step. They bought Shaftesbury Music, a publishing house, primarily to acquire the services of Geoffrey Everett, an old colleague from Decca, to run the record side. Their first record, MAM 1, *I Hear You Knocking* by Dave Edmunds, was released in November 1970 (Mickey Gee played rhythm guitar). It went to number one. MAM 3, though less successful, only reaching number eight, was of far greater importance.

Nothing Rhymed introduced Gordon Mills's latest protégé to the world. He had none of the hairy-chested machismo of Tom, or the lounge lizard romance of Engelbert. Gilbert O'Sullivan looked like nobody else. He looked ridiculous, like an overgrown child, a refugee from a Depression Bisto advert perched behind a grand piano, dressed in three-quarter length trousers, hobnail boots and a giant flat cap. But there was a plaintive catchy melody in his songs and a wistful look in his eyes that complemented his nostalgic look.

Raymond O'Sullivan was born on 1 December 1946 in Waterford, in the Republic of Ireland, though his family relocated to the cultural wasteland of Swindon when he was a child. Young Ray attended art college, but his ambitions were always to be in music. He could certainly write songs. The Tremeloes covered *You* and *Come on Home* on *Here Comes The Tremeloes*, which snagged Ray a record deal with CBS in 1968. His only single, *What Can I Do*, flopped and he moved on to Major Minor, an independent label run by Phil Solomon, who had just scored a massive number one hit with Jane Birkin and Serge Gainsbourg's *Je t'Aime . . . Moi Non Plus*, to no more success.

Disheartened, scraping a living as a postal worker, O'Sullivan took a demo tape of his songs into MAM, with a note explaining that he had specifically chosen Gordon Mills as his mentor. Perhaps it was the photo of the singer looking most unusual, perhaps it was the opportunity to show Solomon he could reap platinum from hitherto barren soil, perhaps he simply liked the songs, but Gordon was interested.

'I remember when Ray first came to Gordon's house on a Sunday afternoon,' said Chris Ellis. 'Gordon was routining Tom and he came up the driveway with that hat on and a bike and a big pile of manuscripts. He came in and Gordon kept him sitting there for hours and hours then he played a couple of songs. O'Sullivan couldn't play the piano then, he was a two-finger man. Gordon sent him away. Eventually he realised he might have found something, so Gordon installed him up at his house as a babysitter and dog walker.'

Once Mills decided to take the artist on, O'Sullivan, already a two-time loser – the way Gordon liked it – accepted the conditions demanded without demur. Mills became his personal manager, he signed recording, publishing and agency deals with MAM.

'When I signed the contract,' O'Sullivan told the *Evening Standard* soon after his first hit, 'I didn't even look at it. If you respect somebody and they're going to manage you, then you have to trust them. That's the most important thing.'

Even in a time of hard bargains, the management and agency deal was restrictive in the extreme. O'Sullivan signed for a minimum of five years, extendable to seven. Mills controlled the direction of his entire artistic output – live as well as studio work –but also the negotiation of all future contracts. The extent of Mills's paranoia was confirmed in that O'Sullivan could not talk to the media without his manager's consent. In writing. Mills's management cut was twenty per cent, with the understanding that O'Sullivan would cover all expenses. In exchange the singer-songwriter would get Mills to protect him from 'unfair exploitation and act solely in the writer's best interests'.

Naturally Ray had to be renamed and reinvented – it had worked with Gerry Dorsey. So Mills christened him Gilbert O'Sullivan, a punning reference to the nineteenth-century light opera composers. Tom and Enge were less impressed, with the latter suggesting that Gilbert O'Sullivan was a joke name. Displaying his innate obstinacy, the Mule spent a year working on the first album, refusing to release it until both the songs and the image were right.

He had not lost his touch. O'Sullivan's first album *Himself* made number five on the album charts. More importantly, it stayed there for eighty-two weeks. Between July 1971 and November 1973 he had eight consecutive Top 20 hits, six were Top 10, two went to number one.

Even after that first hit, Mills continued to pay him an allowance of just £10 a week. 'I blended in with his family. I was very young and naive,' said O'Sullivan. 'I thought if I was part of his family, there was never going to be an opportunity for anybody to con me. I didn't want to grow up to be a person, I wanted to grow up to be a musician.'

Deliberately eschewing the superstar life, he preferred to stay in reading, and often babysat the four Mills children. 'We installed him in a cottage in our grounds, near the zoo,' recalled Claire Mills. 'I was only three and to me "Uncle Ray" was just my new babysitter. He was lovely – tall and slim with nice eyes. He was always very happy and I liked him a lot.

'The strongest memory I have of Ray is standing on his feet and dancing round the room with him. I used to sit in the lounge and watch him playing the piano. My mum noticed our closeness and told Ray she'd love it if he wrote a song about me, which is exactly what he did.

'I can remember the night he finished it. Although it was past my bedtime we went to his cottage where he played *Clair* to us and I really loved it.

'My dad could obviously tell that it was a great song. He took Ray into the studio the next day and recorded it. Then they needed me to do a laugh at the end of it. They all started tickling me. That's how they got the laugh.'

In November 1972 *Clair* became his first number one in the UK, followed in April 1973 by *Get Down* (a song written not about getting hot and sweaty on the dance floor but ordering his dog off the furniture). More important, in July of that year *Alone Again (Naturally)*, a bittersweet ballad chronicling the death of his parents, confounded all the critics who had dismissed O'Sullivan as too English by reaching number one in the States and selling over a million copies. *Clair* was held off the top spot by Billy Paul's *Me and Mrs Jones* and then Carly Simon's classic *You're So Vain*.

With his image carefully relaunched – longer collar-length hair, dressed in chunky college sweaters, sitting behind a piano singing his wry, melodic songs, Gilbert rode the crest of the singer-songwriter wave. For a while it seemed as if he could rival Elton John or Carole King. His next two albums did very well in Britain. *Back to Front* was a number one that spent sixty-four weeks on the charts, and *I'm a Writer not a Fighter* got to number two.

Following that third album, Gilbert told Gordon he wished to produce himself in the future. There were four more British hits but not one Top 10; in America his career was remarkable in that he succeeded in rising to the top without leaving a trace.

Neither Tom nor Engelbert have ever had an American number one single. But, thanks to their huge shareholdings, both enjoyed a healthy slice of the £14.5 million Gilbert earned for MAM. The pecking order was confirmed by looking at the shareholding: Tom had a few more than Gordon and two per cent more than Humperdinck. Gilbert had none.

In the tax year ending 31 July 1973 Tom Jones's twelve per cent of MAM (872,950 shares) earned him a dividend of £96,042.50 before tax (£67,217.15 after it). Gordon Mills' 851,450 shares earned him £93,659.50 (£65,561.65 after tax). Engelbert, who only had some ten per cent (731,550 shares), bagged £80,470.50 (£56,329.35 after tax). Two years later when the hits had dried up for everybody, the dividend had dropped by a half, earning Tom a mere £45,396 after tax, Engelbert £38,142 and Gordon £44,252.

For its first five years MAM seemed touched by the gods. Everything it did turned to gold. At the end of 1969 Bill Smith had renegotiated Tom and Engelbert's deals with Decca. At the time of the flotation they had a pretty good deal – ten per cent royalties on both UK and US sales, and eight per cent in the rest of world until 31 December 1970. The new six-year deal guaranteed total royalties of £2.5 million at a rate, almost unheard of at the time, of 14.5 per cent, payable from that moment. In return for which they sold 500,000 MAM shares to Decca.

The royalty rates also applied to any other artist signed to MAM. This gave the company an instant profit on any hits. A fair return one might think for investing in new talent. Except the initial record royalties paid to Gilbert O'Sullivan were only five per cent in Britain and 3.5 per cent overseas. So for every £1 of royalties paid to MAM by Decca for *Nothing Rhymed*, Gilbert was due 27.6p, Gordon Mills earned 6.9p and MAM kept 65.5p. Lynsey de Paul, who signed in 1972 and took legal advice, was on an eight per cent royalty worldwide – pretty much standard for an unknown at the time. As long as MAM kept selling records, they were onto a winner.

In 1970 the publishing division acquired Paul Anka's publishing company, Spanka Music, for £90,452, as well as paying off £85,667 in debts. Two years earlier, Anka had composed new English lyrics to *Comme d'Habitude* by French composer Claude François. He bought the copyright, called the song *My Way*, and sent it to Frank Sinatra. Over the years the song has earned Anka £5 million. In 1972 Donny Osmond's cover of Paul's 1960 hit *Puppy Love* sold millions.

But in the end MAM must be considered a failure as an entertainment conglomerate. In 1970 the record business was in a major state of flux. Album sales were becoming increasingly important and the business was expanding very rapidly. The British companies that had carved up the industry throughout the sixties were losing ground to the Americans. Decca had lost the plot, Pye was no longer in the game. RCA, CBS and Warners had all opened British offices, which as well as giving American artists a bigger share of the European market, increased the competition. In addition, small hungry independent labels, like Chris Blackwell's Island, Tony Stratton Smith's Charisma, Chris Wright and Terry Ellis's Chrysalis and Herb Alpert's A&M, were offering lifestyle choices as well as record contracts to hungry young bands.

MAM should have been able to use its position to become a major player. 'MAM had the agents, they had the attractions,' said Paul Russell, now chairman of Sony Music Entertainment Europe. In the early seventies he worked for Michael Balin, MAM's lawyer. 'There wasn't anybody who wouldn't take a phone call from MAM. They were the biggest player in town. Their first record was a number one record – from there they should have gone on, and really ended up as another EMI.'

The problem was inherent in the company structure. It was highly successful, but fundamentally old-fashioned. Initially, it was modelled on the Grade Organisation. In 1969 Barry Dickins still wore a suit and tie to the offices in New Bond Street, and called his boss 'Mr Davison'.

MAM flaunted all the trappings of a successful organisation. MAM House was in the heart of Mayfair at 24–25 New Bond St (the entrance was in Conduit Street). The directors were on the fifth floor, the fourth floor was accounts, the record company occupied the third floor, the agency the second. The chairman, Gordon Mills, had no office; he preferred to run everything from Little Rhondda in East Road, St George's Hill.

'When he went there he just walked into Bill Smith's office,' recalled Paul Russell, 'sat down in his chair, and everybody ran around him.'

'He looked like a star, he really did. You put him in the room with Tom Jones and Engelbert and you'd think Gordon Mills was the star,' confirmed Barry Dickins. 'He was a very charismatic individual, very tall, very good looking, always immaculately dressed but not in a traditional style. He looked like a multi-millionaire.'

Like many successful men Gordon was always impatient, quickly moving from one idea to the next, but never hung up on the right or sensible way to do things. Bill Smith described working with him as constantly invigorating. Smith would state the obvious then Gordon would come up with something out of left field, and while he was thinking through the possibilities Mills would have moved onto a dozen other things.

'He wanted everything to happen quickly, he wanted it to happen now,' explained Paul Russell. 'He was very strong-willed and full of ideas. Quite showbiz as opposed to a street record guy. And he was very amusing, sometimes when he didn't intend to be. He could be quite funny because he was so impatient. He had some pretty wild ideas.'

On one occasion when waiting at Balin's office to sign his will, Tom's chair disintegrated. He ended up on the floor and hurt his back. An hour later Gordon was on the phone demanding Russell sue his boss. Finally he calmed down with a begrudging, 'You must get better furniture.'

Gordon arranged for Tom to do a charity show for Newport County, a football team from South Wales who were struggling to survive. The deal was that Tom would pay all his own expenses, would perform for nothing but that the club would pay the PRS (Performing Rights Society) fees for the songs that were played that night. After six months the PRS got on MAM's case, because it hadn't been paid the £4,000 it was owed.

Russell tried to talk Mills out of suing but, as he was adamant, a writ was issued against the club. If they did not pay within fourteen days they would be put into liquidation. A couple of days later Russell got a call from the chairman of the club who said, 'Will you tell Mr Mills that we'll pay the money, but we've got to sell our striker first. We can get a good price for him. It's going to take a couple of months, so would Mr Mills agree that he would give us a little time.'

Russell relayed the chairman's message. The manager's instant reply was, 'Are you joking?' 'No,' replied the lawyer, 'I'm serious.'

'Oh fuck it, we'll pay for the PRS. We can't have them sell the centre forward.'

Man management and motivation were never among Gordon's skills. Those close to him still talk of him with admiration, a few even with love, but his brusque mannerisms added to his aura of unapproachability. Never one to make friends easily, he was fiercely loyal to those who served him well. At MAM they were the men on the fifth floor.

'The directors at MAM were all very tight,' said Russell. 'Barry Clayman was very close with Harold, Harold was very close to Dick Katz, and they were all very close with Gordon and Bill Smith. When they brought Geoffrey Everett in to run the record company, he was somebody that they had dealt with previously. They employed people that they already knew and trusted, but as the industry got bigger, their world view contracted.'

Barry Dickins found the 'us and them' attitude of the directors increasingly frustrating. 'My salary was OK, I travelled first class, but compared to the money I brought in, it was crap. It was a conglomerate run by accountants. One day an accountant came to me and said, "Why did you lose money on the Deniece Williams show?" Believe it or not it wasn't something I set out to do.

'By the mid-seventies the problem was that everybody had their own company under the MAM umbrella. There was no structure, everybody was out feathering their own nest. The leadership wasn't there.'

While publicly the top men at MAM gave the impression of unity, they still operated as they had always done. Putting the most powerful agents in London all on the same floor did not change their habits. Individual agents continued jealously to guard their own fiefdoms.

Because of the need for a public company to maintain growth MAM began to diversify – out of the music industry. They bought into jukeboxes and slot machines, doubling their turnover, but cutting their profit margin. In 1972 MAM owned 9,000 jukeboxes and 5,000 slot machines as well as the sole distribution rights for Wurlitzer. They bought part of a new marina in Bradwell-on-Sea, got set to develop a hotel chain, invested millions in trying to set up a West End theatre chain and even started a charter airline.

The airline seemed a vanity project for Tom, Engelbert, Gilbert and Gordon, that did make some financial sense if the artists were touring in Europe. It worked in America. But the planes did not have the fuel capacity to fly across the Atlantic, which was where the artists were based. Legend has it that MAM Aviation lost a fortune but Bill Smith insists that MAM Aviation always turned a small profit. Initially the three stars provided interest-free loans of £300,000 to buy an HS125 executive jet. The loans had to be extended to three years and they had to pay a proportion of the costs. They had up to nine planes, four of which were more or less permanently travelling to and from Nigeria. When the Nigerian oil boom collapsed and the price of aviation fuel went sky-high, the company was closed.

The nuts and bolts were not of interest to Gordon. His ultimate loyalty was to Tom, Engelbert and Gilbert. To him they were the foundation of the company, the principal shareholders and the principal owners. They always came first.

In his 1972 report to the shareholders, Mills showed his priorities. In a year where his company made a radical change in direction and investment by moving into jukeboxes, he spent time denying industry gossip about Tom Jones and Engelbert Humperdinck. 'I would like to dispel certain doubts that have been expressed in the past with regard to the success of the television series made for the USA. Not only were the entire series of both artists shown throughout America on the major network but they were also repeated.'

In 1975 MAM appeared to be a successful company, but their percentage profit on turnover had declined from a high of almost eighty per cent to nineteen per cent, even though turnover had tripled. While the agency and record royalty profits remained constant, diversifying into other projects added to turnover but not to profitability.

MAM had moved away from what it knew best and consequently spent more time trying to fix the problem areas than exploiting the profitable ones. In 1975 Tom Jones was still making a lot of money in Las Vegas, so there appeared to be no need to address the problem of his recording career. The royalties coming in had remained constant, but most of them came from Gilbert O'Sullivan, not the two singers on whose fortunes the company was built. The decline in MAM's profitability against turnover mirrors almost exactly the fall in Tom's record sales.

But when Gordon, Tom and Engelbert went to live permanently in the States in 1976, their sales did not get any better. By 1978 only half of Tom and Engelbert's earnings were being paid to the company. The agents began to leave one by one. Davison retired, Clayman got into promoting. And with Gordon's absence MAM had lost its resident lateral thinker, its glue.

'I very much got the impression,' recalled Russell, 'that if it wasn't right for Gordon, Tom and Engelbert then it wasn't right. I never got the feeling that Gilbert was one of the partners. He didn't have a piece of MAM. Maybe that's where the rub came, the reason for his eventual unhappiness with them.'

CHAPTER THIRTEEN

THIS IS TOM
JONES

Stardom is a twentieth-century conceit. The advent of the mass market for performing arts requires constant, increasing supplies of fresh blood, new faces, new voices and perfect bodies, all manufactured to order. Prestige and wealth are no longer an accident of birth or the reward for a lifetime of personal struggle, but are available to anybody with the requisite looks, sufficient talent and the luck to be discovered in the first place.

Nothing much has changed since the silent movie days. Film stars were discovered waitressing in coffee shops just as super-models are spotted standing in airport queues. In 1999 a hit song can be manufactured for a pretty face and a pierced belly button. In 1966 the singer might have had a beehive hairdo and a miniskirt. Today celebrity can be conferred by something as mundane as appearing in a TV commercial for instant coffee or introducing pop videos on a cable TV station. The demand for new media fodder is so all-encompassing it might even surprise Andy Warhol. Perhaps soon everyone will be famous for 15 seconds.

As in everything there are degrees, levels of brightness in the cosmology. Tom Jones had got lucky when Gordon Mills turned up at the Top Hat Club. *It's Not Unusual* was a huge international hit, but that in itself was not enough. There are thirty-six acts who have had a British number one and never had another chart hit. During the sixties the rule of thumb was that an artist needed three signature tunes – instantly identifiable big hits – to make a career. After *Delilah* Tom had reached that level. Soon afterwards he was joined by Engelbert Humperdinck.

At some point during 1969 Tom Jones became a superstar. To this day Engelbert remains a star. The precise difference between the two is hard to quantify... but the gulf is immense and fundamental. While stardom may be fleeting, superstardom is perpetual.

Superstardom cannot be created. It is bestowed by the public, not by the media, and then only to a very few. Once granted it cannot be taken away. Once somebody becomes a superstar, he or she will always be one, no matter what fate befalls them. Some basic natural talent is a prerequisite. But the essential ingredient is timing. It is not enough to build a fan base year by year, tour by tour, film by film. It has to appear to be an overnight success even if it has been years in the making. Eventually a star reaches a point of total celebrity where the normal rules and laws no longer apply.

Part of their appeal is that a superstar is a *tabula rasa* for the world – a blank screen on to which people can project all their different fantasies, their desires, hopes and ambitions. What the star is really like, how they behave, what they actually think, if they actually think, these things are no longer important. The superstar has become all things to – in Tom's case – all women. Even when the magnitude of celebrity has faded the memory remains. A superstar is forever.

Back then superstars only existed in a country where it has never been enough to be merely famous. Nowadays the global market and instant communications allows the whole planet to worship simultaneously at the same altar. In 1969 only the States had the necessary media infrastructure, the huge self-perpetuating market, the money and the sheer, single-minded, self-abasing devotion to the concept of stardom to confer such accolades. Tim Rice, whose lyrics to *Jesus Christ Superstar* helped push the word into common usage, lays the credit for that on a *Melody Maker* headline that proclaimed 'Tom Jones – The World's Number One Superstar'.

Exactly when it happened to Tom Jones is impossible to say. By early 1969 everything was in place. He had a proven track record of solid hits, and the word was spreading fast about the sexual dynamite of his live shows. However, the catalyst, the final ingredient in the rocket fuel mixture that propelled him into the celebrity cosmology was a television variety series: *This is Tom Jones*.

Once Tom began his calculated move into the MOR (middle-of-the-road) market, Gordon Mills realised that he had to find some other avenues for promoting his artist in Britain and America. The pop package tours of the early sixties were beginning to diminish because acts wanted their performances to stretch beyond twenty minutes. Simultaneously managers and promoters realised they could earn more money from just one artist filling their halls. Tours were time-consuming and increasingly expensive ways of reaching a relatively small audience. Every time Tom appeared on *Top of the Pops, Ready Steady Go* or the *Ed Sullivan Show* it guaranteed him sales.

Those were product-sensitive shows, a means of promoting hit singles. By the late sixties the pop market was shifting towards album sales. The Beach Boys and then the Beatles had started the trend with *Pet Sounds* and *Sergeant Pepper's Lonely Hearts Club Band*. It was nothing new. Frank Sinatra had shown in the fifties with his series of 10 inch long-players for Capitol (including *Come Fly with Me*, *In the Wee Small Hours* and *Songs for Swinging Lovers*) that there was a huge market for longer works. Teenagers bought singles — three for £1 — adults bought LPs.

Throughout his career Tom Jones has recorded brilliant songs. Songs that he has made his own so effectively that nobody else can approach them no matter how many times they try. Yet while he has made several good albums, he has never made a great one. He should have done.

Tom's forte has always been performance. Singing in the studio was too easy for him, he never had to try to get it right and in some sense he never cared enough about the frame for his pictures. The Voice was all that matters, except sometimes that is not enough. Movies were not the answer.

TV was different. It was free. Sitting in front of the box people have a decision to switch channels or to switch off. Often they do neither. Inertia is a wonderful thing.

As pop music swept variety out of the nation's theatres it had come to rest on the small screen. *Sunday Night at the London Palladium*, the *Black and White Minstrel Show*, the *Val Doonican Show*, the *Lulu Show*. All followed the same formula: musicians, dance numbers, comedians, a magician or a ventriloquist, culminating with the star guest and the host sometimes duetting, sometimes not. Gordon understood variety. It was where he came from, and where he was guiding his protégés.

If Lulu could host her own show, Gordon reasoned, Tom certainly could as well. Gordon never thought small. The trick was to break the mould. British television broadcast the *Andy Williams Show* and *Perry Como's Christmas Special*. So why not make a show with a British host and sell it to an American network? To realise his idea Gordon turned to a man who thought the same way as he did and smoked even bigger cigars. Gordon had learnt a lot from Larry Parnes, but what he really wanted to be was Lew Grade.

Sir Lew (as he was then) liked a man who thought big. With his brothers Boris (who became Bernard Delfont) and Leslie, he dominated showbusiness for over forty years. Together they were impresarios, agents, theatre owners and producers. Lew was one of the first to realise the potential for commercial TV and invested huge sums early on in ATV (Associated Television). Lew had started out as a dancer and he always loved variety performers. He also had a reputation for backing hunches and then leaving professionals to get on with it. 'All my shows are great,' he famously remarked. 'Some of them are bad but they're all great.'

ATV was the first port of call for any Tom Jones spectacular. Lew liked the idea and what he had seen of Tom. 'I wanted Tom to do a TV series because I thought he had a great talent, tremendous verve, flexibility and he could really belt out the songs,' he recalled.

'Gordon Mills was a very tough negotiator. It took us three meetings to get the details ironed out. He guided Tom remarkably well. He was always very polite and charming, but he was determined to get the maximum he could for his client. Tom came to all the meetings, but he never said a word other than "hello" and "goodbye". He had just started to smoke cigars, so I'd offer him one when he came in and he'd sit there happily puffing away.

'We were negotiating and I had gone to the maximum I could. I said to them both, "This is my final offer, but for every show you do I'll give you a box of cigars." Tom didn't even look at Gordon, he just said, "You have a deal." It was the first time he'd said anything in all our negotiations.

'I suppose it was a cheap deal-maker, but he eventually did sixty-five episodes. So I had to give him a box of twenty-five Monte Cristo Number Twos every week. Each show took a week with rehearsals and recording, and he couldn't do anything else during that time. No concerts, no recording sessions.'

Marty Starger of ABC (one of the three networks in the States) was keen on Tom, but before ABC would sign they had to shoot a pilot show. The obvious man for the job was Jon Scoffield, the producer/director on *Sunday Night at the London Palladium*. A sharp-dressing, handsome man with upper-class manners, sophisticated tastes and an eye for the right shot. In 1968 Scoffield had devised and shot four fifteen-minute films for Tom called *The Face*, working in big close-up on his head and shooting in black and white. He knew all about the singer and his weaknesses, on and off camera.

The pilot was shot in late 1968, with guest spots from the Fifth Dimension (an American band, hot after the Top 10 success of their single *Stoned Soul Picnic*), actress/dancer Juliet Prowse and comedian Dicky Cavett, whom ABC were trying out for his own show. There were two British writers working on the show and ABC flew in three of their own. 'It was a bit of a push and pull,' Scoffield recalled. 'They wanted Tom to sing *Green Green Grass of Home*, but they wanted him sitting alone outside a log cabin in a rocking chair. I told them, "That is not the point, the song is about a man who is about to be hanged!"'

Scoffield was pretty happy with the result and was stunned to discover that the ABC ratings expert was breathing doom and gloom. 'The Americans were obsessed with ratings. Marty Starger invited me back to his hotel to meet this expert who had been studying audience reaction of the pilot. They had a theatre in New York with buttons in the seats. You pressed the buttons as the show went on. A was very good, B was OK and C was not interested.

'This man spread his sheet out. It was like a huge graph, marked off at the various parts of the show. He spread it out and announced, "This is interesting . . . but very worrying. Fifth

Dimension there, not bad, fairly level, Dicky Cavett (who I had thought was dull as toothache), scored very high indeed, Prowse OK. The problem is that every time Tom comes on the graph dips. Interest goes."

'I was getting pretty worried, when this man suddenly discovered that he was looking at it upside down. I swear to God if I'd handed Marty a gun he'd have shot him in the head without even thinking. One graph with a scratchy pen and Tom was nearly down all the way.'

'After the pilot,' said Lew Grade, 'I persuaded ABC to take one series of twenty-six episodes. They went down so well they asked for another twenty-six.' The deal Lew structured with Marty Starger was worth £3 million a year for three years – the largest contract to that date between a TV network and an artist. Tom would shoot the first thirteen shows in London starting in January 1969. A further thirteen would be shot in Los Angeles in the autumn. It was a gamble because it took Tom out of the live market for six months of the year. In return it gave him unprecedented publicity.

On Friday 7 February 1969 *This is Tom Jones* aired for the first time on ABC. Initially the show was very successful. It captured high Nielsen ratings throughout the season and during a summer of reruns, and was renewed by ABC for prime time during the 1969–70 season. By the time Tom arrived in LA to record the second thirteen-week run, he was the hottest star in America. ABC studios on Talmadge Avenue had to lay on extensive security. It was a closed set with a helicopter on permanent standby, twenty-two extra pages, fifteen more guards, three extra police and two more firemen. There were 60,000 requests for tickets to see the concert sequences, which were filmed at the Hollywood Palace, an old variety theatre on Vine Street. On concert days the crowds blocked the street. An appearance on the *Dick Cavett Show* led to an entire block in midtown Manhattan being closed to traffic. TV had made Tom a superstar.

The advantage of the transatlantic deal between ATV and ABC (one of the first of its kind) was that the American money coupled with the ITV network fee allowed Scoffield to shoot on a grand scale. He recalled, 'My above the line budget – everything you saw on the screen, all the talent, the writers, the musicians, scenery, wardrobe, make up, the band – was £72,000 a week. In 1969 that was a lot of money.'

The disadvantage was that ABC imposed some very stringent broadcast and technical standards on the production. There was a censor sitting in every show, making sure there was nothing said, shown or sung that would offend middle America. The double standards did get confusing.

'The wheatbelt ruled TV, what you should do or shouldn't do . . . and you shouldn't do a lot,' said Scoffield. 'Tom was drinking real champagne and smoking cigars. There was no problem with that, but I couldn't shoot his crotch. One night we had a problem with Shirley Bassey's dress which was really low cut. We shot her numbers for the British show and then asked her to go and change. Shirley came back on again wearing a tight evening dress that buttoned at the neck. She had also taken off her bra so you could see her nipples!'

The American NTSC TV system was different to the British PAL system, 415 lines rather than 625. Although the US system was of poorer picture quality, the Americans decided they could not accept the British technicians doing the conversion, so every scene and every song had to be shot twice. 'We had three European cameras and three American ones, and we shot back to back,' said Scoffield. 'Eventually we convinced the Americans that we could shoot on their system and convert it to ours. This was not strictly true. We shot on ours and converted it down to theirs and they never knew. The shows we shot in America were of too poor a picture quality to be broadcast over here.'

Scoffield's first rule was that when they were shooting in front of an audience, everyone, from the director to the assistant floor managers, the cameramen and the spot operators, had to wear dinner jackets. This immediately created an atmosphere, psyched up the crowd into feeling that they were attending a special event. Not that many of them needed any invitation.

'Just before the series started Tom had his face done,' said Scoffield. 'I thought the old Tom was very attractive, that big broken nose and hawkish face. Very much a male face, a real rock and roller in a red shirt and blue jeans. America didn't want that, they were terrified of anything that smacked of too heavy rock and roll. This country rather liked the old Tom.'

When the TV series started Tom wore casual clothes, trousers cut tight with no pleats and flat across the front to emphasise his manhood, or jeans and a leather jacket. He loved boots with the zip up the inside leg, chisel toed with a slight Cuban heel to give that extra inch in height. Before long he was wearing suits all the time. They were always impeccably cut, fashionable rather than classic, but all made in Savile Row mainly by Robbie Stanford, though Tommy Nutter made a few. His jackets were cut long and pointedly waisted with wide lapels, hand-made shirts with long collars and kipper ties.

Scoffield was adamant that whenever Tom put on a dinner jacket he had to wear a proper bow tie. Until then the singer had favoured the elasticated approach, which once he started to sweat and loosened his collar, ended up stuck around his ears. Jon showed Tom how to tie a double-ended bow, which he could undo and leave dangling between the frills on his shirt front. It seldom lasted much beyond the first number.

Tom was aware that he had to tone down his live performance

for TV. 'I used to go wild on the stage, I used to float on a cloud through the music,' he told the *Daily Mail* at the time, 'but you can't do that on television. And I don't want to do it any more in real life.'

It took a six-day week to shoot each episode. Tom would have Sundays and Mondays off, except once every four weeks, when they would shoot the concert sequences that opened and closed each show. For two and a half hours over Friday, Saturday and Sunday nights Tom would record between twelve and sixteen songs. The audience had to be seated by 7 p.m. and the recording finished by 9.30. It almost always overran, in part because Tom loved to sing. He would always warm the crowd up with a couple of tunes they had not got right in rehearsal.

Tom had to be at Elstree studios by 10 a.m. which meant Chris Ellis picked him up in Weybridge by 9 o'clock. For a man who so detests mornings he was seldom late – even when he had been out on the town until dawn. 'Unlike some artists, Tom was very good,' said Lew Grade approvingly. 'He didn't try to interfere or to impose himself. He left it completely up to Jon Scoffield and Gordon Mills.'

For the first thirteen shows Gordon was very hands on. 'Gordon was Tom's controller, his creator,' said Jon Scoffield. 'Gordon and I had a few run-ins. I was a bit pushed for time, and he wanted to do it again and again. I had my eye on the whole ball game, whereas he had a clear idea of what he wanted Tom to be.

'There were various songs Gordon would not let Tom do. He had discovered the truth about Tom – he could sing country and western very well, but we soon learnt that whatever you did you don't call it country and western, because that frightened people silly . . . and yet they liked it. Tom's personal choice was to sing rock and soul numbers, but Gordon was always fighting with him to do standards and ballads, because he could paralyse the crowd with big ballads.

'We gradually developed a formula. We needed three numbers for the end of the show, a quiet spot, a little ballad from Tom, a song for the guest artist and a duet for the guest and Tom. At first the concert spot was chosen by Gordon, but after a while he eased off because he was happy with the show. Gordon used to turn up on concert nights. Sound was his forte. He sat up in the sound booth and had quite a lot to say about the balance.'

The guests that appeared on *This is Tom Jones* provide a remarkably comprehensive list of who was who at the time. The names were from the conservative area, where pop music met showbusiness, but is still an impressive roster. The most notable absentees were Sinatra, Presley, Dean Martin, any of the Beatles and Mick Jagger ('We tried for him but the Americans were very nervous after his drug bust,' said Scoffield). Scoffield only remembered Gordon vetoing one guest – the singer Brook Benton. Strange, as Benton has always been one of Tom's heroes. As there was a similarity between their vocal styles, especially on ballads, Gordon was worried that he might show Tom up.

Tom had some influence on the choice of guests and material. 'In those days, the big singers on American television were people like Perry Como, Andy Williams and Dean Martin,' said Tom in 1997. 'ABC wanted me to be like them, but every chance I got, I would sing something harder than the usual stuff of the time. And I would get great people to come on the show, like Little Richard and Jerry Lee Lewis. Back then, no one would let those guys on television.'

The deal for the featured performers was a good one: $10,000, first-class tickets to London, and a week staying in Claridges or the Dorchester. Other artists, like Glen Campbell, appeared on a *quid pro quo* basis, a nominal fee of $1,000 and a promise that Tom would reciprocate by appearing on their own shows.

The singers included: Burt Bacharach, Ella Fitzgerald, Mireille Mathieu, the Moody Blues, Mary Hopkin, the Bee Gees, Sergio Mendes, Julie Driscoll, Sandie Shaw, Dusty Springfield, Engelbert Humperdinck, the Foundations, Paul Anka, Georgia Brown, Cass Elliot, the Dave Clark Five, Jerry Lee Lewis, Bobby Goldsboro, Stevie Wonder, the Hollies, Sonny and Cher, Esther Ofarim, Cleo Laine, Smokey Robinson, Billy Eckstine, Bobbie Gentry, Shirley Jones, Ray Charles, Liza Minnelli, the Rascals, Joni Mitchell, Kenny Rogers, Jeannie C. Riley, Johnny Cash, Tony Newley, Lulu, Tony Bennett, Jose Feliciano, Charles Aznavour, Glen Campbell, the Crazy World of Arthur Brown, Connie Stevens, Matt Monroe and Joel Grey. There were also actresses, like Shani Wallace, Millicent Martin, Diahann Carroll, Judy Carne, Barbara Eden and Claudine Longet, who were not always great singers.

Anne Bancroft was especially nervous as she had to do a sketch, naked inside a bubble bath, and then sing. Her nervousness at singing was matched by Tom's at having to appear in a sketch with her as a bumbling inarticulate construction worker.

Not all the guests were easy. Bobby Darin turned up wearing Levis, a thick moustache and a cowboy hat. He said, 'The name is Bob now, and I don't sing *Mack the Knife* any more.' They compromised and sang a duet of *Aquarius*, but Bob insisted it be sung at dirge pace. During the rehearsal Johnny Spence jacked up the tempo, Tom went with him and Darin reluctantly followed suit. He was furious and insisted on the actual performance being slower. In on the plan, Scoffield had filmed the dress rehearsal, and that was the version that went out.

Bing Crosby was staying at the Churchill Hotel, and, as was usual, he was picked up by the chauffeur-driven black Daimler that transported guests out to Elstree. On the way he passed a golf course and asked the driver to stop. Bing went to the clubhouse and asked if they would let him play a round. Naturally they said yes, so Bing played a round, while everybody at Elstree waited around wondering where the hell he had got to. Bing finally turned up three hours late, went straight up onto the stage and nailed his part in twenty-five minutes straight.

In late 1969 Joe Cocker was tearing up the charts, and the Americans insisted he be booked on the show. When they saw the tiny Sheffield pipe-fitter, with hair down his back, blessed with the voice of a funky angel and a face only a mother could love, they wanted him cut out of the show.

Raquel Welch's demands proved something of a nightmare. She insisted on having her own hair and make-up people. She was supposed to be ready and due on set at midday. At 12.50, the crew struck for lunch early, because she had not turned up. Raquel then appeared and went off again after a conversation with assistant floor manager, Frank Chapman, who was too busy staring at her chest to look her in the eyes.

She snapped at him, 'Have you never seen a pair of tits before?'

'I've never seen yours!' he replied.

Singing was not her forte, and it took ages to record *Along Came Jones*, a spoof of twenties silent films, where she was sawn in half and tied to rails waiting for Tom to rescue her.

Tom did not socialise with his guests much. He seldom left his caravan, and often met them for the first time on the set, nodded and started reading the lines that were set for him. It was left to Jon Scoffield to meet and greet, to sort out the flowers and champagne.

Gordon, who knew how to turn on the charm, never thought to talk to Tom about it. Watching the old TV shows one can see it in their eyes. There seems little or no rapport between Tom and many of his guests, resulting in clinical, cold dialogue, not helped because Tom could not ad lib to save his life. He only came alive in the performances.

He did not take to Raquel at all, though with other female guests, notably Vikki Carr, Leslie Uggams and Nancy Wilson, he became intimate. During the first series he duetted with Sandie Shaw on the Rolling Stones' *(I Can't Get No) Satisfaction*. He gave her the come-on throughout the recording.

'He asked me back to his caravan for champagne,' recalled Sandie, laughing at the memory. 'I said, "No thank you." He didn't believe someone could say no.'

To give the star some privacy, ATV had built a huge garage, big enough for a caravan and his Rolls-Royce Phantom 6 limousine. This was an imposing silver-grey beast, weighing over six tons, with black leather seats and blacked-out windows. The back contained a TV, a bar and a partition window to close him off from the driver. The garage was directly connected to the studio by a corridor. When he was not required on stage, Tom would retire to his caravan.

It was a glorified seaside trailer, with a bedroom at the back and a kitchenette and sitting room at the front, with a stereo, a phone and a small fridge – big enough for six bottles of Moët et Chandon. One night after the show Ellis was sitting there with Johnny and Marion Spence having a drink, when the caravan started rocking. Marion asked, 'What's that in the back?' He replied, 'I think it's one of Gordon's apes gone mad.' It was, of course, Tom, busy in the back with one of the ATV secretaries.

'One day Tom would not come out of his caravan for a shot,' recalled Frank Chapman. 'We were always careful to knock several times on his door and wait. But this day he wouldn't come out or answer his phone at all. Jon Scoffield told me to get him out anyway. We hammered on the door, but eventually the only way we could attract his attention was to let all the tyres down, whereupon Tom ran out of the door, all rumpled, half dressed and out of breath saying, "What the hell are you doing, boyo?" He had a well-known blonde German actress in the caravan with him. It took two of us the whole of the next day to pump the tyres back up again.

'Tom used to spot attractive girls in the audience and ask the floor managers to invite them back to his caravan for drinks. One night he asked me to invite this very pretty red-haired girl. I did what he asked, but unfortunately for Tom, I had to invite her husband too.'

Tom's behaviour was so well-known to the crew that jokes started to appear about it in the show. His close friend and neighbour, the comedian Jimmy Tarbuck, was the guest comedian on one show and nearly blew the gaff completely. 'There was a sequence,' Tom said, 'when girls had to come on stage with champagne, and Tarby had to say to them, "Tom Jones's caravan? Just outside and turn left." Then the cheeky bastard turned to the camera and said, "That Tom Jones, he's a boy. Do you know that caravan of his has had six new sets of tyres and it hasn't moved three feet?"

'When it was transmitted Linda and I watched the show together. "What does he mean by that?" she asked. I had to think quick. "I don't know, love," I said. "I don't get the joke either." '

ABC's concern was not about morality, but about money and ratings. Their worry was not that Tom was screwing women of every shape, size, colour, religion and race, but the age of some of his consorts. Tom has always had a taste for younger flesh and, however careful he was, some girls do lie about their age. The wheatbelt heartland would not take kindly to his bedding an underage girl, however inadvertently. That would rank even lower than divorcing his wife for a black woman.

In between his caravan dalliances, Tom was kept busy. He learnt his songs with the aid of a tape recorder in the back of the car as Chris drove him to the studio. Sometimes, after a heavy night, he was late and liked to be greeted with a jug of buck's fizz.

He seldom complained if the show ran late and never threw tantrums. John Scoffield recalls, 'We'd been there all day, something had gone wrong and when I said, "Sorry Tom, it's taken a long while," he'd shrug and say, "It's easier than carrying bricks up a ladder." You can't ask much more of a star than that.'

Tom put up with the endless waiting, the dancing and the comedy sketches because he got to sing. If Tom had had his way he would have sung for the full fifty minutes each week. 'He had a tremendous interest in music,' said Scoffield. 'He was up with all the technical developments in recording studios and he loved real musicians, especially Ray Charles and Jerry Reed, who wrote *Guitar Man* for Elvis.'

The week Jerry Lee Lewis was a guest on the show, Tom and his original hero went out every night. 'One morning, Tom came in looking very much the worse for wear,' recalled Scoffield. 'He said they had had a big argument that almost ended in a fight.' It could have become a violent squabble. Jerry Lee could get dangerous when he was drunk. When sober, he was the perfect Southern gentleman. A few too many drops of liquor and the same gentleman could be attempting to force a chair down the throat of somebody who had said the wrong thing.

Tom has never been much of a harmony singer. Complicated flat ninths and sevenths were too much for him, but thirds and fifths he could manage. When he sang with close-harmony groups, like the Fifth Dimension or Crosby, Stills, Nash and Young, they were so accomplished they could slot him in effortlessly, and he would sing with the lead voice. His joint performances with David Crosby on *You Don't Have to Cry* and *Long Time Gone* were simply superb.

Tom loved it when he came up against a really good singer. He took a great deal of pride in being able to hit a high note and hold it – 'It's a man's voice, boyo,' he would say. David Clayton

Thomas, of Blood Sweat and Tears, was another vocalist who could shout a bit, so it became a match and not in the most harmonious spirit. There was a bit of needle involved, which made great television. Jones relished the competition, but he also possessed the manners not to blast his fellows off the stage. Melding his style with the hushed, wispy voice of Joni Mitchell was a tough one.

In September 1969 Tom went to meet Janis Joplin at her Hollywood rehearsal studios, where she was preparing for a tour with her Kozmic Blues Band, to discuss the numbers they would do. The studio was dark, dirty and smelt like a bomb shelter. Janis, who was on her home turf, swaggered into the room and looked Tom up and down as if she was going to eat the Welsh upstart and wash him down with a bottle of Bourbon.

'What key do you sing in?' she sneered.

'I just sing,' replied Tom with a grin, never one to let the side down.

Janis wanted to perform her favourite song, Rodgers and Hart's *Little Girl Blue* solo, but then they had to agree on a duet. She was quite impressed Tom knew all the rock and roll and blues songs she suggested. They settled on the Eddie Floyd–Steve Cropper stomper *Raise Your Hand*. On her own territory with her band laying down the backing, Tom matched her perfectly, note for note, alternating 'Here and now' and 'Raise your hand' line for line as they ripped through to the wailing climax. The version that was taped on 21 September never matched the power and spontaneity of the rehearsal, but Janis, at least, had changed her view of Tom's abilities.

'We had this set built for her,' recalled Tom. 'And she went off. She said, "I can't sing walking through fucking plastic raindrops! Just a simple backdrop. I don't want all this crap!" '

'The only time in sixty shows I remember he had real problems was with Steve Lawrence and Eydie Gorme,' said Scoffield. 'Tom was singing the Marilyn Bergman number *What Are You Doing for the Rest of Your Life*. We were shooting and Tom suddenly couldn't get it. It had gone. So Steve and Eydie took him to one side and taught it to him again. Plenty of artists would have thrown a tantrum, told me, "Fuck that, find another number fast." Not Tom, he ploughed on, and after four takes he got it right.'

The dance sequences and comedy sketches proved much harder. The difficulty was trying to mix the sketches so that they worked on both sides of the Atlantic. The American writers were Tom and Frank Waldman (Frank went on to write the script for two *Pink Panther* movies), and the Ace Trucking Company – an experimental comedy troupe. 'Tom's background was as a singer,' said Scoffield. 'Yet by the time he hit that American show he was expected to do an awful lot for his money: he was expected to dance, chat, duet with anyone, and not always on his own ground. He got better over three years, but he was not a natural chatterer. We were forced to find ways for Tom to be comfortable. The dialogue was tightly scripted and written on cue cards. We had to do that otherwise we could have been on Take 40, waiting for the right words to come out in the right order.

'He was not a natural actor, not very good at reading aloud. He had a lot of nervous mannerisms when the dialogue was tricky. He would cough, fiddle up by his collar or move his left hand in front of his face, which was a nightmare for the sound man.

'He liked his concert spots very much, but he wasn't so keen on the big dance numbers. We had a very good choreographer, Norman Mayne, who devised a series of steps around what Tom could do. He is not a natural dancer and he still moves in exactly the same way he did then, the same movements, the same hip grinds.'

Ironically *This is Tom Jones* had almost the opposite effect on his career in the UK as it did in the States. It turned huge sectors of the British audience off. It wasn't 'Our Tom' up there on the screen. The show was altogether too slick, too corny, too wooden, too glitzy. Too American. The shows that were shot in LA were never shown on UK television, and in 1970 ITV schedulers moved the show out of prime time into the graveyard slot – 11 p.m.

One reason for the relative failure of *This is Tom Jones* is a simple technical one. It was an American show in concept and execution, where celebrity and glamour ruled, and the colours were vibrant. In Britain, where colour TVs were expensive and comparatively rare, the public perception of Tom Jones was in black and white. That was how people saw him on *Top of the Pops* or on *Sunday Night at the London Palladium*. His image was about performance not spectacle.

In America *This is Tom Jones* never became the bonanza ABC hoped for. *A Man Called Ironside* consistently beat it in the ratings. 'The appreciation figures were very high, which they took a lot of notice of,' admitted Scoffield. 'In the end people who liked Tom Jones liked him a lot, but there weren't quite enough. When the time came to end, we had pretty well reached the end of our natural life. I'm sure Tom was relieved.' TV tastes were changing faster than the guests on the shows. Duets with Janis Joplin and David Clayton Thomas might have set the goosebumps rising with every growl and howl, but the whole was too old-fashioned and hackneyed for the Woodstock generation, and too hairy and scary for the white-bread crowd. What the audiences wanted were cop shows and *All in the Family*.

Taken purely on its own merits, *This is Tom Jones* was not a huge success. However, as a statement of arrival it took some beating. In 1969 American radio and newspapers were local and parochial in reach, programming, circulation and interests. The only media that covered all fifty states were network television and a few magazines.

Suddenly, this Brit in a tux and tight pants was being beamed into every American home with electricity. Certainly not all of them watched it, but it made him a household name. Not trendy, certainly, but Tom Jones had abandoned being on the cutting edge of teen hysteria when he first sang about pussycat eyes. Superstars do not have to worry about trends.

What set Tom apart was sex appeal. It never showed through fully on the TV, but it was always there, simmering below the surface, in every move, every wriggle and in the way he sang.

'If we hadn't had the American censors the shows would have been raunchier,' said Jon Scoffield. 'But not a lot. Raunchy singing to me is the words and the music, not the movements. Tom had a lovely way, especially in ballads, of sliding through the notes, a glissando. He delivers beautiful bass notes in *If Ever I Would Leave You*. It's a corny song, but with Tom standing there singing, it was as sexy as his *Proud Mary*.

'Tom was sexy because he thought he was. He had the confidence to get away with it.'

CHAPTER FOURTEEN

SUPERSTAR

———

I t happened every time. Wherever he went, wherever he played in the autumn of 1969, three months, forty-one cities.

The house lights dimmed. The drumbeat began. The audience's chattering and twittering died away. Into its place swirled a rippling, rolling eruption of female screams. Not the shrill squeal of the barely post-pubescent, but a roar that came from the pelvis, from thousands of women who knew what sacrifices sex required, what it meant, and what perhaps – through the medium of this man – it could mean all over again.

These women were not skinny, hippy chicks, with their hair falling straight to their butts. They had not danced naked in the mud of Woodstock, smoking pot and espousing free love. These women were the wrong side of thirty, the plump end of size 12 and counting, and so far from being young, free and single as to make their teenage children giggle at the very concept. In many cases only a generation older than the Woodstock kids, their mindset was far older, paralysed in a place where the white picket fence, the working husband and milk-fed, tooth-braced kiddies still held sway.

Middle-income, middle-aged middle America came to worship the pagan Jones.

He played his shows in the round. He entered the stadium surrounded by an impenetrable phalanx of local rent-a-cops. But when Tom sprang out from within his protective cocoon, the women in their bra dresses and their bell-bottoms, their pants suits and their pearls, their girdles and their wigs, forgot they were supposed to be Stepford wives and became Maenads. He stood there looking almost normal. Another lounge singer in a perfect cut silk-lined tuxedo. But there were oh-so-subtle differences between Tom and Andy Williams or Perry Como. Trousers cut tighter than Ed Sullivan would allow, to highlight that unnatural bulge, white shirt with pleats or frills and a bow tie the colour of blood.

The Maenads knew it was different from Frank, Deano or Perry from the very first song. Bobby 'Blue' Bland's 1962 hit *Turn on Your Love Light*, was a paean to getting those juices flowing. Then came the hits. And the perspiration. He sang *I Can't Stop Loving You* and his voice was swallowed by the wailing, *What's New Pussycat?*, with every transatlantic pun ground out with another pelvic roll. The tie was dangling loose before he ever reached *Delilah*. Then he shed his jacket. The sweat poured off him during an anguished *Danny Boy*. When he promised his women *I'll Never Fall in Love Again* it ran down both cheeks like a river of tears.

As the hits kept coming, so did the fans. They came in suicidal waves, one by one, then a handful, then by the dozen, then the hundred, throwing themselves against the chain of guards. The guards waited. A thin black line of fifty or more, crouched low for balance, determined to hold firm. The fans came and the guards tossed them back like undersized fish. Again and again. Sometimes one of the more determined would break through to plant a kiss on the object of their desire, even leap onto his back, before swooning with ecstasy and throwing herself, a spent lemming, back down into the orchestra pit.

If the women did not break through, their gifts did. It started simply enough. Handkerchiefs proffered to wipe up some of that precious Jones sweat, but as the collective mania took hold, the Maenads would shed their inhibitions and with it their clothes. When the musicians left at the end of the set, the stage appeared to have been the testing ground for some new and terrible weapon, one which obliterated human flesh, to leave only female garments – belts, tunics, cotton dresses, flowers, sometimes a home-baked cake, tights and panties by the score.

It was worst coming into the home straight. The guards got tired, tempers frayed, but the women kept coming. *Green Green Grass of Home* might calm the fever, but *It's Not Unusual* fanned the flames, until only *Twist and Shout* was left. The musicians too, the best money could buy, were caught up by the madness. Sweat pouring over his eyes, Johnny Spence conducted furiously, his hands lost inside the moment. Chris Slade, the only Squire left, kept the rhythm loud and hard, the only thing that could always be heard above the hubbub, the beats mimicking, accentuating, every thrust of the singer's hips. Big Jim Sullivan, calm and stolid as his nickname, unleashed his guitar riffs, while John Rostill, no stranger to adulation, pumped his bass and knew it had never been this good with Cliff and the Shadows.

Off stage, in preparation, Lloyd Greenfield wriggled through to the guards, alternately ordering and begging them not to hurt the fans. In the wings Rocky Seddon bounced on the balls of his uneven legs, an uncertain last line of defence. Chris Ellis waited, his arms full of towels and jugs of water, poised for the signal.

'C'mon baby,' screamed Tom, pushing his voice to its very limit, 'twist a little closer and show me that you're mine.' Derek Watkins's manic trumpet took over the theme. With a verse and two choruses left to go, Tom saw Lloyd standing in the wings drawing his hand across his throat, giving him the nod. Tom always hated to stop, and when it was that good, he wanted it to go on for ever. He turned to face the crowd one last time, sodden shirt unbuttoned to the waist, crucifix glinting in the lights, his arms spread wide in supplication. Then he twisted on his Cuban heels, passed off the microphone to a roadie and the lights went out. When they flashed back up, he was gone. Gone to another city, to another show.

That was 1969. A year later he was the biggest solo star in the world.

In America Tom Jones fever had become a raging epidemic. Where had it all come from? He had had hit singles, but nothing like the number he'd had back home. But he was selling albums, lots of albums. In 1969 six of the nine Tom Jones albums available were in the American charts.

The short answer was, *This is Tom Jones* did more for Tom's profile in the States than a dozen bad movies. The show might have been anodyne compared to his live performance, but ten million viewers in living rooms right across America gave him a public profile. Publicity and word of mouth had taken care of the sex angle. The crowds who came were primed, panties ready.

The second time Jones played the Copacabana, the entire season was sold out three weeks in advance. He broke the box office record Sinatra had set in 1951. The scenes outside the club were scary. Hundreds of fans lined the streets, held back by police barricades. Inside the tiny club, he was protected by a hundred security guards. The only way to get to the stage was through the tables, surrounded by armed guards. 'It's frightening having a couple of men with revolvers walk you on stage, but I suppose someone thinks it's necessary,' said Tom. 'I don't really want to be ripped to pieces.'

Tom was at his most vulnerable in the Copa. One woman grabbed him by the hair and was appearing to pull it out by the roots until a guard knocked her off. Another night, a blonde of about twenty-five in a white silk trouser suit made her run to the stage leaping from table to table. She almost made it before a bouncer slung her across his shoulder and carried her out into the foyer, screaming, kicking and beating her fists on his back.

'It was a frightening minute, I can tell you,' admitted Tom. 'I could see her starting to come across the tables and I thought I had had it. She looked pretty determined and was moving fast. I don't know what my singing was like. My mind was so distracted by what might happen if she reached me.'

Whenever fan mania reaches those levels, the incidents feed off each other. One woman started to climb on stage and was pushed back on to her table. Her boyfriend pulled out a switchblade and was promptly laid out by the guard. He was carried out unconscious, while his girl, oblivious to all but Tom, stayed on to watch and scream.

'We even got attacked in the car,' said Ellis. 'They were trying to turn the car over, trying to get into the car. Hundreds of people were swarming round the car, on the roof and on the bonnet. They would have torn us to pieces, Tom too. He was shit scared, yelling, "Go, go." '

Tom remembered, 'For a while in the early seventies I was one of the world's highest paid entertainers. I had a weekly TV series, records in the Top 5, a number one with *She's a Lady*. I was touring six months a year, earning a guaranteed $100,000 a night. I was as far to the front as anyone could go. I was playing Madison Square Garden, the Forum in LA, the Cow Palace in San Francisco. No single artist had been through those venues before, only the Beatles and the Stones had played places that big.'

In 1970 Jones embarked on the biggest tour in American showbiz history. It earned him in excess of £2 million. The itinerary dwarfed the Beatles' tours of 1965 (which began at Shea Stadium) and 1966. Its thirty-four one-night stands doubled the Rolling Stones' tour of the previous autumn (there were no free concerts and therefore no Altamonts). The tour was put together by Buddy Howe, the president of CMA. Howe was Jones and Humperdinck's American agent until he died. The deal was done on a simple handshake with Gordon Mills.

The 1970 tour started in April with a month's residency at the International in Vegas. The showroom had a capacity of 2,000, and Tom was earning almost the same as Elvis – $100,000 a week, plus all the perks. In May the road show moved to New Jersey's Latin Hill Casino for two weeks. At the 4,500-seater nightclub, just outside Philadelphia, they did not bother advertising his shows, they just put up a billboard with the legend 'He is here'. The tickets went within a day. (The following year they put up a sign saying, 'A man and a half', and sold out again.)

On 12 June the tour began in earnest with two nights at Madison Square Garden, followed by a further two weeks at the Copacabana. At the time, the Garden was the apex of a performer's career, one sold-out night would be trumpeted in banner ads across the trade press. With takings of $364,743, Tom broke the box office record. A month later he smashed the box office record in Holmdel, New Jersey, netting $250,000 over six nights.

The penny-pinching days touring with the Squires were gone for ever. No expense was spared to make the Tom Jones show an extravaganza that blew the competition out of the circuit. It certainly offered value for money. 'Nobody else spent that kind of money to put a show together,' said Ben Segal, who has promoted

Jones shows in Connecticut for the past twenty years. 'He always had the best musicians, the finest conductors.' There was always a support group of the calibre of Gladys Knight and the Pips and a comedian/compere (either Norm Crosby or Pat Henry).

The Count Basie Orchestra toured with Tom for four months. Old men set in their ways, they did not fit that well. Basie himself never said a word for four months, never said 'Hello', never said 'Goodbye', just sat there with one of the members of his band, and played cards every night.

For the 1971 tour his backing singers were the Blossoms. Darlene Love, Jean King and Fanita James had been the best vocal trio on the LA recording scene for a decade. Love, who has one of the great underrated soul voices, had been Phil Spector's favourite singer, and sang the lead on the Ronettes' *Be My Baby*.

During the two years Love sang with Tom Jones she was earning $2,000 a week. Gordon expected full value for that. 'We opened the show for fifteen minutes on our own, before Pat Henry, and we didn't waste a second of it,' said Love. 'Our medley of current Top 40 stuff shocked the crowd out of their seats.' They were doing so well that in 1973 their manager decided to ask for a raise and a couple more numbers. Mills had not changed his hard-nosed attitude.

'When our manager took our "demands" to Tom's manager during a break in the tour, the response was, "Who do these three niggers think they are! They should consider themselves lucky just to be in the show." Of course, we never heard any of this from Tom; all of these deals were done — and undone — by the men who cut off the performers from the dirty work of the business. And before we could even negotiate, they hired some other girls to sing.' Love went off to work with Dionne Warwick, and when the Blossoms went back to work for Jones, she was replaced by Cynthia Woodard.

(Tom has always been opposed to racial discrimination in any form. In 1976 he became the first star to play to multi-racial audiences in South Africa. Initially he refused to perform unless all the eight concerts at the Three Arts Theatre in Cape Town were open to all races, but he eventually compromised on three. The Blossoms had to be made 'honorary whites' for the dates so they could stay at the same hotel and eat at the same restaurants.)

What Love remembers best about touring with Tom was the meticulous planning that went into the tour. Gordon had leased a Boeing 727 from United Airlines, and there were limousines on call twenty-four hours.

'I had never seen luxury like it before or since. It was astounding. Of course, Tom was the hottest act in America,' she recalled, 'but it was planned like a military operation.'

'We were working ten months of the year, at least. We travelled so much, we would do ten days in a row, and then Tom would leave the country for a couple of days. Something to do with income tax, then he would come back and we would work for another ten days. It was constant.'

In their scope, the size of venue (stadiums and large arenas played in the round), their execution and logistics, Tom Jones's American tours of 1970 and 1971 were way ahead of their time. Indeed they set the benchmark for the organisation of the large arena tours that were to become the norm. Private planes between gigs, vintage champagne on tap and girls by the score are the kind of superstar excess usually associated with the Rolling Stones and Led Zeppelin. Tom was there first.

There were two differences. The first was primarily that of public perception. The journalists allowed on the road with rock bands were from music or counterculture magazines whose role was to promote the outlaw image, to increase the gap between vibrant youth and petrified establishment. Throwing televisions out of hotel room windows or licking cocaine off the naked breasts of young women were considered as radical political statements not just the perks of the job.

But if such excess was expected from Keith Moon, Jimmy Page, Fleetwood Mac and Aerosmith, it was not expected of Tom Jones. He had an older audience who espoused conservative values and might have been shocked by such revelations. Jones's PR man, Chris Hutchins, either kept journalists away from the backstage parties, or they kept very quiet about what they saw.

While Tom has always hated drugs of any kind, others were less fussy. 'I was brought up on light ale and I have always believed that pop is better than pot,' said Jones. 'The thing about a drink is that you can consume it and not show it. Whereas, with drugs, perfectly normal people are reduced to blithering idiots within an hour. Seeing people take drugs upsets me. I've been at showbiz parties where I've been the only one drinking and everyone else is on drugs. You can't be a performer and do drugs. I remember my bass player trying pot and going to pieces on stage. He was just incapable of playing. If he'd been drunk we could have propped him up against a wall and he could still have played.'

The routine was tight. Although the local fan clubs spent hours decorating the dressing room with candy, cakes and flowers, Tom spent as little time in it as possible. He arrived with a tuxedo on after the show had started, got on stage, did the show, and got the hell out. The stage was as small as possible, surrounded by every seat that could be crammed in. Some nights it took 150 policemen to form a corridor to get him on the stage.

When it was over he ran off stage, escorted by Lloyd Greenfield, Chris and Dai Perry. They were gone before anybody could get out of the front door of the venue. It didn't always work, and sometimes they got trapped trying to get out. The limo was always full of towels. Tom was soaked to the skin, so Chris pulled off his shirt and trousers. By the time they reached the hotel, he was in a dressing gown. He was escorted up to his suite immediately, and then the floor was sealed down.

For one-nighters Tom had a Winnebago waiting outside for him. At the airport, the mobile home parked on the tarmac while Tom took a shower. When he was finished he got on to the plane and ate his dinner waiting for the rest of the musicians and the crew. There was no first class, everybody got the same food and there was free drink in abundance. Within an hour and a half of the show finishing the plane took off.

The plane had a couple of near misses. Once, when landing in Lake Tahoe and another time in Canada, the stewardess, Carol, started shouting, 'Oh my God, oh my God,' and they discovered the plane had taken off with only ten metres of runway to spare.

'On board there would be fifty to sixty people,' said Love. 'It was a great atmosphere, very free and fancy. When you got on board a lot of people were tired, but before too long, they were lively and would start singing. Not Tom though – he would sleep from the time he got on the plane. I have pictures of Tom asleep on board, wearing a blindfold. We'd clown around and he slept.'

The next city was never more than an hour and a half away. The plane landed between midnight and 1 a.m. Limos and coaches were waiting to take everybody to the hotel, where it was party time. When Tad Dowd was really cooking there would be a whole bunch of girls waiting for the party to start. It ended around dawn. Tom would surface about 2 p.m. and go down to the gig around 6, by which time the equipment was all installed and the sound check done.

'It just repeated itself night after night, six nights a week,' said Ellis. 'Sunday was always off, because it was laundry day.'

Sex was Tom Jones's primary indulgence, and a tour was a hotbed of sexual activity. There were plenty of girls and women in their twenties who were able and willing to bed a star. If Tom was not available, but his road manager, a roadie or one of the sound men was, they would do. This was still a close part of Tom Jones . . . and just maybe they could get closer to Tom by being with one of the crew.

Tad Dowd became the tour party's own social director. Dowd, who appeared in the movie *Planet of the Apes*, was a small man with boundless energy, constantly smoking a big cigar. He had special cards made up, and before the show started he roamed the stadium eyeing up potential candidates and handing out the cards inviting them to a drink in Tom's suite after the show. Usually about half of them showed up.

'Tad didn't drink,' said Ellis, 'and he was mad as a hatter, but he had a fantastic way of talking to women. His favourite trick was to get on the phone and call up the nearest stewardess training centre, and invite like thirty girls over. His philosophy was out of thirty or forty, there must be at least five who were going to fuck. And he was usually right.

'Sometimes Tom would come off the stage and say, "That chick in the front row with the miniskirt on, go and . . . " I did it a couple of times, until I said, "No, I'm not doing this for you," so he had Tad or somebody else go and do it.'

In Vegas the crowds were more restrained – though after one week's shows at the International, the stage manager collected 5,000 keys. Tom was well protected from obsessive fans. The International's hotel security guards simply cordoned off entire floors. Entertainers' suites were serviced by private elevators and guards stood by twenty-four hours a day at the fire exits. On the road anything went.

'Tom was very nice, very quiet – as a matter of fact I think he was very introverted, because he never really had a lot to say,' said Darlene Love. 'He loved the women, God he loved the women. Tom was such a great singer, but a lot of times I wondered if women were really hearing him sing, because he did all the sexual bumps and grinds, and the women threw their panties and their bras up on stage. I asked him about it one day: "Tom, how could you wipe your face with them?" as I thought women were actually taking their panties off, and throwing them on stage. I just couldn't imagine doing that. And Tom said, "Oh no love, no, they don't wear them. They're brand-new panties." And in most cases they were.

'In a perverse way women were his religion, his gift from God. To him it was almost a sin to turn them away.'

The saddest sight of all were the groupies who came not to offer their own flesh but the bodies of their teenage daughters. 'I want Tom Jones to be my little girl's first,' they said. It has happened throughout human history – the *droit de seigneur* in the Middle Ages – but such is the cult of celebrity in the last quarter of the twentieth century, so desperate are people to feel it and taste it, that they are prepared to prostitute their own children. To lay claim to fame by association.

'There were lots of funny stories about young girls and their mothers,' said Billy Glaze, production manager on *This is Tom Jones*. In America another member of the TV crew came across Tom having a bath with a mother and daughter combination.

Chris Ellis recalled one particular incident in Indianapolis. 'We were having a party at the hotel, and there was a woman up there in her late thirties. She was drinking and talking to Tom, and about 2 o'clock in the morning she tells him that she's got a daughter, and that if she's going to lose her virginity to anybody she'd rather it was to him than to anybody else. Tom says, "Get her over here," so she did. Tom had to go to bed with the mother first, so he did.

'I was outside the door keeping guard for about forty-five

minutes. Whether he actually bedded the daughter I don't know, because he would never come clean about it. But they were both in the same room and he came out looking pretty pleased with himself.'

'Mums and their teenage daughters,' sighed Love. 'Tom Jones was a star. Women would do anything to go to bed with him. If they couldn't, he could have their daughter.'

Funnily enough, Tom and Gordon attempted to keep the women who worked in their office away from the parties. Nanci Eisner, who worked for Lloyd Greenfield, was firmly told, ' "When Buddy [Howe] leaves why don't you and Sylvia [Harrison] go too?" And we'd leave. I was truly an innocent in those days. Whatever happened, I don't know.'

Darlene found out eventually. The promoter of the season, at the Westbury Music Fair on Long Island, asked Darlene and Jean if they would do the cooking for the party that night. They cooked all day, and after the show returned to finish off. Then they asked if they could stay the night.

As she recalled in her autobiography, *The Name is Love*:

And after we were finished, Jean and I went upstairs and locked ourselves in our rooms. We didn't want anybody getting ideas if the proceedings got too out of hand . . . After a little while we tiptoed out of our rooms. From the landing, like two kids peering between the slats on the banister, we finally saw what when on at Mr Tom Jones' parties.

We felt as if we'd just stumbled into a porno film. Naked men were chasing naked women everywhere. And in the middle, on top of a round glass table, a woman, who must have weighed maybe 200 pounds, had one man underneath her and a couple of others taking turns on top. Jean and I dubbed this woman 'Tabletop Tessie'. Finally they had gotten so heavy that the table just shattered underneath them.

Post-show orgies and casual flings may have been fine for others, but what Tom loved to do was to target and seduce a particular woman over a long period. In 1971 he tried it on with Darlene. The first step was charm offensive. After one show in Tacoma, Washington, the Blossoms retired to their rooms, took off all their make-up, set their hair in rollers, and got into some passion-killer pyjamas. Tom knocked on their door a few minutes later and tried to convince them to come to the party. Later he tried a more subtle physical approach.

'I often sat right behind him on his jet,' said Love, 'and when he was awake he gave me some fabulous foot rubs. I would stick my leg up on his chair from behind, and he would slip my shoe off then go to work. No words or eye contact would pass between us. When he was finished, I'd pull my rejuvenated foot back and then fall asleep, thinking, "This man has great hands," and believe me, honey, it went beyond the kind of feeling you get with any good massage or physical therapy. He knew it, too. It was almost as if he was playing with me, trying to bring me to a climax. A few times I finally had to yell, "Hey, give me back my foot." He let my toes slip through his fingers, waiting for his next opportunity.'

'I was never really attracted to Tom, but after seeing all these women around him I had to wonder what the big deal was,' said Love. One night in Vegas, after she saw him walking around with the singer and Broadway actress, Leslie Uggams, she asked him, 'What's with Leslie? I saw her leaving with you guys. Are you sleeping with her too?'

'Why are you surprised?' Tom replied. 'I've had a lot of black women. Leslie was all right, but . . .'

Love promptly let rip at Tom, 'You low-down sucker, are you telling me she wasn't that great?' Then she laughed. 'That's probably what has made me not go to bed with you. I don't want you to tell how good I was, or bad I was, to the next person.' Instead of slinking away with his tail between his legs, Tom simply turned on the charm offensive, grinning, 'Why don't you come up one night and see for yourself?'

As she recalled, again in her autobiography:

> I just had to find out what all the fuss was about. I had worked with a lot of entertainers, but no one who had as much sex as Tom. Either he was the greatest lover in the world, or the greatest liar. I told myself I was simply on a 'fact-finding mission'.
>
> I got into bed, next to this hairy white man, thinking, 'OK, just get it done with.' But before he could really even kiss me, I knew it was all wrong. Luckily I still had my underwear on. 'I'm sorry,' I said. 'I just can't.'
>
> Tom got that wounded-puppy look in his eyes. 'What's wrong?' he said. I don't think he was used to women being dissatisfied with his performance, and in this case we hadn't even really gotten started.
>
> Tom was very nice. He didn't try to force me to stay.

Success in America breeds adulation. Adulation often attracts a more dangerous kind of fan. The killing kind. Tom had a couple of narrow escapes. The Hollywood Bowl in LA is an open-air venue surrounded by woods, hills and canyons. On 17 April 1968, while Tom was on stage rehearsing for his concert, a passerby saw a man carrying a rifle with a telescopic sight in the hills overlooking the venue, and tipped off the law. Tom was hustled off stage while police helicopters and armed cops searched the ground.

In August 1969 Tom rented a house on Mulholland Drive, which looked down the valley directly on Sharon Tate's house. He and Ellis were staying there when Charles Manson's gang stormed into Tate's house and slaughtered her, her friends and her unborn child, and used their blood to scrawl 'Pigs' and Beatles' lyrics all over the walls. Tom was even more horrified to learn that he was on the gang's death list, along with Frank Sinatra, Elizabeth Taylor and other stars Manson considered part of the establishment.

Manson had arranged for one of his beautiful girl disciples to get herself backstage at one of Tom's concerts and talk him into bed. 'I was supposed to take her back to my hotel, and while we were making love she was going to cut my throat with a razor,' said the singer. 'That rather put a block on any thoughts in that area for a while.'

With such threats it became harder for Chris Ellis to drive Tom and act as his minder. Tom's first full-time bodyguard was Rocky Seddon, a Liverpudlian boxer cum occasional bouncer at the Empire, who Tom liked. Tom was playing at the London Palladium when he announced, 'We've got to get hold of somebody who's a bit handy. Rocky's a boxer, why don't we call him up?'

While Rocky was a real character, a Scouse comedian, his hard-man credentials were soon exposed. His ring career had been hampered by having one leg shorter than the other. Ellis joked, 'Rocky rented advertising space on the soles of his feet because he spent more time on his back than he did on his feet.' His primary job was to stay in Tom's suite to answer the phones and order breakfast, giving Chris more freedom to get on with the lights and sound.

'His nature was to steal as much as he could, though not in a vicious way,' said Ellis. 'Every hotel we stayed in he would nick the silver, until he made the mistake, in the Waldorf Astoria, of stealing a whole dining set. When we were leaving he got caught and was forced to hand it back again.'

Because Rocky could not run quickly enough his body-guarding abilities were limited. So Tom had Chris call up his old mate, Dai Perry, who naturally enough was having a pint at the

Wheatsheaf. Less than a week later Dai, who had never left Britain, was backstage at Caesars Palace standing next to Sean Connery, Elvis Presley and Sir John Mills.

Once Dai was on board Rocky was history. In many ways Dai was the perfect bodyguard. Built like a rugby forward with tattooed muscular arms the size of hams, he was not frightened of anyone or anything. He would have taken a bullet for Tom and would punch out anyone who threatened his friend. However, Dai was out of his depth, he only knew Valley rules and tactics – get your punch in first. Tact was one four letter word he did not understand.

In June 1971 the tour stopped at Madison, Wisconsin, for a couple of days. Around 11 p.m. the party room was in full swing. Perry answered the door to Michael Maret, a local boxer who claimed he was going to be the 'next light-heavyweight champion of the world'. Unimpressed, Dai told him to shove off. Twice more Maret returned, pushing, shoving and demanding entry, eventually calling them 'a bunch of pumped up Welsh factory workers'. Tom had seen what was going on and, after a few drinks, was in an aggressive mood.

Tom said to Dai, 'Open the door and let me have him.' Dai swung the door open and Tom just hit Maret, smack in the face, and he went down. Dai and Tom jumped out of the door, out of the suite and started kicking him down the corridor. They got to the lift, kicked him into the lift and pressed the button for the ground floor and sent him down. The next morning the police came around wanting to talk to the people who were responsible. Dai Perry, not wanting to get Tom involved, took the blame. When the police told him that Maret was the son of the local judge, Dai thought he was in real trouble. Then the cop added, 'The judge sends his regards and thanks you very much for teaching his son a lesson.' It transpired that Maret was the town bully and in trouble all over the state.

That was a lucky escape, but the incident demonstrated how Dai was an explosion waiting for somewhere to go off. Dangerous baggage for a global superstar to be carrying. Perry was a really bad influence on Tom. Tom, who had been out of the Valleys for years, had all but forgotten about how to behave in a Saturday night brawl, but suddenly, egged on and backed up by his old mate, it was like old times. He was ready to take on all-comers. Gordon knew what Dai was all about and wanted him out from day one.

On 16 October 1973, Dai was an integral part of a fracas in the first-class cabin of a Pan Am jumbo jet. Tom's American tour had finished the night before and the party had continued beyond dawn. By the time they got into the limo to catch the morning flight to London, Tom, Dai and Linda – who had come out for the last show – were both an hour late and blind drunk.

On the way to Kennedy Airport the singer and his wife started a major row. Nanci Eisner, who worked for Lloyd Greenfield, was sitting in the front of the car and recalled how it started. Linda had told Tom she wished he had never made it to the top, and that they could have been just as happy in Pontypridd.

'What more do you want? Don't I give you everything?' said Tom, pointing at the gold and jewels that adorned her neck and hands.

'I don't care. None of this means a damn thing to me,' Linda retorted. She pressed the button to open the car window and proceeded to take off her rings, necklaces, bracelets, and throw the lot on to the highway.

'Finally,' said Nanci, 'Linda got to a ring Tom gave her, this gigantic diamond ring. Everyone held their breath. I don't know how many carats it was, but it was worth a lot of money. Suddenly, as she was about to throw it out, she just couldn't do it, she started to giggle and the two of them burst into giggles. Of course a lot of jewellery was left on the Long Island Expressway.'

As the car was travelling in the fast lane there was no way it could stop — not even with $50,000 of gold and diamonds at stake. Linda's jewellery was ground to bits in the heavy traffic. The party reached the airport with twenty minutes to spare where Ellis met them with a golf cart to speed through customs. 'They were all extremely drunk, staggering all over the place, shouting and yelling.'

In the first-class cabin Tom kept on drinking. He was in the window seat next to Dai, with Linda and Mark behind and Chris across the aisle, sitting next to an elegantly dressed woman. When the movie came on, Tom, who was listening to the rock and roll channel, started banging the ring on the little finger of his right hand against the side of the plane. It was very annoying, so the woman sitting next to Chris asked Tom to stop it as she was trying to watch the film. Tom told her to fuck off. Several times.

'Eventually the woman got really angry and threw her coffee over him,' said Ellis. 'Tom got up and threw his brandy back at her, half of which landed on me. I was soaked with brandy and coffee, so I went to the toilets to try and wipe it off. When I came back a couple of minutes later, there was absolute mayhem going on up in the first-class compartment.

'There's Tom, right up at the very nose of the plane, brandishing both his fists, shouting and screaming, "Who fucking wants it? Anybody who wants it they can have it." He was totally out of his head. And on the floor is a person in uniform with Dai Perry kneeling on him.'

Dai had awoken from his alcoholic stupor to see his boss apparently under attack. Without pausing to think, he lunged at the attacker and grabbed his tie (a favourite trick which enabled him to head-butt or knee the victim). Unfortunately, it was a clip-on tie and came flying off, so Dai grabbed the uniform and wrestled the man to the floor, preparing to punch his lights out. 'You'd better let me get up,' he told Perry. 'I'm the captain.'

In fact he was a steward trying to keep order, though the captain did have to come down from the flight deck. Peace of a kind was restored, though Tom continued to drink all the way to London. 'He was drunk to the hoof,' said Ellis, 'and very, very obnoxious, both him and Dai. "More champagne," he kept shouting for the next five hours. Linda was embarrassed to hell, even though she was as drunk as them, but it shocked her, sobered her up. I was pretending I had nothing to do with them whatsoever. They were that pissed, there was no trying to talk sense into anybody.'

The captain had radioed ahead and air piracy charges were being filed against Tom and Dai. When the flight landed the police were there to meet it. They escorted Tom and Dai, under open arrest, down to the baggage area. The airline managed to convince the captain to drop the complaint, while the woman who had been drenched in brandy did not press charges, but it took two hours to clear customs who 'went through us like a ton of bricks' and charged the party £850 in excess duty. When they eventually came out, the press and photographers were waiting. Still drunk, Tom and Dai, who had no intention of repenting whatsoever, started shaking their fists, shouting and bawling at the photographers.

The next day Tom could not remember a thing, could not believe what he had done. In today's climate, where any form of reckless behaviour on a plane is severely treated, Tom and Dai would be very lucky indeed to escape without a prison sentence.

Dai survived that, but not the South American tour of April 1974. It was a gruelling three-week itinerary, with gigs in Buenos Aires, La Paz, Bogota, Lima and finishing up in Venezuela. A threat to kidnap Mark added further tension. At Lima the core group were supposed to take a charter flight to Bogota, even though Tom had to be on scheduled flights because of his insurance policy.

'The airport got quieter and quieter until there were just five of us standing there,' said Ellis. 'Finally, someone produced these two guys wearing leather jackets and goggles round their neck. They were crop dusters. They had a twin-engined plane and they were going to hop us over the Andes into Bogota, which is ringed by mountains. At night! So we went into Lima city centre, checked into a hotel, and left the next day.'

By 2 May when they reached Caracas, Dai was operating on a short fuse. The airport was bedlam, with fans desperate to touch Tom and people shouting questions. One man asked Tom if he was losing his voice. Fed up with being jostled and kicked Dai flipped, turned round and punched him in the face. Unfortunately, his target, Manuel Olalquiaga, was a journalist on *El Universal*, a local paper. Olalquiaga promptly filed a $65,000 lawsuit against Tom's party and a court order against the singer.

With rumours flying about that Tom was going to be arrested, Greenfield phoned Gordon Mills. His advice was swift: 'Get Perry out of there.' Dai was taken out to the airport and booked on a flight to Miami and then on to London.

Back at the Caracas Hilton, the situation had taken a distinct turn for the worse. The guards, hired to protect the party, were now pointing their machine guns into Tom's suite. Everyone was too scared to move. Having finished the shows, they headed for the airport, where they were told they could not leave the country.

Now under virtual arrest back at the Hilton, Tom remained calm throughout. He never shouted at anybody. After the British Embassy was unable to offer help, Chris Hutchins sent a cable to Harold Wilson requesting assistance. Finally a deal was struck with a local judge. While the party waited outside in cars, Lloyd Greenfield and Ellis went into his chambers at 7 a.m. An envelope containing $12,000 was handed over and the group told to get out of the country within the hour, while the judge enjoyed a leisurely breakfast. They did.

That was the end for Dai. Tom knew it, telling Chris in Caracas when Dai was sent home, 'This is the best thing we can do, this can't go on.' When Gordon told him that Dai had to go for good, Tom did not raise any objections. Dai blamed Gordon. 'He always wanted me out,' he said, and remained good friends with Tom.

CHAPTER FIFTEEN

TOR POINT

I n 1967 Tom, Linda and Mark had left the three-bedroomed house in Manny Gate Lane in Shepperton for a newly built £25,000 home in Sunbury-on-Thames. Springfield House had five bedrooms, two bathrooms and a double garage big enough to accommodate Tom's grey Rolls-Royce. The sitting rooms were stocked with antiques and a grey leather three-piece suite that cost £1,000 – a year's wage for some. A little pool was placed on the front lawn for Mark.

In the late sixties property prices in Britain had not started to boom, and the area where you lived was indicative of your social status. In suburban Surrey people stayed for life or until they had made so much money it was embarrassing to remain. Sunbury was for comfortable middle-class professionals.

However, in 1968 Tom, Linda and Mark moved house for the third time in three years. Tor Point, Tom's new mansion in St George's Hill, Weybridge was a serious address, an indication of how far he had come from the basement rooms in Cliff Terrace. To a snobbish Englishman, living in St George's Hill was a sign not of breeding but of new money. John Lennon and Cliff Richard lived nearby. Gordon and Jo Mills moved into a sprawling Tudor manse, while Engelbert and Pat were just down the road in Glenbrook.

Tor Point was the biggest, a seventeen-room sprawling turn-of-the-century pile. It never could make up its mind whether it wanted to be grand or comfortable – the front porch was surrounded by white doric columns. It was secure from rabid fans behind electronic gates and set in five acres of woods and carefully sculpted lawns overlooking St George's Hill Golf Club, one of the most exclusive courses in southern England. Despite his proximity to the first tee and unlike many of his friends – comedian Jimmy Tarbuck is an avid golfer and both Gordon and Engelbert became very keen – Tom never showed any interest in picking up a putter. Instead he invested thousands of pounds in building a state-of-the-art fitness centre, which contained a double tennis court, a squash court, fitness room, a sauna bath and an indoor L-shaped 25 metre swimming pool. The pool had a kiddie slide and a Welsh dragon in red mosaic tiles on the bottom of the pool.

No expense was spared in doing up the house. The interior decoration was closely supervised by Linda who showed sophisticated taste for a Valleys girl. She eschewed modern furniture for classic, antiques and tropical hardwood panelling. There was an enormous drawing room with three chintz sofas and matching armchairs, a chandelier and a marble fireplace. The dining room contained a mahogany dining table that could seat sixteen, a crystal chandelier, silver candelabra and gilt mirrors. The kitchen was all mod cons, an electric hob in a melamine-covered central island and an old-fashioned Aga topped with a beaten copper lintel.

Downstairs at Tor Point there was masses of stuff. Each piece sitting dust-free and proud in its appointed place – Linda did most of the cleaning herself. Copper ornaments, antique bellows, carriage clocks, bowls piled high with porcelain fruit, antique firearms on the wall, the mantelpieces crowded with ornaments, each tasteful in its time and place but indicative of mass purchase. Tom's wood-panelled study was packed full of little knick-knacks and a phone with a gold leaf receiver and a mahogany base that is best forgotten. There were very few books. Instead, the glass cabinets were full of framed gold and silver discs, his Grammy Award and other assorted medals and presentation scrolls. The grate in the white marble fireplace was replaced by an electric fire and surrounded by copper kettles and antique bed warmers, while the coffee table featured a green onyx lighter, with a matching ashtray and cigarette box. There were always vases full of flowers and bowls of fresh fruit on display.

'All the homes Tom and Linda lived in were immaculate,' recalled Terry O'Neill, who was Tom's most favoured photographer for nearly twenty years. 'It was always beautifully done. Even though Linda definitely didn't want anything to do with the parties, she always kept up appearances. Tom was never untidy. He had that working-class thing, he was always immaculately dressed. Even if he was casual he looked like he'd just walked out of the band box. He was a dandy, very particular about his clothes, the fit and things like that.'

The first floor contained four bedroom suites and a separate wing with two further bedrooms, a bathroom, Mark's playroom and a kitchenette for the live-in staff who never came. The top floor was Tom's playground with its full-sized billiards room, a bar with proper bitter in the barrel and a sixteen-seat cinema, plus an upstairs toilet so guests did not have to fall downstairs to recycle the beer.

But for all its luxury accoutrements it was not a happy house. Jimmy Tarbuck and his wife went for dinner a few times, the lads came over for a few drinks, but Tom and Linda never threw a party in the seven years they stayed at Tor Point.

Something changed inside Linda when she moved there. The open, friendly, pretty Welsh girl who would make anybody a cup of tea, who would chat to acquaintances in the street, retreated back into herself. Behind the electronic gates of Tor Point, alone in a five-acre prison of her own devising, with no staff, unable to drive and unwilling to learn, she shut out the world.

Linda enjoyed the money, but she hated the fame. She would have been far happier to have won the football pools so she could remain swathed in anonymity. She had married Tommy Woodward not Tom Jones, and the two inhabited increasingly alien worlds. She did not make friends easily, but then neither did Tom. Linda liked Johnny Spence's wife Marion and Ellis's Swedish girlfriend Eva, but was uncomfortable with the other MAM wives. She never trusted herself to make the leap to become one of them. She could have done it easily for she had good taste and was a genuinely nice person. But in her own mind Linda was a Valleys girl, while Jo Mills was a woman of the world, more at home with the stylish demi monde.

Linda felt inadequate, because she couldn't keep up with the conversation and was convinced the MAM wives were bitching about her behind her back. When she left the house at all she drank for courage. Once Linda had finished decorating the house there was nothing left for her to do. She didn't want to go out and be seen on Tom Jones's arm. She was very pretty but felt that she might let him down. After the Mary Wilson incident, Linda was convinced that everybody knew about Tom's infidelities.

She had never liked to watch her Tom perform. It had been fun at the Green Fly, dancing with Jean Evans, Vernon's girlfriend, with the boys up there on stage, close enough to touch. They'd dance together. As soon as they took the floor, they wouldn't get more than ten seconds together without being tapped, two guys in there right away. 'Oh she was a right cracker,' recalled Chris Ellis, who used to protect her. But then Linda was nineteen, and now she was a thirtysomething, and the nineteen-year-old writhing on the dance floor in front of Tom was Miss World.

'Linda always says that one of the reasons she doesn't like to come to the show is that she gets very excited and frightened for me knowing I have to go on,' said Tom. 'She says, "I get very nervous and when I see the women the way they are, I understand why. I know what's on their minds and I don't really want to see it." When I started off and had the first hit and I was doing TV shows, she couldn't watch me for a long time. She couldn't accept the fact that it was me up there. She never wants to be part of what I am when I'm working. She only wants the part of the me I become when I am at home.'

Except Tom was seldom home for more than a few days. During the recording of the TV shows, Tom and Linda's marriage was stretched to the limit. The singer stayed out all hours and took risks almost as if he did not care if he was caught. 'There was obviously a serious problem because he would just not go home,' said Ellis. 'His favourite trick was to either try and pull something over at Elstree so he could stay in the caravan, or he would go to the bar and just stay there drinking until they threw him out at 11 o'clock. Then it would be like, "Let's go clubbing," so we went to the Bag [o' Nails] and Tramp. Sometimes he'd sit there at 3 a.m., alone with his bottle of champagne, the waiters clearing up around him, anything rather than go home. At home he'd go down to the swimming pool, which is down the drive from the house, and carry on drinking there, so he hadn't got to go in the house. He actually took Joyce Ingalls down to the pool house one night when Linda was up in the house. What kind of a chance was that to take?'

Linda hated the star lifestyle. She was wary of people,

especially of other women, worrying, 'Do you want me for who I am? Or do you want me because I'm married to Tom Jones?' She would deny that she was Tom Jones's wife to avoid the hassle. Naturally shy, she became more and more nervous about meeting other stars, until she refused to go out at all. As her world view contracted still further, aware of her husband's infidelities, she felt there was nobody to trust. So she trusted nobody.

'One night at Elstree,' said Ellis, 'Tom asked me to call Linda, to tell her he wasn't coming back, make some excuse that he was drunk. So I called her and told her that he wasn't coming home. She said to me, "Please don't do this again. If he wants to call me, let him call me. I don't want you to call me like this again. I'd rather hear it from him."

'In her eyes I became no better than he was. She never really trusted me after that, just tolerated me. Previously I used to be invited in in the morning, to have a cup of tea while I was waiting for Tom, but then she saw me as a rat, so she wouldn't open the door.'

While Tom was out all night at Tramp, Linda stayed at home drinking vodka, watching TV and playing her husband's records. Drink was her solace. Linda became increasingly reclusive. She had a temper, and when it flared Tom ducked for cover.

One time Tom, his great friend American plastics magnate, Burk Zanft, Ellis and Linda were playing snooker. More than a few drinks were downed and the arguments began. Linda lost her temper and started throwing vodka bottles at her husband, who was ducking down behind the tables. 'Linda looked at me,' Tom recalled, 'and said, "Who the fuck do you think you are? You don't really think you're Tom Jones do you?" Burk was on the floor laughing his bollocks off because he had never ever seen anybody have a go at me without my going nuts. I was like going, "I'm sorry, love" and he was pissing himself.'

'Linda could really give him hell,' said Ellis, 'but only when she'd had a few drinks. It was like Dutch courage. When she was stone-cold sober she didn't seem to have that fire in her. He was scared of her, she had a good aim. She used to call him every name under the sun: "you bastard, you philandering pig", anything that came to mind. She would build up this hate, and it would all come out, but the next day it was all forgotten again. And he had no defence because everything she was saying was right. She knew exactly what was going on out there, she wasn't stupid, and the anger would come out in bursts.'

Her closest companions slowly dropped away and she had nobody to replace them with. When Blackie the dog was run over, both Linda and Tom cried a lot. The final straw came in 1973 when it was agreed that Mark should join his father on the road. Although Linda rationalised that it was for Mark's good – which it was – it was as if Tom had taken the only thing that she had left, as if she no longer mattered at all. Chris Ellis was present at one argument when she yelled at Tom, 'You bastard, you took the only thing I had left in the house.'

When Mark left home Linda was thirty-one. Her misery and loneliness were compounded because she could not have any more children. A couple of years after Mark was born she had suffered a miscarriage. When they could afford more children it was too late, her Fallopian tubes were scarred, and despite numerous tests and operations there was nothing medicine could do for her.

'Linda had a miscarriage after Mark and didn't do anything about it,' Tom said. 'I'm sure if she'd gone and been seen to, and we had the money we had a few years later, she could have had others. The time came when my wife wanted a daughter – I would have liked one too – but the son is always important for the man. We looked into it and the doctors said the tubes were blocked. She had an operation but it was a long shot in the early seventies. It couldn't happen.'

It was important to Tom to know he was not at fault. 'I went for tests to see if I was firing blanks. The fellow called me over to have a look, and the slide was wriggling like crazy. He told me, "There's nothing wrong with you, sir." '

But there was for Linda. Try as she did, Linda did not want to be married to Tom Jones. She wanted Tommy Woodward.

'I sometimes think I wouldn't mind going back to the way we were before — poor — with me working and Tom on the building sites,' she said in a revealing interview in 1967. 'I'm really a strange person and that's the truth. I've grown up with Tommy and I think more or less like him. His ways are my ways — and I hope it stays that way. But, you know, I'm sort of living in snatches between visitors and between Tom's personal appearance tours. When he is home and the last visitor has left, I start to live.'

Then she went on to explain how she felt when she watched Tom sing. 'I get this burning feeling inside. It's just nature isn't it? How do you think it makes me feel to see all these women setting their caps at Tom? It makes me feel insecure and jealous. I suppose I could take a view that if everybody is after him he must be a good man, but it seems to make it worse. It's no comfort to me. There are all kinds of women after Tom. Some are genuinely interested in his singing and some are interested in him. I just can't stand to see them — that's why I rarely go to watch him work.

'Yes, I need lots of reassurance from Tom. Every woman needs reassurance from her husband — but I suppose I need it more than most. Sometimes I wonder how long he will be able to stand all the attention. I put myself in his place sometimes and I think I couldn't resist it for long. But Tom's stronger willed than me — that's what I'm counting on.'

It was a theme Linda returned to in an interview after she had moved into Tor Point. 'There was a time when I was jealous and I felt embarrassed to see it happening,' she told Don Short. 'I was frightened to go to the door without putting on make-up first. You see I didn't feel I was good enough to be Tom's wife. Well, all those more glamorous girls . . .

'Tom knew my fears and he helped me come through it. He said I would grow out of it, and well, now I have. It was just a complex I had at the time. Now I never worry, because I always know that Tom is coming home. I am sure of him . . . Tom loves me, I'm sure.

'Well, I know I am lucky. It's like a dream, Tom, and our son and this house. Sometimes I wake up and I can't believe it. It's not that Tom or his manager Gordon Mills or his press agent Chris Hutchins have deliberately put me into cold storage. Or that they are unhappy I am around. It's just that Tom does all the talking and I prefer to remain at home.

'I do all the cleaning myself and cook the meals. When we grow long in the tooth we might have servants. But while I've got the energy I will cope myself. I do a lot of cooking. Tom is a big eater. He likes steak and sprouts, although his favourite is lamb curry. But although I may sound domesticated, I don't tie myself to the kitchen sink. I love Tom's records too. Even if he wasn't my husband I'd go out and buy them.'

Rattling around alone in Tor Point with her husband and then her son gone for months on end, it was hardly surprising that Linda should turn inside herself, repeatedly burying, uncovering and gnawing on the festering bones of Tom's infidelities. All the time fretting over whether she was worthy of him. Linda looked at Tom Jones the Superstar, and then she looked in the mirror and saw Linda Woodward, a timid little housewife from the Valleys.

Nanci Eisner, who worked for Lloyd Greenfield and Gordon Mills from 1969 until 1987, remembered one particular incident vividly. 'I'd got to know Linda a little bit in those days. I was in Las Vegas but I can't tell you what year it was . . . 1972, or it could have been 1974. She was in a dressing room with Leslie Uggams and Dionne Warwick. Everyone was talking about what it's like to be in the public eye and Linda was talking about how they used to vacation in Acapulco. One day she was in a restaurant with Tom and she overheard some people talking about her. They were saying, "You know for Tom Jones's wife she's not too pretty, she's kind of chubby," and Linda said, "Didn't they understand that I care and I'm a human being, that I have feelings too?"

'As she said it you could almost feel her withdrawing from the room, deciding she no longer wanted to go out, to be around.'

Tom and Freda Woodward had moved to Weybridge too. Tom's family, not Linda's – her mother Vi flatly refused to leave Wales. It was not like back home, everyone dropping into each other's homes for a cup of tea. While the Woodwards accepted Linda, there was always the unspoken 'you trapped my Tommy because you were pregnant' hanging in the ether. For Freda, her Tommy could do no wrong, and now he was a superstar, little Linda was not really good enough for him.

Linda got on well with Tom's sister. Sheila and Ken Davies lived in the gatehouse. Sheila, like Linda, was unassuming and shy, and she could not drive either. But when Linda preferred to shuffle around the house in her dressing gown all day, they did not see each other for weeks. Ken, who was employed as the groundsman, eventually found the whole situation increasingly stressful. Used to his mates down the pub in Ponty, he felt as isolated at Tor Point as Linda. Chris Ellis remembers him crying into his beer, saying he could not stand it any more.

Eventually in 1974 Ken found himself a lady friend. That did not worry either Tom or his dad. They joked, 'Ken's off having his nooky.' Until Ken broke the code and ran off. He left Sheila.

Tom was furious, and threatened to sort him out. Infidelity was acceptable, divorce was not.

Despite Tom sitting in the car of a morning complaining, despite Linda rattling around in her palace, cleaning, cooking and communicating with nobody, despite everything that happened, divorce was not an issue. It was never an issue.

'I don't think that it ever got to the point of divorce,' said Chris Ellis. 'For a while up at Tor Point, Linda sank into the deepest despair. There have been times when she's said, "I'm going, I'm going to leave you," but it never got any further than that. She threatened to pack her bags, and if he got in the car in the morning in a foul mood, then obviously there'd been a big fight in the house. They were just an ordinary married couple sometimes at war, and sometimes in love.

'Tom had this wonderful knack, when he saw that it was getting really bad, of being able to talk to her, and being able to convince her that everything was OK. He could go home, and he could actually turn it around and convince her that he loved her and that there was nobody else really in the entire world, and then it would all be fine. She wanted to hear this, and she heard it from him, and he was good at that. In the end, she loved Tom . . . and where else did she have to go?'

While 1969 was the start of a miserable time for Linda, it was a fantastic year for Gordon, Tom and Engelbert. The hits kept on coming, *This is Tom Jones* was a success, Engelbert had his own TV series commissioned and the MAM flotation made all three of them millionaires overnight. Gordon's next move was to turn Tom into a movie star.

At the same time Ray and John Boulting, from British Lion Films, were looking for investment income. The Boulting twins had written, directed and produced a highly successful series of satirical comedies in the fifties and sixties: *Lucky Jim, I'm All Right Jack* and *Heaven's Above*. They had become directors of the British Lion Film Corporation, which, while it had reasonable success as a distribution company, failed to get enough hits off the ground.

At that time Roy Boulting was casting and prepping a film called *There's a Girl in My Soup*. While Peter Sellers and Goldie Hawn were locked in for the leads, supporting roles were available.

The conduit between the Boultings and Gordon Mills was Les Reed. Les had written the score for *Girl on a Motorcycle*, an Anglo-French erotic romp with Marianne Faithfull in a black leather jumpsuit and Alain Delon. British Lion were making a movie called *Les Bicyclettes de Belsize*. Les and Barry Mason had written the title song and Engelbert had agreed to sing it. The Boultings approached Les saying, 'We'd like to get our hands on Tom Jones, can we have lunch with Gordon?'

'I'm not sure they actually wanted Tom to star in the movie,' said Reed. 'I think they wanted a business deal, either some investment from MAM, or for MAM to take them over.'

The meeting took place at Wheelers fish restaurant in Old Compton Street, Soho. It went wrong from the start. Gordon was suffering from his ulcer. His face was pinched and pale and his comments were more acerbic than usual. In the restaurant toilets he told Les he was as sick as a dog and could not eat a thing.

'I told him to try,' said Reed. 'I told him, "The Boulting brothers are big people, they could give Tom a good part." '

Over lunch, the Boultings brought up the subject of takeovers. Gordon, in his arrogance and pain interrupted, 'Well what have you done?' This was not the most tactful remark to make to two of the major players in the British film industry. Ever the peacemaker, Les jumped in with, 'They've just made *Girl on a Motorcycle* with Marianne Faithfull and *The Family Way*.' John Boulting said, 'No, Les, we distributed that, we didn't actually make it. The last movie we made was *Twisted Nerve* with Hayley Mills and Hywel Bennett.'

The atmosphere deteriorated from bad to poisonous as Gordon drank more and more. There was no communication between the two parties, and what potentially could have been a historic union between pop music and film ended in social bickering when Gordon asked, 'Well, what's for pudding?' and John Boulting snapped, 'Don't you mean sweet?'

As Reed put it, 'That's when the deal finally went out of the window. The vibes were all wrong.' A great opportunity had been missed for both MAM and Tom. MAM never capitalised on the natural affinity between the two mediums. Thirty years later Tom has never played anyone other than himself in a feature film.

Following his American tour in 1969 Tom topped the bill at the Royal Variety Performance. After the show Tom was presented to the Queen and Prince Philip, who with his usual tact asked, 'What do you gargle with, pebbles?' Tom laughed it off, until the next day when the Prince managed to put his royal foot in it. At a lunch given for the Small Businesses Association, he said, 'Last night we went to the Royal Variety Performance. The last man to come on was Tom Jones. Now there is a young man of about twenty-five or something, worth probably about £3 million. It is very difficult to see how it is possible to become immensely valuable by singing what I think are most hideous songs. I would not say this about the Beatles.' The audience collapsed in sycophantic laughter, which the press gleefully reported.

Tom was livid and embarrassed. 'I was giving my services to charity,' he complained. 'What did he think it was – a bloody royal audition?' Chris Hutchins calmed him down, and Tom later issued a more anodyne statement to the papers.

'I don't know what happened,' he said diplomatically. 'The thing I was annoyed about was that the Prince ran down the whole show. It doesn't matter what he thinks about me, there are a lot of people who don't like my music. But the show is for charity. I wasn't doing an audition for the Duke. The show's got to be disjointed. You cannot look at the whole show because there are too many artists on stage and it's not like television.

'I pay a lot of taxes. I earn a lot of money for this country and I give my services to charity.'

When asked what he thought of the Royal Family, he replied, 'If the country can afford them I think they are a good thing.'

Prince Philip, for once aware of the situation, had Buckingham Palace officials write a letter to Tom disclaiming the remarks in apologetic if pompous terms. A year later, Tom did another charity show for the World Wildlife Fund at The Talk of the Town, and was invited to a cocktail party at the Palace. Philip, always one for plain talking, came straight over and said to Tom, 'Look, I would like to set the record straight. I was misquoted. What I said was that you sing so hard you must gargle with pebbles. But I am not criticising the sound. I just don't know how you do it.'

Tom, who was pretty chuffed to have extracted both a written and a verbal apology from the Prince, said later, 'He told me he wasn't criticising me but that he was at a small businessmen's meeting – they were warning that they couldn't make enough money, that they couldn't survive, and he said, "When somebody like Tom Jones comes along, when a man can make that sort of money, I don't see why you can't do it." He explained all that to me, and I thought it was very nice. He didn't have to.'

Gordon had renamed his sprawling mansion in East Road 'Little Rhondda', and ran his business from a small study on the ground floor. In contrast to Tom's, the house had very little furniture – Gordon hated extraneous clutter. Having escaped the city he disliked going into London, whether to visit MAM or to record.

He built a recording studio on the side of the house. And then he set about building a private zoo.

'Gordon loved animals. He had Great Danes,' said Larry Page, 'whacking great dogs, which would stand alongside me and just lick my ear as I sat there talking to Gordon. I understood the dogs, because they offered protection, but the zoo bit I never understood. People in the area were worried.'

The zoo was Gordon's two-fingered salute to the world. A statement that he had arrived as a multi-millionaire and was going to flaunt it in the most extravagant way. He was a regular at John Aspinall's private casino, the Clermont Club in Berkeley Square, but was never allowed to become one of the aristocratic inner circle, where Lord Lucan, society painter Dominic Elwes and Jimmy Goldsmith held court. Aspinall had two private zoos, at Howletts near Canterbury and Port Lympne on Romney Marsh where he bred rare Siberian tigers, gorillas, rhinos, leopards and other endangered species. Gordon was determined that his zoo would be better.

Gordon's zoo put him on an equal footing with Aspers', but it never made him a gentleman. In the early seventies Britain was still class-obsessed, and for all Gordon tried to cultivate the airs and affectations of the upper classes, to them he was always *nouveau riche*. He dressed immaculately, but in casual fashions not bespoke suits. He drank fine wines and dined on gourmet food, but those were not prerequisites for boys who had been brought up on nursery food and public school dining. Crucially his Welsh accent never quite disappeared. When he got agitated, the Valleys rushed into his mid-Atlantic drawl, marking him forever as an outsider. (Tom, on the other hand, has never had any illusions about who he is and where he came from.) America, where they judge a man on the colour of his money and the degree of his success rather than his breeding, was always Gordon's natural home.

The zoo had tigers, chimpanzees, orang-utans and Ollie, a one-eyed silverback gorilla, who preferred women so obviously that only Jo could go into his cage. Gordon and Jo loved their animals, nothing was too good for them. Nanci Eisner was dispatched to Korvettes in New York to buy disposable nappies for the baby orang-utans, who were given the run of the house. 'They didn't have Pampers in England at the time,' she recalled. 'I had to buy tons of them, and this woman looked at me and said, "Girl, you're not pregnant, what's the story?" When I tried to explain to her they were for a baby orang-utan in England, she looked at me like I was out of my mind.'

The animals became part of Gordon's party games. One time he caused havoc by installing two tiger cubs as attendants in the ladies' cloakroom. On New Year's Eve in 1972 he threw a huge party. Everybody was there: Tom, Linda, Engelbert, Pat, Gilbert O'Sullivan, Barry Mason and his girlfriend Sylvan and Troy Dante. They were all flying high on champagne, and decided it was time to visit the animals. Barry encouraged Gordon to go and hang out in the chimpanzee cage. Troy – the Face – volunteered instead.

'I'm an animal lover,' he said, 'so I went in with the chimp, who started getting very passionate. He locked himself round my leg and I had white trousers on at the time, and I will never forget it, he just ruined them. Everybody was having hysterics because Gordon closed the bloody cage and I couldn't get out.

'Unfortunately, no one was taking any notice of Ollie in the cage next door. Looking more and more like King Kong, he put his hand through the cage and grabbed Sylvan by her dress. Barry got hold of her arms and pulled her back. Ollie ripped her dress off and started swinging it round his head and going absolutely berserk. Needless to say, everybody stopped laughing because he nearly killed her.'

On another occasion Dante was over at Little Rhondda with

Barry, Sylvan, Leapy Lee and Tom. Gordon announced, 'I'm going to wind the Face up — he's to go in with the tigers today.' What Dante did not know was that Leapy had a big bet with Gordon that he would never do it.

'I never had a fear of tigers,' said Dante. 'I was convinced they wouldn't hurt me. I went in and the little ones were fine. It was great until their mother crept up behind me. I felt a cracking weight on my shoulders, and thought, "I mustn't fall down." But the mother was obviously quite big, and she pushed me down on the floor.'

Outside the cage Leapy was screaming, 'Get him out, they'll kill him!' Sylvan, who was a photographer, was calmly shooting a roll of film. Troy came out with nothing more than a few scratches on his arm. Tom, white-faced with shock, rounded on Gordon and said, 'You're bloody mad, Gordon, you'll kill him. He's mad, the Face, you know he's mad.'

While the animals all lived in extremely good conditions, tragedies — as John Aspinall has repeatedly discovered — come with private zoos. A few weeks after the incident with Sylvan's dress, the keeper was inside mucking out the cage and Ollie attacked him, nearly tore him to pieces. Gordon was furious. He rushed into the cage, punched Ollie on the nose and then repeatedly hit the gorilla over the head with a shovel until he let go of the unfortunate man. The keeper was very badly injured and in hospital for six months afterwards.

After that incident Gordon's interest in the zoo languished. With all his commitments, it was a toy he could not properly keep up. Coincidentally in 1975, John Aspinall sold the Clermont to invest more money in his animal collection. When Gordon made his final move to the States he had the largest private collection of orang-utans in the world. It was impossible to transfer the zoo to his new home. The good citizens of Beverly Hills were much less understanding than those of St George's Hill, and the arid climate of California would have made the animals extremely uncomfortable. So he donated all his primates to San Diego Zoo. One of his five gorillas promptly fathered the first baby born at the zoo in over twenty years. It was named Gordon.

After that he would get his wild animal fixes by going on African safaris with Jo, and once their marriage started to crumble, with Gog Jones and Johnny Spence. The bush was the only place he was ever still. He sat in the jungle for hours waiting and watching for gorillas. In many ways he was more comfortable with animals than with people. He discovered that while he loved wild animals he could not change them as he always had to do with humans. He respected them more.

The arrival of Gilbert O'Sullivan in Mills's galaxy in the early seventies should have improved the relationship between Enge and Tom. For all Pat Dorsey said to *Cosmopolitan* about how Tom and Engelbert and their respective families all went on holiday together, it was PR flannel. Pat and Enge had four young children. She hired nannies and staff so she was able to join her husband on the road. It never worried her seeing him perform.

What is strange is how their professional lives reversed their private ones. Enge has dozens of friends and acquaintances who play golf or darts with him and happily announce what a good fun bloke he is. Tom, on the other hand, has few close friends and no outside interests. But, no matter what they think of him, virtually everyone who has ever worked for Tom has nothing but admiration for his professionalism, while Enge is regularly described as a hypochondriac and a whiner, constantly in need of reassurance.

'We once did a test in the dressing room between Tom and Engelbert to see how they would react to being left alone,' remembered Nanci Eisner. 'They shut the inner door on Tom, who fell asleep. When he was called for his show, he got up and got dressed. Engelbert was out the door in ten seconds . . . he cannot be alone. Tom didn't care what anyone else was doing. He is probably one of the least insecure people I've ever met. Not just performers, people.'

It was Humperdinck who took umbrage, who believed he was getting poorer service from Gordon. Now his friend treated him like a meal ticket, even abused him in public. Once he reduced Enge to tears after the singer turned up late for a meeting.

'It wasn't my fault,' Engelbert explained, 'the car broke down.' 'Then why didn't you take a taxi?' retorted Mills. 'You're number one in the charts. Are you telling me you can't afford a taxi?'

Gordon always treated Tom better, gave him more attention, routined his shows, selected his material. Humperdinck was second – and when Gordon was making Gilbert's albums, a distant third. In 1968 Enge sold more records than Tom, but even after that he was still the other medallion man. 'He always used to complain to everybody who would listen to him that Tom was treated better,' said Ellis. 'He'd sit in the dressing room and say, "I'm not going on," and they really had to persuade him.'

Their rivalry took concrete form. Tom did get riled in 1969 when he and Chris Hutchins were listening to Humperdinck's latest album. 'Just listen to that bastard record,' said Tom. 'Just listen to it. That's *my* phrasing.' When Tom bought a Rolls-Royce and then a Phantom 6 limo, Enge followed suit. He even tried to drink Tom under the table.

'The problem,' recalled Chris Ellis with a grin, 'was that Humperdinck could only drink brandy. Tom could drink anything.' One night Engelbert and Pat were over at the Woodwards'. Engelbert looked at his double vodka and said, 'Bit mean with the drink aren't you, Tom?' Tom poured vodka to the top of the glass and kept on doing so until his colleague passed out. Tom carried him out to the car, took him home, and helped him to bed.

Tom was always happy with his dual identity, as 'Tom Jones' and 'Tom Woodward'. Engelbert apparently was not. Having finally accepted his new identity he erased the old one from his life and his memory. He refused to open any letters addressed to Gerry Dorsey, or even answer to the name.

In July 1973 when the relationship between the two was really grim, a darts match was arranged between them. Enge was playing in Lake Tahoe and Tom was at the Circus Star Theatre in San Francisco, so they met up halfway, in a pub in Sacramento in the early hours of the morning. Enge flew in on a private jet, while Tom and his crew went by road. Enge was the better darts player, but Tom had one advantage.

'Tom wasn't drinking at the time, he had the clap and was on antibiotics,' said Ellis. 'Everybody else was drunk and throwing badly. Humperdinck and his team won the first match, we won the second and eventually we managed to win the decider. It was very, very serious, a real battle of the giants. Humperdinck was not pleased he got beat.' Chris Hutchins, however, recalled Enge winning.

Soon after the medallion men and their manager moved into St George's Hill, it became apparent that neither of the singers was going to spend much time there. When *This is Tom Jones* was cancelled in 1971 even staying at home those thirteen weeks a year became unnecessary. America could not get enough of Tom and that was where the big money was. He concentrated less on recording and more on live work – the bestselling album *Live at Caesars Palace* managed to combine the two. His UK tour of 1972 was to be his last for eleven years. The tax man made sure of that.

Originally MAM had been a tax efficient way of writing off a lot of expenses, and dividends were taxed at a lower rate. What nobody had envisaged was that ninety per cent of his income would be earned abroad. All the earnings from record sales, tours and lucrative Vegas seasons was returned to Britain and channelled into MAM. The money he received from MAM in the form of dividends was more heavily taxed than normal earnings. It was classed as unearned income on which, at the height of the Labour government, he had to pay 98p in the £1.

In February 1974 Bill Smith told Tom he could not afford to come home, a bad situation compounded after Labour won the General Election. The maths made no sense. If Tom earned $1 million playing Vegas, the US Government held on to fifteen per cent. In Britain Tom paid income tax of eighty-four per cent on the remainder, and ninety-eight per cent on any dividends he received from MAM. Because of the way Tom's tax affairs were organised he could not come back to the UK. The moment he stepped off an aircraft on to British soil he became liable for a tax bill that would sweep away most of his fortune. From 1974 Tom was basically homeless.

For the previous two years his time in the States had been perpetually interrupted. Because he could only spend 180 days a year there, every tax day saved equalled a small fortune. Every effort was made to get Tom out of the country by midnight. Any break in the schedule, no matter how small, and he would be shipped out to Bermuda, Barbados, the Caymans, Acapulco or cruising outside the twelve-mile limit after chartering John Wayne's boat, the *Wild Goose*, a converted minesweeper.

'For years,' said Ellis, 'we wandered around the world. I was away for eleven months of the year. At Christmas I would go into Barbados, dump Tom there and take the passports back to London. I was given power of attorney to get his passports at the American Embassy, then in the New Year I would head back out to Barbados, and then off we'd go again. Tom got really fed up.'

Especially at Christmas – family time. 'If it wasn't for the fact that I'd be committing economic suicide by returning home, I'd be there like a shot,' said Tom at the time. 'You could keep all the sunshine and plush suites and give me some Christmas pud and a pint with the lads in the local. I really am very homesick and at Christmas it gets almost unbearable.'

On 13 September 1974 Tom checked in secretly to the Beverly Glen Hospital on West Pico Boulevard in Los Angeles. The following afternoon at 5 p.m. Dr Franklin L. Ashley, a plastic surgeon, operated to remove fatty deposits that were building up underneath the singer's chin. The bill was $6,000. Three weeks later, on 10 October, Tom flew to Barbados to recuperate. He hired a house in Holetown near the golf course and invited out the whole family – Tom and Freda, Sheila, Vi Trenchard, Chris Ellis and Eva. It was, Ellis recalled, a very happy holiday. Linda was relaxed because her mother was there, while Tom even grew a beard for anonymity – it also helped to hide the pink scars. Everyone stayed there until 8 November.

'It was a lovely house, big swimming pool, eight bedrooms, a cook and a cleaner,' he said. 'Linda loved jumping in the pool with her mum, and Mark was a real devil with her, you know, splashing her in the pool. When she was lying on a sunbed in the pool Mark would get underneath and tip her off into the water. Vi was a barrel of fun, great sense of humour. Really, really funny. And Linda loved having her out there with her.

'We had lots of fun, we were in a normal family house. Everyone sat down for dinner together but as soon as dinner was over, it was like, "Right, let's go out." Tom would drag off his father, Mark and myself, and we'd leave the wives behind and off we'd go and play darts. Jump in the Mini Moke and off we'd go to a pub called the Coconut Creek, down the road, and stay there and play darts until 3 o'clock in the morning.'

The only solution to Tom's homesickness was for him to apply for a Green Card and become an American resident. 'If I had been living in England I would have paid all the tax – no problem,' he said in 1976. 'But I was working in America so much, going home for such a short time and then paying all that tax was pointless and I was advised to stay out. I was in limbo for a while before I decided to become an American resident. I couldn't come to England at all, and at the same time I couldn't stay in America for more than six months at a stretch, or they would have hit me with more tax plus the English tax. I was like a gypsy.

'Before, the government used to tax us only on a certain portion of money earned outside the country. Now they want a bite of the rest. It really makes my blood boil because most of my earnings are made abroad. I don't like the hand I've been forced to play [getting a Green Card], but what can I do? They've got me by the you-know-what and there's nothing I can do. I love Britain and I love living there. After all, it's home, but I've been forced into exile. When I get my Green Card I'll be able to visit Britain for three months every year, but I still won't be able to work.

'The British tax men are absolutely daft, they're cutting their own throats and they don't seem to realise it. I would be quite happy to pay fifty per cent of my income in taxes. The way things are now the government is getting Sweet Fanny Adams. I just don't understand them.'

Tom's relationship with money has always been strange. He seldom carries cash. Said Ellis, 'As far as he's concerned, it's all invisible money, he doesn't want for anything. Most of the time when we were out he never had any money. I had his money, he was like the Queen of England. As long as Tom didn't have to put his hands in his pocket and actually pull out hard cash and pay for a meal, he was content. It didn't matter if I paid for it with his money. But if he had to do it himself, that he didn't like at all.

'One day we went out shopping in Acapulco to buy gold, and he bought loads of it. But it was me who was pulling out the traveller's cheques to pay for everything. As long as he could sign his name, it was like an autograph. It wasn't money, it wasn't hard cash.'

Tom's Midas heel has always been for gold and jewellery. Dealers used to come into his dressing room in Vegas with trays and seldom left without making a sale. Yet at the same time Tom was very tight when it came to tipping. Waiters, who restocked the bar on his dressing room or brought him breakfast, never got cash as was the custom. Instead their tip was added to the bill — which the hotel paid.

When Chris Ellis married his long-term Swedish girlfriend, Eva, in Las Vegas on 18 September 1973, Tom was the best man, Linda the bridesmaid. After the ceremony they returned to Caesars and went to the bar. Tom put a case of champagne on the table and proceeded to drink most of it himself. At 4 a.m. Frank Sinatra, who was around the corner playing the tables, wished them good luck. The hotel gave Chris and Eva a car for a couple of days. Despite Chris's years of service Tom never gave the couple a wedding present.

Tom was not alone in resenting the iniquities of the tax system. It was a misguided attempt to redistribute wealth that only succeeded in driving high-earning entertainers into what for many became permanent tax exile. Once he made the decision to become an American resident his finances became much easier to control. He and Engelbert won their long battle with the IRS over the withholding of their money and they received several million dollars. In the UK financial advisors had worked out how to deal with the problem.

'It was horrendous, because anyone who started to make any real money would immediately leave the country,' said Paul Russell. 'There were odd things that existed at the time, where if you worked so many days outside the UK, you could apportion part of your income and you'd pay less tax on that. Everyone had split contracts: you had a contract for UK services and a contract for ex-UK services.

'In the case of artists that was very easy: all foreign royalties were foreign earnings, all UK royalties were UK earnings. It was very simple and the only way to get out of the 90 per cent tax issue. Financially it was very significant.'

What it did mean was that Tom Jones no longer lived in Britain. And that a lot of his income no longer went direct to MAM. He bought Dean Martin's old house, at 363 Copa d'Oro in Bel Air, for $1 million. Linda did not want to move to LA, but she was fed up with meeting her husband for snatched weekends in France or Belgium.

In June 1976 the furniture in Tor Point was shipped to LA and the house put up for sale. The asking price was £350,000. Linda must have been glad when the electric gates closed behind her for the last time. It had never been a happy home for her.

• CHAPTER SIXTEEN •

MISS WORLD

———————

I n late 1973 Tom Jones embarked on what was to become the
most public scandal of his career. What began as an attempt
to get one over on Engelbert ended up as a jet-set soap opera.
It involved four major celebrities, a fatal car crash and a suicide
attempt. The British tabloid newspapers had such a field day that
even Linda, locked inside Tor Point, could not have escaped the
story.

The catalyst for the whole drama was Marjorie Wallace, a
nineteen-year-old beauty queen from Indianapolis, who was
crowned Miss World in November 1973. Back then the Miss World
competition was a big deal, front page news. The newly crowned
Miss World was tightly controlled by Julia Morley of Mecca
Entertainment. Like a prospective royal bride she was expected to
be demure (tricky parading in a tight-cut swimsuit), preferably a
virgin, to possess the IQ and expectations of a Barbie doll and the
smile of a saint.

Marji always had a different agenda. Already the girlfriend of Formula One racing driver Peter Revson, she was no Midwestern ingénue. Instead she was determined to make the most of her time in the media spotlight. At the Miss World ball she danced with British heavyweight champion Joe Bugner. Engelbert Humperdinck, one of the judges, made sure his photo was on the front pages the next morning by kissing her full on the lips. Enge was clearly taken with her and invited Marji to his show at the Palladium a few days later.

Because Enge was chasing her, Tom's natural competitive instincts took over. He got on to Chris Hutchins and told him, 'You've got to fix me up with her.' A month later she came to see him in his dressing room at the Palladium. He joked, 'Do I have to get down on my knees for you?' She retorted, 'I thought you already were.' Sparks flew between the two of them, and later that night she joined him at his London hotel.

In February 1974 they both flew to Barbados to film a BBC TV special *Tom Jones on Happiness Island*. The script, such as it was, called for the two to stroll hand in hand along a beach lined with palm trees. Tom was to sing the hit song *I Want to Make it With You* to her, and then kiss her passionately. Julia Morley, officially Miss World's chaperone though she treated them more like employees, put her foot down and banned such intimate contact. Marji went ahead regardless. Terry O'Neill's pictures of the kiss made front pages all over the world. Everybody naturally assumed that Tom and Marji were having a serious affair.

They were, though Marji continually denied it, telling the *News of the World*, 'that kiss was as close as Tom and I ever got, or wanted to get throughout our week in Barbados'.

However, Chris Ellis recalled, 'They got together at a hotel in London, it got more serious the closer we were getting to going to Barbados, and, of course, Linda had got wind of it as well. So she wasn't too happy that Tom was jetting off with her. He told Linda, "It's just a television show, she's not on the same plane as me. I'm on one side of the island and she's in a hotel on the other side, they're keeping us miles apart. They won't even let us get near each other, so you haven't got to worry."

'Of course, she was on the same plane, and they kissed and cuddled all the way from London to Barbados. The BBC had rented a house for Tom, and they were both living in it. I was living in the same house. That's where the romance really blossomed.'

Tom already liked Marji enough to buy her a birthday present. In January he had asked Chris Hutchins to go shopping with him. 'Whose birthday?' he asked. 'Linda's,' replied Tom. 'And Marji's.' Linda was thirty-four on 14 January. Marji was twenty nine days later. They went to a jeweller's shop in Richmond, Surrey, where Tom chose two bracelets. One was made of cultured pearls and cost £220. The other was in gold and pearls for £416. Marji got the cheaper bracelet though Tom later gave her a mink coat as well. 'Evie Fay, a woman from Manchester, who knew a lot of jewellers and people like that, got this coat for Tom,' recalled Nanci Eisner. 'I remember it coming to the office in a box, and I shipped it to Marjorie Wallace. It was unusual for Tom to feel he actually wanted to give someone a present.'

Back in London, while Tom was gigging in Amsterdam, Marji got herself entangled with George Best. In his prime the Ulster-born Best was the greatest footballer in the world, but his talents on the pitch were matched by a self-destructive streak off it. He loved booze and beautiful women — in that order. What actually happened between them is a mystery, but Marji reported he had stolen her fur coat and jewellery. In the tabloid frenzy that followed, gossip columnists reported that her diary, in which she rated her lovers, had gone missing. Tom apparently scored a nine, while George only mustered a three. In the subsequent court case, in which Best was acquitted, he claimed that though they were lovers she was still playing the field and had even phoned Peter Revson, while he was in the room.

Tom, no stranger to bedroom chicanery himself, always believed Marji's story and offered to go round and beat Best up. Mecca, meanwhile, had had enough and stripped Marji of her title. Two weeks later Peter Revson was killed while racing in South Africa. Marji soon bounced back from this savage one-two and fixed her sights firmly on Tom.

The affair reached its dramatic crescendo in May and June. Tom arrived in LA on 7 May; Marji had flown in to stay with Revson's sister Jennifer and brought her along to a lunch party at Le Bistro. 'She [Marji] told me Tom Jones was a friend – just a friend, nothing more – and I believed her,' said Jennifer Revson. 'She wanted me to meet Tom and his entourage, and a crowd of about nine or ten of us went to a restaurant in Beverly Hills for lunch. It turned out to be a nightmare of a meal.

'Tom kept talking about his career, and Gordon Mills, his manager, seemed mesmerised by how much money he'd made. Honestly, it was a colossal bore. They just weren't my type of people at all.

'Tom and Marji kept kissing each other full on the lips with arms entwined. It was quite obvious that Marji had not told me everything about her friendship with Tom. We stayed in the restaurant from lunchtime until 2 a.m., when Marji asked me to drive her back to the house Tom had rented. When we got there we had a drink and I turned to Marji and said, "I think it's time we headed home." She gazed at me calmly and announced, "You can go home but I'm staying here." '

Soon afterwards Tom moved to Las Vegas for his season at Caesars Palace. Tom and Chris were staying in a house Caesars owned behind the Desert Inn golf course. It was very secluded with its own pool, and Chris put silver paper up on all of the windows to stop the sun coming in.

'We were like the odd couple living in there,' said Ellis. 'I'd get up about 12 o'clock and sit by the pool, and I wouldn't see Tom until 3 or 4 o'clock in the afternoon. He'd get up and say, "I'll have my bacon and eggs now please." Then I'd drive him over to Caesars Palace where he would pop into the health club. After the show we'd go into the hotel kitchen and steal all the steaks, then have barbecues at 4 o'clock in the morning with Susan George and her boyfriend Jack Jones.'

Marji joined them. She was seen with Tom frequently in his dressing room, in his limousine. Chris Hutchins warned Tom it was too open, tongues were wagging. He paid attention. 'Marjorie Wallace was living in the house, until the big crunch came,' said Ellis. 'She had given an ultimatum, "Who's it going to be? Me or Linda?" That's when Tom gets really scared, that's when he really starts thinking. I think if he ever lost Linda, he'd be totally lost. Tom told Marji that it was over and she had to leave. I drove her out to the airport. She was crying. I put her on the plane and there was a big tearful goodbye, she was hugging me, and she said, "I love Tom." '

Marji had not left empty-handed. When Tom was preparing for bed at dawn the next morning he went to take a sleeping pill and noticed that his bottle of Mogadon was missing. Two days later the phone rang. It was Marji's family in Indianapolis. 'I spoke to her sisters, who asked me, "What the hell has she taken?" They were walking her about,' said Ellis, 'trying to wake her up. She was out cold, so eventually they had to take her to hospital and pump her stomach out.'

Marji was in a coma for two days and in intensive care for a week. The press happily speculated that she had tried to commit suicide because her relationship with Tom had ended. Her family insisted the pair were just good friends. A press release was issued. 'Tom is very happy that Marji is getting better and feels that things are being said about her character when she is not in a position to defend herself.' Tom sent her a get-well telegram, and then threw a thirty-fourth birthday party at Caesars, which was attended by Liberace, Joan Rivers, Sonny Bono, Dionne Warwick and Debbie Reynolds.

For the first six months of 1974 Marji had been living on an emotional rollercoaster. She was only twenty, and she was playing with international superstars not small-town boys. She might have been at the end of her tether, but her suicide bid could also have been an attempt at changing Tom's mind. He has never been swayed by dramatic gestures. However, that was not the end of the romance. The pair were more discreet, but they continued to meet in secret.

Some months after the overdose Tom and Chris flew to Acapulco and rented a house in the exclusive Las Brusas Estates high up on the cliffs overlooking Acapulco bay. Ellis picked Marji up from the airport the following day and she stayed with Tom for the next three days. On another occasion Tom, Chris and Dai Perry were staying in a white clapboard house on the beach in Bermuda. Marji joined them and repaired to the bedroom with Tom. The walls were paper thin and the couple soon attracted a Welsh chorus.

'Tom was in the bedroom giving her one,' recalled Ellis, 'and we were all outside the door singing, "I'm sitting on top of Miss World." Tom was swearing at us to go away, but Marjorie Wallace thought it was very funny. I could hear her laughing. She had a great sense of humour.'

Marji also joined him for an excursion on the *Wild Goose*. It was moored at Newport Beach so the crew could escape Vegas and be in international waters by 9 a.m. The boat would then cruise around for a couple of days, while Tom and his friends mucked about on speedboats or put ashore on Catalina Island.

Another visitor on board the *Wild Goose* was Pamela Sue Martin. Within a few years she was a major TV star, first as the heroine of *The Nancy Drew Mysteries* and then as Fallon in *Dynasty*.

'We went out on the boat for four or five days,' said Ellis. 'We didn't see very much of her actually, perhaps he was frightened we might jump on her. She was only eighteen or nineteen, a very quiet girl.'

Tom's affair with Marjorie Wallace lasted for two years on and off. While he was very smitten with her, in the long term she was never going to settle for being a secret mistress. Her next boyfriend was tennis star Jimmy Connors.

For Tom, the affair marked the high point of his global fame. His career was just beginning its twelve-year decline. Tom did not know it yet. He was sleeping in the mink-lined coffin of Las Vegas, secure in its neon embrace.

CHAPTER SEVENTEEN

THE MINK-LINED COFFIN

I n 1978 gambling was made legal in Atlantic City. The crumbling boardwalk was restored to play host to bigger stars. It attracted a different clientele from Vegas, with fifty million people living within a six-hour drive, so hotels like Resorts International could offer higher fees – Dolly Parton was paid $350,000 for a week, Frank was earning $50,000 a show. Tom was not far behind.

A reporter from *Time* magazine asked Tom what was the big difference between Atlantic City and Las Vegas. 'Everyone,' said Nanci Eisner, 'held their breath because they didn't know if he'd say the right thing or not. He really thought about it for about thirty seconds, and he just turned to the guy and said, "Humidity." ' To Tom that was the answer to the question, because though he is careful with his money, it has never been his driving motivation. Singing is.

Tom's biggest concern in Vegas had always been the air. It

dried out his voice so badly that a couple of his big ballads were dropped from the set. Air-conditioning exacerbated the problem so it was turned off in his suite. Instead, half a dozen humidifiers sprayed water into the air. Outside, the temperature could reach 110 degrees, so entering Tom's room was like venturing into a tropical rainforest. It never worried him.

In Las Vegas Tom developed a routine which has hardly changed in thirty years. He rose late, never much before 3 p.m., and had his breakfast wearing a hotel towelling robe. The bacon and eggs of his early years gradually gave way to healthier alternatives. When everybody else was obsessed with ingesting narcotics, Tom watched what he ate. Unlike Elvis he always refused chemical assistance to keep his weight down. Forget fads. The only way to lose weight and keep it off is to eat a sensible diet and take exercise. It requires an iron will and self-discipline.

'I eat only two meals a day — breakfast and dinner,' said Tom in 1976. 'I'm pretty careful about what I eat, too. I breakfast on steak and eggs — plenty of protein, nothing fattening — and then go straight for a work-out. It's important to prepare myself physically.

'After breakfast I take steam or sauna to sweat out the alcohol from the night before, then have a good massage for at least two hours. It's like training for a prizefight. The two shows I do every night, seven nights a week, are each as physically demanding as a fight. I have to be prepared for them. There's no need for mental preparation. The words of the song and the reaction of the audience make that instinctive.'

A former boxer, who ran the health club at Caesars, was the first person to tell Tom he must go to the steam bath to protect his voice. As soon as he walked into the steam room at 5 p.m. everyone else ran out complaining, 'The man's crazy.' Tom turned the heat up full and chucked water everywhere, creating dense clouds of boiling steam. After the steam Tom had a two-hour massage, any tight muscles being pummelled into submission.

In the seventies the Vegas norm was two shows a night, seven nights a week, for fourteen days. At Caesars, Circus Maximus shows were 7.30 p.m. and 11 p.m. Showtime for Tom was about 8.45. Pat Henry warmed the crowd up for half an hour, until he heard two bangs from behind the curtain. That was the signal to wind up, perhaps by telling the lady in the front row, 'From where you're sitting, if Tom's got a quarter in his pocket you can tell if it's heads or tails . . . you can also tell if he's Jewish or not.' The band were all ready to go on stage, and the Blossoms would open up with fifteen minutes of soul classics.

To Tom Jones singing is a very simple business. Going on stage at Caesars Palace was no big deal. He arrived in his dressing room in time – often as late as 8.30 – to put the stage make-up on, to pull on his boots and his tux. He did not sit in the dressing room gargling and doing singing exercises. Five minutes before showtime Chris knocked on the door and, everything ready, with Tom mumbling, 'Oh, here we go again', like he was going on a shift down the pit, he stumbled out of the door half asleep.

Which was where the transformation began. As he heard the band strike up the opening theme the shuffle stopped, his back straightened, the walk became a strut, hips swinging, pelvis grinding, fingers clicking soundlessly. At the side of the stage the stage manager handed him a microphone and, fully transformed, he burst on to the stage for seventy sweaty minutes.

Every evening Tom came out he would address the audience, 'Good evening ladies, and good evening gentlemen.' Certain nights when he said. 'Good evening ladies,' two Welsh voices replied, 'Good evening, Tom' – his mum and his sister. One night when he said, 'Good evening ladies,' there was no response, so he started worrying, until they rushed in having been delayed at an earlier show.

On stage Tom drank a minimum of eight glasses of water. 'I once weighed myself before and after a concert and found I'd lost six pounds,' he said. The level and energy of Tom's performance meant he came off stage with his clothes completely drenched in sweat. To help rehydrate his body he then spent a minimum of half an hour under the shower, however pressing his later engagements or the people waiting in the dressing room might be. Sometimes when his voice was bad he would drink only water for a month – but he still stayed up until 7 a.m.

The star dressing room of the Circus Maximus was as well appointed as his suite. The dressing room was divided into two parts. The outer part for guests, with a fully stocked bar, couches and a table with food on. Tom's inner sanctum was smaller, with a shower, comfortable chairs, a full-length mirror and a bed that he christened 'the workbench'. Concerned that Linda might come in and catch him working out, Tom decided that he should have a concealed escape door built behind the mirror. Chris Ellis conveyed the star's request to the stage manager, who, after years in which he thought he had heard everything, thought it was a joke and said, 'Tell him to behave himself.'

Early in the evening room service would come down and replenish the drink. There were two fridges, one full of vintage Dom Perignon for Tom, the other with non-vintage for everybody else. Every night fresh smoked salmon *canapés* and caviar were provided for the guests. Tom was afforded the privileges given only to the top flight performers: he could have anything he wanted – within reason.

Tom never drank alcohol before a performance. Nothing was allowed to stand in the way of delivering his best. He only ever cancelled a show if he was genuinely too ill to sing. Gordon Mills seldom missed a show in Vegas. He'd wait with Tom in the dressing room, then watch the show from the wings or from his booth fifteen feet from centre stage. Gordon kept his eyes and ears on everything, from sound and lights to the singer's banter between numbers. 'Keep it short,' he'd tell Tom, 'they've come to see you sing, not tell jokes.'

In the early days after the first show, Tom had a quick shower, and rushed out to the stage door parking lot where Charles Mather waited in his convertible Cadillac Eldorado. Mather, who managed Lovelace Watkins and boasted that he had a better locker than Moe Dalitz at the Las Vegas Country Club, was a Vegas insider.

'After his first set Tom would come out and we'd tear up and down the Strip, going to the different lounges to see the different entertainers, like the Kim Sisters, Nancy Wilson and Don Rickles. It was fun, a relaxation for him. Tom was very strict about not drinking, he'd just have a soft drink or a cup of coffee. We'd wait until the last minute and race back like mad.

'He'd charge into the dressing room, and who'd be standing there but Gordon, who would shout at us like a couple of schoolboys, "Where have you been? You should know better, you're a manager." After the second show we'd go and have dinner — usually in the gourmet dining room of a hotel. They would keep it open especially for him. We'd be the only people in there, and they'd keep a chef on for our party.'

After his second show, Tom would spend even longer in the shower, because he had to wash his socks. 'Every night,' said Ellis, 'there would be socks hanging everywhere. Tom washed them in the shower. He would strip the suit and shirt off and then wash his socks and underpants, then he'd hang them up. Then they would be there for the next night. He'd wear clean ones for the second performance, and the next night the same ones would go on again. He had three or four pairs going round at a time.'

Savile Row tailor, Robbie Stanford, regularly flew out to America to measure Tom. He would make six mohair tuxedos, with the trousers cut extremely tight. There would always be four revolving. Two would get absolutely soaked every night and would eventually split and rot because they had to go to the dry cleaners so much. Ellis always kept two new tuxes in reserve.

By this point Ellis had learnt enough to let celebrities into the dressing room. At the Flamingo he had turned everybody away, having no idea who they were. 'It is very much the done thing in Las Vegas, a compliment to the artist,' he laughed. 'And I managed to tell them all to go away, not very politely. It became very embarrassing, because these talk-show hosts and film stars would go back and phone their agents, and tell them, "There's a guy working for Tom Jones, and when you knock on the door he tells you to piss off."

'One night there was a knock on the door. Edward G. Robinson was standing there with a stunningly beautiful woman, at least twice as tall as him and half his age. I recognised him, so I said, "Hello, Mr Robinson, come on in." Tom was in the shower, so I shouted into the shower, "Tom, Edward G. Robinson's here to see you." Tom shouts back, "Fuck off, he's dead."

'I went red. I turned round, said, "I'm very sorry," and he said, "It's OK, everybody thinks I'm dead." When Tom came out, he was embarrassed to hell.'

Outside, in the dressing room, the usual suspects gathered, drinking champagne – friends, record company and Vegas business associates, other stars, fan club members, sometimes family, and if there was no family, girls. Girls spotted and plucked from the audience or brought along and presented to see if they tickled the star's palate. 'He'd like the women,' said Chas del Guercio, now stage manager at the Circus Maximus, 'so he stayed in his dressing room and had a lot of lovely ladies coming back. They had to have a pass but that was easily arranged.'

Often there were fan club organisers desperate to meet Tom.

'Some of the fan club ladies were a pain in the neck,' said Ellis. 'He would go, "Hello, girls, how are you? Lovely to see you, what do you want?" and then throw a look at me that said, "Get them out of here." He was Mr Nice Guy, and I was the arsehole.

'Tom's behaviour towards women was always very courteous. If girls got drunk and started getting obnoxious, I would get the nod or he would shout "hatchet" to me. I was known as the hatchet man. If somebody was getting out of order he shouted "Get the hook" and I had to get them out of the room. That was as angry as he got.'

Many nights at Caesars they ate in the dressing room, partying until 6 or 7 a.m. Another favourite hangout was an Italian restaurant up the street called the Leaning Tower of Pizza. Dinner seldom started before 2 a.m. It was in the gourmet restaurants of Vegas that Tom completed his education in fine foods and wine. He left steak and stodge behind to sample grilled prawns, frogs' legs, escargots, caviar, smoked salmon rolled with caviar, langoustine flown in from France, rack of lamb, sweetbreads, all the finest dishes from classical French cuisine. 'He liked to try every dish we could prepare for him,' gushed Ilario Pesco, now the *maître d'* at Gi Gi in Bally's. 'He is a food connoisseur. Mr Jones has very great taste.'

Guided by Gordon, who had a particular penchant for Petrus, Mouton Rothschild and Château Lafitte, and with a free run at a cellar, Tom would make sure that vintage wines flowed until dawn. As far as Tom was concerned, if it was expensive it was good, so he would order the name of a wine he liked without caring what year it was. The night was finished off with copious brandies, and then Tom would retire, sometimes alone, more often with his chosen companion.

Las Vegas brought out the worst in Gordon Mills. At Caesars he was treated like a Roman emperor and whenever possible he behaved like one. He loved to appear escorting Anne Marie and Aase Brekke on each arm. The girls were identical twins, who both worked for Pan Am as stewardesses. Tom christened them 'the bookends'. While Tom would have loved to try his luck with them, he always left well alone. Gordon never let them out of his sight, and whisked them off as soon as he had made his impact. Presumably Gordon could tell the girls apart as Anne Marie was his regular girlfriend until 1982, while Aase eventually married Gilbert O'Sullivan.

There was a mean streak to Gordon. He had his assistant, Gog Jones, change dollar bills into coins, as he refused to tip bellboys and room service waiters more than a quarter. He treated Ellis and Dai Perry with cold contempt. 'Sometimes you wouldn't see him for three months, and then he'd suddenly show up in Vegas,' said Chris. 'I would open the door and he would ignore me. To speak to me or Dai Perry was lowering himself, so he wouldn't talk to us, he would just come in and grunt, "Where's Tom?" and he'd go straight in to Tom. There was no real warm greeting between them either. Tom just did everything that Gordon told him to do.'

Gordon spoke down to all his artists. Tom kept taking it right until the end. He would mumble, 'But Gordon,' to which the reply came, 'Don't Gordon me, this is what we are going to do.' Gordon liked to employ the royal 'we'. Gordon needed to dominate proceedings, while Tom seldom stood in the middle of the room holding court. While not exactly shy, Tom was wary of people. It was difficult for an outsider to get near him, or gain his confidence. He loved to hear people talk and to get into arguments. Tom and Gordon would argue about politics, gun laws, all kinds of things, well into the night, until there was nothing left to argue about.

Occasionally Mills would overreach himself. 'We were in the dressing room at Caesars once when Tom and Gordon started having a serious heated argument,' said Ellis. 'They used to argue a lot so I didn't take a lot of notice of what was going on, but all of a sudden Gordon jumps up and says, "I don't fucking need you, I can do everything myself."

'Tom started laughing at him, "What do you mean you can do everything yourself? There's a midnight show in half an hour, are you going to go out and sing for me? Are you going to be Tom Jones at midnight?" Gordon actually believed what he was saying. It was the most ridiculous statement. Gordon was convinced that he could go on at midnight and be Tom Jones. The man had an ego like you could not believe. When he came into town, everybody was supposed to knuckle down and bow down to him and polish his boots.'

While Mills was used to getting his own way there were certain people he was wary of. One was the *Las Vegas Review Journal* columnist Joe Delaney. 'My first dealings with Gordon Mills was a fight over the decibel level of Tom's shows at the Flamingo,' said Delaney. 'I told him they were way too loud, and Mills told me to mind my own business. So I complained to the Office of Safety Hazards Administration. They came round to the Flamingo with an audiometer which registered 105 decibels. He was fined $12,500. For years after that, whenever Tom was playing at Caesars Palace, he had someone in his employ at the casino whose job was to warn the stage manager whenever I came in. The sound was always turned down which was much more pleasurable for me and the audience.'

Nor was Mills always as sharp as he pretended to be. In the early seventies, promoting a Tom Jones show in North America was a licence to print money. Mills got talking with some gentlemen from Montreal and promised them Tom would do a show north of the border. They took him at his word and started inquiring as to when the singer would be available. Gordon told them he had not signed any contract. The reply came back that if Tom didn't come to Canada they would come and get him.

Mills promptly sent Norman Weiss, from CMA, north of the border. He was told, 'It's a verbal contract, he's going to come here and he's going to play for us.' Weiss, smart enough to know when he was dealing with organised crime, came back and told Gordon, 'He's going to play . . . or you are going to pay.'

Despite everything, Tom was fiercely loyal to his manager. In 1970 he nearly fell out with his idol Jerry Lee Lewis over Gordon. 'We were getting along fine, when suddenly he insulted my manager,' said Tom. 'Jerry Lee said he'd have to send a friend of his to sort my manager out. I told him that he would have to sort me out. I wasn't having that, so I said, "Before you have a go at my manager, why don't you try having a go at me?" So Jerry Lee gets up swinging a champagne bottle, going, "You motherfucker, you faggot, I'll kick your ass!" I'm like, "Come on then. You try and use that champagne bottle on me, I'll ram it up your fucking arse!"

'Jerry Lee phoned me next day and said, "Tom, what happened last night? Let's meet and have a friendly drink." I said, "Only if you promise not to talk showbusiness," and at that he sang the first lines of one of his early hits, "Come on let's talk about us."

'I fell about laughing at that, and we've been pals ever since.'

Like any good Welsh boy, Tom was an admirer of Tommy Farr and loved to watch boxing. Both he and Gordon became very friendly with Gene Kilroy, who worked with the Philadelphia Eagles and then for Muhammad Ali. In 1974, when Ali was preparing for the famous Rumble in the Jungle with Joe Frazier in Zaire, they flew up in a private jet to his training camp in Deer Lake, Pennsylvania.

'Ali talked Tom into sparring with him,' said Kilroy, who now works for the MGM Grand. 'Tom's a pretty tough guy, he could really go in a street fight. Ali was sparring and said, "Hit me." So Tom hit Ali and Ali took the fall, went down, Tom laughed about it and everything, then we started to get fan mail telling Ali, "You'd better retire, Tom Jones knocked you down. Get out of boxing, you've been in there too long now." A lot of people thought it was serious.'

Six years later Tom, accompanied by his father, was back sparring in the ring as Ali was preparing for his fight with Larry Holmes. After two rounds Ali accidentally hit Tom on the mouth and drew blood. Tom shouted, 'I've got a thousand dollars' worth of capped teeth.' That night, Ali drove him back to Atlantic City and attended his show. 'I am very honoured that Muhammad would break training to come and see me do my thing,' Tom said. 'I am also very happy that during the two rounds we sparred he didn't have murder on his mind, because in the excitement of it all I forgot to ask for a mouthpiece to protect my capped teeth . . . my front teeth almost took a count of ten on the floor.'

Throughout the seventies Tom Jones was consistently one of the highest earning performers in Vegas. By 1970 he was earning $125,000 a week, and once Caesars had poached him from the International, he joined the select band of performers – Sinatra, Presley and Streisand – on 'favoured nation' status. The casino undertook to match an improvement in salary or perks that any other Vegas headliner might get. By 1973 his salary was up to $160,000, earning him $4,480,000 for a fourteen-week season. Vegas had other financial attractions. It was all very well playing Madison Square Gardens, but in New York State there was a stage tax of six per cent of the gross, and Tom had to pay all the equipment and hotel costs for his crew. In the desert, everything was found for free.

The hotels picked up an agreed amount of the costs, put the artist up in the hotel (the musicians were shipped out to a hotel off the Strip) and comped them to various levels. While this may seem generous, it's actually very tax efficient. The exotic penthouse suite that Tom inhabited at Caesars would be hired out to a paying guest at $1,500 per day. The actual cost to the hotel of running the room per day was maybe $150, the rest, $1,350, was offset against tax. It is the same with the dinners: the actual cost of the $5,000 bill, even including several bottles of Petrus, was under $1,000; the remainder was a tax write-off.

What the casinos liked best of all was to get their money back on the tables. Hooking a star meant free entertainment. Tom and Elvis had one thing in common: their managers loved to gamble. They didn't. Even if he had been interested, Presley could never play the public tables. The fans would have mobbed him instantly and disrupted gaming (the most heinous crime in town). It was the same for Tom. He never saw the point. One day he was walking across the floor at Caesars with Nanci Eisner. She found a quarter on the floor, and gave it to Tom saying, 'Why don't you throw it in the slot machine?' Tom didn't hesitate. He did not look at the chattering, clattering slots or even at the coin in his palm, but with a flick of his wrist he tossed it across the casino. 'Same as gambling,' he said.

Another time Linda came up to him in the dressing room with some friends and asked him for some money to go gambling with. She was expecting him to hand over a couple of thousand dollars. Instead he gave her a single $5 bill and said, 'Go and gamble with that. Be a good girl, don't spend it all at once. Don't leave the country.'

Tom knew all about Gordon's love of gambling. Whether he knew how much he lost is another matter. Gordon played blackjack, he fancied himself betting the spread on American football and other games offered on the sports book. 'Gordon liked to bet sports, he thought he was a football coach,' said Gene Kilroy, who gave the eulogy at Gordon's memorial service in LA. 'He was a good handicapper and a big better. He won, he lost, he won, he lost. Most of all he loved baccarat.'

In Caesars Palace the baccarat tables are an ocean of calm, situated right by the entrance to the Circus Maximus. Baccarat is a high stakes game for the serious gamblers. There are only two players involved: the dealer, who is put up by the house, and the person putting up the bank representing everyone else round the table. Because the house takes a percentage only of the dealer's winnings, a serious gambler feels he has better odds. But the longer you sit at a table, the more certain it is you will lose. The longer you play, the bigger the percentage you will lose.

The difficulty for a gambler is knowing where to draw the line. Paul Anka, who has been playing Vegas for years, gives himself a limit. He is a serious high-roller, prepared to lose $50,000 a week on the blackjack tables, but at the end of his month playing Vegas he will still take home half a million dollars. 'However much you win, you always lose,' he said. 'They always get your money. Never chase your losses.'

Anka is the exception. For many Vegas entertainers it has always been hard to resist the lure of the tables. Mary Wilson won enough playing blackjack to buy herself a Rolls-Royce, but she also watched Motown executives rolling away a small fortune with the dice. Fats Domino got into debt so deep at the Flamingo that, for a while, he was doing four lounge shows a night seven nights a week to pay it off. Fats looked fed up for the entire set and to finish used his large stomach to bump the baby grand piano off the stage. There was never any question of an encore.

Presley's manager, Colonel Tom Parker, the mysterious Dutchman born Andreas Wilhelmus von Kujik, was a travelling carney hustler who had struck gold once. He had protected his investment until he brought him to Vegas. Parker played everything: dice, slots (he liked to play four Double Diamond $25-a-pull slots simultaneously) and blackjack. Perversely, another of his favourites was the Wheel of Fortune, which offers the worst odds of winning. Usually there was a $1,000 limit on a single bet, but when Parker played the limits were taken off. Dealers remember him losing $10,000 a turn for over an hour. Liberace's manager, Seymour Heller, believed that the Colonel lost a million dollars a year on the tables. 'He played roulette. They had to set up a private table for him and you dared not talk to him – no matter how much he liked you – while he was gambling.'

Sinatra was a very heavy loser. Paul Anka saw him lose a million dollars in one night, and he would regularly blow $100,000. Vegas legend has it that the casino would write down his losses so he only had to pay forty per cent. But he ended up playing his seasons almost for free.

The casinos put the hook in by giving high-rollers and entertainers a line of credit. All they had to do was sign a chit; when the money had gone, they just called for more. At the MGM in the mid-eighties Mills's line of credit was a quarter of a million dollars. It was possible for him to lose in a night what his artist made in a week.

'Gordon lost a lot of money, he loved to gamble,' recalled Nanci Eisner. 'Sometimes with the cheques from Vegas, it could have been Tom's, it could have been Engelbert's, there would be a gambling deduction, $50,000 or more came right out of the cheque. The agent's commission also came out, with the balance left from Gordon's gambling.'

Like any addiction gambling is insidious; it starts slowly and becomes all consuming. In the early seventies Vegas was only a small part of Tom's schedule. Even a week in Vegas cannot match up to the gross from three sold-out shows at Madison Square Garden. Once Gilbert O'Sullivan had peaked, Tom and Engelbert's hits started to dry up and MAM started its slow decline, Vegas became increasingly important to the cash flow.

When Gordon moved to Los Angeles in 1976 he had much less to do. When his artists played Vegas he came too. He was bored with Tom asleep all day, and focused on his performances. Naturally hyperactive but also shy around strangers, in baccarat Gordon found the ideal game. During one of Tom's engagements at Caesars, a dealer recalled Gordon and Anne Marie sitting at the baccarat tables for a week. Then, one day, he took her to the lobby to put her in a limo for the airport. As her car pulled away another drew up disgorging Jo Mills and their four children.

'The next thing we saw,' said Denny Walker, 'was Gordon pushing this buggy through the casino like the proud father he was. That night he was back at the table, sitting next to his wife, drinking champagne as if nothing had happened.

'Gordon wasn't always a big loser. He was way too smart for that, but in the end the odds favour the cards. The more you play the more you lose. He would also drink too much and then the judgement goes.'

Gambling became easier and easier for Gordon. When anybody plays in Vegas the drinks are free. For high-rollers ordering vintage Dom Perignon by the magnum is not a problem. When the wine flowed, inhibitions went, caution got tipsy and the bets got higher. Fuelled by booze and bravado the Mule would reassert himself, determined he was right as he called 'Bank' and the cards fell. Losing threes, losing fours, no problem – just sign another marker, bring another ten grand.

Gene Kilroy acknowledged that Gordon was a heavy gambler but disagreed that he would ever gamble away Tom's money. 'Gordon never spent Tom's money on the table. No, not at all. It was always, "This is mine, and that's yours, Tom." '

In 1974 Gordon lost so much money gambling at Caesars that the terms of Tom's contract had to be changed. 'Lloyd Greenfield told me that Gordon had lost a lot of money, over a million dollars, and that it would mean cutbacks for everybody,' said Chris Ellis. 'Members of the band were not able to sign for drinks and food any more. The shoe was on the other foot. Once you were in debt to the casino, they could do what they liked with you.'

Just as Colonel Parker's love for roulette helped keep Elvis in Vegas, Mills's gambling addiction goes a long way to explaining why Tom Jones was to spend so much of his career in a gilded cage off the Strip. That is certainly Paul Anka's take.

'Gordon Mills used to gamble at Caesars Palace,' said Anka. 'At one point he had a marker outstanding for a million dollars which meant Jones had to come back and sing again. He performed in Las Vegas to pay off Gordon Mills's gambling debts. But, of course, all the time he was running up more debts. That is why Tom played Vegas for so long. Tom was a hostage to Gordon's gambling and as Gordon did all the deals Tom was none the wiser. He was unaware that he was singing, not for his supper but for Gordon's.

'Tom Jones would have been nothing without Gordon Mills. He had the talent, but he didn't know what to do with it. Without Mills, Thomas Woodward would never have been Tom Jones, Dorsey would never have been Humperdinck. Tom could never have done it on his own, he needed help.

'He needed an industry around him to build him up, but the trouble is for all the money made, it left him with almost nothing.'

CHAPTER EIGHTEEN

TOM AND THE KING

J ust as Tom Jones was poised to become the capo of Vegas entertainers, he was faced with the one competition even he could not handle: the King of Rock and Roll. On 31 July 1969 Elvis Presley opened at the showroom at the International Hotel. For the next eight years, whenever he was in town, he was the main man. Elvis was the first act in the history of Las Vegas to earn a hotel a profit on its show.

Tom has claimed for many years that he was instrumental in showing Elvis how to play Vegas. 'I was the reason that Elvis started to play Vegas,' he said. 'He saw me in Las Vegas and really wanted to crack it there. He'd tried in the fifities and failed, because he was too much of a rebel then. He saw me doing something similar and realised he could do it too.'

In 1968 Colonel Tom Parker was eyeing up the pot of gold he could earn in Las Vegas – $400,000 for a four-week residency. Elvis was less convinced. His ego went cold at the memory of how his 1956 foray at the Frontier had ended in ignominy after only two weeks. After their daughter Lisa Marie was born on 1 February Elvis and Priscilla had stayed on in LA, four hours from Vegas and ideal for Presley to scope out the opposition. He had no stage show, little inspiration and his confidence had been eroded by that soul-destroying run of dreadful movies.

The showroom at the International had the potential to become a performer's graveyard, designed with all the sensitivity of an indoor arena scaled down to the size of a town hall and with the acoustic properties of a giant machine-gun bunker. Comedian Don Rickles took one look and told Alex Shoufy to forget it. Barbra Streisand opened the hall doing her usual show and died a death. It needed something special.

Then the news filtered through to Elvis about Tom Jones fever. About this sweaty, crazed Welshman with a black voice, a neo-Afro hairdo, trousers cut so tight the audience could see every vein, ridge and curve of his genitalia, who was burning up the stage at the Flamingo.

Elvis was determined to see for himself what all the fuss was about. Late on the afternoon of Saturday 6 April, he had his bodyguard, Joe Esposito, phone to request a table for the midnight show. Just before midnight, Elvis and Priscilla, having flown to Vegas in a private jet, walked through the casino flanked by eight companions. Vernon Hopkins, who was playing a one-armed bandit, saw him come in and rushed backstage to tell Tom. 'Elvis is here? Don't wind me up,' Tom said, until Vernon insisted. 'Jesus, we've got to do a good show, lads.'

Elvis and his party sat at a table right in front of the stage. That set the room buzzing. Elvis did not make many public appearances, especially at a rival's show, and fewer still with Priscilla so soon after the baby. Tom Jones has never shrunk from a challenge and so, according to Chris Hutchins, he gave it everything he had:

When he did the first up-tempo number, *Don't Fight It*, Elvis slapped the table and rolled his head in time to the beat. Several times during the song, he turned to comment to Priscilla, a broad smile on his face and a long, thin cigar clamped between his teeth.

Later in the act, Tom announced, 'Ladies and gentlemen, we have in the audience tonight a man I have admired for many years, Mr Elvis Presley.' The audience cheered Elvis, who stood up to wave and take a bow. 'OK, that's enough – sit down,' Tom commanded jokingly. When Tom finished with *Land of a Thousand Dances*, the wildest number in his repertoire, Elvis jumped up and led the audience in a standing ovation. After the curtains had closed, I took Elvis and Priscilla backstage to meet Tom, who was soaking wet in his stage suit. Elvis took Tom's hand in both of his and offered his congratulations.

Backstage, Priscilla chatted to Linda, quickly producing her pictures of Lisa Marie. One by one the Squires found excuses to come into the dressing room and to be introduced to the King.

'It's a great pleasure to meet you, sir,' he said to each of them. Elvis was always polite, he called everyone 'sir' and happily gave them autographs.

Linda was not impressed by everybody sucking up to Presley. 'What are you making such a big fuss of him for?' she complained to Vernon and Chris Slade. 'Tom's better than him. You should make more of a fuss of Tom than him.'

'Linda always defended him on everything,' said Vernon. 'But she couldn't understand that although we respected Tom as a singer and great artist and everything, this was special. It was Elvis Presley and she couldn't understand that.'

Later that night, after Elvis and his party had dined at Caesars

Palace, he surprisingly agreed to pose for pictures with Tom for photographer Peter Borsari. 'Most of the shots were very similar,' admitted Borsari. 'They were standing together, sitting on a couch together. I know they were talking, and I think it was about music. I don't remember, because I was trying so hard to concentrate on taking as many pictures as I could in the time I was allowed.'

Elvis saw how Tom had broken the rules set by the Vegas crooners. Sure he wore a tux, but his bow tie never stayed done up beyond the first couple of numbers. Tom played it hard and sexy, the only way he knew how, played it rock and roll, but did not preach revolution. Elvis saw in the swaggering, the posturing, the sweating and the pneumatic groin a flashback to his own teen idol days. But he also saw that it worked as well, or perhaps even better, on the maturer audience. Elvis realised he could do that too.

It was all image, all attitude. The scales fell away from his eyes, showed him the key to the stage. He did not copy Tom's show. He simply appropriated and magnified those elements of it which he could use effectively. (Fifteen years later Prince was to do the same. While planning his *Purple Rain* tour he went to Vegas and watched Tom's performances every night for a week.) Elvis did not just have three girl backing singers, he had two sets, one male, one female. He had a full orchestra and the best rock band money and his legendary status could buy. Tom had Big Jim Sullivan – one of London's top session guitarists – the King hired James Burton, the greatest of them all.

Elvis took to wiping his forehead on a towel – he drew the line at panties – and then slinging it into the screaming crowd. Elvis never had any intention of showing the outline of his regal cock to the crowd. Instead of Tom's tuxedo jacket and pocketless skintight pants with double sewn reinforced seams, Elvis preferred a karate suit in black mohair (later he went for his glitter suits). Tom, who has never been a natural dancer, preferred to keep it bump and grind while Elvis, altogether more graceful, went through a whole gamut of martial arts moves until finally his weight made them appear ridiculous.

'What Elvis got from Tom was the trick of working the Vegas show stage,' said Nick Naff. 'Tom showed him that you have to be dynamic and sensual in a way that gets through to the over-thirties. You gotta hit 'em right between the legs. Tom gave Elvis those head shakes, the vocal accents on the bridges, the freeze poses at the end of the songs, the trick of wiping the sweat with a cloth and then throwing it out in the house – all those things.

'The big difference was that Tom did all this stuff instinctively. He just didn't know any other way to work. Elvis wasn't so spontaneous, but he knew a good thing when he saw it. He took Tom's stuff, translated it into his own style, rehearsed his ass off and went over big with it.'

Since they had first met on the sound stage at Paramount Studios, Elvis had kept abreast of Tom's career. Watching him gyrate on the *Ed Sullivan Show* had struck a chord of memory deep in the King's pelvis. 'Elvis really liked *It's Not Unusual*,' said Marty Lacker, Elvis's best man. 'We didn't know that Tom was from Wales because of the way he sang. As a matter of fact, at first, Elvis thought Tom was black.'

'Elvis was positive Tom was black,' wrote Priscilla Presley in *Elvis and Me*, 'No white singers could belt out a song like that, except the Righteous Brothers, who much to his surprise were also white.'

On 29 November 1966 Elvis was reminded that Jones could sing more than rock and soul. Driving back to Graceland they managed to pick up local Memphis radio station WHBQ, just outside Little Rock, Arkansas. The radio was playing *Green Green Grass of Home*. Elvis stopped the bus and had one of his guys call the DJ, George Klein, and ask him to play the song again. He was so taken with the song he also called Priscilla back home in LA and told her to go out and buy a copy of the record.

A little further down the road Elvis put in another call to WHBQ, and kept it up all the way to Memphis, with George – another high school buddy – dedicating each play to Elvis and all the boys. Everyone was laughing fit to bust, except for bodyguard Red West, who had heard the song on Jerry Lee's album a year earlier and brought it to Elvis. Elvis had told him it was far too country for him to consider recording.

Soon afterwards, in May 1969 Elvis took Priscilla, Lisa Marie, her nanny and a small entourage – only seven friends – to Hawaii. Coincidentally, Tom was doing a short season at the Paradise Lounge in the Ilikai Hotel. Elvis, who was still preparing his own Vegas debut, could not resist a further opportunity of studying his Welsh pretender. At the Ilikai Elvis was especially taken with how Jones mixed and matched his powerful voice against the range and subtlety that only comes from a full orchestra. The electric guitar chords gave his show balls, but those soaring strings were what gave the audience goosebumps and sent them shivering into the night begging to come back again. That was the night that convinced Elvis that he, too, must employ a full orchestra, no matter how much Colonel Parker might cavil at the extravagance.

'After the show Tom invited us to his suite, along with our group,' wrote Priscilla. 'Within minutes the champagne exploded and the party was on. We laughed, drank, joked, drank some more (lots more), jammed and reeled back to the Ilikai at dawn. Elvis had had such a good time, he personally invited Tom and his group to join us the next day at our beach house.'

'I went over the next day and he wasn't there,' recalled Tom. 'Priscilla said, "He knows you're coming today and he hasn't got any guitars with him, so he's gone out to find guitars." Elvis comes walking through the door with a guitar in each hand and says,

"You have this one and I'll have this one." We sat down, I play the guitar as well as he did – maybe a bit better, a couple more chords.'

During the jam session Chris Ellis had surreptitiously tried to tape the proceedings. The ever vigilant Joe Esposito saw the recording light was on and removed the tape. Esposito himself recorded the Hawaiian summit on an 8mm film camera with the duo singing, *Hound Dog*, *Heartbreak Hotel* and *Blue Suede Shoes* together. That too has been lost – or destroyed – for Priscilla Presley has tried to find it without success. The three of them also went down to the beach where Elvis, despite the sticky summer heat, kept his Hawaiian shirt on. In preparation for his TV special he had been over-dieting and he was too embarrassed to strip off.

It is hard to gauge the exact nature of the relationship between Elvis and Tom. For the Welshman, Elvis 'was my ultimate hero. There were similarities in our backgrounds, which is why we became friends.' The Jones legend has it that after the Flamingo show Elvis told him, 'Man, that was terrific. After seeing you, I want to get back up on stage myself.' Seeing Tom Jones is why Elvis made his comeback. That is the way Tom remembered it.

The Memphis Mafia, who surrounded Elvis, have a different take. Because they too have their place to keep in the Presley legend, they deliberately play down what Tom meant to Elvis.

'Tom was a nice enough guy,' said Marty Lacker, 'but Elvis didn't think of him as some big pal. And I'm sure Tom didn't really consider himself such. Not really. One time in Vegas, in the seventies, Tom came backstage to the dressing room after one of Elvis's shows. There were a lot of other people there, some entertainers, like James Brolin, the actor, and his wife, who were nice people. Elvis was in the back changing his clothes, and Tom sat there, being Mr Macho, Mr Cocky.

'After a little while, the doors opened and Elvis walked in. And Tom got dead silent. He wasn't Mr Macho anymore. Tom

Jones is one of these entertainers who became Elvis's big friend after he died. You know what I'm saying? He was part of that documentary I worked on, *Elvis: the Echo Will Never Die*. We went out to Vegas to interview him for it, and his public relations guy, John Moran, told me that Jones said he could've straightened Elvis out and gotten him off pills if he'd had the opportunity. I looked at Moran and I said, "You tell Tom he's full of shit." Jones would never have opened up his mouth in front of Elvis.

'During the interview, Jones had the nerve to say, "If Elvis had had a few more friends around" – intimating himself – "he wouldn't have died when he did." I just shook my head. Elvis was the same way with Tom Jones as he was with the Beatles. He liked their music. And that was about it.'

Presley certainly respected Tom's talent and enjoyed his company, but there were always all those other guys getting in the way. 'One of Elvis's outstanding attributes was his conviction that there was room for anyone with talent in the entertainment field,' wrote Priscilla. '[In Hawaii] That was the night a friendship was born, a friendship of mutual respect and admiration.'

Tom and Elvis had more in common than one might think: both were from poor backgrounds with an almost unnatural affinity for black music. Elvis told his guys, 'Tom is the only man who has ever come anywhere close to the way I sing. He has that ballsy feeling, that "I'm gonna shove it up your ass" attitude.' Elvis did find the blatant sexual posturing in Tom's show offputting. 'I think that's very lewd,' he complained to his guys, 'showing his cock and his balls.' 'Hell, Elvis,' Lamar Fike replied, 'you did the same shit in your time!' 'No,' Elvis denied vociferously, 'I was never vulgar.'

They both despised John Lennon. 'The one time Elvis met the Beatles, he hated the way they sat worshipping at his feet,' recalled Jones. 'He said to me once, "Tom, we should do a special, just the two of us, it would be the biggest thing ever. We could get the Beatles to be the band . . . no, we'll just let them do some backing vocals." '

When Elvis was in town, Party Central was the Imperial Suite on the thirtieth floor of the International (later the Hilton). Elvis liked to throw parties and Tom liked to go to them. (Elvis always had the prettiest girls on tap, but never seemed very interested in getting to know them.) There were certainly drugs around, which Tom abhorred. Elvis had experimented with marijuana, LSD and cocaine – 'I tried everything before John Lennon even knew what a stimulant was,' he boasted – but his heaviest addiction was to prescription drugs, amphetamines and barbiturates. (When he died Elvis was swallowing between one and two hundred pills a day.) When he offered cocaine to Tom he was warned, 'One day you'll overdo it with those drugs and none of us will be around to help you. I love you, Elvis, but if you don't stop sticking that stuff up your nose, you won't be around to love much longer.'

Once the party was settled in the Imperial Suite, the Memphis Mafia would take off their coats. As all of them wore guns the suite often resembled the prelude to the gunfight at the OK Corral. Elvis's bodyguards, Red and Sonny West, got on with Dai Perry like a house on fire. One night they asked him, 'Have you got a gun, Dai? What happens if someone comes for Tom?'

'I fucking use these,' said Dai brandishing his fists. The Wests offered to get Dai a .357 Magnum. For the rest of the night he tried on various shoulder holsters and different weapons. Dai thought it was a great idea. Tom and Chris Ellis thought otherwise.

Hanging out with Presley was full of surprises. He gulped down vodka and orange while Jones sipped champagne. One night he asked Tom what he thought about Robert Goulet's singing on a television show. Tom, who actually found Goulet to be amusing company but knew better than to argue, shrugged his shoulders. Presley announced, 'I think it's a piece of shit.' He calmly took out his .357 Magnum and blew the television to bits.

Other nights Tom and Elvis would visit each other's dressing rooms and kid about. Once they got to discussing self-defence. Tom teased Elvis that karate was little better than street brawling and that boxing was a far more noble martial art. Elvis took this as a challenge and they began showing each other various moves in their respective sports. The moves became rather excited, especially when Tom pretended to demonstrate that well-known Welsh martial arts move — the head-butt.

One night Tom came off stage and went straight into the shower. The Presley entourage had invaded the dressing room, and Elvis, who was wearing a fashionable buckskin suit with tassels hanging off the sleeves, just walked straight into the shower, and started talking to Tom.

'Tom's standing in the shower naked,' said Chris Ellis, 'and there's Elvis, fully clothed, soaking wet, saying to him, "What a great show, man." He was oblivious to the fact he was standing in the shower. After Charlie Hodge had the hotel send him over a change of clothes, he sat on the sofa drinking a bottle of mountain spring water, slurring all over the place, like he's totally, absolutely, drunk. Of course, he wasn't drunk, it was the pills.'

On another occasion, Elvis used an adjoining toilet cubicle and they carried on a conversation through the glass partition while each did his business. After a few minutes, ready to get dressed again, Elvis screamed out 'Red'. Red West knew what was required of him. Cursing Elvis to his face, he entered the cubicle, pulled up the skintight leather trousers and, while his boss sucked in his belly, laced them up. Afterwards, Ellis went into the cubicle and found a small revolver that Elvis had dropped on the floor.

Ever since he had conquered his own expanding girth Tom had become a purist about exercise and fitness. When Elvis confessed he was having weight problems Tom advised him to watch it daily by checking the bathroom scales. He could see the way the King was letting himself go, ordering a dozen burgers at a time and eating the lot, destroying himself with every mouthful. Tom resolved never to let it happen to him.

'Towards the end it looked like nobody had any control over him,' said Tom. 'He just got bigger and bigger. I'd been seeing Elvis since 1965 and every time I saw him he was never the same weight. He would either be thin or heavy. He only seemed a normal weight once, around 1969 when he was first playing Vegas. Elvis used to go on eating binges, but he would kid himself it was all right because he was exercising. He wasn't, of course. He'd got one of those exercise bikes but the pedals were driven by an electric motor. He'd be sitting on the bike, which was pedalling itself, eating wedges of pizza. "Yeah, Tom," he'd say, deadly serious, "I like to keep in shape."

'Elvis's mistake was that he never left the country,' he said. 'He wanted to, but Colonel Parker wouldn't let him. He wanted to play overseas so badly. I told him, "You would love it. The people are dying to see you — you would be the biggest thing they've ever seen." He wanted to do it, but life caught up with him. I did see him starting to fall apart. I saw when the weight started coming on him and he was getting vague. If he wanted to talk about something he'd beckon me over and we'd go and chat. This one night I walked into the bedroom and asked what was the problem. He'd forgotten what he asked me in there for, and he started looking around the room and there was a silver buckle somebody had given him on the sideboard. It caught his eye and he said, "I want to give you this." I know it wasn't his original thought.'

Elvis was a compulsive gift giver. He gave Tom a book called *The Impersonal Life* saying, 'It really has been a great source of inspiration to me.' He had written a message on the flyleaf, but his handwriting was so illegible Tom never could work out what the inscription was. He gave him a pistol with 'Tom Jones' engraved on the barrel, and a big blue lapis lazuli medallion inscribed with the initials 'TCB' ('Take Care of Business') and a lightning bolt. On another occasion he handed him a beautiful black sapphire ring (which later vanished from Tom's hotel bathroom along with an attractive young lady). In return Tom gave Elvis a tiger's eye ring he had admired.

In 1975 Tom made a tactless remark on stage about the Ku Klux Klan which seriously upset the Blossoms. They went on strike. Elvis heard about the problem and in one of those characteristic flashes of impetuous generosity sent a plane to Nashville to pick up a vocal trio and another plane to Los Angeles to collect three more girl singers. 'By the time I got up next day he had assembled a choir for me,' recalled Jones. 'But by then Gordon and I'd sorted out the problem, so he just kept his six on for the rest of the week to sing for us and with us at our after-show get togethers.'

While Tom and Elvis were very friendly, their organisations conducted the semblance of a publicity war. The Vegas hotels were far too sussed to have them play in the same town at the same time. For the most part their rivalry took the form of huge billboards. One of these said, 'Elvis Presley is at the International', while Tom's placards stated simply, 'Tom Jones is in town'. There were similar games with any photographs they had taken together. Colonel Parker would only send out the ones where Elvis looked good and Tom was squinting or looking rough, while the British would not send out any shots where Elvis looked taller than Tom.

Occasionally the competition took a more personal tone. Gordon was annoyed when the Colonel started using comedian Sammy Shore, whom he had discovered. On the two occasions Chris Slade was approached to join Elvis's backing band, Gordon refused to let him go. He could not have Tom losing his musicians to the only artist who was bigger than him. Impossible.

Despite that, Gordon flirted with the Presley camp. By that stage the relationship between Presley and Parker was virtually non-existent. Elvis had his Memphis Mafia, while Parker employed Joe Esposito to make sure the shows worked.

'To Elvis,' said Chris Ellis, 'Parker was a complete joke. Outside the theatre there was a line of people going in to see Elvis, and there was Colonel Tom Parker wearing a funny hat, with a table selling postcards and other merchandise, with buckets of quarters and dimes. As soon as the crowd had all gone in, Parker would take all this loose change and go up to the desk and change it into gambling chips and go and gamble with it. It was an incredible sight. Here was the biggest star in the world, and his manager was selling postcards to make some extra money to go gambling.'

Between 27 October and 1 November 1971 Mills exchanged letters with Tom Daskin (Parker's right-hand man) and the Colonel himself. Rumours flew around that Mills was offering to buy Parker out and take over managing Elvis. Where that would have left Tom is an interesting source of speculation.

More likely is that Gordon and Barry Clayman – who had established a very close relationship with Jerry Weintraub who promoted Elvis's American tours – were seeking the holy grail, getting Elvis to play overseas. MAM were the obvious partners for Europe. Owing to his status as an illegal immigrant, the Colonel would not countenance going abroad.

When Elvis joined Tom on stage at Caesars they would laugh and joke about in front of the audience, but they never actually sang together. The Colonel would have gone spare because he was forever warning his protégé about the danger of bootleg recordings, which sparked off Elvis's own paranoia. There are no known recordings of Tom and Elvis singing together at their post-gig parties.

They could not resist sniping at each other's performances.

Tom told Chris Hutchins, 'Look, he's like a big chorus girl up there.' Elvis, too, would say something to knock Tom, comment on his singing; he would pretend to sing along with Tom, making out that he could hit the high notes, which he could not.

According to Sonny West, 'Elvis was never critical to Tom's face, but he did ask him once, "Why do you sing the high notes?" "Why? Because they're in the bloody song," Tom replied, wondering what point Elvis was making. "You can't sing it without them."

' "I leave 'em to J.D.," Elvis explained, referring to J.D. Sumner and the Stamps, his backing group. "It's a lot easier that way. The audience sees me with my mouth open in front of the mike and no one knows who's singing what." '

There had to be a competitive edge to their relationship. They were both superstars. On stage there was the danger that Tom would not be able to resist the opportunity to prove he could blow the King off stage. Elvis might have been the first artist booked to appear on *This is Tom Jones*, but there was no way it was ever going to actually happen.

It was when they sang late into the night that the results were magical. 'It got difficult talking to Elvis because there was a lot of garble coming out of him,' said Chris Ellis. 'But he could sing – no matter how stoned he was, he could still sing, so those sessions were absolutely fantastic to hear. They would go into all kinds of things, a lot of gospel. And the harmonies together were really good. Tom definitely came out on top with the stronger voice, but Presley used to do better harmonies.'

Elvis never recovered from his divorce in October 1973. Losing Priscilla and Lisa Marie sapped his spirit and his behaviour became more extreme. As his indiscriminate consumption of pills and junk food spiralled out of control, he stayed longer and longer in Vegas. Even when his engagement at the Hilton finished, he stayed on at the hotel commandeering the thirtieth floor, with its intimate nightclub with panoramic views overlooking the city that never sleeps. When Tom was playing at Caesars, Elvis would come over to watch the show almost every night.

'Towards the end,' said Ellis, 'when Tom was told Elvis was coming over again it would be, "Oh fuck." The guy became a pain in the arse because he was so irrational you didn't know what he was going to do. Elvis would leave the booth with his guys before the show finished and come backstage so he wouldn't get jumped on by autograph hunters. Elvis used to grab the spare mike and wander on to the stage. The sound man would see him come out and push up the fader. It never bothered Tom about being upstaged, he took it all in good heart.'

It got so bad that Tom told Chris to 'hide the spare mike so he can't find it. He's a pain, he's ruining the end of the show.' The spare mike, already plugged in with a long lead, was kept in a box next to the stage manager who, in the days before radio mikes, would be feeding out the lead. Hiding the spare did not work because Elvis simply came on, mini-cape flapping on his shoulders, and used Tom's mike.

'Elvis was a southern redneck who used to hang around at Tom's Vegas shows, always managing to steal a few cheers,' recalled Burk Zanft, who never shared Tom's warm feelings for Presley. 'He wouldn't go out anywhere unless he was in his white suit, and then he would complain he felt trapped. He liked to watch the show from the wings, make sure he got seen by the crowd. He could never resist that, then he'd go into the dressing room for a drink about ten minutes before Tom came off stage.'

He told Burk once, 'Tom sure sweats a lot, doesn't he?' Burk replied, 'I remember when you used to.'

After the show Tom was virtually kidnapped back to Party Central where Elvis's entourage had given up trying to reason with him. One night Tom was sitting next to the 300-pound Lamar

Fike, when the King disappeared into his bedroom to swallow another handful of pills. 'Can't you stop this?' Tom asked. 'How do you stop a madman from himself?' came the bitter reply. 'He ignores everything you do or say to him.'

As Elvis's dependence on drugs increased, his behaviour grew more erratic. 'He would have his [backup] group come up and sing,' Jones said. 'We would do gospel unless Elvis had an obsession of the moment. There were two songs: *Why Me Lord?* – a Kris Kristofferson song – and *Killing Me Softly with His Song*. We'd do either song continuously, all night – like from 2 to 6 a.m. I'd sing it once, he'd sing it, we'd do it together. Then he'd have the tenor do it – he'd want to sing as high as the tenor did.'

'I used to back off a bit to save my voice,' said Tom, always aware how the desert air could sandpaper the life out of his vocal cords. 'He'd get it out of me though.'

At 5.30 one morning the party was still happening. Elvis was in full flow giving his private rendition of *Killing Me Softly* accompanied by Per Erik Hallin on the piano and Charlie Hodge on his guitar. Chris Ellis realised he had to get Tom back to Caesars.

'Tom was still singing his head off,' said Ellis. 'He didn't care, he had no idea of the time as he was as gone as Elvis, but I had to get him out of there to get some sleep. He had to sing the next night. So quite playfully I took hold of the piano player and we just gently slid down to the floor. It was a joke, and everybody was laughing. Except Elvis, who thought I was attacking Per Erik or something, and he went nuts. He started doing all these karate chops at me, kicking and chopping away but nothing was coming anywhere near me as he was so out of it. I just kept jumping out of the way. It started out as a laugh, but it got nasty and serious.'

Elvis was upset. So everybody in his entourage had to be upset or pretend they were upset. In the fast-souring atmosphere Tom sobered up and they split fast and went to bed. At ten in the morning the phone rang in Ellis's room. His wife answered and passed the receiver to her semi-comatose husband.

It was Khang Rhee, Elvis's Korean karate trainer, whose English was marginal, shouting at him, 'You come over here 2 o'clock, apologise hands and knees to Mr Presley, you upset him very much last night.'

Ellis told him to fuck off and put the phone down. Five minutes later he called back again, 'You come back over here 2 o'clock on hands and knees, you come in here apologise on hands and knees to me and Mr Presley.'

Ellis repeated his insult, but then realised that the situation was getting out of control. So he called up the sleeping Sonny West and told him what was going on. 'If I come over there at 2 o'clock, there will be a couple of really nasty bastards with me,' snapped the Welshman, who had made some interesting connections at the Copacabana, 'and that guy is not going to go very far today, or any other day.' Sonny said, 'Listen, just forget it, he's a fucking idiot, leave it, we'll sort it out.'

News of the incident reached Tom via Elvis's doctor, Dr 'Nick' (George Nichopolous). Tom was livid. When asked what would have happened if Ellis had been beaten up, the singer replied, 'I'd have gone over there and rammed his fucking karate belt right down his throat.' A few days later he had Chris Hutchins get Elvis on the phone to sort the situation out.

'Everybody became friends again,' said Ellis. 'I met Elvis again, and everything was fine. I don't think he really remembered what happened.'

The friendship was patched up, but by that stage the King was almost beyond help. Tom has claimed in interviews he could have helped Elvis, but that is wishful thinking. Elvis lacked Tom's self-discipline and absolute sense of self. Having let himself go, the King could see no way back. Sure they were friends, as much as two celebrities inhabiting a goldfish bowl amid the neon, window-less kingdom they ruled can be. But Elvis's death, and their respective entourages, prevented any chance of it becoming more than that. Tom was deeply upset when the King died, but he had lost a man even closer to him the previous day. On 15 August, 1977 his musical director Johnny Spence died of a heart attack. Tom, Gordon, Gilbert O'Sullivan and drummer, Terry Jenkins, acted as pallbearers. 'The next day,' recalls Tom, 'I was still in shock over Johnny's death then somebody came up and said that Elvis had died. I was shaking. It was terrible.'

'That day in Hawaii Priscilla told me that when I was around him he was very natural and happy,' said Tom sadly. 'She said, "I never see him on a downstroke when you're around." I felt very happy about that. He would have these moods, I'd see them a little bit later, when he'd get withdrawn, and there looked like flashes of fire there. We kept in touch until he died. Well, about two years before he died – he pushed everyone away from him. He wouldn't answer the phone and he fired everybody because he was getting so big and taking so many drugs. They were trying to tell him the truth, so he fired them.'

The King had forgotten how to listen. For all his faults, Tom Jones never did.

CHAPTER NINETEEN

THE SEX
MACHINE

T he waitress in the Rihga Royal Hotel Bar was total New York cool. All of twenty years old, hard-bodied from blading through Central Park, every flick of her shiny black hair, every roll of her hips telling the world 'don't-mess-with-me-buster-I'm-too-beautiful-for-you'. A waitress whose attention you dared not attract in case she ignored you. She sashayed between the tables, strangled 'pleases' and 'miss . . .' and hands waving vaguely in mid-air behind her, leaving a trail of the unfulfilled.

It was 1994. Tom Jones had just finished recording the *David Letterman Show* and was chatting to an MTV executive before going to dinner at Lutèce. Desperate to impress, the executive tried to attract the waitress's attention, in vain. Feeling thirsty, Tom raised a finger. She materialised by the table ready to chew the digit off. She took the order, bit her bottom lip as if to prevent herself saying something and rushed off.

Two minutes later she was back, with three glasses of

champagne and a Manhattan. This time she could not hold it in. 'My God,' she stammered, 'you are the sexiest man I've ever met in my life. Please, please call me.' She handed over her phone number written on a napkin before retreating, knees trembling, tray shaking, glasses clattering but always facing the singer. Bowing his head of grey curls in acknowledgement, Tom Jones unleashed that special smile he reserves exclusively for the ladies, full of both promise and regret. A smile that says, 'I'd much rather be making sweet music with you darling, than talking business with this schmuck . . . but you know how it is . . . later, who knows . . . ?' Removing a silver swizzle stick from his jacket pocket, he stirred the bubbles out of his champagne. He raised the flute to his mouth. Gently he wet his lips.

Had he asked, the girl would have stripped naked and gone down on him, right there. A twenty-year-old mesmerised by a man of fifty-four. That was the way it was in 1994. The way it always had been and probably still is. Some men have sex appeal. It's just there, threaded into their DNA. They exude it like musk. Throw fame, money and a raging libido into the mix, and you have Tom Jones.

In recent years Tom has toned down his stage act so it no longer appears as the posturing of an old bloke long past his sexual sell-by date. These days he has learnt to ignore the panties that still appear as regularly as the moon's cycle, freshly laundered and neatly ironed, plucked from handbag and thrown on to the stage. But even self-censored, he is still a perennial flirt. Not so long ago when the inevitable lingerie landed at his feet, he buried his face in them, while the audience roared with appreciation with not a little lust threaded in.

It all appeared a tease, a well-trodden, oft-repeated one-liner, part of a *Carry On* burlesque, but it went further than that. For Tom Jones, sex comes second only to singing. And the girls have stayed young, while he is getting older. Because he is a star, he has been presented with temptations which would enthral most men. And because he is a star who does not have to resist temptation, he does not.

Back in the Valleys his desire for sex had got him into trouble at a very early age. He married Linda, had Mark, and then settled down to wait for better things. Once Tommy Scott and the Senators became popular, they attracted a large female following. In the Valleys, most girls were wary of losing their virtue in a community where gossip had wings and lived next door. Though not all of them. Once *It's Not Unusual* hit, so did the girls. It was not a difficult leap from having his clothes torn off by a mob of screaming girls to voluntarily removing them for any favoured adoring fans.

Musicians have always exchanged their talents for sex, and in the twentieth century as their status and wealth grew, so did their excesses. Jazz began in the whorehouses of New Orleans. Music encourages members of the opposite sex (or indeed the same sex) to dance, which helps cast aside inhibitions. Viewed from a politically correct standpoint, the sexual behaviour of Tom Jones and the Squires was exploitation. But they were doing little more than following the sexual mores of their profession and of the time. Anyone expecting a bunch of Welsh boys, escaping from a culture where premarital sex was frowned upon, to behave like monks, also expects bonobo chimpanzees to take a vow of celibacy.

Rock bands have always been, and will always be, sexually promiscuous. However, as the success of a band increases so does the security around it. It becomes increasingly difficult to get casual sex. As Tom moved from rock to MOR, he exchanged champagne for beer, Cuban cigars for Woodbines, *filet mignon* for fry-ups. So did his taste in women change.

To paraphrase Thomas Edison, life on the road is ten per cent excitement surrounded by ninety per cent boredom. Constant travelling, sleeping, eating, waiting in hotel rooms, waiting in dressing rooms, waiting for Godot to lead them to the stage. Everything merges into a long blur. Casual sex is one way of alleviating the boredom, fine as a physical release, but in the end the artist wants something more. Happily married musicians fall in love on the road all the time. It is something to do, along with drinking too much, taking too many drugs and supergluing the tour manager's bed to the ceiling.

From the late sixties Tom Jones developed a *modus operandi* with his women that, according to the latest tabloid newspaper reports, he was still using in 1999. Tom's numerous dalliances can be divided into distinct types, with consistent patterns of behaviour. There are the celebrity 'love' affairs which petered out by the mid-seventies. These were superseded by pseudo-romances with ordinary, much younger girls, which occasionally developed into longer-term relationships. Punctuating these affairs have been a constant stream of pure sexual encounters, which have all added to the legend of 'Tom Jones, Superstud'.

Cassandra Petersen, best known as Elvira, Mistress of the Dark, a heroine of B-movie horror flicks, told Howard Stern's radio show how she had lost her virginity to Tom Jones back in 1971 when she was nineteen. 'My God, it was enormous,' she told Stern. 'We ended up in the sack but it was no fun for me. He was so big. It was like having sex with a horse. I crawled out of his bed and drove straight to a hospital emergency room. I needed immediate attention in my most intimate place.'

Jones happily admits that the best rumour he's ever heard about himself is that he is 'very, very well endowed'. He is, he laughed, 'very but not very, very'. Flaunting a large bulge in tight pants, whether it be a Tudor codpiece, rolled-up football socks or an extra-large penis, is part of any rock singer's image. According to Billy Smith, Elvis's cousin, the King was very suspicious of Mr Jones's endowments. 'Elvis called him "Sock Dick". He thought Jones put a rolled-up sock in his pants to make himself look more well-endowed.'

Chris Ellis puts it down to Tom's love of tight trousers, not to extra padding. 'I've seen him naked hundreds of times, he's just a normal guy,' he said.

Another rumour about Tom Jones is that after a hard night's horizontal jogging, he will soak his manhood in the antiseptic mouthwash Listerine. The story began when his former minder, Chris Montgomery, sold his story to the *News of the World*. 'I could always tell if the girl he'd chosen to sleep with was too demanding in bed, because he'd send me out to buy some Listerine the next day. He insisted the antiseptic was perfect for restoring parts he'd worn out the night before. He reckoned it helped him ease the agony. He'd fill a glass or a sink with it and plunge in his afflicted appendage. After that he was ready for anything.'

The whole Listerine story smacked of headline-grabbing embellishments (as when David Mellor was reputed to wear a Chelsea shirt in bed with his mistress), which Tom himself found laughable. He denied he had ever used the green stuff – being Tom it would at the very least be vintage Remy Martin. However, much of what Montgomery recounted as Tom's *modus operandi* has been backed up by other former employees and ex or spurned girlfriends.

Like many a sailor Tom has come to have a regular girl in every port. For years whenever he played in Toronto a limo was sent to pick up an Italian girl who worked at a Zellers Department Store. When Prince Andrew visited LA in 1983 Annie Toomaru sat at a table with Gordon Mills, Tom, Roger Moore and a nineteen-year-old brunette with short hair who told her: 'I've been with Tom for three years on and off.' She showed off her expensive jewellery and a gold watch that were all presents from Tom and said, 'He's really nice to me, wonderful.' Gordon later told Annie that Tom liked the girl enough to invite her to an important function, and he would fly her in for weekends, but that was the extent of the relationship.

'It's the one thing Gordon always told me,' says Annie. 'He will never divorce Linda, never, never.'

A very long time ago Tom Jones decided that he was never going to leave his wife. But nor has he ever made any pretence about being faithful. In the sixties and early seventies, he had a string of celebrity lovers, including singers Nancy Wilson and Vikki Carr.

Tom was not always successful in his pursuit of his fellow stars. Dancer Juliet Prowse turned him down, and an attempted seduction of Dionne Warwick in his New York hotel room did not go according to plan. For a while Tom vigorously pursued Lulu. One night when they were both working up in Manchester and staying at Milverton Lodge, Tom made his move. He had Ellis place a bottle of champagne on ice and put the fire on to create a romantic atmosphere. Lulu was less interested, writing in her autobiography, 'Tom Jones was convinced by the way I danced and the way we sang together and got along professionally, that I had to fool around a little, and I think he was disappointed to discover that he was wrong. I was very aware of his animal magnetism, but to be truthful he frightened the life out of me.'

Tom preferred to do the wooing. Predatory women scared him. Ava Gardner came backstage at The Talk of the Town. Sinatra's second wife was forty-five, and heavier than in her prime, but still formidably sexy. With eight people in it the wedge-shaped dressing room was full to bursting, but Ava, who had had a few drinks, was all over the singer. Around 1 a.m., as she prepared to leave, she went up to Tom and whispered in his ear,

'I want to fuck the ass off you,' while slipping him the number of her hotel room.

Tom was stunned, not by her coming on to him, but by her language. 'I couldn't believe my ears,' he said to Ellis. 'This elegant lady saying that to me.' In Tom's world, women did not behave like that. He never took Ava up on the offer.

On at least two occasions Tom got hot and heavy with Diana Dors. On their first meeting in 1965, he had pulled her on to a nightclub dance floor and, as she wittily put it, 'His discretion went right out of the window.' Diana continued to flirt with Tom until he played a most unlikely card. He took Linda along for dinner and after inviting Diana and her then boyfriend back to their house for drinks explained why he could not have an affair with her. 'I would always be afraid to make love to you. You always treat me like a child and I'd be frightened that you would laugh at me.'

He did try one more time. At Elstree. 'He tried to screw Diana standing up against the bar,' said Ellis. 'He was so drunk, and she was so drunk. It was a pretty pitiful sight really, he was there with his tongue down her throat and humping up and down the bar with her.'

One of Tom's strangest affairs was with a Persian princess, who took a fancy to the singer. A strong-featured attractive woman in her twenties, used to getting her own way, she called Chris Ellis whenever she was coming to London. Wilful and extremely rich, she stayed at the Ritz and had her own chauffeured Rolls. Tom met her several times in London, and once in Bournemouth.

'It was a very secret thing,' said Ellis. 'Tom had this special telephone number to call her if he had to. She thought of me as some kind of go-between and she would call me from Iran, at all hours, to say she was coming in and ask could she see Tom. She gave my wife a turquoise ring and a turquoise bracelet and me a gold diamond ring. Tom was not particularly enamoured with her, but she used to give him lots of gold and jewellery she brought in from Tehran. He loved the gold.'

In the late sixties there was a series of full-blown affairs that ended in tears. In 1968 *Top of the Pops* launched the career of Pan's People, five leggy, sexy dancers who soon became stars in their own right. In the middle of his phenomenal run of thirteen consecutive Top 20 hits Tom was constantly on the show where he and dancer Babs Lord became very close. They used to meet in secret at Jack Le Claire's, an after-hours drinking club just off Putney High Street where Jack, the one-eyed owner, had a couple of upstairs rooms he used to rent.

'It was a love scene,' said Ellis, 'another one he could have run off with quite easily. He loved her a lot, and she loved him too, but she could see there was no future in it. Babs put an end to it after she met a guy and got engaged. I remember Tom at the BBC bar — he was really heavy on Babs, trying to get her to give this guy the elbow so that they could get back together again.'

In his own way Tom Jones is a romantic, one who likes to woo his women, not drag them by the hair into his cave. He has consistently held the view that a woman's place is in the home — which never endeared him to the feminists. The cardinal rule is that Tom is boss and should not be taken for granted. Relationships are conducted on his own terms, and he expects his women to obey his rules.

Joyce Ingalls pushed her luck too far in January 1970. After the break-up of his affair with Mary Wilson, Tom was consoling himself with her while filming *This is Tom Jones*. One afternoon the Phantom 6 got stuck in a rush hour traffic jam on the North Circular. Tom was in the back with Joyce and, secure behind the blacked out windows, the pair started to make love. 'I was getting some very, very strange looks,' said Ellis. ' The traffic was at an absolute standstill and the back of the car was jumping about all over the place.'

Joyce was a beautiful blonde American model, turned actress. Tom called her 'Clogs' because she did not appear to own a pair of normal shoes. Joyce was very goofy, so he never knew what she was going to do next. The final straw came when she installed herself in his caravan at Elstree and started issuing a series of increasingly eccentric orders. When she refused to allow the dresser in she was given her marching orders.

'The next afternoon when Tom was on the set recording, I went over to the caravan,' said Ellis. 'I saw that the Rolls-Royce was moving about. I opened the back door, and there was Joyce, who had somehow got back on to the lot. She was in the back of the car with a big bag of boiled sweets wrapped in cellophane, and a roll of sellotape, and she'd taped them all over the back of the car, the doors, the windows, the bar, the television. She just sat there like a naughty little child.'

Joyce flew back to America the next morning. They did meet up a few times in New York, but the affair was over. Some eighteen years later, Melanie Spradlin, another petite blonde American model, drove Tom's staff, especially his minder Chris Montgomery, mad by ordering everybody about and acting like she was his wife not just a girlfriend. Melanie was only twenty-two when she was employed to work on the video of one of Tom's songs in Britain. Tom became obsessed with her and she moved to Los Angeles so she could be close to him. 'She was always blabbing and boasting about their affair,' said Montgomery. 'Then Cindy Montgomery came along, and that meant curtains for Melanie.'

Cindy, a twenty-one-year-old Californian student, caught Tom's eye at a show at the MGM Grand (now Bally's). 'She was a lot taller than him, and he loved that,' said Chris. 'She was big too, in fact to be honest, she was quite fat. But Mr Jones thought she was the most gorgeous thing he'd ever seen. For more than a week she refused to sleep with him, and it drove him absolutely wild.' As Linda was away in Wales, Tom flew her back to his mansion in Bel Air, where he finally seduced her. According to his minder, the couple went on holiday to Hawaii and the affair lasted for nearly a year.

None of Tom's flings had a high public profile until the Marji Wallace affair. Since Marji, he has preferred to find ordinary girls who are less demanding.

Tom has a distinct penchant for 'petite blondes', perhaps they remind him of Linda when they were first courting. But then he also likes black women and very tall girls. All women. Any women. According to Montgomery, he had a three-year road affair with Cynthia Woodard, who replaced Darlene Love in the Blossoms. 'Cynthia was a lovely girl, huge,' reported Montgomery. 'But then the boss likes big girls. The problem was she also snored like a train and could rattle the walls with the noise.' Cynthia – who played her final gig with Tom and The Blossoms in 1990 – laughs it off, dismissing the suggestion as 'outrageous'.

One tall young girl he failed with was Brooke Shields. In 1981 she was turning sixteen when she flew up to Vancouver to tape an appearance on *Tom Jones: Coast to Coast*. For their sketches Tom would flirt with Brooke – best known for her series of sexy jeans ads with the strap line 'nothing gets between me and my Calvins'. She would then deflate his ego by reminding him how much 'My mom and my grandma love your music'. Tom, smitten by both her innocence and her beauty, had other plans.

'He was absolutely besotted with Brooke,' recalled Nanci Eisner. 'He actually went into a jewellery store and picked out a sixteenth birthday present himself – a strand of pearls and matching earrings. He never bought presents personally. At a salute to Buddy Howe, Tom's agent, Brooke was there and sitting next to him. Tom said, "Oh, Brooke, wait till you're twenty-one." "Oh, I don't know about those things," she giggled. He was absolutely nuts about her, but Terri, Brooke's mother, kept an eye on her. There was just no way he was getting to Brooke.'

'I got the feeling he had a crush on me,' laughed Brooke, remembering the story with the benefit of hindsight and experience. 'I had a crush on him because here was this dynamically sexual man and I was so far from that – being America's most celebrated virgin. Tom was two different people. On stage he was very sexual, he exudes it, but off camera he was very solicitous, very gentlemanly, taking care of my mum and my girlfriend. I had no knowledge of what was going on, though I expect my mum was probably telling him to keep away from me.

'He was a man and I was used to the kids at school. I didn't have a boyfriend. The way he moved made me want to dance with him. I was never alone with him, the closest I ever got was when he asked me to dance. He danced really close to me and I remember thinking, "I've never danced like this with a man before." There was this little *frisson* and I just shuddered and went "Ohh". Tom said, "Are you OK?" He knew, but that was it.

'He still has that animal magnetism,' she said. 'I met him after a concert in the summer of 1998. He was worried I wouldn't remember him. He was flirting with me as much as the girl I was with. I was married and he mentioned that he had missed the boat. First it was my mother and then my husband that had got in his way.

'He certainly has charm. I could see him being wonderful to a young girl. There is a sensuality, a sensitivity and a sexuality all in one, plus he's an old-fashioned gentleman. I can imagine him really courting a girl – even if it's just for the hour – with flowers or a gift. That goes a long way with a girl.'

Ellis concurred, but with some reservations. 'Tom wasn't a grab and run guy. He would talk to them as well; he liked to woo them, give them the eyes. He would go four or five hours working on a chick if he had to. One night he spent hours trying to get this fan club lady into bed. There was no way it was going to happen in a million years, but he kept going for it. The next morning he woke up terrified she might have been a reporter, and Lloyd Greenfield had to nail her in the hotel corridor and find out who she was.'

Yet for all his wooing and cooing there is something cold and calculating about Tom's approach to women. He never forces, but he does use them – as much as they use him. In today's parlance he is a sexual obsessive. He will sleep with anyone who will have him.

'In Germany once there was a woman who worked for the record company,' said Ellis. 'Because she was getting on a bit Tom decided that with her clothes off she wouldn't look great. He was horny, so he had her, but he made her keep all her clothes on "so she wouldn't fall to bits".

'That was Tom. He'd fuck anything to get his end away. He's slept with hundreds and hundreds of women; if they were willing, so was he. He would fuck anything, but he wasn't sick – there was never any question of very young girls or young boys, never anything like that. Though he prefers more mature women, maybe eighteen or nineteen years old!'

After forty years the Jones seduction technique is very well honed. In his hotel suite there is always vintage Dom Perignon and the complete works of Tom Jones on the CD player. He may well serenade his intended with his greatest hits, changing the lyrics of *Delilah* to fit her name. In bed he prefers not to use contraceptives, because they reduce his pleasure. In more recent years, because of a fear of AIDS, he has been content with giving and receiving oral sex. Being a creature of habit, the next day he is happy to invite them to his shows or dinner.

With some, like Nicole Hall, a fitness trainer in San Antonio, Texas, he will have a long-distance affair. When Nicole was fifteen, her grandmother took her to Las Vegas and introduced her to Tom. According to one source, who wishes to remain anonymous, 'There was an instant attraction between them, and every year Tom has flown Nicole to Vegas when he performs there. They dated for the first time two years ago [when she was eighteen] and since then they've been together two or three times a year.'

Despite being exposed by tabloid newspapers both in Britain and America as having spent seven days sharing hotel suites with Tom, Nicole, twenty, in 1994, valiantly insisted their relationship was entirely innocent. She said, 'Tom is not my lover, he is like a father to me. I have known him since I was fifteen and we're just very good friends. We were introduced by my grandmother, a great fan, who took me to several of his concerts. He's been a friend of my grandmother's for twenty years and that's the nature of our relationship.'

In his own terms Tom sees himself as a gentleman. He treats women with courtesy, showers them with his attentions and surrounds them with the trappings of fame. He kisses them, looks deep into their eyes and tells them they are special. He gives them his personal card with his phone number on and promises to call. At the moment he says it he means it, but the moment the limo door shuts or the plane takes off he has moved on to the next date and the next girl. The phone number is for Tom Jones Enterprises, his office in LA.

In Tom's terms his women know he is married, they know he is passing through, they know it's a one-night stand and should accept the consequences of their actions. Most of his women do enjoy their time with him. 'I don't think I was just another notch on his bedstead, I think I was someone special to him,' insisted Christina James, a lap dancer he picked up in Stringfellow's after she stripped off to his version of *You Can Leave Your Hat On.* 'I'm a big fan of Tom's and it was like a dream come true to meet him.'

All Christina was doing was echoing a string of Tom's lovers, convincing herself she was special. She had no regrets. But for a few, especially the younger girls, the consequences of sleeping with Tom Jones can be much more damaging. Not everybody can take being dumped back into reality after being romanced by a superstar.

In 1983 Sally Anne Williams was seventeen. Tom spotted her at his show at Revesby Workers Club in Sydney, Australia, and invited her backstage. Then she was invited to join him on Queensland's Gold Coast for a few days. A man with Tom Jones's reputation does not pick a pretty little blonde out of the audience and offer her a holiday purely out of the goodness of his heart but Sally Anne, and her parents, were naive.

'My father asked him, "Can you promise me as a true Welshman that you won't take advantage of my daughter?"' Sally Anne told the *News of the World* in 1990. 'Tom gave his word and the next afternoon I was whisked from home in a Rolls-Royce. Tom's minder Chris Montgomery told me: "You'll be a very spoilt little girl for the next few weeks." We all flew to the Gold Coast in a charter plane. I was so naive that when we arrived at the Currumbin Palms and I saw the plush penthouse suite, I thought it was just for me.

'Then as he started to unpack his things next to mine I panicked, thinking, I hope he doesn't expect me to sleep with him. He said, "Relax, it'll be OK." We had a drink. There was always lots of expensive Dom Perignon champagne around. I didn't like drink but I took it for courage. I'd always been too frightened to sleep with boys and I wanted my boyfriend Tyrone to be my first.

'We went to bed but I couldn't relax. I just didn't fancy him. But the more alcohol I had the nicer he began to look. He was stroking me all over and telling me how beautiful I was. I began to relax and he was a good lover. He didn't even ask me if I was on the pill till after we'd had sex. I wasn't but we still didn't use any contraceptives.'

Over the next few days Sally Anne and Tom made love, talked about Wales, where she was originally from too; Tom called her 'Baby' and 'Baby Doll', sang *What's New Pussycat?* to her and changed the words of *Delilah* to Sally Anne. He made her feel special in a way no Australian boy ever could.

When it ended she 'cried and cried and he cried as well. He told me he wasn't going to Australia the next year but would change his plans to see me. He gave me his phone number and card. Tom told me he loved me and I thought he might stay in touch as a friend even if not as a lover. Then we flew back to Sydney before we parted. I was driven home and I cried all the way back.'

To begin with Sally Anne obeyed the rules. When the *Sun* started sniffing around the story she denied she had had any relationship with Jones. But, of course, he didn't call. Her life began to unravel: she miscarried, had a major row with her parents, left home and started drinking and taking drugs.

Eighteen months later she met Tom again after his show in Brisbane where his attitude was very different. 'He said I'd talked to the press about him and caused trouble for him. Actually I'd denied the affair.' Jones then compounded the situation by offering her some money whereupon she stormed out of the dressing room in tears.

Eventually Sally Anne got some measure of revenge by selling her story but the effect of that short affair coloured her life. She made the error of mistaking a romantic fantasy for real life. Tom knew differently, but then he has had rather more experience in such matters.

Tom developed a taste for threesomes – or more girls if he could. He generally prefers to be the only male engaged in these intimate performances, though on at least one occasion, at Janie Jones's house, he joined in with Gordon Mills.

'Two girls, that was his favourite thing, Janie Jones's house was where he got the taste for it,' said Chris Ellis. 'He'd go there, but it was mainly Gordon's domain. Tom didn't like people watching him having a bunk up, while Gordon didn't care. He was very much a one-to-one, or him and two chicks. After that it was his favourite thing: Tom in the middle and two girls on him. He liked to get them at it as well and watch. He'd love to get two straight chicks to try it. Sometimes he'd succeed, often he'd fail but he would go for it.'

In the News International cuttings library (which services *The Times*, the *Sunday Times*, the *Sun* and the *News of the World*) there are as many files devoted to the career, or should one say exploits, of Janie Jones as there are to Tom. During the seventies the career of Janie Jones, who was born with an altogether more exotic name (Marion Mitchell) in a less exotic place (County Durham) was temporarily halted by a prison sentence following trials for blackmail, prostitution and payola. (She was also immortalised in a song by the Clash – so things weren't all bad.)

In the sixties Janie started out as a Windmill Theatre girl, before attempting a pop career. Thanks to pirate radio – and her friendship with a great many DJs – she had a minor hit with *Witches Brew* in January 1966. Stars would gather down at the Revolution in Bruton Place, Mayfair. The Revolution was run by Rick and John Gunnell, who also owned the Bag o' Nails and the Flamingo. Despite its name, the Revolution was anything but. It was an up-market version of the Flamingo – expensive and exclusive, but not where the Beatles and their friends liked to hang out. The Revolution's clientele was more conservative, drinkers not drug takers: record company bosses and TV celebrities.

'Then they'd say we'll all go back to Janie's,' she said. 'So the party always used to be here. I used to give fantastic parties.' Her parties in Campden Hill Road were extremely popular with stars and DJs.

'Everyone who was anyone came. The doorbell would ring and there would be Tom or Engelbert Humperdinck, Paul and Barry Ryan and many disc jockeys, like Ed Stewart and Johnnie Walker.' The star attraction was a homely but extraordinary woman called Zelda Plumb. She was an exotic striptease artist who would employ a brace of doves or a chinchilla in a performance for which nature had not intended them. Tom, Engelbert and others would clear a space in the living room for Zelda to do her act and jaws would hit the floor as she squirmed naked on the carpet.

'Tom Jones,' said Janie, 'had an insatiable appetite for sex. Often he would be on my seven-foot bed upstairs with two or three girls at a time.'

Janie had a two-way mirror fitted in one of the upstairs bedrooms, which proved very popular.

'Not everyone joined in, of course,' she said. 'Paul Anka came to one of my parties on a visit from America and Tom Jones could not wait to take him upstairs to look through the two-way mirror. On the bed was Tom's manager, Gordon Mills, with two pretty girls. Paul Anka was shocked. He turned to Tom and asked, "How could you let someone like that hold the whole of your career in the palm of his hand?" Tom laughed and went in to join his manager while Paul went downstairs in disgust.'

Paul Anka, a strait-laced, happily married man with a puritan work ethic, confirms the story. He said, 'I don't know what Tom was into or why he'd want to watch Gordon having sex. I wasn't interested, so I went downstairs and left them to it.'

Tom's taste for the exotic erotic has not changed much over the years. In 1995 Jones met Michelle Ferrara (described by the tabloid newspaper to which she sold her story as a 'part-time actress') in Sydney during his 'Three Decades of Cool' tour. She and a girlfriend were invited to join his table at the Cauldron club. At 3 a.m. the three retired to his suite at the Ritz-Carlton.

'He had the best champagne waiting in his suite,' said Michelle, then twenty-seven. 'I asked him if he'd like to see our act and he said, "I'd very much love to". While my girlfriend and I got ready, Tom went into the bathroom to change. The only music he had in the suite was his latest CD, so we started stripping to *She's a Lady*. I gave Tom Jones the striptease of his life.'

Then the girls rubbed each other with oil and began caressing each other intimately. 'He was sitting on the couch devouring us with his eyes. We began tongue-kissing each other and crawling around the floor. He was really loving it. We crawled up to him and began touching his body. He leant back spread-eagled on the couch, while the three of us kissed. My friend began massaging his body while I continued kissing him. He has a really big mouth, it just sucks you in. I told him I thought he had bigger lips than Mick Jagger.

'Tom took off his underpants and handed them to me. I said, "You're supposed to throw them at me." So he did and then I joined my friend in giving him oral pleasure. He was satisfied with that.'

Following their all-night session, Tom told Michelle he found it 'more fun playing sexual games'. The next night the girls had dinner with the singer, and he told them that he liked to watch at least two girls, sometimes as many as five. 'He certainly is a voyeur,' she commented, 'he likes to watch women getting off together.'

Tom Jones has always preferred not to use a condom, claiming it diminishes his enjoyment of sex. While he has been lucky, he has not escaped unscathed. 'He paid for it a few times with some social diseases,' recalled Chris Ellis. 'It was nothing serious, gonorrhoea was like a cold for touring musicians, part of the life. He caught it about four times, had a couple of injections and then steered clear of girls for a few weeks. He didn't want to take anything nasty home with him.

'Running around somewhere in the middle of England there's one little Tom Jones, that's for sure. I'm surprised there aren't more. One of his regulars was a girl who lived up in the Potteries. She drove an E-type Jaguar and Tom told me he'd always thought it was impossible to screw anybody in an E-type, "But we managed it." She always told him that if she got pregnant she would send him a telegram with just one word in it — "bullseye". One day, the telegram did arrive, but there was never a demand for money or anything like that, she was just happy to have Tom Jones's baby.'

In the case of Katherine Berkery, Tom's dislike of condoms was to cost him dear. On 29 October 1987 in Regine's Nightclub in New York, he and Montgomery invited Katherine Berkery and her friend Alicia to his suite at the Ritz-Carlton Hotel for drinks. 'We didn't leave the nightclub until 4 a.m.,' she told a New York court during her paternity suit in 1989. According to Berkery, Jones suggested a threesome, but she refused. 'I was a little angry with him over that, but we went into his bedroom and I had sex with him. I did not have any contraceptive protection.'

Katherine was twenty-four, a part-time model, the illegitimate daughter of a Korean girl and an American GI. When she was eight, her mother gave her up to a New York businessman and his psychiatrist wife, who took her from the Seoul slums and adopted her. Although she left home as a teenager to try her hand as a model and became a regular at Studio 54, a club in the middle of Manhattan's decadent heart, she insists that she was not into one-night stands.

'I really didn't know much about Tom Jones except his name. I certainly didn't know he was married,' she said. 'I think the reason

I finally went to bed with him was that he was very quiet, almost like a father figure.'

For four days and nights they were inseparable, spending hours in his suite at the Ritz-Carlton Hotel. 'He would set the mood by playing his own songs on a tape recorder he kept in a silver briefcase,' she said. 'I found that very funny and rather conceited. But I thought he was really fond of me. I will never forget how once when we were making love he said, "Where have you been all my life?" I suppose I was gullible.'

Three months after Tom left town Katherine discovered she was pregnant. Despite increasingly hysterical phone calls to Tom Jones Enterprises in LA, nobody ever called back. Vowing to start a new life, she moved to Florida and gave birth to Jonathan on 27 June 1988. Two months later, she called the office again.

'I spoke to someone who kept fobbing me off saying Tom was not available to take my calls. In the end I was so upset, I blurted out, "You tell Tom that he has a new son." There was a long pause and I received the reply, "That's showbiz, darling. Do what you have to do." '

If that sounds callous, it has to be put into perspective. The office of a major star can receive thousands of calls a day from fans, girlfriends, college buddies or potential stalkers. Whether the caller dismissed Katherine's call as a prank or followed it up nobody knows.

Ms Berkery was made of sterner stuff. Determined that he should recognise his son and pay child support, she engaged the services of New York's divorce Rottweiler, Raoul Felder. Felder was no stranger to high profile, messy divorces: he had handled Robin Givens' divorce from Mike Tyson.

Tom Jones Enterprises issued a statement saying, 'Mr Jones has been the victim of an irresponsible and scurrilous allegation.' In court their attorney tried to paint Berkery as a lady of easy virtue by linking her with Mafia don, John Gotti. She admitted she knew Gotti, but denied she had sex with him.

'I have not seen John Gotti for several months. I never slept with him or took money from him. He is someone I met at a club called Club A.' Later, when she was accused of being a prostitute, she fought back tears before snapping, 'I have never been a prostitute, worked for an escort agency or lived off men. I have had to sell my gold Rolex watch, put my fur coat in storage and live off the charity of friends because Tom Jones hasn't paid a dime to me.'

The court insisted Jones take a blood test which was 99.67 per cent positive that he was the father. A further DNA test suggested it was 99.9 per cent positive that Jonathan was his child. In July 1989 Tom's lawyers were told they had lost. Although she had turned down £50,000 to drop the case, in a subsequent confidential settlement Jones agreed to pay Berkery $2,000 a month in child support, plus Jonathan's school fees. Despite the DNA test Tom Jones has always refused to acknowledge his paternity.

'You have to understand that we get letters and calls from women claiming all sorts of things,' said Tom. 'There is one woman in Belgium who thinks I should own up to having her child, and she writes to me all the time and sends tapes and things telling me about her life. But I never even met the woman.'

When pressed about Jonathan Berkery's DNA test, Tom conceded, 'Well, we couldn't disprove them.' Then, to the surprise of interviewer, Michael Shelden, he blurted out: 'At least it's natural. I mean, the sex. At least these things are all about natural stuff. You know, nobody's suggesting that I had sex with kids or anything. Or sheep.'

In 1996 Berkery took him back to court in Florida demanding more money. She played the single mother card brilliantly. 'It's not the money, it's the principle. It is heartless for a man not to acknowledge his own son. No amount of money can compensate for the damage that does to a child.' The judge ruled that the New York settlement was not binding in Florida. In August 1998 it was reported Tom had paid a further £50,000 to stop being sued over child maintenance.

Even with the money Katherine has not stopped embarrassing Tom. Every year or so there is a newspaper article talking about how well Jonathan can sing, how he studies videos of his dad, or how he has been to see him in concert. The message hammered home, with all the subtlety of a sledgehammer, is of how much the boy needs a father and how that father refuses to acknowledge that Jonathan is his son.

Despite Katherine's unrelenting campaign, Tom has not, and probably never will, meet his son. He has refused to accept the consequences of what he did and has continued to lead the life he did before. Age not desire is slowing him down. At the end of it all there is a little boy living in Florida who will never understand what he did wrong.

As the aide said, 'That's showbiz, darling.'

CHAPTER TWENTY

THE FAMILY
CRUMBLES

———————

When Tom and Linda moved to LA, Engelbert bought the Pink Palace, Jayne Mansfield's old house. Gordon Mills came too, though Jo stayed behind in Little Rhondda. But Chris Ellis was no longer in the picture.

On 5 March 1975 Johnny Spence, Mark, Tom and Chris flew from Los Angeles to Paris. Because of the tax situation they had rented a rambling farmhouse about twenty miles outside Paris, to act as the headquarters when the orchestra came over to rehearse for the start of a European tour. Ellis was given an extra open ticket to London and told he had to return to collect a white Mercedes to use on the European tour.

On the Monday evening (10 March) Tom said to Chris, 'Let's me and you go out for a drink.' They embarked on a pub crawl through the French countryside. In one bar, Charles Aznavour was chatting to a friend, so they joined him for a while. Early in the morning, with just the two of them left, Tom became particularly maudlin. He was depressed with the way his career was going, how his records weren't hits any more.

'You mustn't worry, the hit records are going to start up again,' said Ellis, noticing how the singer had tears in his eyes. 'Everything's going to be fine.' After that Tom grew very quiet, very down, and wouldn't talk very much any more. Eventually the duo, well pissed, drove back to the farmhouse. The next day Chris and Marion Spence flew back to London.

For the next two months Ellis was kept busy running errands. He drove down to Wales to pick up Linda, helped Jo Mills out by taking her children to school, picked up passports, Tom's trousers. The usual stuff. He was told he was not needed on the European tour. On 20 April he called Lloyd Greenfield in New York who told him there had been 'cutbacks' in the touring party and that Mark was now filling his position. Eventually, on 12 May he had a blazing row on the phone with Gordon Mills who told him, 'I can't be dealing with this. Bill Smith will take care of it.'

'When I was summoned to the MAM offices a couple of days later, Smith suddenly started babbling about Mark, how he's running wild, how we have to get him a job,' said Ellis. 'All of a sudden these words start sliding in, about me driving Bill and working at MAM. And it dawns on me that he's telling me that I'm going to be his chauffeur.

'So I said, "What's this all about? What you're telling me is that you've given Mark my job. Why didn't Tom tell me this? I only saw him a couple of days ago." '

Ellis lost it, told Smith he 'wasn't going to be a chauffeur for no fucking Indian', and stormed out of MAM. At home he dialled Weybridge 51051 and spoke to Linda. It was obvious that she knew. 'Hasn't Tom talked to you?' she said, surprised that her husband had not broken the news himself. 'What do you want me to do? What do you want me to say?'

'Talk to Tom and tell him I want him to call me, I want him to tell me what's going on. I want to hear what he's got to say about this.'

'Right, I'll call him, and I'll tell him,' said Linda.

Of course, the call never came. Chris tried to call Tom in Las Vegas. Where once he could get through immediately, there were now barriers. He spoke to Jeanie King and Johnny Spence, who, while deeply embarrassed, were unable to do anything except promise to pass on the message. Chris Ellis has never spoken to Tom Jones since the Monday morning he left for the airport, offering support and blithely saying, 'I'll be back in a couple of days with the car. I'll talk to you later, we'll sort everything out.'

Two days after he quit, MAM called Chris to tell him that they were going to pay off the £7,000 mortgage on his house. A nice gesture? Yes, except that it had a sting in the tail. 'Nobody at MAM,' said Ellis, 'bothered to take the time to inform me that I was going to be due for this horrendous system, called top slicing relief, and all kinds of things. Two years after all this happened, the tax man caught up with me and told me I owed them £5,000 and threatened to bankrupt me. They took me to court and at the last moment I had to remortgage my house.'

Chris had been on the road for ten years and paid a pittance (£100 a week at the end), what could he know about tax matters? Tom probably never knew how his gift backfired. It was indicative of the attitude of MAM to its employees. Companies tend to reflect the personality and attitudes of the man at the top. While Gordon Mills would never have deigned to 'hate' Chris, he always disliked him.

How much Chris discovered in 1977. Before the tax debacle, he had been holding a job together driving and working for a lighting company. In 1977 he was employed as the lighting designer on a Gilbert O'Sullivan tour. A week before the tour went out,

Jerry Maxim from MAM rang up to get the crew list to arrange backstage passes. Ten minutes later he was back on the phone, adamant that Ellis could not go on the tour. The reason given: 'Gordon Mills is going to be there and if he sees Ellis I'll get my head kicked in.' As at the time Mills and Gilbert barely spoke – the singer was already demanding his songs back – it is unlikely that the manager would ever have been to see the show. Chris had been placed on a blacklist. He was kicked off the tour. 'After all those years, they still got me,' he shrugged.

Nearly a quarter of a century later, Chris Ellis was no longer angry over the money. At least, unlike Vernon, he got something for all those years of graft. What saddened him was the way in which his loyalty and friendship were repaid. He should not have been surprised, he had seen it enough times. But, being human, he was surprised.

'During my meeting with Bill Smith,' he said, 'it suddenly dawned on me that on the pub crawl it had been Tom's intention for him to tell me what was going on. But, as usual, and as it was with the Squires, with Vernon, Dai and everybody else, he got somebody else to do it for him. It didn't surprise me one little bit. Maybe Gordon had told him it was a sign of weakness.

'All those years I was with him, if there was any dirty work to be done, it was me who did it. He loaded the gun, I fired the bullets. Now it was my turn. I think of all the people who got kicked out, I probably got the closest for Tom Jones to actually tell me himself. But I think that at the last minute his bottle went. He couldn't do it, and that I can't forgive.'

'Tom was pained because he and Chris went back for ever,' said Nanci Eisner, who maintains a sanguine view of the relationship between employee and star. 'Some might say he has never taken responsibility but there was always this childlike quality about Tom and people there to jump in and do it, so he was never the hatchet man. There were many things done to people who worked for him that Tom knew nothing about. It is a mistake ever thinking you are really close to a star if you work for them. I don't think anybody is ever that close.'

Like all empires, the edifice that Gordon Mills had so carefully crafted had begun to crumble long before the cracks were visible. Dick Rowe had noticed unhealthy changes in Gordon and his charges when he visited the States during the seventies. 'He believed in Tom Jones like Brian Epstein believed in the Beatles,' said Dick, 'then he went to LA and things started falling apart. He was living in cloud-cuckoo-land. I watched it from a distance and I thought, "This is sad." '

The MAM empire had been built on the illusion of being a family. It was – for the people at the top – but for the agents at the coalface the rewards were not enough. In February 1978 Barry Dickins left to form his own agency, ITB, taking Fleetwood Mac, then the biggest rock band in the world, and the Kinks with him.

'By the late seventies, Harold Davison was moving to America and Colin Berlin decided to go,' said Barry Dickins. 'I went, Alan Field went, the company had diversified into the wrong directions. I have a simple theory – only diversify into things you understand. Why diversify into marinas when you are Gordon Mills? All the mainstays had gone, except Barry Clayman. The records weren't hits any more, Tom wasn't as hip as he had been and they hadn't brought anybody in to replace him.

'This is a business that reinvents itself all the time, it's primarily a young person's business. If you don't have young blood – which they didn't – it's your downfall. MAM should have reinvented itself in the people business. They should have got involved in film and TV. The fact is that they let people become their own company within MAM. It was never a united company.'

The final nail in the Family's public image was hammered in, ironically, by the man who had been hired to create it. Back in 1966 Chris Hutchins had been the news editor of the *NME*. After seeing a magazine picture of Tom dressed in a pinny washing the dishes at his kitchen sink while Linda did the drying up, he realised the boy from the Valleys needed a serious image rethink. After inveigling lunch with Gordon, Hutchins made his pitch to turn Tom into an unattainable sex symbol. He walked out of the restaurant with a new job.

However, by 1976, Hutchins was tired of being a salary man. He could see the huge amounts of wealth being generated at MAM for the top men. But it never trickled down. He wanted a piece of it. He determined to start his own record company and wanted to run that out of New Bond Street in conjunction with his publicist duties. Typically, Mills was not interested unless MAM owned everything – publishing, record contracts, image making, the works. That was the way he did business, and if Hutchins did not like it he could walk. He walked.

The record company never happened. Instead, Hutchins delivered a devastating six-part series in the *Daily Mirror* in which he exposed the myths he had built up around Tom, Engelbert, Gilbert O'Sullivan and Mills, as the PR sham they were.

By the standards of what has come since, Hutchins's supposed revelations were pretty tame stuff. Compared to the extraordinary *fin de siècle* decadence and excess that drenched contemporary rock bands, like the Rolling Stones, Led Zeppelin and Aerosmith, in orgies of women, drugs and alcohol; or record companies like the cocaine-fuelled colossus that was Neil Bogart's disco label Casablanca, tales of the Family were suburban tittle-tattle.

That Tom and Engelbert both slept with as many women as they could was hardly a surprise. It was Hutchins's version of events, the little details about their petty behaviour and personal jealousies, that struck home. About how Tom was so lazy he would

Tom Jones and the Squires – (left to right) Chris Slade, Mickey Gee, Dave Cooper and Vernon Hopkins – in 1965 (*Scope Features*)

An early publicity shot (*Scope Features*)

Backstage at the Paradise Lounge, Pearl Harbour, Hawaii on 16 May 1969 (*Chris Ellis*)

Chris Hutchins and Tom (with Lloyd Greenfield behind) clowning around on the private jet during the US tour of 1971 (*Chris Ellis*)

Linda in Acapulco in 1970 (*Chris Ellis*)

Tom in Barbados in 1974 (*Chris Ellis*)

Tom with Jo Mills in the South of France in 1967 (*Chris Ellis*)

On tour in Canada in July 1972 – Tom, Derek Watkins, Terry Jenkins, Dai Perry and Big Jim Sullivan at the front, having fun on Lake St Clair (*Chris Ellis*)

With musical director Johnny Spence on Catalina Island, with John Wayne's boat *The Wild Goose* in the background, 1974 (*Chris Ellis*)

Chris Ellis, Tom and Rocky Seddon looking the part in Acapulco in July 1970 (*Chris Ellis*)

Tom, Mark, Linda, Ken and Sheila Davies and Eva and Chris Ellis at Lake Tahoe, California in 1974 (*Chris Ellis*)

Tom, the best man, and Linda, the matron of honour, with Chris and Eva Ellis at their wedding in Caesars Palace on 18 September 1973 (*Chris Ellis*)

Linda, Violet Trenchard (Linda's mum, just visible), Freda, Tom senior, Mark, Eva and Tom on holiday in Barbados in October 1974 (*Chris Ellis*)

Chris, Eva, Freda, Tom (now with a beard!), Vi, Linda and Tom senior (*Chris Ellis*)

Tom, Mark and Alexander at home in LA in the summer of 1983 (*Scope Features*)

By the pool in LA with his parents and a friend in 1981, just before Tom senior died (*Scope Features*)

At Tor Point in the early seventies: in his study, by the swimming pool (note the Welsh dragon) and in the kitchen demonstrating his healthy diet! (*Terry O'Neill*)

'The kiss' – Tom and Marjorie Wallace, in February 1974 (*Terry O'Neill*)

Through the decades: On stage for the BBC in 1968… (*David Redfern/Redferns*)

Looking good in the USA in the early seventies… (*Michael Ochs/Redferns*)

In concert in 1983… (*Syndication International*)

Singing with Robbie Williams at the Brit Awards in 1998 (*Syndication International*)

always sleep with 'the plain girl who was a pushover. Those who didn't ask, didn't get'; or how Engelbert was so envious of Tom. It made the medallion-laden superstars seem so ordinary.

As the series continued over six days, Mills and his lawyers tried without success to injunct the *Daily Mirror*. Justices Denning, Lawton and Bridge ruled for the newspaper. Stoking up the fire, Hutchins then claimed he had received a death threat from America, while Mills raved about how he would pursue his former employee through the courts, even if it took him ten years.

'Chris Hutchins was there and saw what was happening,' admitted Mills in the *Daily Mirror*. 'He was very good at his job — very, very good. But I don't know what has happened to the man. He was more than an employee, but now . . . I'm going to find out. I know where he lives. I know his haunts. I know the nature of the man. I may take a swing at him. It depends how I feel. I come from Tonypandy where Tommy Farr was born. We know about action in the Rhondda Valley.' A few days after the series had ended, Mills flew into Heathrow on business, screaming revenge. 'I may attack him,' he shouted to the gleeful newsmen, 'I may take a swing at him.'

Tom was embarrassed by the Hutchins revelations. 'I told my wife about it,' he admitted in a transparent piece of damage control. 'Her mother also called her and warned her that terrible things were being said. Linda said she never wanted to see the stories, and she never did. But I felt betrayed even though the things that were written were not terrible, terrible things. He gave Humperdinck a harder time than me. I don't know what I would do if I saw Hutchins again. I think the best thing is for me not to see him. It might get me into trouble because I don't know whether I could control myself.'

As usual it was Enge who came out of it the worst. He'd been unhappy for a while, and using the exposé as an excuse, appointed Harold Davison as his new manager. Although he was still contracted to MAM, Mills commented ruefully, 'I'm still his manager in name and law, but that's all. He doesn't listen to me any more.'

Worse was to follow. The following year Humperdinck challenged his management contract in the High Court claiming it was illegal on the grounds of 'oppression and bargaining power'. He also claimed he had signed the deal, giving Gordon Mills thirty per cent of his earnings, without ever reading it.

Meanwhile, the career of the triumvirate's junior member had also stuttered to a halt. Gilbert O'Sullivan had not had a hit since 1975. All he had were the songs he had written, and he wanted them back. What started as a minor disagreement over music publishing, ended up as a landmark case in pop history.

Copyright ownership is one of the most vexatious and litigious areas in pop music. To this day Les Reed deeply regrets he let Gordon insist on *It's Not Unusual* being published by Leeds Music, rather than by his own publishing company Donna Music. It was not just a case of the money – though he would probably be tens of thousands of pounds better off – but a question of who controlled the exploitation and legacy of the song, what TV ads it could be used in, which movies and so on.

Early on in his legal wranglings with MAM, O'Sullivan had been offered fifty per cent of his copyright back. In today's publishing world, where an established writer can demand – and get – ninety per cent, such an offer seems miserly. In the early seventies that was, if not generous, a standard royalty. However, the massive sales boom the industry enjoyed from 1976, with albums such as Fleetwood Mac's *Rumours*, *Saturday Night Fever* and *Frampton Comes Alive* selling over twenty million copies, had raised an artist's expectations. They had better lawyers too. In 1979 Gilbert O'Sullivan went for broke. He issued a writ against Gordon and MAM, demanding the return of the copyrights of all his songs, millions of pounds in back royalties and damages, as well as the cancellation of his employment agreement with Ebostrail and his recording contract with CBS in New York.

The case came before Justice Mars Jones in the spring of 1982. History and legal precedent were not on the side of MAM. The very nature of any contract between an unknown artist and a major company mitigates against it being fair. In a court of law those fundamental inequalities become only too apparent to the public.

The media had a field day. Mars Jones was appalled to discover that Gilbert had been living on £10 a week pocket money even after his first hits. In 1973, the year after he had been voted the world's most successful solo artist, his allowance was still only £150 a month. When he suggested buying a modest £95,000 house near Weybridge, he was told he could not afford it and that the money would have to be borrowed. He was reprimanded for spending £1,000 on a brass bed. 'I had the impression I was living beyond my means,' he told the court. When he queried his royalty statements, Mills, 'like a schoolmaster, gave me a good rollicking for going behind his back'.

Used to the diffident young man of a decade earlier, MAM believed Gilbert to have been well coached by his lawyers. When Mars Jones asked O'Sullivan if he used a synthesiser on his tracks and confessed to playing a little guitar himself, they realised the case was lost. The judge found Gilbert to be an impressive witness and an honest and sincere man. 'I regret,' he said forthrightly, 'I cannot say the same about Mr Gordon Mills and Mr William Smith, chief witnesses for the defence.' Inadequately prepared, they were torn apart by O'Sullivan's lawyers.

After the accountants' files were prised open and millions of pounds appeared to have disappeared, Mars Jones concluded that the singer had been 'fleeced'. The documents revealed that from

1970 to 1978 O'Sullivan's recordings had grossed an estimated £14.5 million, from which he had actually received £500,000 before tax.

On 5 May 1982 Mars Jones delivered a damning historic judgement. He set aside the agreements between O'Sullivan and MAM as 'oppressive, with inequality of bargaining power and an unreasonable restraint of trade resulting from undue influence'. The master tapes of all the recordings had to be returned, while Mills was ordered to repay every single penny he had made from the singer, with the added penalty of compound interest. O'Sullivan's costs, estimated at £100,000, were awarded against Mills. Headlines put the judgement at over £7 million.

Worse was the damage to Gordon's already fading reputation. The fight appeared to have gone out of him. In court there was no sign of the man who had been the most powerful personal manager in the world. Dick Rowe recalled, 'I was one of the witnesses in court. It was very sad for Gordon. I thought, "God, now we know the real strength of the man." He didn't know what to say. The opposing counsel just tied him up in knots and made him look like a fool. It must have been sad for Gilbert's people to see this man, the managing director of MAM, made to look like an ignorant office boy.'

Naturally, the case went to appeal. On 14 February 1984, Mills and MAM won a partial victory. Justice Dunn acknowledged that it was significant that 'until Mr O'Sullivan had met Mr Mills he had achieved no success and after they effectively parted company in 1976 he achieved no success. During his years with Mr Mills his success was phenomenal.' Mills's QC, Michael Miller, pointed out that, contrary to the original calculations, O'Sullivan had received £1.4 million, and after meeting his own expenses was left with £960,000. The three Law Lords changed the original ruling allowing Mills and his companies a share of the profits for the work they had done in exploiting and promoting the artist worldwide. They also concluded that Mills should receive credit for the tax that he had paid on behalf of the singer, so the original order to pay compound interest was amended to simple interest.

The submissions of fraud and fleecing, though not overruled, were placed in a new perspective because Mars Jones's criticisms had been based on the assumption that publishing agreements dated February 1972 were made at that time, whereas in fact they had been made in 1970, before O'Sullivan became a star. Mills's culpability was therefore modified. His counsel reckoned the appeal had been about one third successful.

But the crux of the matter was that Gilbert was entitled to keep the copyright of all his songs and the master tapes of his records. The judgement was worth some £5 million. Money Gordon did not have readily to hand. There are rumours that he had to borrow from Tom.

For MAM it was already over. In the changing environment of the late seventies and early eighties, the company had been struggling to keep up. The agency had fallen from its all-powerful position to be also-rans. The other interests — gaming machines, hotels, marinas and airlines — had diluted its purpose too far.

The 1982 judgement effectively killed MAM. While the City knew that the judgement was likely to be modified on appeal, it was not prepared to invest any further in the company. MAM desperately needed £2 million to finance its latest scheme. In 1981 Burger King had awarded them the franchise for south-eastern England (excluding central London) — one of the richest areas in the country.

Instead of opening seven Burger Kings, as Bill Smith had planned, they were forced to open just three. At the time, Burger King had not got its advertising act together, and with no further finance available the restaurants were sold back to the parent company. It could have been one of the shrewdest investments MAM ever made, but instead the world was spared from having to eat a flame-grilled Tom-burger.

In early 1985 MAM was the victim of a reverse takeover by the private Chrysalis Group run by former agent Chris Wright.

Gordon Mills's empire-building days were over. After twenty years it was back to the beginning.

Just him and Tom Jones.

CHAPTER TWENTY-ONE

LIVING ON THE FAULT LINE

———————

J ust as Tom was on the verge of finalising the deal to buy the Bel Air mansion at 363 Copa d'Oro, Linda got cold feet. The prospect of being away from Britain made her homesick, so she asked Tom if there was any way they could pull out. She cried for twenty-four hours after Tom refused, telling her, 'It's too late now – you saw the house, you liked it, everything's final.' He was fed up living out of a suitcase and damned if he was going to sacrifice his hard-earned fortune to the tax man. He pointed out to Linda that if she was in LA it would be much easier for them to spend time together. He even suggested she come on the road with him and she could go back home whenever she wanted.

'Listen,' he told her, 'we haven't been sent here. It's not the colonies. You can go back home to visit whenever you like.' Linda, unfortunately, however much she missed her mother and sister, will not travel on her own. Her reclusive tendencies increased, the only difference being that now Tom was around enough to notice them.

She refused to learn to drive, which in LA is tantamount to committing social suicide. Every time she wanted to go out she had to call a limo and driver.

In many ways Linda was more trapped than in England. Beverly Hills society makes its judgements based purely on success and the trappings that come with it. They might be able to accept that she was not a trophy wife, but then she had to get involved in a charity, anything to validate her position. LA is a company town where who you know shapes who you are.

To Linda, her husband was not a star, just the same cocky boy she had met when she was ten. But if she met a 'real' film star she was struck as dumb as any Welsh housewife. It drove Tom crazy.

'Moving to LA put strains on the marriage – more so for her – because when I'm busy, I'm busy,' Tom said. 'When I was living in England, I was away for seven months a year, so when she moved to LA she was seeing more of me because I would only tour for a month at the outside. Linda is a very introverted woman. She always has been. She doesn't feel comfortable with people she doesn't know. And because of this she doesn't go out to parties or restaurants. And I rarely invite strangers into the house.

'She is not a showbusiness woman, she's scared stiff of it. I would say to her, "I'm not the only man in showbiz, other people do it and their wives get friendly." She didn't like it, didn't want to. I know a lot of people in the business well enough to invite them to dinner, but I have never got close to them in Los Angeles because of my wife.'

'An estate agent friend wanted to show us a property he was selling to see if we would be interested. It turned out to be owned by movie producer Robert Evans, who invited us to stay and watch a new film he was screening. Jack Nicholson and his girlfriend also turned up and we all had a really great time. She did not get all uptight because it was done on the spur of the moment. But if I'd said to Linda, "Let's go over to Bob Evans's to watch a new movie and we'll be sitting with Jack Nicholson," she would have said, "No way." '

This theme continued throughout the eighties. 'She's a misfit,' Tom told Lynda Lee Potter. 'A lot of women would love to have the money and all the socialising, but it doesn't do a lot for her. She doesn't like travelling, she can't stand crowds, she is a bit agoraphobic. If she does go out, she has to get some Dutch courage. In order to go anywhere she has a drink. She doesn't like to go to parties because she says, "I'll only have a few drinks to give me confidence and then I'll make a fool of myself." My life really goes against the grain for her, what she'd really like would be for me to have a nine to five job and she'd rather be in Britain.'

Following the Hutchins revelations, a new line started to creep into interviews, best summed up by one of Tom's favourite one-liners, 'Being married keeps me single.' He no longer made any secret of the fact that he had affairs and that Linda knew about them. 'If it hadn't been for my wife I'd have been married five or six times now. I've weighed it all up and I don't think there's anything with more advantages. If we separated I wouldn't be any better off, and she's never said she wants to leave, so why should I change? She accepts I'll have affairs, although she doesn't go along with it, doesn't say, "Oh it's all right." She just tells me to be careful.

'My wife doesn't want to know,' he said. 'She has never been unfaithful to me and I don't ask any questions that I don't want to know the answers to. And she doesn't ask me. It's fair that way. "Don't you go running off with some young girl," she says. It's the young thing that bothers her — all women worry about that. Men age gracefully.'

Perhaps he should have said 'stars'. Unfortunately and infuriating as it is for feminists, Tom, for all his posturing and bragging, understands a fundamental truth about women.

'A lot of women around me are very sexy and would be very good in bed, but there must be more than that to the kind of partnership that marriage is,' he said. 'When you're in the process of making love, the woman seems everything to you. After you've made love, she is one of two things. Someone you want to keep with you, or someone you want to crawl away from. A wife must be in the former category.

'A man is more likely to have casual encounters. A woman looks for something deeper in her relationships.'

For all Tom's complaining about Linda's shyness, it worked for him. He, too, is not naturally gregarious. A creature of habit, very self-contained, aware of who and what he is. He enjoyed being at home in Copa d'Oro. 'I like to be out by the pool and get some sun,' he said. 'I don't often get the chance. I love to catch a few rays to look healthy rather than like a bloody ghost. I go very white and pasty, then you have to start with the make-up and I don't like wearing that. In LA, if I'm not working, I'll get lazy, get up at noon, have lunch round the pool. Then I have to convince myself to go into the gym in the basement. If I'm off for a week, I put on weight. I fluctuate by about ten pounds, which I can put on over a Christmas.'

Tom and Linda lived at 363 Copa d'Oro for 21 years. He paid a million dollars for it – $200,000 below the asking price – and eventually sold it to film stars Nicolas Cage and Patricia Arquette. In an area where the favoured style is white Spanish hacienda, Copa d'Oro was built in 1940 in the style of the eighteenth-century Scottish architects, James and Robert Adam, and constructed entirely of red brick.

Because Dean Martin had lived there, the sixteen-room house was already a gawping stop for the tourist buses. Autograph hunters, lurking outside with cameras, freaked Linda out. When one couple spread a blanket out on the front lawn and ate a picnic lunch, Tom had had enough. High fences were installed and electric gates, decorated by Welsh dragons, were constructed at the entrance.

A fountain, shipped over from Italy, stood outside the front of the house. In many ways the house resembled Tor Point, a Beverly Hills vision of how an English manor house should look, with oak and mahogany panelling on the walls, high oak-beamed ceilings and chandeliers.

Gold records hung in the hall, next to awards from music papers. In the pool room hung photos of Tom with celebrities. Traces and memories of home were everywhere. Brass and pewter ornaments – reminiscent of the front room in Laura Street – in the library/TV room, Union Jack mugs in the kitchen. The living room, with its Victorian furniture was strangely formal, except for the shelf with a bobby's blue helmet on it.

To the right of the hallway was a dining room, furnished with a dining table which sat twelve people. Beyond the dining room was a family breakfast room. Next to that was a large old-fashioned kitchen with sparkling copperware hanging everywhere, and a red-brick hearth and a gas range. At the end of the hall was a film screening room with a bar, which was well stocked with champagne and beer.

A broad, winding staircase led to the four upstairs rooms, each with its own private bathroom. The master bedroom suite was dominated by a giant mahogany four-poster bed. Upstairs was Linda's domain. Often she did not come down for days. In the basement, Tom had a fully equipped gymnasium. Inside a medieval turret attached to the house was more fitness equipment, punch bags and a rowing machine, easily accessible from the swimming pool.

The pool was the house's crowning glory: 45 by 25 feet, big even by Bel Air standards, it was surrounded by terracotta sculptures, statues of Roman maidens and open-mouthed fish at each corner. A Jacuzzi pool bubbled away at one side. The flower beds were filled with oleanders, hibiscus and bougainvillaea, as well as blooming red roses, grown to make Linda feel at home even though they did not take well to the southern Californian climate.

Wonderfully kitsch, at the side of the pool was a red telephone box, the old button A and button B 'four penny' type. The very one that used to stand in Tower Street, Treforest, from which Tom phoned the hospital to see if Linda had had their baby. When he heard it was going to be replaced, he bought it from the GPO for £250 and had it shipped over. It still worked.

'When I was eighteen, if you dialled Pontypridd 3667, the chances were you'd have got me in that box,' said Tom, in a nostalgic mood. 'That was my first home. My first office. I courted girls from it. My family began in it (not literally, mind you), and it is as much part of my life as my first gold records. On visits home at the weekends Gordon would call me there.'

By 1983 Linda had come to a grudging acceptance of life in LA. Having abnegated the role of Mrs Tom Jones, Mark's marriage and the birth of her first grandson helped give her back a family focus. In a rare interview with the *Sun*, she said, 'At first I went everywhere with Tom, but now I am content to sit home and wait. Sometimes, when he is away touring in Las Vegas or somewhere like that, I get lonely so I phone up my mum for chats that can last as long as three hours. It's pointless wishing I was there with him, because I've done all that before. I no longer want to be sitting in some hotel room while he is out on stage. I am much happier being a housewife, making sure everything is ready for him when he comes home exhausted.'

At their home, the cook was given weekends off, so that Linda could prepare Tom's favourite meal — chicken curry — and take him his 'early morning' cup of tea at around noon. The rest of their time together was spent watching old movies and sports programmes on TV, just like 'any other ordinary, middle-aged, happily married couple'.

Linda gave up worrying about her weight, about how she looked. She knew she could not compete with twenty-year-olds, so what was the point of trying? Her anonymity had its advantages. When photographers and reporters were outside her hotel waiting for Tom and his family, she could walk past them without being recognised.

Together they were as comfortable as ever. Linda still gave him hell. 'She doesn't want to be with Tom Jones the singer,' admitted Tom. 'She wants Tom Jones the husband. She knows I'll always come home to her. And she knows that, when I close the front door behind me, I'm hers. I'm not the star with my wife and she's certainly not in awe of me. In fact she bullies me. She's always shouting at me to do things round the house. I said to her recently, "I take more crap from you than anyone else in the world." '

'You only have to see them together to know how much they still love each other, they really do have the most extraordinary marriage,' agreed Linda's mother, Violet Trenchard. 'The funniest time of all is when they have a row. Tom stalks to the telephone, rings me up, and says, "It's all your fault. She's your daughter." It's that type of humour injected into their marriage that keeps it so fresh for both of them. Besides being husband and wife, they are wonderful, marvellous friends.'

Tom needed Linda desperately when, on 10 October 1981, forty years of inhaling black dust finally caught up with Tom Woodward Senior. He was seventy-one. Miners call it 'the black lung'. Coal dust never completely goes away – it lingers behind, trapped at the bottom of the lungs, biding its time before returning in late middle-age, to kill tens of thousands of former miners. Suffering from emphysema and pneumoconiosis, Tom Senior had been having difficulty breathing for years. During a visit to Bel Air his lung disorder grew so bad that doctors warned him against travelling home. He died in LA and was buried at Forest Lawn

Memorial Park, a few miles from Tom's home.

'When my father was alive, I always thought I was all right,' said Tom later. 'You just always expect your parents to be there. Then, when he went, I started believing that I would be next.' It is always hard to lose your father, but to a superstar it is a reminder both of mortality and the fickle nature of fame. Tom was deeply upset. Fuelled by grief and alcohol, he even talked of giving up singing. But it was never a serious option.

As Gordon Mills said to Tom, endlessly, while he nursed his artist through his grief, 'Because of your success, you were able to get him to retire years early from the mines. That alone doubled his lifespan. How many other former miners from Pontypridd have drunk with Presley, Sinatra and Jimmy Tarbuck? Think of your poor mother. Think of your fans.'

Tom bought another house nearby, and moved his mother and sister to LA. For the first time in her life Freda Woodward was no longer required to be at a man's beck and call. She missed her husband but loved the climate. 'I've had enough of rain and grey skies,' she told her grandson. Best of all, her son took them with him whenever he played his Vegas seasons. Linda, generally, stayed at home, while Freda and Sheila had a great time.

In 1982 Mark married Donna Polom. Their son, Alexander, was born in June 1983. They also had a daughter, Emma, in 1987. They, too, moved into the neighbourhood. The death of Tom Senior had the effect of bringing the Woodward family closer together, physically, in a foreign environment, and focused them on the undisputed head of the family. This created a Welsh laager, cemented by blood and absolute loyalty, inside which Tom was utterly secure.

He needed the support. By 1983 Tom Jones's career had sunk to its lowest ebb for twenty years. It was going nowhere.

CHAPTER TWENTY-TWO

GORDON'S LAST DAYS

On the evening of 20 June 1982, just as Annie Toomaru walked back into her apartment in Santa Monica, the telephone rang. It was Michel Willow, one of the owners of Le Dôme, a long-established and chic West Hollywood restaurant. 'Please come and meet me this evening,' he said. Hot and exhausted after a long flight from Tahiti, Annie was in no mood to go out.

'I've just landed, I'm tired and I want to sleep,' she protested. 'I don't want to see anyone, I don't want to dress up.'

'Please come,' he insisted, 'it's going to be just the two of us.'

Annie still wonders whether it was a set-up. She arrived at the restaurant, where Michel said to her, 'I want to introduce you to a friend of mine.' There were two men at the table, Gordon Mills and John Moran, Tom Jones's PR manager. Gordon's first words were, 'Oh, you're from Tahiti? You are the first Tahitian I've met, and it was always my dream when I grew up to go to Tahiti.' So they talked for a while and, at the end of dinner, Gordon asked Annie to go on with them. They moved on to the piano bar of the Bel Air Hotel, where they drank vintage Dom Perignon and talked, until her jet-lag was forgotten.

For the next month they dated three or four times a week. 'He was spending his time with his girlfriend and me,' said Annie. 'A month after that we were steady, every night together.' They were together for the next four years.

Annie was certainly different. A single mother in her early forties with two school-age children, running a small travel business, she stood out like a beacon from the surgically enhanced, bottle-blonde, Beverly Hills starlets. An enticing mixture of Polynesian, French and English ancestry, a soft, sexy accent, a cosmopolitan, cultured upbringing and an unbridled lust for life made her irresistible to Gordon. He always had a taste for the exotic.

She was the best thing to happen to Gordon in years, at a time when not many things were going right. His personal life had been floundering since his separation from Jo (their divorce was not finalised until 1985). Their marriage had slowly disintegrated during the seventies as Tom and Engelbert's careers demanded he spend his time in the States. Jo hated Los Angeles.

Gordon had had his affairs, including his fourteen-year relationship with Anne Marie Brekke. Gordon had introduced her twin sister, Aase, to Gilbert O'Sullivan, who, after years of an on–off relationship, married her in 1980.

From the start there was no secret about Gordon's relationship with Annie Toomaru. Soon she knew his kids and his feisty mother Lorna. (After Gordon died, Lorna tried to persuade Annie to move to England, but after she started to date other men, Lorna never spoke to her again.) Annie loved to travel, so they travelled all the time. For her he conquered his fear of flying: weekends in Acapulco, camping on her family atoll in Tahiti with his kids, fishing at Fort William in Scotland. They went to Australia and New Zealand, when Tom was on tour there, and to Vancouver for recording sessions.

However much Gordon loved her, some parts of his character never changed. His desire to control and his paranoia remained. He never liked her to leave his side. There would be dinners at Le Dôme with the William Morris Agency. 'There are fifteen men at the table,' she recalled 'I'm sitting right next to him, and he'd say, "OK, half an hour of business, and after that we do whatever you want." I was friendly with John Moran, but Gordon would always keep him at a distance.'

Gordon owned a large mansion at 340 North Faring Grove, in the chicer-than-chic Holmby Hills. He had an office in Century City – a few minutes' drive away – but all his meetings and deals were conducted from home. Whereas St George's Hill had also been home to everything he loved – his family and all his animals – his mansion in the hills was a soulless place. He had no live-in staff, unusual for LA, and only employed a couple to clean on Annie's insistence. A naturally solitary man most of the time, he was alone and brooding.

'The last time I saw Gordon was in the early eighties,' recalled Barry Mason. 'I was working in Los Angeles, and because I'd not seen him for a year I rang him up. I said, "Hi, it's Barry. Do you fancy a drink?" "Oh yeah, OK," no enthusiasm. So I go to his house in Holmby Hills, his beautiful, fancy LA home, and we sit down. So we make conversation. Twenty minutes go by. Finally I say, "Yes Gordon, I'd love a drink." It's the first thing you do when somebody comes to your home, isn't it?

'Anne Marie was off somewhere, the house was desolate, empty. He is in this great bloody place, totally alone. I sit there talking to him. The conversation is hard work really, he's not really very relaxed, and finally it's time to go. I said, "Well Gordon, you've done bloody well, haven't you?" He said, "Yes, I've done all right." "Well done, my old mate," I said, light-heartedly, "but you want to give up smoking."

'He exploded, "What?" I said, "Smoking." All this money and yet still smoking, it seemed insane to have everything and risk it. And he let off at me, "Fucking smoking, my grandfather smoked until he was ninety-eight and it did him no fucking harm." He really attacked me, so I said, "Hey, no problem, see you later, goodbye." '

'I hated that house. It was beautiful, beautiful, but all just for decoration,' remembered Annie. He had a room where you could view movies, a big screen like a theatre, and he had his office next to it, with a living room, and another living room where we never sat. Five rooms upstairs and a huge swimming pool. Empty except when the children came.'

Annie refused to sleep in his house. When he complained she told him 'to go, you know the f-word'. Nobody else, except Jo, had told Gordon to fuck off in years. He loved it. A year after they met, her tour company was bought out. Rather than continue to work for the new owners, Gordon suggested Annie run the Tom Jones fan clubs. Although he seldom came in to the office, he called her several times a day, even checking up on who she was having lunch with. 'He would always call me around 5 p.m. and say, "What are we going to eat tonight?" One night I say, "I don't feel like going out," so he says, "How about if I cook a curry? You just have to lay the table." Before I came home, he opened a bottle of wine – a bottle of Château Latour '61 or '66 – and he would have just one glass and wait for me for the rest.'

Tom was as concerned as he had ever been about his career. He worked constantly in America – Vegas for two months in four two-week stints, a week or two in Atlantic City and at least a hundred one-nighters across the country. The venues were getting smaller. There were no new songs on the TV or radio. Tom was aware that his career was in trouble. In the past he had been saved by recording a great song. The problem was finding one.

'I had got preoccupied with live performances,' he admitted, 'they didn't dwindle away like the hits. A year went by, two, three years went by and the audience was still there. Playing the big venues, I got caught up in thinking that everybody can hear me. I was singing the songs, but it was not being recorded, not being captured for others to hear.

'I was always moaning to Gordon, "What the fuck happened? I'm still singing." I knew my time would come again. We had a song in 1978, *Say You'll Stay Until Tomorrow*, which made some noise in America. I thought, "Here we go. Things have come around my way again." I followed it with an album, but there weren't any other hit songs.'

Gordon, too, found it frustrating. In 1978 they built Britannia Recording Studios on Cahuenga Boulevard. The plan was to control the recording process and give Tom access to the strong new material he craved, while at the same time buying and developing scripts, and also doing some TV packaging.

'Most songwriters today seem to be recording their own material or giving it to people who are on top of the charts,' Gordon said in an interview in 1978, before moving on to the attack, 'so I'm going to develop a really big music publishing company. I'm trying to find new writers who will write for the company, so that Tom and I can have first choice of anything they write. But finding these people has not been easy.'

Mills complained that in an era where hits only happened if they had a disco beat, there was no room for a ballad. 'There's no chance of getting airplay on a ballad unless you get a song from a picture like Debby Boone did. [*You Light Up My Life* won Boone both an Oscar and a Best New Artist Grammy.] Why, if Barbra Streisand hadn't had motion pictures as a vehicle for her songs, I don't think she would have been as popular.'

Mills was bitter about the trend record companies had followed – looking for something new, while abandoning the old but proven winners. 'I hate to say this, but they're more interested in turnover. If you get a big hit and the second record doesn't happen and the third record doesn't happen – it's on to the next case. They just do not stick with the artists and build them like they did in the old days.'

That comment showed how out of touch Gordon had become. The music business has always been, always will be, obsessed with the new at the expense of the old. He had forgotten how Decca were considering dropping Tom after the failure of his first single. He reserved the rest of his anger for the movie business. 'Film producers and directors are totally unaware of our business. They don't even know one singer from another – and they couldn't care less whether they can act.'

Gordon's obvious frustration was apparent because he realised that he had missed his chance of establishing Tom as an actor. Although not many have actually succeeded in running dual careers, there is a natural affinity between pop singers and movie stars – leading men, not actors. Tom Jones looked a natural to be in the movies, he had the right look, rugged, working-class, not too good-looking, but sexy, a coarser, darker Michael Caine. Why did Tom Jones never make a movie?

One problem was that Tom was a lousy actor. On one Christmas special, where all he had to do was walk on with a pile of Christmas presents and say, 'I've been shopping,' it took dozens of takes. The idea of learning whole scripts filled him with dread. Song lyrics were easier. They rhymed.

Talent is not a pre-requisite for a film star. A great deal of the art of screen acting is saying very little and moving less – both of which the Welshman excelled at. He could hardly have been any worse an actor than Elvis Presley.

The spectre of Presley's films haunted Tom, and particularly Gordon, who did not want to surrender control of his protégé to the Hollywood wolves. 'I always thought he should have done a lot more movies,' said Gene Kilroy. 'Gordon remembered Elvis doing all those shit movies. For Gordon, it had to be the right script. He was overly protective of Tom there.'

Making movies takes up a lot of time. Time in which a singer could be singing or recording. People have to make a conscious effort to go to the movies. They have to pay. And for all his talents, Tom wasn't a legend, he wasn't Elvis.

Tom wanted to be a film star; he had fancied himself playing a cowboy or a secret agent. 'The parts I've been offered always have no meat in them,' he claimed. 'I've always been offered these Elvis-type roles. The only thing that would have appealed to me was if I'd been offered a part in *The Wild Bunch*.'

The trick was to find him a role that allowed him to stay in character. In August 1971, Herb Jaffe, a vice-president at United Artists, announced that Tom had signed a three-picture deal. His first movie, *The Gospel Singer*, was being adapted by screenwriter Robert Thom, and would be shot the following year.

On the surface *The Gospel Singer* was a perfect fit. The original novel, by Harry Crews, tells the tale of a golden-haired young preacher with the voice of an angel who meets with a violent death. It was a part Tom could empathise with, familiar territory. He had the down-home southern accent – grits and all – down pat. Elvis had coached him. But there were a couple of major drawbacks from Tom's point of view. He did not want to be blond, and he did not want to die. Although Crews was aghast at the idea, neither of those were insurmountable objects to the movie world – Hollywood loves a happy ending. *The Gospel Singer* was never made, although a shooting date of May 1975 was announced. And Gordon was still talking it up in 1980, by which time Tom was way too old for the part.

When, in 1976, he was offered the lead role in *The Stud*, based on Jackie Collins's bestseller, Tom was horrified by the script. The sex was bad enough: he was supposed to leap from bed to bed, sleep with both men and women, but it was the four-letter words that really upset him. 'I don't mind swearing to emphasise something, but just to throw words in for no reason is another matter,' he said. 'I wouldn't like my mum and dad to see that sort of film. It's just short of being pornographic.'

In July 1976 Tom finally started a movie, cancelling eleven weeks of concert bookings to do so. He was the lead in *Yockowald*, an off-beat spy thriller, directed by Russell Rouse and produced by Clarence Greene, a well-respected team who had made *DOA* and *The Oscar*.

'I play a sort of unsophisticated James Bond,' he told reporter Gordon Lindsay on the set. 'I'm an undercover agent for the CIA, and get my leads from people living in the ghetto. So I look like a bum who is always hustling, playing poker and shooting dice.

'I really am thrilled at starring in my first movie. I've wanted to do a movie for years, but I never seemed to work it around my concert schedule. What I would like to do is to make at least one, maybe two movies a year, and spend the rest of the time on the road. I haven't done a lot of dialogue yet, but the director has told me he's very pleased at what he's seen in the daily rushes.'

Three weeks into shooting the film's financing fell apart and the plug was pulled. Tom was desperate to continue, but the money and distribution deals were so muddled, it would have cost him millions. 'This was a terrible thing in my career,' said Clarence

Greene, 'because I just knew that I could have made a star out of him.'

In the end Tom's acting career was limited to TV vehicles such as *London Bridge*. Made in 1972 and co-starring Kirk Douglas, Terry Thomas and the Carpenters, it was filmed in London (where Terry drank the bar in Tom's limo dry at 8 o'clock one cold morning) and Lake Havasu in Arizona where London Bridge had been re-sited. (Its owner thought he was buying Tower Bridge.) Although Tom had to do various stunts, like being towed behind a speeding car wearing full cowboy regalia, it was hardly Oscar material.

Finally, in 1979, he took the part of a nightclub singer and part-time smuggler in a TV movie for NBC. *Pleasure Cove*, an uneasy mixture of *The Love Boat* and *Fantasy Island* set in a classy California beach resort, was the pilot for a TV series. The fact that it was never picked up speaks volumes. Tom acquitted himself adequately. 'He wasn't the world's greatest actor,' said director Bruce Bilson, 'but essentially he was playing himself, and he plays Tom Jones quite well.'

But the bottom line was that he sang Tom Jones much better. Alan Woodward summed it up best, telling his cousin, 'If I were you I'd stick to singing!'

However much money the music business brings in, LA is first and foremost a movie town. You have to strike while your star is burning bright. Miss that moment, hit records or not, horny matrons notwithstanding, and film producers stop returning calls. By 1980 Tom Jones and Gordon Mills were no longer serious players in Hollywood.

The following year Gordon agreed to make a new TV series in Vancouver. On paper, *Tom Jones: Coast to Coast* was an attempt to recreate the glories of *This is Tom Jones*. The deal was fronted by Bert Rosen – who had been involved with *London Bridge* – and Clancy

Grass, and was signed with 32 Records in New York.

The end result was tawdry. 'We recorded only twelve thirty-minute shows, but it seemed to go on for 300 years,' sighed Mark Woodward.

The formula was the same, but cheaper. Much cheaper. The comedy sketches were at best lame. When he shared jokes with his stick-thin dancers, the repartee was so forced and the jokes so obvious, the punch lines could be seen from outer space. Tom's outfits plumbed new depths of sartorial disgrace. Pastel sports coats, black bolero jackets, topped by a rhinestone belt. The trousers remained alarmingly tight.

Songs like *Lady Madonna* and *Do You Think I'm Sexy* were all blurred into one, thanks to a consistent and irritating disco beat. Nobody had dared to tell Gordon that disco was dead, far beyond outré. Some of the duets – with Tina Turner, Dusty Springfield, Dionne Warwick, Chaka Khan and Teddy Pendergrass – were redeemed by the sheer class of the singers. Others, with Brooke Shields and Paul Anka, are best forgotten.

As a career reviver the TV shows were not a success. But far worse was a clause in the small print of the contract, never spotted by Gordon or his advisers, which allowed the songs to be sold off separately, as albums. Dozens of different albums have since been released at budget prices, often with titles which were very similar to the original studio albums, such as *The Ultimate Collection*, *It's Not Unusual* and *Fever*. Containing poor versions of his best-known songs recorded in a TV studio with an inferior band, they confused record buyers and retailers alike.

In one deal Mills managed to devalue twenty years of Tom Jones recordings. His current recording contract did not help the situation.

In 1978 *Say You'll Stay Until Tomorrow* had hit number fifteen in the American pop charts. It had been his first country number one, which helped Gordon negotiate a substantial new deal. In 1980 Tom signed with the European record conglomerate Polygram, who were determined to establish a presence in America. 'They didn't know what to do with me,' he recalled. 'In the studio there has to be direction, particularly when the record companies have so many different divisions. The first record I did for them, *Darlin'*, became a country hit. So the country division said they'd got me a hit and they wanted the next album to be country. I said, "Fine." '

That could have been an inspired decision. The record industry was still obsessed with the hangover from the disco era and country music was enjoying a solid revival. Its audiences had always appreciated a man with a big voice and the ability to wring every available teardrop from a lyric. For the cover picture of *Darlin'* Tom posed in western duds. He looked deeply uncomfortable. On songs like his remake of Elvis's 1959 hit *One Night* he sounded it too. The *LA Times* critic suggested he had hit a low point.

'It wasn't country enough,' admitted Tom. 'We didn't dive in the deep end. We sat on the wire. It wasn't my *Ray Charles Sings Country* and it should have been. I had a contract with them for five years, but it didn't say what kind of music. That was it, country album after country album. The other problem was that they were only releasing them in America, because Polygram worldwide said, "We can't release these records – country doesn't sell anywhere else." I was getting country hits and wishing the next one wouldn't be a hit.'

It was, according to Annie Toomaru, purely a 'money, money situation'. The country market was, and still is, a huge one, and Gordon was banking on being able to re-establish Tom and give him a record-selling cushion again. From 1981 Tom had a succession of minor country hits: *It'll Be Me*, *I've Been Rained on Too* (which peaked at number thirteen), *This Time, I'm an Old Rock 'n' Roller (Dancing to a Different Beat)*, (which did have an appropriate title, though it only made it to number sixty-seven) and *It's Four in the Morning*.

Albums like *Don't Let Our Dreams Die Young, Love is on the Radio* and *Tender Loving Care* all did reasonably well. They went on the country charts and sold enough to keep the option being renewed.

'I had some success on the first one,' said Tom, 'and they wanted another one and another one. I was digging my own grave, covering myself in cow pats. I didn't want to make a bad album, and they just sold enough to keep me in that country thing. I was playing smaller venues, but it didn't dry up. It didn't panic me as long as when I stepped out on stage the place was full. I don't think about it. What kept me going without the hit records was that the people were there.'

Tom had a production deal with Polygram through Gordon Mills, who produced the albums and chose the songs. In the studio the old magic had evaporated. For the first time in years the star and his manager would argue openly about the choice of material and the direction they were taking. Mark Woodward was always suggesting to Tom he try some contemporary material. Believing he was being undermined, Gordon became even more entrenched.

Gordon had made Tom, moulded him, taught him about stage craft and performance. He knew best. But he had forgotten the one fundamental rule about managing a singer – times change. If you do not change with them, you will die.

'Why,' he would rave at Annie, 'should I change him? This is what the people want to see, this is what the fans like. That is his image, I don't see him doing anything else and he will stick to that to the end.'

'Tom wanted to change the music, people would ask for him to do something different,' said Annie. 'Gordon never wanted him to. I was handling the fan club, there were hundreds throughout the USA. The majority were old ladies and that is what they liked, but there were young ones too, who appreciated other kinds of music.'

When Gordon informed Tom that Polygram wanted to pick

up the option for a sixth album, he was stunned by the reaction. 'No,' said Tom, 'I want out. I like country music, but this is ridiculous. I like other things as well.' Over the years there had been many arguments, usually about songs and interpretations, but never before had Tom exerted his power over a business decision.

They fought over it for months, Gordon insisting he get another record contract and Tom, who was secure financially, saying 'Don't worry about it.' For Gordon it was a different matter. With his expensive tastes and his addiction to gambling, he did not have the same financial cushion. MAM was no longer earning big money. He was beset by legal problems. His divorce from Jo was eventually settled in 1985.

He needed Tom to keep working, and Tom loved to work. In 1983 Tom made his first UK tour for over ten years. There is nothing Britain loves more than a star returning in triumph. Especially if for the past fifteen years its media had, like a Roman slave, been whispering in the public's ear how human he was.

The tour was designed for maximum publicity, kicking off at St David's Hall in Cardiff on 12 September. The years of tax exile had imbued the hills and valleys with a rosy hue, time conveniently plastering over the wounds of memory. All those bitter words about how he could not enter a pub in Pontypridd were forgotten. While, in the pubs and clubs, the locals reminisced about that 'good old boyo'.

It was, Tom insisted, a tour in memory of his father. 'It's hard to talk about Dad's death, even today. I loved my dad, I miss him still. For years he kept asking me when I was going home to Wales to sing to the people there. I wanted to badly, but it just never worked out. My home, my family, my body, is in Beverly Hills, California. But my heart will always belong in Wales.

'There's another reason I've never been back to Wales. I was afraid that if I did I would want to stay, and my career is in

America. Maybe I'll go back to Wales one day, when this is all over. All I know at the moment is that I must keep singing – that's all there is for me. I don't need the money. But this is my life. I'll keep singing until my voice or my body gives out on me.'

The night before the tour started, Tom hosted a party for 150 Woodwards, Joneses and Trenchards at the Celtic Manor Hotel in Neath. It lasted well into dawn and Tom happily footed the £5,000 bill. The reaction to Tom's performances in the UK further convinced Mark that his father's future must lie outside of Las Vegas.

Vegas itself was in the first throes of another major change in its attitude towards entertainers. Even though the major corporations had been taking over the casinos since the early seventies, the old attitudes towards entertainers had remained in place longer than the accountants wanted. By 1983 the big names were drying up. Elvis was dead, the Rat Packers were all pushing seventy, and losing it to the vagaries of memory or the bottle. The spark was missing from Sinatra's shows. Nobody wanted to pay top dollar and get an old guy in an obvious toupee, whining about his review in the *Las Vegas Sun*. Tom, Engelbert, Wayne Newton, Robert Goulet and Paul Anka all filled the showrooms, but they had little appeal to the younger crowd. Established rock artists, kept buoyant by record and songwriting royalties, could afford to turn down the lucrative contracts offered by the casinos.

The corporate bean counters had never understood why the ancillary departments inside a casino hotel should be allowed to operate at a loss. The prices of rooms, drinks and food started creeping up. Show tickets soon followed, as they tried to get artists' fees and receipts balanced on the books. Another tactic was to halve show commitments, down from two shows a night to a single performance, and then renegotiate contracts accordingly.

Tom had been playing at Caesars Palace since 1971, but the

relationship had soured by 1984. Mainly, according to the *Las Vegas Review Journal* columnist Joe Delaney, 'because of Gordon Mills's excessive demands for caviar, and vintage Dom Perignon at $150 per bottle. He wanted it by the case, delivered to his room, and he wanted it comped. If you are a serious gambler you can get away with almost anything, but Gordon was excessive and he didn't take criticism well. The bills for entertainment were running so high that Caesars Palace said they had to put a ceiling on it.'

Incensed, Gordon negotiated a new deal with the MGM Grand, just over the Strip. Part of the deal was they were comped for everything. 'Mr Tom Jones, he had the *carte blanche*,' recalled Ilario Pesco, the *maître d'*. 'He could have anything he wanted. The president had told me, "Whatever Mr Jones orders, he will have." '

In Gi Gi's restaurant it seemed as if the good times were back. The restaurant stayed open especially for their star. The Puligny Montrachet, the Margaux, the Château Lafite, the Haut-Brion and the vintage Dom flowed until dawn. The meals would be finished off with a fine Cuban cigar – 'friends of Mr Jones would bring them from Canada,' said Ilario – washed down with glasses of Remy Martin XO, or Louis XIII. Even the tips were paid by the hotels – so they were very generous.

They were big, convivial parties, sometimes up to thirty people – Freda and Sheila, friends of Tom and Gordon's, Annie and her daughter Vaitiare Hirshon. But for the first time there was an undercurrent between artist and manager. Gordon would never let Annie sit near Tom at dinner after he tried to chat up Vaitiare one night.

Ilario noticed that not all was well between Tom and Gordon. 'He was always arguing with Mr Jones the last couple of years. He was very forceful, Mr Gordon Mills, in the conversation they had. Mr Jones make white and he say black. Mr Jones would be very like a gentleman and say, "Gordon, OK, fine, you made your point." He had arguments with all the staff. He was a little rough.'

Mills drank too much all the time. One night, after everybody left the restaurant, at 4.30 in the morning as Ilario was locking up, he heard a pounding on the door. It was Gordon demanding a bottle of brandy. 'I had to give him the flambé cognac which was all I had left.'

To Ilario Pesco, who has seen all the excesses and flamboyance Vegas money can bring, there was an old-world charm, a sophisticated air about Tom Jones that American artists lacked. He wore a different immaculately cut suit every night he came to dinner, he made imaginative choices from the classic French menu and he drank only the best wine, which a *maître d'* loves more than anything. The way he held himself and treated those who approached him had 'a dignity'.

Tom was in control, but Gordon had lost that charisma that once could scorch a room. To Ilario it showed. 'Gordon's lifestyle was different, Mr Jones has his son, he has a wonderful family, and he was content with that, but Gordon was not content, because something was missing. Gordon I think was very jealous of Mr Jones' success.'

For the first time in twenty years the created had outstripped his creator. Just as there is a point in a boy's life when he knows that he is physically stronger than his father. He still loves him, but the balance of power has shifted for ever.

What Gordon did have was his gambling. At the Grand, Gordon's personal line of credit was $250,000, which he used to the full. He taught Annie Toomaru baccarat and she taught him gin rummy.

When Gordon lost at gin he'd demand to play again. 'Double or quits.' In the casino it was the same. Sign for $5,000 then another $10,000.

There were good nights. One night in Aspinalls, London, he

won £200,000. 'He stuck, which was unusual,' said Annie, 'because when he won, he tended to go on to play again for more. I'd kick him. I said, "Come on, stop it." I'd even say in front of the guys, "Hey Gordon, that's it, let's go home", or I invent that I have a problem. Then we got home and he'd put everything in a brown bag. The next day we went and visited his mum, and he said, "Here Mum, put this in your bank account."

Two months before he died Gordon lost $60,000 playing baccarat at the Palace Court in Las Vegas. By that stage he had resolved to change his life, to marry Annie and retire. 'In those days,' said Annie wistfully, 'I think he loved me more than Tom Jones. He said, "I'm fed up, I have enough," and that's why he plant this pole, "For sale", outside his house. He said at fifty-four, "I'm out, I'm retired."

'Everything was planned, Jo was moving out from St George's Hill, he was taking over their house on 1 August. I booked our reservation for 30 July, to go to England, to go to London. Can you imagine the path of our life, what happened, not only to that life, to our life, and to everyone's life? He was taken away from me. He was taken away from what he liked the most, St George's Hill.'

Gordon never made the flight. In June 1986 he was drinking his morning cup of tea, when he started to burp. It went on and on, followed by a pain in his stomach. Annie asked whether it was too much alcohol. 'There's nothing wrong with my liver,' he told her. Later that month he was in so much pain during a recording session with Tom that he admitted he had something upsetting his stomach.

On 5 July they were in Vegas, preparing to entertain some Tahitian friends of Annie's, when Gordon announced he wanted to take a nap instead of watching the show. Gordon always watched the show, he would check the sound, the lights, the reaction, everything. Annie went back to their room and found him writhing in agony. She called the doctor, who insisted he go to hospital. The next day he returned to LA, where his doctor arranged for him to have a check-up at Cedar Sinai on Monday morning.

Gordon hated hospitals. Whether by accident or design, that Monday morning he drank a cup of tea, and, therefore unable to have a barium meal, had to reschedule his appointment for Friday 11 July. All week he lay in bed, refusing to answer the phone or the doorbell. Annie cancelled all his appointments.

'He was so weak he could hardly eat. At the hospital the doctor came back with a picture of his stomach, and the duodenum was inflamed. He said, "You have to spend the night here, there is an infection." Gordon said, "No, give me some shots and some tablets, I want to go home." But the doctor said, "No, we have to put you on an IV." Gordon wanted shepherd's pie, it was Jo's recipe, but I prepare it. The next morning the pain was still persistent, so they had to keep him another night. So I made a lamb curry Madras.'

The next day the doctors gave him the all-clear. To celebrate they ordered in a meal from Adriano's in Bel Air. When the meal arrived he could not eat a mouthful. 'It's hurting,' he cried. Eventually the doctors diagnosed him as having stomach cancer. They tried to operate, but once they opened him up, they discovered his body was completely riddled. There was nothing they could do except sew him up . . . and wait.

For the next eighteen days Annie slept in his room while his family and friends gathered – even Jo and her new boyfriend came over. On 28 July Tom paid his last visit to the hospital. After seeing Gordon lying there, he realised there was no chance. Beside himself with grief he wept to Beverley Mills, 'Oh God, what am I going to do?'

'I had been to see Gordon several times,' he said a week later. 'This time the doctors told me to be prepared for a shock. He didn't look his normal self. He was no longer there, there was no hope.

'I said, "Gordon, has the doctor told you what you have?" He said he knew and asked me what were his chances. I said they were fifty-fifty. I said this to the man who discovered me. He was dying in front of me. Gordon was a gambler. He said he thought fifty-fifty was reasonable odds. "That's not bad," he said. He was dead the next day.'

According to Annie Toomaru, who along with his children was one of the beneficiaries of Gordon's will, he left an estate valued at $10 million. Inheritance taxes of sixty per cent in England and fifty per cent in the USA and Zimbabwe reduced that to some $4 million. Not a huge legacy for a man who had guided the careers of three of the biggest artists of the early seventies, on a commission that varied between thirty and fifty per cent, as well as being chairman of a major entertainment conglomerate. Conservative estimates of Tom's wealth at the time were in excess of $50 million. If Gordon was on a fifty-fifty split there should have been much, much more.

Perhaps there was. In 1994 Chris Hutchins, who had reinvented his career as a gossip columnist, declared that Gordon had had a series of secret Swiss bank accounts, but that he had taken the numbers with him to his grave and that millions of dollars remain in vaults in the Alps. That Gordon had Swiss bank accounts is almost certain. In the sixties and seventies the swingeing British tax laws and foreign exchange controls meant that anybody who earned money overseas would try and keep as much as possible outside the country. Ebostrail, the private company set up in 1968 to handle the foreign earnings of Tom and Engelbert, only sent a proportion of its income back to MAM.

It would have been typical of Gordon to have kept a secret line of credit that only he could access. Even in his last days the

Mule thought he could beat the odds. He had forgotten where the greater part of his fortune had been dissipated.

On the green baize tables of Vegas, waiting on the turn of a card.

CHAPTER TWENTY-THREE

HERE COMES
THE SON

———

T om was devastated by Gordon's death. On 6 August 1986, the day of the funeral, he told the *Daily Mail*, 'I was not just close to Gordon, he was as near to me as a brother, my dear, dear friend, my adviser. He was part of my life. He taught me just about everything. He groomed me, he taught me my pacing. He tried to be me, sitting in the audience watching myself, and then he would tell me how I would have criticised myself. There are parts of me which he totally created.'

Tom's reliance on Gordon was well known in the business. Los Angeles is not a sensitive city. Even before Gordon was buried, the vultures were circling, for there were Vegas contracts available until the day after Tom passed on. There was money to be made . . . and to the outsiders, there was no clear successor to Mills, the control freak.

'As soon as Gordon was in the ground – even before,' said Jones bitterly, 'I had these other managers saying, "Tom, if there's anything I can do for you." Then came the vultures and so-called friends he had, who were all of a sudden telling me, "I knew Gordon very well and I think he'd have wanted me to help you." So I said to Mark, "Have a pop at it." He said, "I'm not experienced." I told him, "Don't worry, I'll help you do it." And he did, Mark jumped straight in.'

How they laughed in the bars and restaurants of Beverly Hills. Mark Woodward was twenty-nine and appeared to have no management experience. He had been working as daddy's lighting man for several years, but what did he know about management?

But Mark Woodward was not to be underestimated.

If one was to be cruel – and when he was a fat insecure teenager desperate for his father's approval, many were – Mark Woodward appeared to have inherited little of his father's physical presence. When Tom Jones is your father you do not try to compete. You try to complement.

Until he was eight Mark had lived in the Trenchards' damp basement in Cliff Terrace. He had never forgotten how tight money was, or that horrible year when his father was in London and his mother had to go out to work in a factory to put chips on the table. Nor had he forgotten, when success finally came, how he and Linda had been told to disappear into the woodwork while the management pretended they did not exist. When real fame came and Mark moved from Surrey houses into Surrey mansions, attended private schools and went on luxury holidays, there was one other ever present constant: he seldom saw his father.

Mark Woodward always knew the price of fame. After Chris Hutchins took over PR duties, he decreed that the family should remain firmly in the background. That was fine with Linda. Not for Mark. He was a good boy, but he did not like being an only child, raised single-handedly by his mother.

'I tell my wife that she's the boss at home, not me,' Tom told

Godfrey Winn. 'That's right isn't it? When I was a kid and I came home, it never worried me if my dad wasn't there but at the pub or the miners' club. But if my mother hadn't been there, why it'd be the end of the world. And my wife is always there, she is someone to come home to, and that's why I think she should have the big say over Mark, our son. He's eleven now, but I always tell him, "Now listen to your mother," and I never interfere.

'What do I want for him? He's very bright. He might make a comedian. The really funny thing is that he sings quite well, so his mother says, but I've never heard him because he stops the moment I come into the house.'

A telling anecdote in itself. It is tough being the son of a superstar, tougher still to be a small boy who cannot show off a natural talent to the one person he wants to impress most. Daddy. When Winn suggested that it could not be easy for Mark having such a famous singer as a father, Tom's reply swiftly changed the subject. 'I know that . . . but it isn't so easy for me either. That's why I don't go back to Pontypridd any more. When I did and went into my favourite pub, if I offered drinks all round they called me a big show-off, while if I didn't, they thought I had become a mean skinflint. I can't win. They think I've changed, but I haven't. It's Pontypridd that has changed towards me.'

Putting feeling uncomfortable about not being able to drink in a pub in a town you no longer live in on a par with the problems your only son is having living in your shadow, might seem a mite selfish. Yet for Tom Jones that was not a tricky dilemma. It was the ways things were. Like his mother, Mark accepted that the household was run solely for the benefit of one person, Tom. Fortunately, Mark was tougher than he looked. He learnt young that to earn Tom's approval he would have to sublimate his own ambitions so that his father could continue to enjoy the good life.

Mark took every opportunity he could to be with his father.

When Tom was recording *This is Tom Jones* in the first quarter of 1969 and 1970, it was blissful. For thirteen long weeks at a time he was at home. Sundays and Mondays he did not go to Elstree, so it was almost like having a normal dad. They played squash together in the sports complex at Tor Point, and provided Tom did not have some more pressing assignation in his caravan, went to Elstree to watch the recording.

'Mark used to run around at full speed,' recalled Frank Chapman, 'dodging between all the cables and cameras and lights. It was full of signs saying, "Do not touch", which to a twelve-year-old boy was simply calling out, "Touch me". He was a pain because he was always getting in the way or fiddling with the wrong things, but he wasn't a spoilt brat.'

Mark soon learnt about life on the road, joining his father for those frenetic American tours in 1969 and 1970. The experience blasted the boy's eyes wide open. Tom never tried to hide what happened. Perhaps he was a little bit more discreet about the women, but the longer Mark stayed on the road, the more he saw. He was an inquisitive boy, always watching and learning.

'I wanted him to see exactly what went on. I had nothing to hide from him,' said Tom. 'It was an education, but he liked it. It might not have been the same if I'd had a daughter, I suppose, but he was my son.'

Adolescence did not treat Mark kindly. From the age of ten, he was seriously overweight. He looked like a fat, over-indulged kid, but his size was due to a thyroid problem, not over-eating. By the time the problem was diagnosed, his puppy fat had turned to real fat, and it took him a long time to get it under control. Tom, the super-slim sex symbol, might have been embarrassed by his boy's size, but he never put him down about it in public. Tom loved Mark, no doubt about that.

In 1972 Tom made what was to be his last tour of the UK for

eleven years. The TV series was finished. His work was almost exclusively in America and his tax situation had him hopping over the border whenever time allowed. He could not afford to spend time back in Weybridge and would meet his wife and son for snatched weekends in France or Belgium. Mark was no great academic, he chafed under the discipline of his private school. He loved his mother, but he wanted more.

'I've only ever wanted what made him happy,' recalled Tom. 'When he was sixteen, I was travelling a lot, wasn't seeing him much. I got home, we went out to dinner. I could see he was moody and I asked what the matter was. He told me he wanted me to spend more time with him. I talked to his headmaster and he said, "Let him leave school and take him on tour with you."

Though it broke her heart, Linda agreed with the decision. She hoped it might curb Tommy's wilder excesses, but at the core she was just being a dutiful Valleys wife, sacrificing herself for the good of the men. So Mark left school and went on the road, while his mother stayed at home.

By the time he joined his father, much of Mark's fat had turned to muscle. He would run down the aisles of these theatres, and clear the people out of the way, a tank coming through, with Tom and Chris following in his wake. Mark loved it on the road. He ran around smoking huge cigars and drinking. Drinking too much.

The band and crew liked Mark. He was a funny guy. He did a brilliant Dai Perry impression, standing there with his fist up in the air shouting, 'Who wants it?' Welsh accent spot on. Mark could take the piss out of anybody: Lloyd Greenfield, Gordon, even his dad. He'd start singing, *With These Hands*, shaking his arms and bringing the house down.

Mark never pulled any power trips, never played the 'I'm Tom Jones's son' card. In fact, the opposite. When people asked him he denied it and walked away. Naturally, he enjoyed the power of the magic pen at Caesars Palace, where he could order anything he wanted to drink or eat. He palled up with bass player, Alan Morgan, who had a similarly warped sense of humour. The pair wandered around the casino at 2 a.m., drunk as lords, laughing like hell.

Mark was not a great chick-puller, but he was a great chatterer. When it came to the crunch, he would often back off, or invite her to the dressing room. If she then disappeared with his father, that wasn't his business.

Mark could party. If his father was up, he was up. Sometimes even longer. He could keep going all night long, no trouble at all. He was a big guy, he could hold his drink. He was never a falling down drunk. In the early days before they gave him Chris Ellis's job, Mark would vanish all day, then turn up in the dressing room after the second set, with shining vodka eyes and a big smile on his face.

There was one golden rule everyone kept. Gordon Mills was always right. Especially when he was wrong. However, Mark had ideas and opinions of his own about the business, and was not prepared to keep them to himself.

Mark did not like what his father was doing on the stage. Musically he was from a different generation. He discovered new bands, and played them to Tom, and told him, 'This is the way you should be going.' Gordon got to hear about it, and he didn't like it at all. Mills was extra dogmatic when it came to choosing songs. Then Mark had the effrontery to stand up to him, to argue like hell – with him and with Tom. All Woodwards have a genetic disposition to argue beyond dawn. Mills never dared treat Mark the way he treated other employees.

A lot of the things that Mark was saying were right, and some of his suggestions started to creep into the act. But most times he lost, because Gordon held the power. Secure in the rectitude of youth, Mark kept banging on until Tom would just look at him and say, 'Mark, just leave it there now.' Whereupon Mark would get exasperated and stomp out of the dressing room, go to the bar and have a drink . . . and another drink.

Everyone realised Mark had to have a job or he was going to get into trouble. So he started working as Tom's unofficial minder and drinking companion. After Caracas, Mark eased into Dai Perry's position, until Chris Ellis found himself without a job.

After a couple of years, Mark moved on to become lighting director. 'The best I've ever had,' acknowledged his father in 1980. 'Having him with me all the time has made us very close – almost like brothers. Best of all he has never found a reason to rebel against me the way most sons do. And I like to think I set a good example for him. That's why he doesn't take drugs like so many young people.'

Mark had a good role model after all. He liked to drink and chase girls. His two-bedroom apartment, above the garage in Bel Air, became 'Party City'. Once he had an established position, his confidence grew by leaps and bounds.

Part of Mark craved stability. In 1982 he married Donna Polom. The wedding party at Copa d'Oro was a major event. Gordon got so drunk he fell on top of Anne Marie and broke her arm. The band were ripping through Tom's favourite sixties soul classics, and for once Tom refrained from leaping on stage and hogging the limelight. 'He told us it was our day and he waited until we'd left,' said Mark, 'and then he tore the place down. I heard it was one of his best performances ever.'

Donna was a transplanted New Yorker, four years her husband's senior. She had been around the Jones camp for a while, having previously dated Barry Morgan, Tom's drummer and the brother of Michael Morgan, who had succeeded Johnny Spence as musical director. Donna had a strength of character and a sense of personal self-worth a million miles removed from Linda. Once married, Mark's tomcatting days were curtailed. Tom bought the couple a house in Bel Air, where together father and son discussed and planned how to resurrect Tom's fading career. While he retained enormous respect for what Gordon achieved, Mark never liked him. He never forgave the man who had told Tom to deny his very existence, nor forgot he had kept Tom away for much of his childhood.

By 1986 Mark was secure. He had a family. He had fought for and earned his position. He knew his job inside out. He knew everybody's job inside out. With the confidence and arrogance of youth he believed he could do a better job than Gordon. But Gordon was the only man who told his dad what to do . . . and his dad would do it. Mark wanted that power because he loved his father and he knew that his father loved his career above all else.

According to Annie Toomaru, Gordon had long recognised Mark as his natural successor. 'For two years before Gordon passed away he was trying to get close to Mark,' she said. 'He said to me, "Mark will be the next one." He said, "I want him to follow." But he and Mark didn't click. Gordon wanted to be like a father, but he was too dogmatic. Mark had his own vision of how he wanted to manage Tom Jones.'

Whether Gordon would ever have been able to step aside, or indeed afford to, is debatable. When Mark took over managing his father's career many people in the Tom Jones entourage jeered and sneered. The sneers turned to shock and complaint when Mark, quietly but ruthlessly, set about expunging the old guard and creating a new career for his father. Mark determined to make Tom cool again.

Whatever personal doubts he expressed to his father, Mark seized his moment and displayed a ruthless certainty that smacked of long-laid plans. He quickly let many of Gordon's key personnel go. The signs were apparent at Mills's funeral.

'After the funeral we went back to Gordon's house,' said Annie Toomaru. 'John Moran told me, "Go ask Tom about your job." He told me, "There is a rumour that you are not going to be working there any more." I went to Tom and said, "I want to know what happen to me about my job." The only thing he said to me was, "We'll take care of that. We'll see when we get back to LA. I can't think about that right now." It made me feel very uneasy.'

Within two weeks she was fired. PR man John Moran followed soon after. Donna Woodward took over his position. On the touring side, Lloyd Greenfield stayed on the payroll until he died in January 1999. Some of the older musicians were not so fortunate. Three were let go at the end of the year when their one-year contracts expired. One, Jimmy Nuizo, filed a lawsuit alleging age discrimination, which had no chance of sticking. Sax, oboe and French horn player Steve Romanelli was let go after seven years with the band. He was fifty-six. They were too old for the new look Mark was contemplating.

'We had to let a few people go, not just for the sake of it, but because it needed to be done,' said Mark defensively. 'Tom is notorious for being a loyal employer.'

Annie Toomaru was, and still is, deeply upset. She accepts she would have left at some point, but would have liked to have made a dignified exit. 'I was lost at the moment because I considered them as family. Yes, it hurt. For Tom it was only *his* family and once Gordon was gone that was it.'

Neither Gordon Mills's children nor his mother have heard from Tom since Gordon's funeral. Not a personal phone call, nor a word of comfort. They find it hard to understand why. It was part of Gordon's legacy. For twenty-two years he had cocooned Tom inside a specially created family, taught him that he need do nothing except sing. Now Gordon was gone and the Family had been replaced by a smaller, tighter unit: his real family bound together by ties of blood not money. For Tom it made perfect sense.

Soon after Gordon died Mark renamed the business Tom Jones Enterprises, and started negotiating with the Mills family to buy Gordon's half. Both sides wanted to do the deal, but once lawyers got involved it took a long time. Among the assets now wholly owned by Tom was Valley Music, the publishing company set up by Gordon in the sixties to administer his songs. Every time *It's Not Unusual* is played on the radio, used in a TV commercial or in a movie, fifty per cent of any royalties still go to Valley Music, whose directors are Thomas John Woodward and Mark Woodward. Valley Music also owns half of *Help Yourself* and a proportion of *Without Love (There is Nothing)*, as well as other assorted songs shrewdly accumulated by Gordon throughout the sixties.

Nanci Eisner quit a year after Gordon died and returned to New York. 'The organisation was changing,' she said. 'Gordon had built this dynasty, but now it was like an era had come to its end. I could understand it because when a new president comes in, he brings his own people. If anything Mark gave it a shot in the arm. He lent a perspective of youth, and maybe something fresh and new. Change is difficult, but intrinsically I didn't have the same respect for Mark as a manager as I had for Gordon. I'd known him since he was thirteen.'

It has long been assumed that Gordon's final legacy to Tom was a bona fide hit record. Mark Woodward, however, is adamant that the first time he played Tom the demo for *A Boy From Nowhere*, they both knew it was a hit in waiting.

'I listened to the songs and thought they were fantastic,' said Tom. 'The voice was the thing, these wonderful songs showing off my voice. They are slightly operatic, I was rather flattered. Originally they went to the London Opera and the singers were all too stiff. There were problems with the range – mine is two and a half octaves, full voice without falsetto.'

'Gordon never thought much of it,' insisted Mark, 'but after we received the demo cassette for *Matador* I played *A Boy From Nowhere* to Tom in his hotel suite in Atlanta. From the first time he heard it Tom loved the song, he was desperate to record it. The last thing Gordon Mills said to me as we were walking down the stairs in Ballys after Tom's opening night was, "I can't believe that Tom wants to record that song."

'Gordon might have let Tom record the song, but I don't know if he would have committed him to the promotion time that was the crucial element in breaking that song.'

That song was to breathe new life into Tom's career. In 1985, composer Mike Leander – the man behind Gary Glitter in the early seventies – and lyricist Eddie Seago, wrote *Matador*, a musical based on the life of Spanish bullfighter, El Cordobés. Their initial plan was to record a star-studded album, which would create enough buzz to raise enough money to actually stage the musical – the method Andrew Lloyd Webber and Tim Rice had pioneered with *Jesus Christ Superstar* and *Evita*.

'We hadn't cast it, but we were looking for the right lead voice for it,' said Leander. 'It became increasingly obvious that Tom Jones was the singer we should use. The singer we used on the demo tape even sounded like him.'

A West End musical might not be the movies, but who knew where it could lead? Throughout his career, Tom has made too few musical decisions based on his gut feelings. That was Gordon's job and he had ended up with his guts riddled with cancer. But everything was right about *Matador*. This was the world he knew, a haunting melodramatic big ballad.

El Cordobés was Tom. Despite the cultural and career differences, his life story mirrored that of the boy from the Valleys.

Manuel Benitez, born into grinding peasant poverty in a village just outside of Cordoba in southern Spain, was a wild child, always in trouble with the Civil Guard for stealing chickens. An arrogant upstart desperate to break into the traditional world of bullfighting, he caught the public imagination by jumping into the main Madrid ring in front of General Franco, armed only with a red rag and a stick to take on a huge bull. Before his first official fight he promised his sister, 'Don't cry for me, for tonight I will buy you a house or I will dress you in mourning.' He bought her the house.

In his glittering suit of lights, topped by an unruly mop of black hair, Cordobés's flamboyant style led to him being christened 'the Beatle of the Bullring'. For a short time he became one of the highest paid entertainers in the world. In his heyday in the sixties and seventies, he was renowned for his lust for life and love – he would slaughter six half-ton bulls in an afternoon and seduce six señoritas all night. El Cordobés was no graceful artist of the corrida, he was a natural showman, full of stunts that angered the purists – a frog-leap on to his knees as the bull snorted past, putting his face close to the horn, and a trademark grin that melted more than female hearts.

A Boy From Nowhere was a massive hit in Britain (it was never released in the States). In April 1987 Tom Jones made his first appearance on *Top of the Pops* for fifteen years, and the record roared up to number two, and was only just held off the top spot by Starship's *Nothing's Gonna Stop Us Now*. One of Tom's more unenviable records is that he has only had two number ones, and five number twos. The British media, who had so lapped up his 1983 'comeback' tour, jumped on the 'boy from nowhere' tag.

The key to its success was timing. Tom was wanted on all the TV chat shows, and he did them all. The hunger to succeed was back. 'It wasn't the money, the money was always there,' said Tom.

'Gordon always used to bring that up, he'd say, "What's the matter? You have a lovely house, you've got cars, look what you've achieved." I said, "Yes, but I want to keep proving I can do it, I know I don't have to prove it to you, but the rest of the world is out there." It wasn't financial, I just had to prove I could do it.'

He wanted to do it. After Tom had gone into tax exile he appeared to have turned his back on Britain, so Britain had turned its back on him. The 1983 tour had reminded everybody of just how good he could be, but now he was back and charming. The brash medallion man had been replaced by a witty, self-deprecating and charming star. An unreconstructed man among pop boys like Rick Astley, Boy George and the Pet Shop Boys, he could laugh at himself, which the British always like, and he so obviously loved to be loved.

Despite the massive success of *A Boy From Nowhere* and the *Matador* album – which went on to sell over 100,000 copies – Epic Records had not signed Tom to a long-term deal. Even when he played the Royal Albert Hall in March and the company was inundated with requests for tickets, they did not take the hint. When the request came for Tom to appear on *The Last Resort*, they put it on the bottom of the pile.

In 1987 *The Last Resort* was the hippest show on British TV. Although viewing figures seldom topped four million, it became a must-see programme, the one everyone discussed at work the next day. The fledgling Channel 4 had commissioned a British clone of *Late Night with David Letterman*, complete with a sharp-suited lisping host in Jonathan Ross. Ross's interview technique was rich in post-modern irony, often more about the host than the guests. It was a million miles from the reverential approach used by Terry Wogan and Russell Harty.

'*The Last Resort* was an alternative show,' said Jonathan Ross. 'You had to go out of your way to be different, and sometimes we'd fall into the trap of adding some superfluous and rather stupid gimmick to it, which we tried to do on a regular basis. Sometimes it worked, but often it became embarrassing.'

One basic rule was that singers had to perform with the house band, and were not allowed to plug their new single. This had two effects. The first was that artists experimented with new material or intriguing covers which made for interesting viewing. The second was that record companies were very loath to let artists appear if there was a danger either of them making fools of themselves or if there was nothing to sell.

Ross and his producer Graham Smith were desperate to have Tom on the show. 'In early discussions we had agreed there were only two people we would die to have on the show – Michael Caine and Tom Jones,' recalled Smith. 'In our minds, Tom was already a legendary figure, who was stuck doing this understandable but not very exciting cabaret career. Tom was around promoting *A Boy From Nowhere*, and we attempted to book him on the show.'

To Epic, Tom Jones was a one-off project that was coming to an end. Appearing on *The Last Resort* was not going to sell any more singles. It would have been very easy for Richard Evans, head of promotions, to bump the request off the list. But he liked the show and so did not actively oppose it.

'It was the very last thing on the list,' said Mark Woodward, 'and the record company didn't care if he did it or not. If he wanted to do it that was fine.' Mark's determination to introduce numbers by new chart-topping artists – such as Billy Idol, INXS, Huang Chung and Prince – into Tom's act was starting to bear fruit. *The Last Resort* was exactly what he wanted to do, it hit the right demographic, and Tom, after years in the States watching Letterman, knew exactly what to expect. Singing was good, chat was not.

'Jonathan and I went to see Tom at the Albert Hall,' said

Smith, who, lulled by childhood memories of watching *This is Tom Jones* and the Vegas legends, was expecting a tux and supper crowd performance that a Channel 4 audience would laugh at. Instead, he saw the Tom Jones fever zone in full flow. A little more knowing, a wink here and showers of panties there, but still full ahead. 'He had started doing a few contemporary numbers, including *Kiss*, which impressed and surprised us. It was clear he had to do *Kiss* when he came on the show.'

Tom Jones's appearance on *The Last Resort* in early April 1987 was to be the defining moment of the second part of his professional life. His career renaissance began there. He demonstrated that he was not too precious by duetting with Jonathan Ross on *It's Not Unusual*, which, given the host's vocal prowess, consisted of him 'arseing around' while Tom sang. 'Tom was great,' said Ross. 'He had the right attitude and a sense of humour – especially about my singing.'

And then Tom sang *Kiss*. The contrast between the glorious kitschness of *It's Not Unusual* and a leather-encased Jones blowing audience, host and band away, was extraordinary. The final touch that elevated the performance into the incident that had all of trendy London calling each other up and saying, 'Did you see *The Last Resort*?' was pure Tom. As the band started on the instrumental break, he spontaneously – and he is not normally a spontaneous man – announced, 'Think I'd better dance now.' With that he started a glorious series of pelvic thrusts, hip flexes, legs going back and forth. The way he always danced, but never before was it the perfect comment on both the song lyrics and his performance. Suddenly a superannuated lounge singer was doing Prince better than His Purple Majesty. This was not two-dimensional cabaret, this was the real, rocking thing. Vintage Jones, just the way he used to be before he got fitted for that tuxedo.

'The drive and the ambition came from Mark,' said Graham

Smith. 'Mark saw an opportunity to do something different to try and attract a younger audience. The vast majority of artists of the calibre of Tom Jones, when confronted with a noisy, youthful, sarcastic Channel 4 show, wouldn't have wanted to go on a show like that. The fact that Mark was prepared to trust his instinct paid off enormously.

'Suddenly a performer, who has not really had significant hits since the early seventies, was reinvented in the most aggressively modern, youthful style, carrying it off, but not looking sad, tragic or out of his depth. It could have been a disaster.'

Instead eyes opened wide across Thatcher's Britain. Tom was suddenly hip again. *It's Not Unusual* became a dance-floor favourite in the clubs, because its distinctive rhythm matched that of the current Euro-beat trend. It was reissued and climbed back up to number seventeen. Telstar Records quickly jumped on the Jones wagon by aggressively promoting a Greatest Hits compilation on TV which reached number sixteen.

The eyes that opened widest of all belonged to Anne Dudley, J.J. Jeczalik and Gary Langan. All three were noted producers, arrangers and musicians, who had worked for producer Trevor Horn, before recording as the Art of Noise. Their name was taken from an Italian futurist manifesto, and their original intention was to produce original instrumental music behind a faceless image. This pre-techno approach had led the Art of Noise into film and TV theme work. A clever remake of Duane Eddy's 1959 instrumental classic *Peter Gunn* had hit number eight, while *Paranoimia*, a collaboration with the virtual TV presenter, Max Headroom, had made it up to number twelve.

Watching *The Last Resort* gave Dudley and her cohorts the spark of an idea. Reinvent *Kiss* in their inimitable style. It certainly helped that *Peter Gunn* had won the 1986 Grammy Award for Best Rock Instrumental Performance, but the idea took months to bring to fruition. Eventually, the backing tracks were recorded in London, while Tom, in the middle of his Vegas and Atlantic City touring schedule, laid the vocals down in LA. Dudley, who did not meet the singer until after the record was in the shops, then mixed the two together.

Because it was due to appear on the band's compilation album *The Best of the Art of Noise*, *Kiss* was not released until October 1988. The second single from *Matador*, *Born To Be Me*, another old-style pop ballad, had been released in January 1988 and had died. In the fickle world of pop music there was a serious danger that a magical TV moment eighteen months earlier could have been forgotten. However, a characteristically bravura performance on *Live from the London Palladium* swept the record into the charts, peaking at number five (one place higher than Prince's original version).

The initial record company thinking was that this was a comedy record – like Cliff Richard and the Young Ones or Weird Al Yankovic – not a club classic. The first storyboards proposed for the video were predictable post-Vegas nonsense – glittery showgirls grinding around Tom in a tuxedo. Eventually Polygram let Mark have his way and they ended up playing the song straight (it was cheaper that way). In a tongue-in-cheek homage to David Byrne, Tom wore a suit that appeared several sizes too big, dancing, bumping and camping it up against a plain white backdrop, laughing and singing, 'Act yo' age Mama, not your shoe size.'

Kiss was a hit all over the world. The video was immediately snapped up by MTV in the States – it won their Breakthrough Video of the Year award – who played it enough to get the song into the US charts. *Kiss* only made number thirty-one, but that was enough. Young America now knew that Tom Jones was more than a Vegas dinosaur. For the first time they glimpsed the power that the Voice possessed. And they liked it.

'When I did *Kiss*,' said Jones, 'I thought, "That's it, this is what I've been looking for for a long time, a good-sounding modern record. I thought, "Let's get songs like that, with producers who could do it." '

To that end Tom signed a record deal with Jive Records, a small British independent label. In Britain, Jive were best known for having made big tits into big hits, successfully turning *Sun* page three girl Samantha Fox into a pop singer. In the States, they were far more cutting edge, involved in the rapidly burgeoning rap and hip-hop scene. As the Fresh Prince, Will Smith, now one of the hottest actor/singers in the world, made his teenage debut for Jive with his partner DJ Jazzy Jeff.

Finally Tom was in a position to make albums that Mark knew he was capable of. Records that would place him in the rock pantheon, and grant him the respect that was his due.

CHAPTER TWENTY-FOUR

THE RIGHT STUFF

'I think I know this woman,' announced Tom Jones, raising his face from a scanty pair of crimson knickers. 'I forget names, I forget faces . . . but there are some things I never forget.'

The audience in the Melbourne Entertainment Centre on 7 November 1990 roared their approval. The girls — girls not grannies — at the front of stage showered the singer with the contents of a lingerie counter. The Jones banter was temporarily nonplussed by the arrival of a pair of longjohns, so he moved straight into another song, tight black jeans grinding out the beat.

'You don't have to be beautiful . . .'

Pause. One beat. Two beats.

'. . . to turn me on.'

Cue applause. Blue-rinsed matrons squeezed their husbands' hand tightly, twenty-year-old blondes let their jaws fall slack and wriggled suggestively on their seats. *Kiss* did that to an audience. For the hip kids, Tom was the hottest ticket in town. Sure, he was fifty and a bit cheesy, but the Voice had a real power. Class will out.

Filling sports arenas and entertainment centres meant that the Australian tour was a big success. Seven years earlier Tom had been playing the Revesby Workers Club in Sydney, the equivalent of the Batley circuit. Good money, but zero credibility. That had been the old Tom. Now post-*Kiss*, he was heading on his way back up the charts, reinvented, revitalised for the young.

In truth, Tom was still in transition.

It was late afternoon, the day after his first show, and Tom Jones was eating breakfast in his two-storey hotel suite in the Melbourne Hilton. He wore, as he always does, a white towelling dressing gown, supplied by the hotel, that barely covered his knees. His legs were brown and very hairy. Perched on the end of a nose, now far straighter than any Welsh coal miner's son's had the right to be, was a pair of black-rimmed spectacles. A brace of gold chains and a crucifix, large enough to qualify as an offensive weapon, snuggled together amidst his greying chest hair. He wore a £50,000 solid gold Cartier Pasha watch on his left wrist, but the chunky gold rings and diamond and sapphire encrusted bracelet were left upstairs.

'Mark doesn't like me to wear my jewellery for interviews,' he explained. Four years after he took over managing his father's career, Mark was in control. Not everybody agreed with him. Ever-present in the background lurked Chris Montgomery, an ex-soldier with a handshake that mangled bones. Since 1986 Chris had lived with Tom 365 days a year, part-valet, part-bodyguard, part friend and part domino opponent. He was unhappy with the new direction, feeling it did not sit comfortably with 'Mr Jones'.

Mark's influence was most apparent when the singer was fully dressed. The dinner jacket had been deep-sixed, replaced by a plethora of trendy designer labels — baggy Versace suits, double-breasted Armani jackets, Yamamoto blazers, iridescent Thierry

Mugler shirts, plain black Gap T-shirts, cowboy boots, leather jackets, leather trousers and jeans, either blue Levis or black designer label, but always cut skin-tight. Some things, at least, had not changed. At times, Tom appeared uncomfortable with the new minimalist image, for his personal tastes have always tended towards the florid.

Mark shrewdly understood that, if Tom was to attract a younger audience, he had to acknowledge his age, not hide behind it. The singer's hair was allowed to go grey, happily acknowledged by Tom. 'I was rinsing it before,' he said. 'I was using the darkest brown colour. I tried a shade lighter, but it never looked quite right. Tarbuck said to me, "Your hair's blacker than it was at twenty-five." My wife said, "For God's sake, stop dyeing your hair, it looks like someone's slung a bucket of soot on your head." So I thought I'd let it go and see what happened.'

In April 1990 Tom had plastic surgery to remove bags from under his eyes and reduce his chin. 'I've had operations on my teeth to make them look better,' he admitted. 'One was twisted, others were decayed, and I needed them to look right. Same thing with my nose, it had been broken a few times in fights and it was crooked. It's still a little crooked now. I had the bone broken and reset twice. I had it done in 1966 and it didn't turn out very well, the right nostril was still collapsed. Then in LA, I went to see a fella and he fixed it.'

Chris Montgomery, who left his employment six months later, claimed Tom had been through five scalp operations to conceal his thinning hair. 'When he began to go grey and thin on top, he used a really dreadful hair dye that looked so unnatural it was laughable. He came to breakfast one morning in a dressing gown, and his hair, sideburns and even chest hair, were all this improbable blue-black colour.

'He started using a more natural-looking product that he

could spray on his bald patch to make it look less thin. But eventually he decided to go the whole hog and have scalp reduction operations. A strip of skin was taken from the centre of his scalp and then the skin on each side, which is blessed with nice thick hair, was pulled over to cover the balding bit, and then stapled into place.

'I arrived in the middle of one session and saw his skull with all the skin peeled back and the man himself blissfully unaware and fast asleep. Afterwards it was only a little sore. He performed on stage several times with fifty or sixty of these metal staples still in his head. I had to take them out for him with special scissors as it healed. It cost him around £750 a time. His most recent visit was in February [1991], and it worked so well he gave up the hair spray and allowed himself to go naturally grey.'

Montgomery also insisted that Jones always denied that he had had the bags under his eyes cut down by cosmetic surgery, joking, 'If these are what I got after having my eyes done I'd sue!' He had, in fact, been operated on in 1987 by Dr Harry Glassman, cosmetic surgeon to the stars and husband of *Dallas* star Victoria Principal. 'I've also always wondered if he had had a face-lift,' said Montgomery. 'He has two little scars under the ears, usually a telltale sign.'

By 1999 it was apparent that Tom had indeed had a face-lift, and a chin job, to postpone the ageing process. In an era where nobody laughs when French performance artist Orlan announces she is changing her body as part of an ongoing artwork, and women wish to remodel their bodies to look like Barbie, an anatomically impossible children's doll, the fact that an ageing pop singer might wish to hold on to some of his youth scarcely passes comment.

The full-out way he sings has caused Tom problems with his

neck and with nodules on his vocal cords. 'He sang so hard with his head back that the skin would stretch,' recalled Chris Ellis, 'and he would get a tremendous build-up of fat. He was in danger of looking like a pelican. He's had it cut out several times – that is why he wears high-necked collars to hide the scars.'

In 1989 Tom had an operation to remove the nodules. 'Singing hard, like I do, I really should take better care of my voice,' he said. 'Vocal cords were not designed for being pressed together to get that clear, hard note. Mine looked like I was smoking three packs of cigarettes a day and it gave it trauma. Some nights it was hard to sing. The doctor told me I had a nodule coming and going. When I rested it was going.

'One day it didn't go away. I had this vision of it all being over,' he said in the tones of a man who had looked at the end of his career and had been scared to death by the sight. 'I had to have an operation which was very frightening because the doctor told me, "There's no guarantee that your voice will sound the same." But I haven't slipped yet. He took twenty years off my voice.'

Previously very modest about his vocal abilities, Tom now deliberately sang his own praises. 'I would hate people to think of me as being a jack of all trades,' he said. 'I think as far as music is concerned, I am a master of all vocal styles. Except maybe for Elvis, there has never been anybody so versatile. Sinatra couldn't sing rock and roll, Mick Jagger can't sing *Fly Me to the Moon*. I can. I cover all the ground. There isn't another singer who can sing better than I can. Not yet anyway.

'Mick Jagger knows he doesn't have a good voice, so he does the best with the tools he has. Phil Collins makes a monotonous piercing sound with no sex or warmth, while Cliff's mild singing is like going through life on tranquillisers.

'I have to be careful about the songs I pick. When singles come out I get associated with them for a long time, so I choose a good song that is suitable for my voice. At one time, if a good song came my way, I'd record it. But as time has gone on, because I had this Vegas image, this nightclub thing, the songs didn't come to me any more.'

Here was a distinct script to explain away the Vegas years and prove he had been credible all along. 'I am deliberately choosing new material to extend my career for a further ten years, to expand my audience, but most of all it is a proving thing. My ambition is being rekindled. The longer you go on, the less time you have. I don't just want to get on stage and make money. I don't need the money any more. I want to prove my voice is something special.

'The show I do now is a rock concert and the same as I do in Vegas – I might wear a suit rather than jeans and a T-shirt – but my show is basically the same. I don't do a Vegas-type extravaganza. I've got to be more careful about the songs I record, not to be MOR. *Kiss* was a good song, a dance song, a club thing that people could dance to, but still a contemporary song recorded in a contemporary way. Even the ballads now have to be contemporary, not that standard lush arrangement with swelling strings, because otherwise people will say, "Here we go again."

'We're trying to do what Tina Turner did with *Private Dancer*. Though her problem was the opposite, her image was very raw. She was doing funky clubs, so they had to make her more commercial. For me it's the other way around.

'I love to sing. I love all kinds of music, I want to record all kinds. In order to do this you have to have hits. I'd like to do special albums: a late-night album with songs like *My Funny Valentine*, a gospel album, a fifties rock and roll album. But the record companies will not go for me doing an album of authentic Christmas carols. Not until I'm back in the charts.'

The problem Tom Jones was faced with was the same that had dogged him since the early seventies. Before then it did not matter what he sang. It was a hit because he sang it. Since then the songs had only worked when they struck the right note with the public.

Despite licensing *Kiss* to open the album, the Jive album *At This Moment* (*Move Closer* in the States) had not been able to continue the momentum. The album only made it to number thirty-four in the UK, while the first single *Move Closer*, a cover of Phyllis Nelson's 1985 number one, scraped up to number forty-nine. Subsequent releases failed to chart at all. A succession of hot young producers all failed to recreate the Art of Noise buzz. Whether it was the low budget or simply the choice of material – neither Chris de Burgh's saccharine *I'm Counting on You* nor a stripped down, emasculated *(I Can't Get No) Satisfaction* worked – is hard to say. Listening to the album, people felt that Tom's heart was not in it.

'The production of the album was soft. It was good but not great,' Tom lamented.

Jones's career was almost schizophrenic. While American youth was at least aware of who Tom Jones was, there was no way of capitalising on this without a hit album. In the USA hit singles were seen as marketing tools for racking up album sales, and Jive had not had the marketing muscle, or budget, to break the record. Tom continued to work the casino circuit, because that bankrolled his whole operation. That audience did not buy records by the new, improved, modern Tom, they wanted the old, sweaty Tom.

Having ignored Britain for fifteen years, it now became the focus for the reinvention of Tom Jones. Mark's reasoning was that, if Tom could come back in Britain, then he could re-export him to the States.

The situation was helped by Linda. The success of *A Boy From Nowhere* led to Tom spending three months in Britain, and, after her mother died in June 1987, Linda determined to spend more time with her family. There was a big family reunion at Christmas 1988, after which Linda announced she was going to stay on with her sister Rosalind until Tom came over to tour in April. When he arrived, he phoned her from London.

'I said to her, "I'm here," and her answer was, "Yes, but how busy are you going to be?" I had to admit I was very busy, so she decided to stay down in Wales,' said Tom. 'During the tour we stayed at the Holiday Inn in Cardiff, and when I was ready to leave, she wasn't. I said to her, "Is it the hotel, or is it Wales?" She was more in tune with Cardiff than LA. I suggested buying an apartment, but she wanted a house. I wanted some land and a bit of privacy, so we bought a place in Welsh St Donats, just outside of Cowbridge. It's got twenty-five acres in the Vale of Glamorgan.'

Llwynddu House was a bizarre combination of tat and mansion, two council houses knocked into one. The fields were leased off to the dairy farmer on one side and the sheep farmer on the other. 'It looks nice,' said Tom. 'My wife's sister's husband looks after the place, there is a lot of garden and a duck pond behind the house.'

However, not everybody was happy with the new arrangement. Freda Woodward was worried. She said to Tom, 'Now that you've bought this house does this mean we're moving back to Wales?' During the Christmas 1988 visit Tom had asked her, 'Ma, would you like to live here again?'

'I've lived here long enough,' was the tart reply. Even in the twilight of her years, Freda knew how to control her family. She loved living in Bel Air because it was warm. Various members of the extended family would come out every year for a month. Eventually, a compromise was reached. Tom stayed in LA, while Linda lived in Wales six months of the year – longer if she could.

'Linda can't flip-flop and fly very easily,' said her husband in November 1994. 'When she gets set into the Welsh thing, it's difficult to get her out of it, she won't travel by herself. Come

January, I have to get her out the house by turning the central heating off.'

For several years Linda spent more time in Wales than in LA. They were both there in 1989 when the news broke about the Berkery affair and Tom's DNA test. She staunchly defended her husband, saying, 'Tom has told me that he was never with her — and I believe him absolutely. He is a lovely man, the only one for me. It is ludicrous to suggest that I want a divorce. There will be no divorce. That is for the record. I don't know about any tests. I prefer to take the word of my husband. I love Tom just as much as I ever did and he loves me. And nothing that these women throw at him will ever destroy that love.'

Any chill between the two of them had evaporated by 1992. Tom, sensitive as ever, told the *Daily Mail* that his wife was undergoing the menopause. 'Linda is having the change. When things are not happening for her sexually, she tends to feel low. We both do. But do not worry about me, I can control my sexual urges. I am not about to jump on any old thing . . . though sex is very important in a relationship.

'Our relationship is still fresh because I am away touring so much. If I had a nine to five job, and I was home every evening, I think sex could get a little ordinary for us. But being continually on the road builds my hunger for Linda. And hers for me. When I get home things are very hot and sensuous. And they stay that way the whole time I'm here. The fact that we are still good together in bed is the most important part of our relationship. The sexual act is a kind of reassurance for us both. And Linda is very comforted by the fact that I still dig her.'

Spending much more time in Britain enabled Mark to involve Tom in the sort of venture he had never done before. Charity records, big multi-artist concerts (low in financial reward but high in profile) or just intriguing projects that put him into the orbit of other singers and musicians. Tom had never shirked from doing charity performances, but the scope had been small-scale, limited to Royal Variety Shows or one-off Vegas concerts. In the sixties Tom had never been that comfortable hanging out with his contemporary musicians. In the days of flower power and pretension, he had felt both inadequate and uncomfortable. By the nineties the young musicians who might have sneered the most were those who accorded him the most respect, deferred to him as an elder statesman.

In November 1988 Tom appeared alongside actor Anthony Hopkins on George Martin's musical production of Dylan Thomas's *Under Milk Wood*. On 3 June 1989 he took part in *Our Common Future*, a satellite broadcast shown in over 100 countries, which featured live performances by Sting in Rio de Janeiro and Stevie Wonder in Warsaw. Tom's performance was beamed live from Oslo in Norway.

Following the paternity suit filed by Katherine Berkery in New York, Tom kept his head down, while Mark set about finding a new recording deal. A deal was struck with Dover Records, a subsidiary of Chrysalis, the company that had bought MAM in 1984.

Dover specialised in TV-advertised compilations, whose bosses, Phil and John Cokell, were hoping to break into making direct signings with Tom.

Once again the object was to mix the commercial and the credible. The credibility came from four songs recorded with Van Morrison at London's Townhouse Studios in January 1991. 'I knew Van from the sixties, when he was in a band called Them,' explained Tom when *Carrying a Torch* was released in April, 'and in those days we all toured together on package shows. I had lost touch with him, but in January he contacted me because he had a song he thought I might like.'

The meeting of two opposite sides of the Celtic fringe

went well. Both had the same old-fashioned attitude to the studio. Van has always believed that if an album is fifty minutes long he needs about an hour of studio time, while with Tom it's two vocal takes, a maximum three per song. The four tracks written and produced by Morrison, played by his band with brisk, competitive backing vocals from Carol Kenyon, have both a cohesion and a roughness that the rest of the album recorded the previous year lacked.

The commercial came with the first single *Couldn't Say Goodbye*, penned by the Californian hit-making team of Diane Warren, the mistress of the modern rock ballad, and Albert Hammond. Like the other eight tracks, it was produced, engineered and mixed by John Hudson, who had originally stepped into the project when Terry Britten turned it down. Hudson's vision and control (he also arranged seven of the tracks, Terry Britten did the other two) were too one-paced and the choice of songs did not help. Britten and Graham Lyle's two contributions, *Fool For Rock 'n' Roll* and *Only In America*, failed to ignite Tom as they had done for Tina Turner. John Parr's *Killer On The Sheets*, whose lyrics demanded a crunching arrangement and a full over-the-top self parody à la *Delilah*, ended up with neither. Sheryl Crow, who had just been touring with Michael Jackson, appeared as part of the backing chorus on three numbers. Her name was misspelt as Sheril.

The dedication says it all, 'To Van: Thanks for making it real – you've made a happy man.' Despite good reviews, the album sold poorly, and was never released in America. But at least Tom was out promoting something. On 21 March he kicked off a twenty-five-date tour at the Apollo Theatre in Oxford. It finished thirty days later – Tom has never believed in wasting time having days off – at the Hammersmith Odeon in London. There was even an entire issue of *Omnibus*, a BBC2 Arts programme, devoted to Tom. Finally he was being taken seriously.

Then Mark risked it all. In March 1991 Tom agreed to appear on Comic Relief.

The idea was for Jonathan Ross to introduce Tom, singing head-to-head against Theophilus P. Wildebeeste, and viewers were asked to vote which of them was the God of Sex. Theophilus, the creation of English comedian Lenny Henry, was a brilliant caricature with his overstuffed codpiece, spray-on black leather trousers, strutting about with the complete certainty that he was the sexiest singer ever to draw breath. There was the possibility that Tom could fall flat on his face, leaving the audience wondering what the hell was going on, and the organisers trying to bring the curtain down.

Mark trusted his father's performing skills. He was not disappointed. Tom's performance on *Can't Get Enough of Your Love* was judged to a T. He came on looking the part, his red nose stuck firmly on his crotch, matching Theo grind for grind, lingering look for look and smouldering note for note. But after a couple of minutes, Tom began to take control. By stretching the phrases, hitting and holding the high notes a fraction longer, he wrested it away from being a comic turn into a remarkable performance of extreme power and intensity.

Lenny Henry was impressed. 'We actually did a version that is really strong. Tom rocked at the end when the joking was over and he had to sing the last bit of it. I asked him later, "How do you hit the high notes and keep the power?" Tom just said, "Bite at it." When we were singing together I was watching him and he sings from the crotch. I think he should go for a balls-out r&b album.'

Except for a summer performance at Cardiff Arms Park as a soloist with the World Choir, a 7,000 massed male-voiced choir accompanied by the four bands of the Irish, Welsh, Scottish and Coldstream Guards, Tom confined his live British appearances to two benefit concerts. For a man who had never previously shown much interest in matters political or ecological, Kurdish refugees and Amnesty International must have seemed an interesting choice. Both, however, were high-profile projects shown on TV worldwide.

In May, he performed in aid of the Kurds at 'The Simple Truth', a multi-media concert from Wembley Arena in London, arranged by Conservative politician, novelist and self-publicist Jeffrey Archer, which was broadcast by MTV. Tom's backing band included Pink Floyd guitarist Dave Gilmour, and the other artists included Lisa Stansfield, Sinead O'Connor, INXS, Paul Simon, Whitney Houston, M.C. Hammer and Gloria Estefan. In December, he performed at 'The Big 30', a celebration for the thirtieth anniversary of Amnesty International. Again assisted by Gilmour and his band, Tom opened and closed the show, setting a hot pace for Seal, Daryl Hall, Lisa Stansfield and KLF to follow.

His final collaboration of 1991 was *The Ghosts of Oxford Street*, a new Christmas production conceived and directed by punk impresario and former Sex Pistols' manager, Malcolm MacLaren. Tom was cast alongside Sinead O'Connor, Happy Mondays, Kirsty MacColl and the Pogues. He sang two songs within the context of the story, including *Nobody Knows You When You're Down and Out*, which was produced by Dave Stewart of the Eurythmics.

These various projects were to bear immediate fruit the next year when Tom made a new TV series. Many of the names were to appear as guests on *The Right Time*.

'So many years have gone by of me doing the same thing,' said Jones, explaining why he was doing a new TV show. 'I've done Vegas, I've done this, I've done that. I've been so busy, I've lost track a bit. You always think there's plenty of time. But then when you get older you think, "I could have done that, I should have done it when I had the chance." Now I want to cut through the bullshit and get back to basics. I want to do something I really care about, that I'm really passionate about . . . music.'

In the early nineties British TV companies had lost much of the entrepreneurial flair that had led Lew Grade to handshake a deal with Gordon Mills. Networks were controlled by bean counters, not programme makers, so commissioning editors were now obsessed not just with ratings but with targeting specific age groups and income brackets so as to attract the advertising. With profit the name of the game, they thought safe rather than radical, so every successful innovation spawned instant imitators. At Central, who had taken over the old ATV franchise, they liked the idea of doing a new Tom Jones show.

He appealed, so the reasoning went, to both the grannies and the young, which made him ideal for Saturday night prime-time viewing. What Central really wanted was *This is Still Tom Jones*, where Tom wore a bow tie and did duets with Shirley Bassey and the Pet Shop Boys. Mark, however, had different ideas. He wanted a credible music show to capitalise on Tom's new lease of life as a serious artist.

The Right Time was made by TV 21, Graham Smith's production company, for Central. The director was a young Irishman called Declan Lowney, who had his first break directing the Eurovision Song Contest from Dublin in 1989 and had also directed Tom's concert video *Live at this Moment*. On paper, Declan looked a nice, safe choice. In fact, he was youthful, energetic and came with a rock-orientated, creative aesthetic, rather than from a traditional light-entertainment background. He later went on to direct *Father Ted*, Channel 4's iconoclastic, surreal comedy about three Irish priests.

Each of the six forty-minute shows was budgeted at £180,000, not a great deal more than Jon Scoffield's budgets from twenty-five years earlier. They were all shot over a four-week period at Central's Nottingham Studios. All the shows were recorded live, using a band fronted by drummer Gary Wallace. (Tom was impressed, and later used a lot of the musicians for his UK band.)

'*The Right Time* was a compromise show,' said Smith. 'As producers, we had to find a compromise position that satisfied Mark's desire to do something credible, but which also satisfied ITV's demands for something that wasn't wildly esoteric. All the recordings were live.

'As Tom is the world's most easy-going guy, all the creative input was driven by Mark, with us following closely behind. Tom did have power of veto over numbers and guests. We spent weeks trying to get Jerry Lee Lewis for him.'

The mixture of guests was certainly eclectic: soul legends Stevie Wonder and Sam Moore (the surviving half of Sam and Dave), blue-eyed soul masters Joe Cocker and Daryl Hall, anarchic country singer Lyle Lovett, Pink Floyd guitarist Dave Gilmour, Cyndi Lauper, an American chanteuse with a zany fashion sense, Irish traditionalists the Chieftains, Bob Geldof, Al Jarreau, Mica Paris and Curtis Stigers, balanced against current pop stars with pretensions, such as EMF, Shakespear's Sister and Erasure.

The show that had the musicians and technicians most excited was when Stevie Wonder arrived. There was no time to rehearse, as Stevie was only available for one day. The band had routined a lot of his material in advance, but the show was unscripted. Like an old-fashioned jam session, everyone went into the studio and played while the cameras rolled. The result was very impressive.

Tom has always loved singing with other vocalists blessed with a good pair of tubes. With Cyndi Lauper, no shrinking violet herself, they produced a riveting *River Deep Mountain High*, while Daryl Hall did a storming version of *Me and Mrs Jones*.

'In those situations you could see this quiet competitiveness come through,' said Smith. 'He wasn't going to be fazed by anybody. There might have been matching vocal pyrotechnics, but he certainly held his own with everyone. He knew he still had it in droves. For EMF we had a very young audience who invaded the stage. A lot of artists wouldn't like that. When this sixteen-year-old kid launched himself on to Tom's back in the joy of the moment, Tom was totally cool, laughing.'

'He conserved his voice, which is one reason he's a two-take guy. He's not a person who wants to over-rehearse. Off duty, Tom was quiet. For someone of his stature he is one of the least egocentric people I have met.'

Musically it was hard to fault *The Right Time*. It had energy and showcased Tom's abilities perfectly. In England it was screened at 10.30 on Saturday nights and later on VH-1 (MTV for grown ups) in the States. Yet the show lacked sparkle and, more importantly, the raunch that has been a part of the Jones performance since he discovered how to move his pelvis.

What ultimately prevented *The Right Time* from becoming a long-running series was Tom's personality as the host. TV is not his natural medium, because he is not a spontaneous man. His appearances on chat shows work because the questions have been agreed and polished in advance. Over dinner he is an affable, amusing and interesting companion. But once the camera is rolling or the tape machine running, he becomes more guarded and reverts to pre-rehearsed stories. (Which is why the same Tom Jones stories and stock quips crop up again and again.)

'At times doing *This is Tom Jones*, Tom looked like a cardboard cut-out of himself,' said Smith. 'That hackneyed delivery was of its time and place, which you can't do these days because the audience is far too sophisticated for it. When working on links for Tom, we had to pare them down to the absolute bone, so he was comfortable with what he was saying, and people would believe it. We had to make sure that he appeared to know what he was talking about.'

In June, immediately after the recording sessions for *The Right Time*, Tom was invited to perform as the 'special guest' at

Glastonbury. After some twenty-six years, the Glastonbury Festival of Contemporary Performing Arts, held on a farm near the mystical town in Somerset, has evolved from a mudbath for a few score hippies into the largest festival in Europe. Using up to four stages, the festival showcases a mixture of contemporary and alternative artists with more mainstream performers. One of their most successful innovations had been to introduce less predictable old stars to a younger audience. Tony Bennett had been a huge success in 1991. In 1992 Tom Jones was the next logical choice.

'After we finished recording we all got on the bus and went straight down to Glastonbury,' said Smith. 'It was very hot, very relaxed. Tom Jones came on and people literally converged from all over Glastonbury to see him. He stormed it. It was an extraordinary performance.'

It was a great moment for Jones. One of the finest of his career. The memories of adulation all came flooding back, but this time it was different. It was the music they loved, not the snake hips. Perhaps this time the youngsters would not move on again.

'I followed Van Morrison on and I said to him, "What are they like?" He said, "They're falling asleep, they need a kick up the arse." I said, "I'll see what I can do." And what a fantastic reception. I didn't expect them to even know who I was, let alone all my songs.

'I saw thousands of kids running over the hill towards the stage,' he recalled. 'These two young fellas had this banner on big poles which they lifted in the air. It said, "Tom Fucking Jones". Wouldn't it be great to use that all the time. "Ladies and Gentlemen, please welcome Tom Fucking Jones." I'd love it.

'Tom Fucking Jones, that's me.'

CHAPTER TWENTY-FIVE

SWINGING THE
LEAD

——————

D uring the filming of *The Right Time* Tom managed to upset many of his older fans. There was a deliberate policy to attract a younger audience.

'If there was one problem we had in the making of the show,' said Graham Smith, 'it was that there is a very small proportion of his older audience who are a wee bit cross they weren't allowed to throw their knickers on the stage. At that time, Mark was really trying to capitalise on the newfound credibility he'd got, and he wanted to avoid that element on that programme. It's not something you can avoid full stop, because that sector is still a massive part of his audience, people who buy the tickets for his live shows. It is important not to alienate that audience, but it was not appropriate for that particular show.'

Unfortunately, it did alienate them. On 23 May 1992 *Today* reported that fans were not being allowed in to *The Right Time* recording sessions, because they were too old. In a series of interviews, Tom compounded this PR disaster.

'My request to the girls is to keep your knickers on and listen to the songs,' he said. 'The knicker-throwing image has grown much too big. People never talked about my music, they just counted how many knickers were on the stage. It got in the way of music. People can carry on. But I'd rather they didn't. I don't want to become a caricature of myself.'

Suddenly it appeared Tom was claiming that his sexy image was all a mistake, and that he had never enjoyed it. It damaged his musical credibility. 'In the late seventies I suddenly saw myself turning into a buffoon,' he said. 'I kidded myself that it was just fun and games, but I knew deep down that it was taking away from the musical ability I have always had.'

This upset a large number of the older fans. Bringing (clean) underwear, single roses or large bunches of flowers to the front of stage was part of the Jones ritual, the equivalent to the laying down of gifts on the altar. It was not the first time the new regime at Tom Jones Enterprises had upset the fans.

Over the years Tom had always been very good to his fan club, making sure that good seats were reserved for them at his concerts, and letting many backstage to meet him after a show. Backstage gatherings generally resemble a free for all scrimmage, in which the star stays hidden in his inner sanctum and prefers to talk only to select friends and business associates. To be fair, Tom has always been different. Once he has showered, he has always been very gracious and charming to his visitors. He is a natural at the 'meet and greet', exchanging a few words with each person, signing autographs and posing for photographs. For a die-hard fan, a few words from their idol has a remarkable knock-on effect. Everybody in the fan club hears about it. The problem is they all want the same chance.

To a certain extent the new management wanted to protect

Tom. They also wanted to encourage new younger fans. Some of the front seats at Ballys were filled by young girls, recruited in the casino by members of the band, and placed up front, so Tom had some younger flesh to play to. Some of them were invited back to meet the man himself. Naturally, the older fans noted this and started to complain.

At the time of Gordon's death there had been seventy-five US fan clubs, loosely affiliated, and co-ordinated by Annie Toomaru. Two weeks after Gordon died Annie was sacked and Donna Woodward took over responsibility for the fan clubs. It soon became apparent that the new organisation wanted to impose a more central control, and started to lay down certain rules. The first was that Tom was now to be referred to as Mr Jones. In 1989 a letter was sent out. It began, 'To all fan clubs', and announced that it would 'outline our new policies'. Policy number one was enough to get the fans up in arms.

It is not a Fan Club's natural right to demand a backstage visit with their performer. If your motivation for being a club is based on a personal moment with the artist, then your motivation is wrong. Contrary to what you may hear, very few artists ever visit with their fans, due to a tremendous demand on their personal schedules, of which you have no knowledge, nor should you speculate in this area.

Your main function, should you choose to continue in your endeavours, is to support the artist in his endeavours, by word of mouth, by radio station call-ins, and record purchases. This is what matters to Mr Jones, and it is your efforts in these areas that he appreciates most. It is nobody's business who gets backstage, or for what reason. The decision on backstage visits is entirely the prerogative of Mr Jones and his management.

However, the bite was at the end. 'We are now in the process of reorganising the fan clubs to create a more cohesive and effective group.'

> We do pay attention to your letters and calls, and we take many of your comments and suggestions into consideration. To all those who keep the right perspective, we thank you for your many efforts . . . we thank you for your many forms of support. But there are also criticisms that have come to us that reveal pettiness, selfishness and a warped sense of 'understanding' of Mr Jones's business, and it is most annoying for the management to have to spend time with these 'issues'. In our restructuring of the clubs, we will try to help you focus on what is important, and what is most appreciated by all involved.

This letter stated how Tom Jones Enterprises was going to be dealing with the American fan clubs in the future. In 1989, when corporate restructuring and centralising were all the rage, it made perfect business sense: bring the fan clubs all together and use them as a uniform lobbying group to push Tom's records. Secondly, it helped the recruitment of new younger members, who could be used to show how Tom was attracting a younger audience. Fine in conception, but it missed two major points.

Fan club members were not corporate wage slaves. They gave their efforts for free. The letter insulted many fans. It showed a considerable disdain for people who had worked for years promoting Tom in their own way. The fan clubs had contributed $3,500 to buy Tom his star on the Hollywood Boulevard Walk of Fame. Now they were being told their presence was not required. They felt that Tom was cutting himself off from his old fans because he did not wish to be reminded of how old he was.

It appeared that the management had forgotten one of the fundamental rules of stardom, the *tabula rasa*. Tom meant something different to each fan. He was all things to all women. So what if some of the fan clubs had become inward looking, tea party gossipy circles for a small group of ageing fans? If they want to sit in their rocking chairs, making quilts of Tom in Vegas, that is their prerogative.

In 1994 when asked if he would like to stop playing Vegas, Mark admitted, 'Yes I would. It's a great place, but I'd love to stop for a period, stop the routine. The nature of Tom Jones is that he's not routine. He plays there eight weeks a year, and it does help with costs.'

In the brave new world that was Tom's second lease of life, there was room for both the old and the new to co-exist in harmony. But Mark had not realised it yet and, as ever, Tom was happy going along with the ride. The relationship between Tom and his fans has taken some bashes in the last decade. The infamous letter still rankles as Donna is sometimes described as 'the Daughter-in-Law of Darkness'. The centralisation has now reduced the number of official fan clubs to just one. America's Tom Terrific Fan Club is run by Margaret Mariotti, who guards Tom with the unquestioning devotion of a trained pitbull. The rise of the Internet had led to dozens of unofficial websites, varying in quality but not in their loyalty. Links between them and Tom Jones Enterprises are limited in the extreme which the fans find deeply frustrating.

Yet there is a part of Tom that still relishes contact with his public and he can be very generous with his time as this account from a fan, who wishes to remain anonymous, attests: 'On 29 May, 1997 Tom was performing at the Big Bear Arena in Sault Saint Marie, Michigan. My mom, sister and myself had front row seats at the fabulous concert and afterward tracked him down at a small hideaway restaurant in the Kewadin casino where a folding wooden screen separated Tom from the rest of us. He was sitting in a private room with his tour manager, Lloyd Greenfield, and an adorable young female companion (no older than twenty-four). I asked the waitress to take my camera back and take some pictures if possible. Well, when she came back and said we could go back and visit with Tom I just about fainted. Somehow I managed to put on a fresh coat of lipstick and floated back to his dinner table. He was looking just fabulous and smelling fabulous. He wouldn't tell me the name of his cologne but did say it was only sold in Vegas.

'We stayed with him for about forty minutes. Talked about how much we all loved *The Lead*, how much he disliked Engelbert Humperdinck, and that my fantasy of twenty-five years had finally come true. I sat as close to him as I could possibly get and held his beautiful muscular arm with a gorgeous hairy hand attached. I kissed him several times smack on the lips. We had him undo his shirt down to his navel and took pictures in various poses. His chest is so fine and hairy I wanted to lick it. I rubbed his chest with my hand and had a rush. He is more charming than I ever thought he would be, although they had drunk a couple bottles of wine before we arrived so he was feeling no pain.

'I took his wineglass, silverware and he autographed a white napkin for all of us. His little chick "model" girlfriend was very cordial and let us do whatever we wanted to him (without taking his clothes off). She was beautiful and seemed to adore him. I told her I hated her very much and she had better appreciate what she had. You know how they say the day you get married or have kids is supposed to be the most special day of your life? Well not for me. That night was and has changed me forever. I stared at the ceiling all night and didn't sleep a wink. I was in a trance.'

The height of kitsch cool was achieved when Tom appeared

as himself on Fox's animated TV hit *The Simpsons*. Tom was kidnapped and forced to serenade Marge Simpson with *It's Not Unusual*.

The word had spread out from Glastonbury, and Tom's subsequent five-week British tour was a sell-out. His gig at London's trendy Town & Country Club in Kentish Town was recorded for what was intended to be his first live album for twenty-three years, but it has never been released.

Tom began 1993 with a brace of charity records. First was a stirring version of the Beatles' *All You Need is Love*, produced by Eurythmics' Dave Stewart for Childline, a British charity which provides telephone support for children suffering from physical or sexual abuse. The song reached number nineteen in the charts. Next was a raucous cover of the Rolling Stones' classic *Gimme Shelter*, with alternative rockers New Model Army, released on the independent label Food Records in March, designed to benefit Shelter, the national UK charity for the homeless. That made number twenty-three.

None of Tom's new recordings had been released in America since the Jive album. Business continued as usual. Wisely, following the fan club furore, there had been no attempt to enforce the 'no knickers' edict on American audiences. Tom adopted an altogether smarter ploy. When they appeared on the stage he simply ignored them, instead picking up flowers and thanking the donor. Along with his looser fitting, less overt stage clothes – the Jones appendage was no longer rampantly visible – the message started to get through.

Mark still had his designs. In February 1993, VH-1 aired *The Right Time*. People started to take notice, realised there was more to Tom than a wiggle. One of the first was shock-jock Howard Stern, whose outspoken radio show, which insulted everybody regardless of race, sex or creed, was essential listening. Tom, with his prehistoric attitudes to women, both politically incorrect and a notorious stud, was Howard's kinda guy. Howard loved Tom, especially when the singer sprang a surprise on him by singing a cappella with a black gospel/rap group.

Stern even stopped his constant heckling to exclaim, 'Damn, you're good.'

'Either Sting or Trudie Styler heard that Howard Stern show and asked if Tom could come do their rainforest benefit concert at Carnegie Hall in May,' said Mark. 'It was a lovely invitation.'

It certainly was. Tom shared the bill with James Taylor, George Michael, Sting, Bryan Adams, Herb Alpert and Tina Turner. Tom was the surprise sensation of the evening, with only Tina matching him for power and exuberance.

'The benefit started out as a bit of a joke, doing maybe two numbers, then I ended up doing more,' admitted Tom. 'I opened with *It's Not Unusual*, which was Sting's suggestion, because he wanted to play bass on it. Then I did Al Green's *Take Me to the River* and two Otis numbers, *Try a Little Tenderness* and *(Sitting on the) Dock of the Bay*. I have a competitive streak, so I just sang like I always do. It went tremendous.'

The audience was packed full of record industry bigwigs. Not A&R grunts working at the club face, but the guys who wielded the real power and the fat cheque books. Most of them were old enough to vaguely remember how big Tom had been long before *Kiss*, but what impressed them was how good he still was. Being on the bill with Tina Turner, who had reinvented herself for a mass audience only a few years earlier, helped the equation take shape. The scales fell away from their eyes, to be replaced by dancing dollar signs.

The next morning Mark Woodward's phone started ringing. Sony, A&M, Capitol, Mercury and Warners. 'I got calls from everybody, but I didn't want him signed for the wrong reasons. The most intriguing call came from John McLain at Interscope.'

Interscope was a label owned by Jimmy Iovine, perhaps the most successful record producer of the eighties. Iovine had produced massive albums for Bruce Springsteen, Patti Smith, Tom Petty, Dire Straits, Stevie Nicks, U2, Simple Minds and the Eurythmics, before starting Interscope in 1990. Springsteen's manager Jon Landau saw Tom at Carnegie Hall. When he got home he called Iovine in Los Angeles and told him, 'You've got to sign Tom Jones. I just saw him and he stole the whole show.'

When he was urban music director at A&M records, John McClain had put Janet Jackson together with production team Jimmy Jam and Terry Lewis. In 1985 Janet was a slushy wannabe going nowhere in the teen market. In 1991 she signed a $50 million deal with Virgin Records, at the time the most lucrative contract in recording industry history. That was the sort of makeover Mark was looking for.

Interscope appeared to be the answer to his dreams. It was licensed through Atlantic Records — part of the huge WEA conglomerate — so proper distribution was guaranteed, while maintaining the personal touch of a small label. Unlike Jive or Dover, it had the money to make a proper contemporary album and market it up into the charts. And Interscope was so *hip*. The label roster included rappers Dr Dre and Snoop Doggy Dogg, industrial noise merchants and critical darlings, Nine Inch Nails, and hitmakers 4 Non Blondes and Blackstreet.

'Jimmy Iovine understood,' said Mark. 'He asked both of us what we wanted to do. He told us, "I want to do what you want to. You guys know what you are doing," which is very unusual in the record business. It's an artist-driven label.'

Except that throughout his career Tom Jones has been the one who has been driven. Others have always made the decisions. *The Lead and How to Swing It* was Mark's project. Best of all, it gave him access to the best songwriters and producers.

'The hardest thing was finding songs,' he lamented. 'You think it would be easy, but there are so many bad songwriters out there making millions. I wasn't getting the A stuff.

'It has taken eight years to get to this point. I hope I've done it without alienating Tom's established audience. Maybe they don't know it, but as you get older you tend to get a bit of tunnel vision, don't look at things so wide. People of any age love to be stimulated, and that's what Tom always did for people.'

No expense was spared. The album cost over $1 million. Mark listened to everything: boombox fodder, hip-hop, rap, swingbeat and Euro dance numbers, plus proven songwriters. They demoed nearly thirty songs to choose the twelve that actually made it on to the record.

The album starts with *If I Only Knew*, produced by Trevor Horn. It opens with a scream, continues with a rap and ends with the vocal climax of a wild animal in heat. When Tom performed it live on the *David Letterman Show*, the host gasped, 'What the hell was that?'

The eleven other songs and the contemporary producers drafted in to make *The Lead and How to Swing It* resulted in an eclectic mix, perhaps too eclectic. There were obvious attempts to make a big ballad hit out of Diane Warren's *I Wanna Get Back with You*, which featured a duet with Tori Amos. Yazoo's 1990 hit *Situation* was given a makeover by neo-hippy and former Killing Joke bass player Youth. Blackstreet's Teddy Riley aimed to capture swingbeat on *Something For Your Head* and *Fly Away*. *A Girl Like You* was produced by U2 veteran Flood, after Tom listened to Nine Inch Nails and said, 'Who's responsible for that noise?'

The cover pictures by David LaChapelle were, in hindsight, a serious mistake. Tom wears a string vest, through which one can see a perfect six-pack abdomen, and polyester blue pants. He is screaming. His hair looks unnaturally touched up. Next to him stands Barbarella as navvy – a girl in a silver bikini and hard-hat operating a jackhammer. The inside sleeve has Tom in a scarlet PVC suit in front of a Manhattan skyline obscured by dry ice. His eyes are pleading, 'Let me out of here.'

The intention was to create radical, in-your-face, space-age images. The whole concept comes over as contrived, modern for its own sake. It is also high camp.

Not so, insisted Tom, who chose the picture himself. (Twenty years earlier he had rejected a whole session by Harry Benson because it made him look gay. Tom has no problem with gay men as long as they don't try anything on him.) His choice in clothes has always been a trifle suspect, preferring the glitz to the sober. 'It's a striking concept. This is a new album, a screaming album, a hip commercial album, that's hard and blows. I thought the picture summed it up.'

Jimmy Iovine had great hopes for the album, claiming, 'Tom Jones is an animal. A rocker, a great singer. Kids love him! This record will be big on MTV, clubs and radio. Tom Jones represents to young people the kind of vibe they want when they get older.' Unfortunately, the sales failed to live up to the hype.

If I Only Knew did give Tom his first British Top 20 hit since *Kiss*, but the album did very little. In America it never came close to recouping its costs. Commercially it was an unmitigated disaster but this had nothing to do with Tom. Interscope had the rap label Death Row Records, who were involved in a media controversy over lyrics that called for the shooting of police officers. Public pressure and threatened law suits against Warner Brothers led to Interscope making a new distribution deal with Universal. *The Lead* was released in the interim period and fell into the political crack. Warners did not want to spend any money working an album for the competition to reap the profits. Only across the Pacific was the album a big success. In Japan it made the international charts, and in Australia it went platinum. On an ensuing tour Tom found himself for the first time able to play multiple nights at the 15,000-seater entertainment centres.

The Lead and How to Swing It was, still is, a good record. In places, very good. But as a concept it suffered from being so determined to be up-to-the-minute that it forgot what had got Tom signed in the first place.

Singing soul music, better than any other white boy alive.

CHAPTER TWENTY-SIX

ICON TIME AT
LAST

A t the end of 1996, Tom went into the Hit Factory in New York to record an album of r&b and soul songs for Interscope. The session was produced by veteran Steve Jordan, who was the first drummer on the *David Letterman Show* and has worked with Keith Richards. Some twenty-six tracks, a combination of originals and lesser-known covers such as Wilson Pickett's *Engine Number Nine*, *Do Right By Me*, *Can't Stand up for Falling Down* and *Trick or Treat* were recorded live, with session legends such as former Parliament and Talking Heads keyboards player Bernie Worrell, guitarists Waddy Wachtel and Cornell Dupree, bassman Pino Palladino, Mavis Staples on vocals and the Memphis Horns.

Tom's interpretations of these songs show a side to his vocal talents that previously had only been glimpsed. While his voice had contracted and lost some of its elastic, sensuous range with age, it had gained in resonance and interpretation. 'It was a great feeling record,' said Mark Woodward. 'We recorded a lot of stuff, but the bottom line was that the songs were lacking, they weren't traditional r&b covers, there was a lot of original material so Interscope weren't that excited about it. At the time Tom wasn't selling a lot of records, it was difficult to launch an album of unknown, not necessarily radio-friendly, material at that stage in his career. It wasn't ever finished so the material is in a raw state; we were looking for new songs when time ran out.'

Sadly, in America the market for pure soul and r&b is ever-shrinking. Having given Tom carte blanche to record what he wanted, when confronted with the finished product Interscope could not find a single that fitted with the tight US radio formats and so declined to release the album. Timothy White, the editor-in-chief of *Billboard* magazine, was sent a tape by Steve Jordan and wrote a letter to Jimmy Iovine begging him to issue the record. Instead Tom and Interscope agreed to part ways. Tom was very disappointed. 'We were in the studio having a great time,' he said in 1997, 'making a bunch of great music and I'd get into the booth and listen back to what we were doing and it was like, "Yeah this is happening, this is the real deal." Tom has always wanted to make a real soul album. Way back in 1965 he had announced, 'What I'd really like to release is a big blues or r&b number, just to show everyone I can do it, but my manager points out the snags to me and I start thinking maybe he is right and I should stick to the kind of stuff I've been doing.' In 1966 he was offered a contract by Tamla Motown but that deal, which did not fit Gordon Mills' grand scheme, also fell through. Despite various attempts to buy the tapes from Interscope, the New York sessions remained unreleased. Among fans, Tom Jones' r&b album has attained a legendary status – his equivalent to Bob Dylan's *Basement Tapes*.

Ironically, the big-ballad voice married to hip-hop rhythms formula that Mark had tried to apply to *The Lead and How to Swing It* did work. For Engelbert Humperdinck. Enge was now managed by his son, Scott Dorsey, who applied similar principles of career reinvention. First came a single, *Fly High, Lesbian Seagull* for the cult slacker cartoon movie *Beavis and Butthead Do America*. It went platinum in 1997. He then went into the studio with the production duo Thunderpuss 2000 (aka Barry Harris and Chris Cox). *The Dance Album* was a clever mix of six re-recorded old favourites – *The Last Waltz, Release Me* and *Quando, Quando, Quando* were given new up-tempo dance floor arrangements – alongside five new songs. Unlike *The Lead and How to Swing It* the album had a focused sound and direction. It went Top 10 in America, but did nothing in Britain.

Meanwhile, in Europe, Tom's talent was increasingly recognised. In late 1994, the Chieftains' Paddy Maloney asked Tom to contribute to *The Long Black Veil*, a collaborative project which also featured Sinead O'Connor, Sting, Mick Jagger, Ry Cooder, Mark Knopfler, Van Morrison and Marianne Faithfull. Tom recorded *The Tennessee Waltz* at the Utility Muffin Research Kitchen, Frank Zappa's studio in LA. At the time Zappa was terminally ill with the cancer that was to kill him.

Tom arrived in the early afternoon just as the Chieftains were practising the little Tennessee mazurka that Moloney had composed two days earlier. The bouncy Appalachian/Celtic air brought Zappa back to life. He strolled into the studio and started changing the parts, including a new intro for the bass player and a different way of phrasing the song.

Tom was shocked at the way Zappa looked. 'He was on his last legs, that wasn't funny. He left in the middle of the session to go to the hospital to have another check up.'

Tom gave the song three different treatments. 'I sang it straight ahead at the beginning. I didn't know how to treat it and whether to sing it a little lighter because of the instrumentation. But when I listened back to it I thought, "No, I can give it some more. I can give more bite on it." Then I felt, "No I can give it a little bluesy effect. A gospel effect." I knew the instruments would take it. Then I thought maybe I should sing it more like an Irish thing. But because of the way they played I felt I could put some more weight on to it. So I did.'

That was the take used, after which the band repaired to the pool room and tucked into a fridgeful of German beer. Gail Zappa had invited her friend, actress Beverly D'Angelo over, who immediately struck up a rapport with Tom. He was booked to record *Late Night with David Letterman* the following day in New York.

'I almost missed the bloody plane,' said Jones. 'We were drinking and telling stories. It was tremendous, a great night. It's wonderful when you can record like that rather than be too businesslike or serious about it.'

Tom had cornered the British market in self-deprecation. Indeed his whole career was now so wrapped in the shiny armour of irony that it reflected straight back, blinding the unbelievers. The other 'i' word was now regularly attached to his name without a wink.

Tom Jones . . . Icon.

In 1970, when Tom was the biggest star in the world, there was an unbridgeable gap between him and rock groups, with their shoulder-length hair and flared pants, spouting ideology as the money rolled in. A quarter of a century later that barrier had evaporated. By 1995 entertainment was business, so it was acceptable for younger artists to admire Tom Jones, even seek his advice.

Luke Perry and Jason Priestley, the teen hunks from *Beverly Hills 90210*, requested dinner with Tom. They asked him how they should handle living in the white glare of sex symboldom. 'Never,' he advised them, 'never, ever believe your own publicity . . . But, lads, enjoy it while you can because it will never come again.'

From 1995 Tom made another series of forays into the movie world. The first was a guest appearance in *The Jerky Boys* – an unsuccessful vehicle for comedians Kamal Ahmed and Johnny Brennan. At least his performance singing the Lenny Kravitz hit *Are You Gonna Go My Way* gave him a new song for his stage show Then there was a remake of Carl Douglas' *Kung Fu Fighting*, recorded with the techno-punk band Rudy for the soundtrack of *Supercop*, starring Jackie Chan.

The second was a cameo role in Tim Burton's witty science fiction spoof *Mars Attacks*. Finally Tom had got to be in a movie – albeit playing himself. 'Being a singer (and not an actor),' he confessed, 'I think it's easier to play yourself than somebody else.' It has a sequence where Tom is singing *It's Not Unusual* on stage in Vegas when the casino is invaded by ray-gun crazed Martians. Tom flies a small group to safety in his private jet.

'When I was younger I wanted to do meaty roles, I wasn't interested in tongue-in-cheek stuff,' explained Tom. 'So now I've gone right over the top. I did it because I like Tim Burton. He's directed some strange movies.'

In the barely controlled mayhem of the movie Tom is one of many famous faces and, as ever, he does a very creditable impersonation of Tom Jones. Two years later he was to repeat his role as Tom Jones in Anjelica Huston's film of Brendan O'Carroll's Irish bestselling novel, *The Mammy*, renamed *Agnes Browne* for an international market. In the book, Agnes, the widowed mother of seven, dreams that one day she will dance with Cliff Richard, but for the script they changed it to Tom. This certainly appealed to Tom, who has always despised Richard's soft pop and whiter-than-God image. He was more concerned about how he would look.

'It is a small part, but crucial,' explained Donna Woodward, they couldn't do the film without it. Tom had questions, because it is set in the sixties and he is thirty years on, how they were going to portray his career when it first started. The film makers didn't want to use another character or a Tom Jones impersonator to try and pull it off and said they could film in a way that it didn't show.'

Even so, there is something staccato and unnatural about his delivery and performance.

Tom had to perform three songs (*It's Not Unusual, Green Green Grass of Home* and *She's a Lady*) at the Gaiety Theatre in Dublin and make a small speech dedicating a song to Agnes (played by Anjelica). The old gremlins returned and Tom kept fluffing his lines. 'It's these teeth,' he joked to the audience, 'they keep falling out.' Despite reasonable notices the movie failed to ignite at the box office.

A year earlier Anne Dudley from the Art of Noise had asked Tom to record Randy Newman's *You Can Leave Your Hat On* for a low-budget British movie. A brilliant comic tale of unemployed Sheffield steel workers seeking to restore their dignity by stripping in public, *The Full Monty* became a huge international hit. Appropriately, it was Tom's number which provided the soundtrack for the movie's climax. The same year he had even more fun in a television commercial for the American lingerie firm, Victoria's Secret. Herb Ritts directed, while Tom shared the spot with supermodels Helena Christensen, Tyra Banks, Stephanie Seymour and Karen Mulder.

At the Brit Awards show on 9 February 1998, Tom and Robbie Williams duetted on a medley of songs from the *Full Monty* soundtrack: *You Can Leave Your Hat On, Land of a Thousand Dances* and *Make Me Smile*. It was a showstopper that became a career enhancer for both parties.

'Everybody,' said Jones, 'went, "Fucking hell! That was great." Great for him. Great for me. Robbie says to this day that when he put his album out it wasn't going anywhere. Then we did that thing and his album took off.'

Capital Radio's 'Party in the Park' for the Prince's Trust has become one of London's most popular music events. In many ways it is like the package tours of the sixties, in that twenty artists come on for only fifteen minutes each. For newer artists, such as the Corrs, Boyzone, B*witched, and Louise, that is enough for them to showcase their best tunes. For Tom Jones it is like handing him the keys to the front door. On 5 July 1998 he gave a blistering twenty-five-minute performance in front of 100,000 people and met Prince Charles.

At the post-gig party at the Boardwalk restaurant nothing much was happening. A smattering of models and minor pop stars were hardly setting the place afire. After midnight Tom Jones walked in accompanied by Mikey Graham from Boyzone.

'Anything I can get you?' asked the PR, Richard Beck.

'Champagne, boyo,' said Jones. 'Champagne ... and lots of girls.' A bouncer was dispatched to find the latter and returned a while later with some five blondes. They snuggled up to Tom, completely ignoring little Mikey. A couple of hours later Tom announced he wanted to see the edit of the concert. Tom, ten girls and champagne turned up at the edit suite in NADS, where the hapless engineer showed Tom's performance.

One of the girls suggested going back to her flat in Maida Vale. Tom was game for that. Everyone piled into a Toyota Previa. 'Oh my God,' realised Beck, 'we have no champagne and if there is no champagne Tom isn't going to be any fun.'

Suddenly he spotted an all-night supermarket. He rushed out and talked to a bemused Asian shopkeeper who said firmly that he could not sell any champagne at that hour. 'But I've got Tom Jones sitting outside,' begged the PR, 'and I must have champagne.'

'If you've really got Tom Jones in the car and you want champagne,' replied the shopkeeper, 'he's got to come into my shop and sing for it.'

So Beck went back out and said, 'Tom, the guy won't sell us any booze unless you sing him a song.'

'No problem, boyo,' said Tom. 'Leave this to me.' So at 3 a.m. he got out of the Previa and walked into the shop singing *Delilah*, hip movements and all, never missed a note. The shopkeeper did not want to take any money as he'd just had a concert to end all concerts. So he gave Tom a bottle. And they bought a few more and it was on to Maida Vale until 7 a.m., when Tom decided it was time to return to 47 Park Street. Alone.

The announcement that Tom had been awarded an OBE (for his contribution to the world of music and entertainment) in the New Year's honours list was somewhat dampened by the simultaneous tabloid revelations that he had been enjoying himself with lap dancer Christina James. For Tom January 1999 was a series of reminders of his mortality. First Lloyd Greenfield, his American tour manager for over thirty years, died after a long illness. On Saturday 23 January, after attending the funeral in LA, Tom had a long phone conversation with Dai Perry. The pair had remained good friends, and in August the previous year Dai and his girlfriend Glynis McKenna had been Tom's guest on a holiday in America.

Two days later Dai was found dead on Graig Mountain. Perry had had a triple heart bypass operation four years earlier (local legend had it that Tom paid for the operation, which always made Dai laugh) and walked the mountain every day to stay fit.

'Mark called me on Monday and told me that Dai Perry, as we always called him, had died,' a visibly upset Tom told the *Western Mail*. 'He was taking his usual walk over the mountain where we used to play when we were kids, and he just dropped where he was. I had known Dave all my life. We were close as kids, we were close on the road. We went all over the world. We were like brothers. We got into trouble together and out of trouble together. It was a terrible shock because I was talking with him two days before and he felt great.'

Tom cancelled three concerts in New York and Connecticut

and flew over. He joined 200 mourners for the funeral at Court Chapel of Rest in Treforest, singing along with the hymns *The Old Rugged Cross* and *Cwm Rhondda*. He sent a large wreath with the inscription, 'Friends Forever. Tom, Linda and family.'

Dai's death took the last of Tom's closest friends away. Burk Zanft had died suddenly two years earlier. Zanft was a strange figure, a billionaire New Jersey plastics manufacturer with his own private plane who had decided in the sixties that he was going to be Tom's friend and so became it. The Jones entourage found Zanft and his motives peculiar for he could be acerbic and unpleasant, but Tom, as he does, welcomed Burk into his inner circle and enjoyed his company.

'Burk was the best friend he had,' said Nanci Eisner. 'I guess Burk wanted to be Tom, he was happy around him. Tom couldn't do anything for Burk because he had more money than Tom could make in ten lifetimes and he was very generous with it. They were equals.'

In comparison, the rest of 1999 was triumphant. On 9 March he picked up his OBE from Buckingham Palace, accompanied by his grandchildren. On 10 April he performed *She's a Lady*, *Green Green Grass of Home* and *When a Man Loves a Woman* at the Linda McCartney memorial concert at the Albert Hall.

With the opening of the Welsh Parliament and a boom in all things Celtic, Tom was much in demand. Soon after the OBE he made his first political statement in years, attacking Sean Connery's 'divisive' politics. 'The British Isles is small enough as it is, we don't want to make it any smaller,' said Jones, displaying renewed pride in Queen and Country. His lilting words came as his fellow Celt prepared to campaign for the SNP in the Scottish parliamentary elections. 'I'm very proud of being Welsh,' Jones said, adding hurriedly, 'but I don't want to split this island up. United we stand, divided we fall.'

On 11 April he sang with Max Boyce at Wembley Stadium before the deciding Five Nations rugby game in which Wales beat England by one point. England, the commentators noted, were decidedly shaken by the partisan crowd. On 26 May Tom played at a concert in Cardiff Castle to celebrate the opening of the Welsh Assembly. He joined Shirley Bassey, Max Boyce, Sir Harry Secombe, Shakin' Stevens, the Alarm, Bonnie Tyler, Charlotte Church and John Cale to entertain the Queen, Prince Philip and Prince Charles. His singing partners, Catatonia's Cerys Matthews and the Manic Street Preachers, both refused to play.

After twenty-five years on the road Mark Woodward was feeling the strain. Musical credibility was all very well but hit records were elusive. On the road it was gruelling, never asleep before dawn, but for a manager there is no staying in bed until mid-afternoon, no regular steam baths and long massages. There were always calls that had to be taken, deals that had to be fixed, pie-in-the-sky schemes that might unleash a hit record. All the minutiae, all the crap that comes with the job. Worst of all, for a manager there is no release through performance. That greatest drug of all is reserved for the star alone. Which is why rock and roll casualties are generally found in the entourage not on the stage.

For Mark the solution was easy. A heavy drinker since his early teens, his alcohol intake increased with the pressures of running Tom's career. His resistance to it decreased. Where once it had brought confidence, now it brought indecision. Mark had modelled his management demeanour as the opposite of Gordon's. His approach was friendly rather than arrogant, conciliatory rather than dogmatic; rather than give an outright no, he would delay, hoping that time would bring its own answer. That is frustrating enough, but when Mark was drinking it became far worse, and his reputation suffered.

Tom understood but he was never going to change his habits. If people want to drink with him that's great, if they don't that's fine too.

Mark had to do something. The first solution was to stop spending so much time on the road and to start working regular hours. In late 1996 he moved his family back to England into a large house overlooking the river in Henley-on-Thames. Any advances to Tom's career were, he reasoned, going to come out of Britain. LA, a city where status and money are all that matters, is not a good place to raise teenagers, so it was good for Alexander and Emma too. Best of all it was good for Mark, one step further removed from temptation. It was not easy, it never is, but in the summer of 1998 Mark quit drinking. It might have been coincidence but his first project was the *Reload* album.

'Mark gets a lot of flak from a lot of people,' said Guy Holmes, the head of Gut Records, 'but I think that's from when he was drinking. I'm grateful he's not, for his sake, and he has been brilliant to work with. I could not have made this record on my own. Period. My A&R skills weren't enough, it came down to Mark and me as a team. Mark has an exceptional music knowledge, he knows what Tom can and can't do.'

In 1990 Guy Holmes, who was then a successful radio plugger, chanced upon a bizarre demo made by a bald fitness instructor from south London. Unable to interest a record company in Right Said Fred's *I'm Too Sexy*, Holmes started his own record label. The record promptly reached number two in the UK, and number one in America. Gut Records was an indy label because that allowed Holmes and his partners, Don Reedman (who oversees Focus, a label which packages compilation albums) and Caroline Lewis, freedom to do what they want the way they want. Overheads are lower and profits are higher. Guy's instincts have remained commercial.

In late 1997 Tommy Scott, the lead singer with Space, an off-centre Liverpudlian pop band, came in with an unfinished demo of a song he wanted to record with Cerys Matthews, the lead singer from Catatonia. *The Ballad of Tom Jones* is about a warring couple on the verge of murdering each other until they hear Tom singing. Simultaneously a clever record and a kitsch joke, it parodied what Tom had done in the past and complimented him as a performer. As soon as the song was finished Holmes sent a copy to Tom in LA, who faxed back his thanks. The song eventually reached number four in March 1998. Tom now uses it as an intro tune for his show. A tribute record? That confirmed his icon status.

Until that song Tom Jones was just a name to the staff at Gut. Now he had lodged in their consciousness. Early in 1998 the partners were chewing the fat when Caroline Lewis said, 'I wonder what Tom Jones is doing? Maybe he could do a duet with Tommy Scott?' Within a few minutes the proposal had spiralled into something far more grandiose – a duets album with younger artists.

Through a mutual friend Holmes got in touch with Mark and Donna Woodward, who at the time was negotiating with Richard Branson's V2 Records to release the r&b album Tom had recorded for Interscope. 'I'm not going to give you my idea,' said Holmes. 'But if anything goes wrong, can we buy you lunch?'

A couple of weeks later Holmes watched the Brit Awards show. 'Bollocks,' he thought. 'Now someone else is going to do it.' Shortly afterwards, Mark, who had decided the deal with V2 'didn't feel right at the time', called Holmes and at a Japanese restaurant he gave the Woodwards his idea.

'I gave them the idea on Wednesday,' said Guy. 'Mark phoned me the following day and said, "Can you be in LA on Monday afternoon?" Mark picked me up in the afternoon and took me up to the house on Mulholland. I met Linda, met Tom and had a tour of the house. Then we sat down in the kitchen, burbling, drinking coffee – which was a big mistake – for between four-and-a-half and five hours.

'We talked about music, politics, James Brown, Frank Sinatra . . . but not about the record. I was waiting for him to bring it up. I wasn't in there as a salesman. "If he's interested," I thought, "he can ask me about it." But it was more a case of, "Who are you? What's all this about?" Tom's is a family business, and having grown up in a family business myself, I am acutely aware of what that means. Outsiders don't get in with ease, and rightly so. You have to earn respect, earn your place and the opportunity to have your own opinion.'

At the end, just as Holmes was leaving, Tom turned to him and said, 'Shall we do this then?'

'If you'd like to, I would.'

'Yeah, I'd like to, it could be a lot of fun.'

That night at dinner Holmes explained his philosophy. It would be an expensive album to make and he did not have the resources to offer a huge advance. 'You tell me what you want,' he told Mark. Mark sent through a deal memo, Guy signed it and sent it back. There was no further negotiation.

An indy label can offer a much higher artist royalty, as high as twenty per cent. From the beginning Holmes insisted that everybody gets the same royalty. Artists have very fragile egos. If Tom got ten per cent, so would the Stereophonics.

The fact that *Reload* was recorded for Gut does not mean that it is a non-commercial work. Far from it. *Reload* is ruthlessly commercial, right down to the seemingly bizarre choice of some of the artists: Zucchero – big in Italy; the Cardigans – big in Scandinavia; Barenaked Ladies – big in Canada; Natalie Imbruglia – big in Australia; German producer and remix Wizard Mousse T. One quid pro quo was the inclusion of Space (Tommy Scott specially worte two songs for the album which were first recorded, although one, *Reload* provided the album title) and the James Taylor Quartet, who both record for Gut. It was a happy coincidence that Wales had been really rocking for a few years, so Catatonia's Cerys Matthews, the Stereophonics and James Dean Bradfield from the Manic Street Preachers were logical collaborators. The Celtic fringe was further boosted by Van Morrison and Neil Hannon from the Divine Comedy, pop stars Robbie Williams and Mick Hucknall, a soul shouter in M People's Heather Small, indy cred from Portishead, and all sorts of cred from the Pretenders.

'It was not all plain sailing,' admitted Holmes. 'The chairman of one major record label said, "Over my dead body am I having my artist on this." I said, "I'm very sorry to hear that." Well, we were after signing Tom Jones, we wanted to do it. But we got them in the end. The chairman of another record company said to me, "This is not the sort of record an indy label should be making."

There were a few planned duets that never happened. All Saints suggested *What's New Pussycat?*, but Tom had no desire to re-mark his old territory, so countered with Ray Charles's *Hit the Road Jack*. The various differences of opinion inside the girl group meant that it never happened. Tina Turner, who Tom had recently described as the only female singer he would throw his knickers at, was not available. Jay Kay from Jamiroquai wanted to do Johnny Guitar Watson's *A Real Mother for Ya*. Then his bass player left and he had to rewrite, then re-record half his album. Fatboy Slim also bowed out.

The choice of songs was down to the guest artists. 'I asked each band I worked with whether they had any of their own material suitable for a duet, but most of them said they didn't have anything strong enough for my voice,' said Tom.

Neil Hannon initially suggested covering Britney Spears's *Baby One More Time*, which Tom firmly rejected. Instead they settled on Portishead's *All Mine*. Portishead, in their turn, tackled the blues standard *Motherless Child*. Holmes, with dollar signs dancing in front of his eyes, was pushing for Robbie Williams to sing Space's *Female of the Species* (which Tom plays live). 'It was a slam-dunking number one hit. The whole thing added up to a hit formula.' Instead, Robbie opted for Lenny Kravitz's *Are You Gonna Go My Way*.

'I already perform it live,' said Tom. 'It's a good raunchy encore song and gets everyone going. It's got that riff, so it feels brilliant to walk back on stage to it.'

INXS's *Never Tear Us Apart* had a more poignant memory for Tom. He had got on very well with Michael Hutchence before the singer's bizarre death in an auto-erotic accident in a Sydney hotel room. He said, 'I went to the funeral and they played *Never Tear Us Apart*, 'cos that was his favourite song that he'd recorded. That's why I did it on the album . . . with Natalie Imbruglia because, you know, she's Australian.'

I'm Left, You're Right, She's Gone, his collaboration with James Dean Bradfield, was one of the most intriguing songs. 'When I first talked to him he was gonna try and write something,' Tom told the *NME*. 'But he never came up with it. Then the word came back that he wanted to do an Elvis Presley song and I thought, "Oh great," because I know all the Elvis stuff so whatever he picks is going to be fine. Then he came up with this . . .

'It's a real old Elvis thing, y'know, Sun Records. So I listened to it and thought, "I wonder why he would wanna do a rockabilly thing?" But then, of course, I went into the studio with him and he had a totally different way he wanted to do it. And he wanted it high. Like when he said he wanted to do Elvis I thought, "Great, I'll have no trouble with the keys," because me and Elvis had about the same range. But then he did his thing and I said, "Jesus Christ, this is high." And he said, "Well *Delilah*'s high, *It's Not Unusual*'s high," and I said, "Yeah, but that's over thirty years ago!"

'I'm versatile though. I love all kinds of stuff, so I knew I could do it. Whatever these bands came back with I could handle. It wasn't a problem. But it sure was new for them. Like Kelly from Stereophonics, we did *Mama Told Me Not to Come* and his producer said, "How come you don't sing like that all the time?" '

Looking Out My Window, recorded with the jazzy James Taylor Quartet, is a particular oddity, as it was written by Tom himself. The idea for the song came to him sitting in a car on the Cromwell Road, looking out the window at the pouring rain. One of only three songs he has written, it was originally released on the B-side of *A Minute of Your Time* which reached number fourteen in November 1968 (the others were *I Tell the Sea* on the B-side of *Once Upon a Time* in 1965 and *The Words I Would Have Liked to Say* on the B-side of *Sonny Boy* in 1981, both co-written with Gordon Mills). In the early nineties the song was rediscovered by dance DJ Andy Smith, the resident disc spinner with Portishead, who sampled the drum breaks. When Tom was recording *Fly Away* and *Something For Your Head* with Teddy Riley for *The Lead* album, they were playing *Looking Out My Window* in the studio. In 1998 Smith included his remix on an album called *The Document* and suddenly all the clubs were asking, 'What is that new record Tom Jones has out?' The idea to do it with the James Taylor Quartet came from Gut.

Originally Guy felt that to get fourteen tracks that sat together and sounded like an album the project needed one producer. The first producer did not work out and nor did the second, Stephen Hague. In the end the tracks were recorded with almost as many producers as songs. This meant that certain tracks had to be recorded more than once, which added £100,000 to a recording budget already spiralling out of control. *Never Tear Us Apart* had to be recorded three times, *Baby It's Cold Outside* twice.

'We recorded Space and the Cardigans in Scandinavia, and others in studios all over London. Robbie's was a very expensive track to make. It's much cheaper to be an indy label,' said Guy. 'We make albums for sixty per cent of what a major might spend. For a major this would have been a million-pound album easily. I don't resent a penny of it. We got to the point where we thought, "If we have to spend another hundred grand to get this right we will," because you have to.'

Most of the artists were very nervous. Neil Hannon confessed, 'When I heard that voice up close, I suddenly got very nervous and had to visit the toilet.' M People's Heather Small knew Gladys Knight and the Pips' *You Need Love Like I Do* inside out, whereas Tom read the lyrics from a sheet. She told him, 'Look, when you sing with Tom Jones you come prepared.'

Natalie Imbruglia had to do one of the first sessions. She was taken aback when Tom started singing in his usual way – flat out. At the end of the take the five-foot-nothing girl looked up at him and said, 'Fuck me. I nearly fell over in the wind.' Tom realised he was smothering what was, in essence, a great voice and on the next run he held back, leaving room for her. Natalie was unhappy with the original session and volunteered to come back and redo some of her vocals.

There was the same problem when recording Talking Heads' *Burning Down the House* with the Cardigans. The song was recorded in Tore Johansson's Tambourine studios in Malmo, Sweden. Nina Persson's voice is very light and ephemeral, so to accommodate the difference, Tom sang in a very staccato manner, emphasising the syllables – 'burn-ing-down-the-house' – leaving her the space to fit into.

In some ways Tom's instinctive musical approach is better suited to the nineties. Back when he started, musicians read charts and performed the notes precisely, but young bands work on feel. 'Tom loved the rawness and raunchiness of the way the Stereophonics played. What he adores in a musician is balls, pure raw fuck it and do it,' said Holmes. 'He does it without thinking. He works on what he feels, what he loves. That is something people get from Tom. He's much nicer than I thought he would be.

'For some reason Tom is classed as an entertainer because he has always sung other people's songs, yet Frank Sinatra was a singer and an actor. Frank had a very defined idea about how his arrangements should be, so does Tom. He has ideas, but he is very diplomatic in the studio. He won't trip someone up.

'We were recording the Hogmanay TV show with Jools Holland, and they were singing *Whole Lotta Shakin' Goin' On*. It's a classic Jerry Lee number and I knew Jools had been playing it for twenty years that way. Tom was standing at the front of the piano and it didn't feel right, he was uncomfortable . . . but he didn't do what most artists do, which is throw a wobbly. He just wandered over to Jools and said, "Would you just try it a bit differently," singing him the rhythm.

'Jools tried it, and he was beaming. He was playing this right for the first time in his life. Afterwards we were in the Green Room and Jools said, "Thanks very much, but how did you know?" Tom said quietly, "I sang it with Jerry." '

For Gut *Reload* was a serious gamble. It was not just the recording costs. The marketing budget – the ads, the in-store displays, the launch party, the life-size cardboard cutouts of Tom – for the first two phases of the album campaign were budgeted at £570,000, with a further £200,000 to come. If the record did not go at least platinum (300,000 copies) in the UK they were stuffed.

Perhaps aware that this was his last big shot, Tom embarked on a prolific promotional campaign, appearing on all the right TV shows, in all the right magazines. While preparing for the *National Lottery Show* Tom was running through his questions with the host Dale Winton. Holmes warned him, 'Tom, I don't feel we're talking enough about the album.'

Live on the show Winton asked Tom, 'What have you been

doing?' Supposed to say, 'I've been singing and playing,' Tom launched into, 'I've been making an album with Catatonia, Stereophonics . . . ,' listing every artist. After Tom gave his performance he had to press the lottery button. Winton made the fatal error of asking, 'What's your favourite number Tom?'

Without hesitation the singer replied, 'One, because my new single with the Cardigans, which is out on Monday, is going to be number one.' It was so blatant that even Holmes blushed. Tom walked off stage, looked at him, winked and said, 'That all right then?'

It worked. *Reload* went to the top of the album charts. It was his first number one album since *20 Greatest Hits* in 1975. (The *Delilah* album of July 1968 is his only other album to hit the top.) Despite mixed reviews, by Christmas 1999 *Reload* had sold 500,000 copies in Britain, a further 750,000 in Europe and gone platinum (75,000 copies) in Australia. A year later sales were up to a million and a half in the UK, and a further two and a half million around the world, despite having no American release.

Over in the States, few of the artists featured on *Reload* meant anything at all so while, thanks to the Internet, American fans heard the music, most of them did not get it. Throughout 2000 there were constant rumours that Tom was preparing to record duets with various American artists – ranging from names as diverse as the Dixie Chicks and Enrique Iglesias to Janet Jackson and Tina Turner. 'I wanted Tina on the album,' he said, 'but she wasn't working at the time. Her manager said it was her down time . . . The timing was off then, but maybe not next time.' According to Gut Records, Tom will be recording tracks for an American album in the first half of 2001 with release to follow later in the year.

The magic of Walt Disney might have helped to resuscitate Tom's recording career in the USA. Tom sang *Perfect World*, the opening track for *The Emperor's New Groove* which was released in

America in December 2000. The music for the animated movie, set in pre-Columbus South America, was all written by Sting who, remembering Tom's magic performance at his Rainforest Concert, wanted him on the soundtrack.

In June his laconic PR Rob Partridge announced: 'Tom Jones is currently the best-selling British singer of the Millennium.' *Burning Down The House* had been a Top 20 hit all over Europe and number six in the UK. *Mama Told Me Not To Come* continued the good work, but the record that broke wide open was *Sexbomb*. It was the second single released in Europe but the fourth in the UK (*Baby It's Cold Outside* was a minor hit just before Christmas).

Sexbomb was a perfect Tom Jones song. Part parody, part disco anthem it was Tom singing about his public persona, tongue firmly in cheek, but delivered with all his customary power and zest. It became one of those songs that followed you wherever you travelled – in Europe, at home, on the radio, ubiquitous in clubs, weddings, office parties, school playgrounds. Newspaper columnists complained it was ruining their lives and probably frightening the horses. Many of Tom's older fans – especially in America – thought it was demeaning to their idol and at some of his Vegas shows it was greeted with a stunned, almost hostile, silence.

'*Reload* was a challenging thing to do,' said Mark Woodward. 'I'd rather have a Tom Jones record that people either love or hate than just think it's OK. That was the way with *Kiss*, thirty per cent of people thought it was a novelty record and hated it. The others bought it.

'That's been part of Tom's problem over the years, you try and please everybody and end up getting nowhere. When he started he was adventurous in his choice of recordings: *It's Not Unusual* was very different, *What's New Pussycat?* was outrageous, and *Green Green*

Grass of Home . . . well, to take a country song and do that to it. That was what fell flat, too much trying to play safe.'

Reload was a deliberate move to cash in on Tom's iconic status and introduce him to a whole new generation of fans who were not bound by the prejudices of their past. Throughout 2000 Tom toured Australia and New Zealand – where he has been a huge draw for the past decade – the festival circuit of Europe and the UK (where tickets were sold out nine months in advance). The tour was a triumph mixing new and old fans. The raw sexual power of 1970 had gone but The Voice was still there.

Whether the new fans will stick with Tom is a moot point that will be decided in 2001 with the biggest British live shows of his career – outdoor concerts in London's Hyde Park and at Cardiff Castle in July. In January he went into the studio to record the follow up to *Reload*. Initial reports suggested he was following in the grooves of *Sexbomb* and recording a dance-oriented album, consisting of original material, along with a few covers of well-known tunes. As with Mousse T, other artists have collaborated but Tom has sung all the vocals. The first single is due for September release with the album following a month later. It might be taking pandering to the kids a beat too far, but to Tom, even if they never buy another of his records, the success of *Reload* was an essential affirmation of his worth.

'Anyone who says they're not bothered about hit singles is lying basically,' he said. 'People expect me to have hits, and rightly so. I see chart action as a challenge and I tell you I do love a challenge. If I'm not having hits I want to know why. I can play to packed houses every night of my life. I should never be out of the charts.'

Perhaps the greatest compliment to the resurgence of Tom Jones came from Madame Tussaud's. The London tourist attraction is notoriously ruthless for recycling celebrities once their fleeting moments of fame have passed. In August 1999 Tussaud's commissioned a fresh model of the boy from Treforest. Their previous model Tom had been melted down twenty years earlier.

CHAPTER TWENTY-SEVEN

TOM AT SIXTY

―――――――

The Celebrity Deli on Flamingo Road is a Las Vegas institution. Kosher cooking just like Mama did in Brooklyn, set in a parking lot in the desert. Inside its Naugahyde-lined booths sit old Vegas gossips: a deliberately anonymous retired Jewish hotelier with ancient Mob connections he will never discuss; Muhammad Ali's former right-hand man; a one-time vaudevillian who was Jimmy Durante's sidekick for so long he should have a schnozz to match. On the walls are a series of chocolate box portraits of Vegas greats. There is Tom, next to Elvis and Wayne and Julio and Frank.

Like the Deli Tom Jones should be a Vegas institution. He is, after all, part of the fabric of the place, respected and admired for his longevity and consummate professionalism. Yet after thirty years playing there he is not loved by Vegas. Not the way it loves others who entered then embraced this extraordinary hurlyburly of a city – Frank and Shecky and Dean and, in his own tortured way, Elvis.

In the proliferating books about the neon city Tom Jones commands little more than footnotes. It is as though the extraordinary impact and vigour of his early performances have been diluted by over exposure.

Tom Jones never imposed his personality on Vegas, was never interested in burying himself inside the American dream. He does not live in a desert mansion surrounded by wild animals like Siegfried and Roy. He does play eight weeks a year at the MGM Grand, the shows all sell-out, and there is always a queue of expectant, hopeful fans waiting for returns. Tom's performance did not pander to or patronise the audience, the set was virtually identical to that on his British tour four months earlier, even down to singing *Female of the Species (Is Deadlier Than the Male)* which left the crowd bemused.

In Vegas Tom remains in permanent stasis, a waxworks model of what he once was. Part of the tour. Gamble, visit the Hoover Dam, get married in the Little White Wedding Chapel, see Tom Jones, gamble some more, get divorced. 'You can only go to the well so many times,' said Gene Kilroy, sadly.

His home town of Pontypridd appears to care more about the talents of the world-record-breaking rugby player Neil Jenkins (until he too moved on to richer pastures) than they do about Tom. Until recently there was no plaque on the wall outside 44 Laura Street, nor 2 Cliff Terrace nor 57 Kingsland Terrace. Nothing to mark he ever lived there. His name does at least make an appearance alongside other musical luminaries – like Sir Geraint Evans – on the wall of the Mill Street underpass. Tom might have left Ponty but in its insularity it expects the man to give first. Knowing Tom, that is never going to happen.

Initially there were plans to celebrate this sixtieth birthday with a massive concert at Cardiff's New Millennium Stadium, featuring everybody on *Reload* from Robbie and Cerys to the

Stereophonics. There were rumours of a Tom Jones Night on BBC2. Neither ever happened and instead, fresh from a sell-out tour of Australia and New Zealand, Tom celebrated at home in LA with his family.

On the morning of 7 June 2000, student Paul Dixon, who now lives in 44 Laura Street, opened the door to Lisa Rogers of Channel 4's *Big Breakfast* dressed in a towel. He did not appear unduly surprised. 'This is nothing new,' he commented. 'A coach-load of German tourists came past once and we often have people knocking on the door and asking to see around the house.'

The ensuing live broadcast rounded up a dozen of Tom's cousins, unveiled a plaque and a chicken-wire statue of Tom designed by fashion students from Newport decorated with underwear, and featured a chorus of *Delilah* sung by everyone in the street and the Pontypridd Male Voice Choir (who also have their place on the underpass wall). Amusing television, but ultimately tacky and yet another example of how the media world views Tom Jones. With familiarity has come contempt. Tom is worth more than that.

Forty years on and Jones is not bored by singing. In fact the opposite. He loves it, relishes it, attacks it with the same desire he did back when he was the biggest star in the world. It's a rare gift. There are very few singers who go on for so long unless the money goes, before the hunger does. With a fortune estimated at some £50 million Tom does not need the money. Put him in front of an audience and he gives them 110 per cent. He knows no other way.

Tom Jones needs to sing the way humans need oxygen. On Sunday 19 September 1999 the studio at London Weekend Television was packed full of famous faces attending *An Audience with Tom Jones*. A prime time hour was the best promotion the *Reload* album could want and Jones did not disappoint. But the treat came later on, long after the show had finished and the champagne in the Green Room had all been consumed. At three in the morning when Tom and Mick Hucknall, clustered round the piano like a pair of pub drunks, got down to some real singing.

Tom was like that with Elvis in Vegas. He seldom needs an excuse to sing, whether it is on a breakfast interview with Capital Radio or drinking brandy at a West End bar. One night when out with the staff at Gut Records Don Reedman started singing. That was the cue for Tom to launch into an a cappella set at three in the morning. 'He was truly happy,' recalled Guy Holmes. 'Happy because he was performing.'

Tom Jones may be the most contented superstar in the world. Secure in both his fame and, most surprisingly to many, in his marriage.

Nanci Eisner met up with them both in the summer of 1999 when Tom was singing in Westbury, Connecticut. She had not seen Linda for twelve years. 'I was with two friends from work and they could not get over how nice, friendly and open she is,' said Nanci. 'Linda was fabulous, warm, loving, thrilled to see me, and outgoing. She had no make up on, she was just wearing a sweat suit. Tom hasn't changed. Linda told me I should have gone to their hotel where I would have seen all the socks he washed out on the balcony.

'Linda is just not comfortable with a lot of people. For a long while she had a real tough time, dealing with people, the fans, the gossip, and because she doesn't look like Julia Roberts it presented a problem but I don't think she cares now. She loves their new house. I think she is as happy as any human being could be now, she seems relaxed and so genuine. Maybe in her insecurity she is secure that is who she is.'

Some things never change. During his Atlantic City concerts in July 2000, eagle-eyed fans spotted Tom at dinner, accompanied by a tall black woman on several nights in a row. On 1 September 2000, according to the *Sun*, Tom partied until dawn with singer

Andrea Harpham, thirty-six years his junior. After dining at a Japanese restaurant they were photographed outside Tramp before heading back to 47 Park Walk for champagne in his suite. Andrea denied there was any impropriety insisting, 'There were about a dozen people there. Tom was charming but I didn't fancy him. I'm not into older men.' The newspaper headline simply asked 'So Where is Mrs Jones, Tom?'

The relationship between Tom and Linda continues to fascinate after forty-four years in which he has continually strayed and she never has. His treatment of her may appear uncaring, even outrageous, yet she accepts it. He could have left, maybe in the throes of his love affair with Mary Wilson he actively considered it: but he never did. Stars' marriages are fragile things. Clint Eastwood, Robert Redford and Kevin Costner all appeared to have secure twenty-year marriages that eventually disintegrated when advancing years and temptation proved too much.

If Linda really was the downtrodden doormat she is often portrayed as, their marriage would surely have foundered years ago. He would have found somebody else younger and more interesting or she would have snapped and left. Their relationship is deeper and more complex than that.

Years ago Tom came to an accommodation with himself about his infidelities; he gave up love affairs for philandering moments. When he was at home he would be the dutiful husband. To him this made perfect sense, indeed it was a nice thing to do. They have no agreement about this for it has never been discussed. What Linda thought did not especially matter, for Tom is, as he has always been, the master in their relationship while she is mistress of their domain.

Their relationship entered a new phase when they moved house. In April 1998 Copa d'Oro was sold to Nicolas Cage and Patricia Arquette for $6.6 million. The house in Wales was also sold, a major commitment from Linda. The Woodwards paid $2.7 million for a new five-bedroom house in an enclosed guarded community on Mulholland Drive. Small by comparison (only 8,000 square feet), but with high ceilings, a pool and a great view over Beverly Hills, Linda loved it. She had a project to do where she was safe and not rattling around. Finally she was at home in LA.

In it she guards her Tom like a hawk. At his first meeting with Tom, Guy Holmes was in the kitchen while Linda sat in the other room listening. 'After I'd been there a couple of hours she came in and said, "Do you want a sandwich?" She'd obviously been listening, decided I wasn't an arsehole and she could come in and say hello. She's great, a real sweet lady, very kind, very open. When they are in the house she has Tom under control absolutely.'

The relationship between his parents even surprises Mark Woodward. He talks of how they were over at his house, behaving like they were fifteen again, bickering over mindless stuff, making each other laugh, giggling like a couple of schoolchildren at private jokes. To Mark, Linda is entirely her own woman, she does what she wants when she wants; if she doesn't want to speak she won't, if she does you can't stop her.

Yet there is a point at which Linda's idiosyncrasies, her iron determination not to change, her endemic shyness, appear to tip over the edge into neuroses. Propelled by the twin demons of her own fears and her husband's fame she lives a solitary existence in which she will do nothing for herself. Too frightened of strangers to shop for clothes or carpets and curtains for the house without him, nor will she drive or fly unescorted. Although she lives in Los Angeles, the therapy and cosmetic surgery capital of the world, she chooses to do nothing to confront her phobias or (unlike her husband) erase the bags under her eyes.

Her husband does not analyse this deeply. He tries to understand and accommodate her and never thinks to wonder if any of it is his fault. It's the way Linda is. 'I'm on the road so much that I feel that when I'm at home it's her time. Whatever she wants I'll do,' said Tom, who absolutely loathes buying soft furnishings or studying kitchen plans. 'She is a shy person and it's been difficult for her to deal with me socially. She has a fear of being alone with strange people on an aeroplane. I've told her if she's frightened of certain things she should talk to someone who would get her over it. But she won't do it.

'She is a pretty woman still. But I think women dread being older and it doesn't sit well with her. But she won't have cosmetic surgery. She has to do things in her own way. I can't tell her. She said to me recently, "Maybe you need a younger person to travel with." She meant if I wanted a younger wife she would have to deal with it. I don't need to show off with a younger woman like some men do. Whatever flings I've had have never been planned. As long as I reassure my wife that I am married to her and that nothing will alter that everything is fine.'

It may seem bizarre to tell your husband he can have a divorce if he wants but, like her refusal to do anything for herself, this is a vital part of Linda's control. She has paid a high price for his stardom. She wants for nothing and yet has only partial ownership of the thing she wants most.

Some of this is self-inflicted. Linda has not made her own friends and created her own life for when Tom was away. She has divided her life into compartments, so she is often unable to distinguish between the trivial and the important. If Tom was asked to attend a royal film premiere and Linda had in her diary that she was having her sister over for tea she would have her sister over for tea.

Because she hated seeing all those other women screaming at

her husband, she stopped going to his shows. Just as Norma Major was fundamentally uncomfortable being the wife of the Prime Minister so Linda does not want to be Mrs Tom Jones. Perhaps she understood that if she tried to be Mrs Superstar she would be destroyed by it. That the only way to retain her sense of self was to lock it away in a little box. To tell herself she is not married to Tom Jones, that she never was. When he is with her he is randy little Tommy Woodward, the boy with twinkling eyes and roving hands from Laura Street. When he goes out to work he becomes, like an actor, this superstar called Tom Jones.

Tom, too, likes it inside their private little island, the one place he can stop being Tom Jones. Because nobody ever talks to him the way she does, he would be devastated if he lost Linda. 'It is obvious when they talk to each other that there is a huge amount of affection,' said Holmes. 'It's just there, and when you have been with someone since you were a teenager, you have got to have something. I'd say they were best mates, that is the basis of their relationship, they are really good friends.'

Linda and Mark are Tom's best friends. He has never had very many friends and too many of those are dead. Jimmy Tarbuck remains a close pal, for Tom likes people who can make him laugh. Not a great joke-teller himself, nor a spontaneous teller of anecdotes, he likes to hear jokes. Tom has stacks of good acquaintances across the world. He loves hanging out with young musicians who accord him the respect his peers always have. But like Keith Richards Tom never lifts the phone, people have to call and come to him.

He is neither sad nor lonely and has few regrets. Except that he might be on tour when his mother Freda, now eighty-five and bedridden after bouts of cancer, finally slips away.

Tom never loses his temper. He used to get into fights when he was drunk, but otherwise remains preternaturally calm. He cannot get angry. He has been in tight control of his emotions for years, a process begun in his TB cell and cemented by Gordon Mills. This can make him appear reserved, cold and self-centred for all the charm and courtesy he displays.

Vernon Hopkins still does not understand why Tom Jones treated him the way he did. Part of him dreams of the time Tom will say, 'I'm sorry.' He thought it had come when he was pushed to attend a concert of Tom's in 1989. He sat around in the dressing room until Tom started to reminisce, not about the good old days of the Squires but about Gordon Mills and how much he missed him. Because Vernon had been there he must understand. It did not occur to him that Vernon loathed Gordon.

Judged by star standards, which he should be, Tom Jones is a good employer. In the early days he paid poorly but he always treated his staff as fellow human beings, was never rude or abusive in public. He will carry his own suitcases if that is the difference between catching the plane or not. He does not throw tantrums or blame others when things go wrong. While they worked for him, both Chris Ellis and Chris Montgomery were treated as family, privy to both the secrets and the lies. While they worked for him they were his friends and he trusted them. For Tom once they left they ceased to exist, became non people. That is hard for anyone to accept. Yet Tom appears to find it hard to understand that they might want to tell their version of his truth.

By their very nature stars are inordinately selfish. That is one reason for their success. Tom is utterly self-centred yet strangely without ego. Even during the superstar madness when all around were losing their heads Tom kept his. From the time that *It's Not Unusual* rocketed up the charts Tom understood he had found his destiny. He was a singer. A great singer. It was what he was born to be.

'There's an old movie called *The Light in the Piazza* with this girl, played by Yvette Mimieux, who will always have the innocence of a sixteen-year-old,' said Nanci Eisner. 'She reminds me of Tom. There is a childlike quality about Tom. It's not a "Fuck you, I'm going to do what I want" attitude. It's just he goes about his own business. Some people would say it's selfish because there is an unawareness of other people around, but it's not deliberate or calculated.

'He is not stupid, he has a tremendous interest in history, he had loads of books on the American Civil War and was very knowledgeable. He is very down to earth and simple. That's the word, simple.'

Tom Jones knows who he is, he is absolutely secure in himself. There is a Forrest Gump simplicity about him. He has boiled his life down to its basics, does not concern himself with the might-have-beens, nor agonise over things he cannot control. Aside from watching a bit of boxing he has no hobbies except sex (and that he admits is slowing down). His son takes care of business, and as long as there is some point in the day when he can get up on stage and sing and do that well and have a drink afterwards, he's happy.

He is still a night owl and sometimes in unforgiving lighting the skin on his face shows too taut and an unnatural colour, the result of too many years in the sunshine and the cuts and tucks. He moves his shoulders rather than swivelling his neck when talking to people, but he does not try to hide it, to him it is a small price to pay to be still able to do what he loves and be loved in return.

He is genuinely content with his life. Not mad. Not crazy. Not bitter at all, which is not usually the case with people who have been stars for thirty years. Aged sixty his life revolves – as it has for the past forty-five years – around the same three certainties. Singing. Sex. Family. He works very hard and relaxes with the serenity of a man who truly has no worries.

Save one. He is realist enough to know nothing, not even his Voice, lasts for ever. 'When I'm on stage that's when I shine, when

I come to life, that's what makes me strong,' he said. 'I want to sing all the time but I know that one day it's not going to be there. I dread that but I'm not scared. I hope when the time comes I can accept it, that I won't drive it into the ground like poor old Frank Sinatra using big video monitors, so he could remember the words. I really don't know what I would do if I couldn't sing any more. It would be back to Wales. I guess I'd have to take up golf,' he joked, 'go on a giant pub crawl.

'What pisses me off,' said Tom Jones, 'is that I want to do it for ever.'

EARL'S COURT, LONDON, 3 MARCH 2000

Half an hour before showtime the backstage area at the Brit Awards appeared closer to chaos than rock and pop heaven. Famous, once famous and almost famous faces belonging to actors, singers, models, comedians, managers, PRs and record company executives circled round the backstage encampment, flitting in and out of the bar. The presenters and performers were a cunning mix of the old and familiar with the young, fresh and occasionally anarchic: Martin Kemp, Vinnie Jones, Andrea and Jim Corr, Paul Whitehouse, Zoe Ball, Ben Elton, Kylie Minogue, Roger Taylor, Natalie Imbruglia, Ronnie Wood, Thora Birch, Ali G, Cerys Matthews and Robbie Williams.

Interchangeable members of 5ive wandered past with chrome engine mountings welded to their backs — more cyborg than boy band. Macy Gray kept locking herself in the ladies' loo, there was not enough room for Will Smith's eighty-strong entourage, while Ricky Martin's security flinched at every passing wave. The Spice Girls had an entire corridor of private dressing rooms, as far away from Geri Halliwell's as possible. Outside the inner sanctum, dozens of dancers in various states of undress and costume overkill milled in ever decreasing circles. Everybody ignored the rabbit run where a hundred-strong firing squad of TV crews waited behind metal barriers.

First right just inside the backstage area was the band corridor where members of Travis and the Stereophonics hopped about wondering which pair of jeans to wear. Third door on the left led to an oasis of calm – Tom Jones's dressing room door was wide open to anybody, a statement of intent and unshakeable confidence. The Voice might be approaching sixty but his nerves were still hewn from tempered steel.

In 1998, Tom Jones had come to the Brit Awards and conquered. In 2000, he returned as a winner. For a while he had been considered for the Outstanding Contribution to British Music Award – generally perceived by both the record industry and the public as a Lifetime Achievement Award and designed to honour careers that have beaten the Warhol dictum by lasting years, not minutes, and people whose songs, love them or loathe them, have become inextricably woven into the fabric of our lives. The first two choices for the award had turned the invitation down flat. Both Paul McCartney and Mark Knopfler of Dire Straits indicated that their careers had a way to go yet, thanks very much. The third choice was Tom Jones. But, the powers that run the Brits – the major record companies – were unhappy and worried that Tom could not pull the TV audience, that he would not appeal to the young and, the most heinous crime of all, that he was too old. However, Tom preemptively proved them wrong by making *Reload* for a small indy label, duetting with young upstarts and generally earning far more credibility than was good for him. He ended up being nominated for the Best British Male Vocalist and, so the reasoning went, could be held back for the Outstanding

Contribution to British Music Award for another year or two. When he does do it – and he will – he'll give the Brits the greatest finale they could ever want.

At Earl's Court, the Brits certainly got their money's worth out of Tom. He presented the Best British Female Award, walking down the stairway alongside Robbie Williams to the strains of *What's New Pussycat?* – dressed, not in leather, but almost matching well-cut, black, high-necked jackets. Tom let Robbie do most of the talking, then politely pecked Beth Orton on the cheek and returned to his seat.

But not for long. Ben Elton introduced the nominees for Best Male: Sting, David Bowie, Van Morrison, Ian Brown and Tom. There was, of course, no competition – the others have had their moment or perhaps will again. When Ben announced 'Tom Jones', Earl's Court erupted with the warmth and spontaneity, fuelled by alcohol, that only legends ever enjoy. As for Tom, he rose slowly, around him everyone was already on their feet. Guy Holmes from Gut threw his arms around the singer. Tom, never one for public displays of affection, disengaged himself from Guy with a pat on the back. He turned to Mark and shook his hand. Nothing more. He glided through the crowd, shaking outstretched hands, looking straight ahead, no emotion playing on his face. On the podium, the traces of a grin quickly buried, he said, 'This is fantastic. First of all I'd like to thank my manager, who is my son, Mark Woodward.' Then he thanked the record company and added, 'I have won a lot of awards in my career but this one tops them all.' Not completely true. Tom's last major award was his 1966 Grammy for Best New Artist but after 34 years we shouldn't quibble.

On a night where spectacle took precedence over music, what counted was not Tom's award but his performance. Geri Halliwell emerged from between a pair of giant female legs, surrounded by semi-naked dancers. Ricky Martin arrived in an ancient convertible full of bikini-clad babes while forty feet above him the cascading swirls of a dancer's giant skirt imitated a waterfall. Will Smith had an infinity of dancers, Queen and 5ive were ushered in by thunderous Kodo drummers. The Spice Girls descended like stick aliens from their white space ship. Only Travis and Macy Gray played it completely straight, letting the songs work their magic.

Tom came on with the Stereophonics to sing Randy Newman's *Mama Told Me Not to Come*, a massive hit for Three Dog Night in 1970. It was just Tom, the band, a keyboard player and three backing singers. As the keyboard intro began, Tom spoke quietly into the mike, most of his words lost in the music, 'We've got no dancers ... we've got no fireworks ... we've got no waterfalls, no explosions.'

'What are we going to do?' he asked Kelly Jones, half pleading, half teasing, referring to what had come before.

'Just sing, Tom,' replied the guitarist.

'OK.'

And so, as he has always done, he did.

DISCOGRAPHY

—————

ALBUMS

A complete Tom Jones album discography is almost impossible because so many compilation albums with similar titles have been issued. His television series from the early eighties has also resulted in a series of generally poor quality recordings flooding the market place. For a more complete discography, try the Tom Jones Visual Discography on the World Wide Web (www.txhighlands.com).

This is a list in chronological order of his official recordings. Until 1975 his records were released on Decca in the UK and Parrot in the USA. The list does not include compilations or 'Greatest Hits' packages.

1965
ALONG CAME JONES – Decca
I've Got a Heart/It Takes a Worried Man/Skye Boat Song/Once Upon a Time/Memphis, Tennessee/Whatcha Gonna Do?/I Need Your Loving/It's Not Unusual/Autumn Leaves/The Rose/If You Need Me/Some Other Guy/Endlessly/It's Just a Matter of Time/Spanish Harlem/When the World was Beautiful.

Released in the USA as IT'S NOT UNUSUAL on Parrot with *I've Got a Heart* and *The Rose* deleted.

WHAT'S NEW PUSSYCAT? – Parrot[+]

What's New Pussycat?/Some Other Guy/I've Got a Heart/Little By Little/ One More Chance/Bama Bama Bama Loo/With These Hands/Untrue Unfaithful/To Wait for Love/And I Tell the Sea/The Rose/Endlessly.

A-TOM-IC JONES – Decca, Parrot

Our Love/Face a Loser/It's Been a Long Time Coming/In a Woman's Eyes/ More/I'll Never Let You Go/The Loser/To Make a Big Man Cry/Key to My Heart/True Love Comes Only Once in a Lifetime/A Little You/You're So Good for Me/Where Do You Belong/These Things You Don't Forget.

Released in the USA with *It's Been a Long Time Coming/The Loser/To Make a Big Man Cry* deleted and *Thunderball* and *Promise Her Anything* added.

1966

FROM THE HEART – Decca

Begin the Beguine/You Came a Long Way from St Louis/My Foolish Heart/ It's Magic/Someday/Georgia on My Mind/Kansas City/Hello Young Lovers/ A Taste of Honey/The Nearness of You/When I Fall in Love/If Ever I Should Leave You/My Prayer/That Old Black Magic.

1967

GREEN GREEN GRASS OF HOME – Decca

Ghost Riders in the Sky/He'll Have to Go/Funny Familiar Forgotten Feelings/ Sixteen Tons/Two Brothers/My Mother's Eyes/Green Green Grass of Home/ Detroit City/Field of Yellow Daisies/Say No to You/All I Get From You/ Mohair Sam/Cool Water/Ring of Fire.

Released in the USA as FUNNY FAMILIAR FORGOTTEN FEELINGS with *Green Green Grass of Home* deleted.

GREEN GREEN GRASS OF HOME – Parrot[+]

Green Green Grass of Home/A Taste of Honey/Georgia on My Mind/That Old Black Magic/If Ever I Would Leave You/Any Day Now/Someday/You Came a Long Way from St Louis/My Mother's Eyes/My Prayer/Kansas City/When I Fall in Love.

TOM JONES LIVE AT THE TALK OF THE TOWN – Decca

The Star Theme/Ain't That Good News/Hello Young Lovers/I Can't Stop Loving You/What's New Pussycat?/Not Responsible/I Believe/My Yiddishe Momma/Shake/That Lucky Old Sun/Thunderball/That Old Black Magic/Green Green Grass of Home/It's Not Unusual/Land of 1000 Dances.

Released in USA as TOM JONES LIVE with *Thunderball* and *That Old Black Magic* deleted.

13 SMASH HITS – Decca

Don't Fight/You Keep Me Hanging On/Hold On I'm Coming/I Was Made to Love Her/Keep On Running/I'll Never Fall in Love Again/I Know/I Wake Up Crying/Funny How Time Slips Away/Danny Boy/It's a Man's, Man's, Man's World/Yesterday.

Released in USA as THE TOM JONES FEVER ZONE with *Yesterday* and *I'll Never Fall in Love Again* deleted and *Delilah* added.

1968

DELILAH – Decca*

Delilah/Weeping Annaleah/One Day Soon/Laura/Make This Heart of Mine Smile Again/Lingering On/You Can't Stop Love/My Elusive Dreams/Just Out of Reach/Only a Fool Breaks his Own Heart/Why Can't I Cry?/Take Me.

HELP YOURSELF – Decca, Parrot

Help Yourself/I Can't Break the News to Myself/The Bed/Isadora/Set Me Free/I Got Carried Away/This House/So Afraid/If I Promise/If You Go Away/My Girl Maria/All I Can Say is Goodbye.

Released under same title in USA with *Laura* and *My Elusive Dreams* added.

1969

THIS IS TOM JONES – Decca, Parrot

Fly Me to the Moon/Little Green Apples/Wichita Lineman/The Dock of the Bay/Dance of Love/Hey Jude/Without You/That's All Any Man Can Say/That Wonderful Sound/Only Once/I'm a Fool to Want You/Let It Be Me.

LIVE IN LAS VEGAS – Decca, Parrot
Turn on Your Love Light/Bright Lights and You Girl/I Can't Stop Loving You/Hard to Handle/Delilah/Danny Boy/I'll Never Fall in Love Again/Help Yourself/Yesterday/Hey Jude/Love Me Tonight/It's Not Unusual/Twist and Shout.

1970
TOM – Decca, Parrot
I Can't Turn You Loose/Polk Salad Annie/Proud Mary/Sugar Sugar/Venus/I Thank You/Without Love/You've Lost That Loving Feeling/If I Ruled the World/Can't Stop Loving You/The Impossible Dream/Let There Be Love.
I WHO HAVE NOTHING – Decca, Parrot
Daughter of Darkness/I Have Dreamed/Love's Been Good to Me/Try a Little Tenderness/I Who Have Nothing/What the World Needs Now/With One Exception/To Love Somebody/Brother, Can You Spare a Dime?/See-Saw.

1971
SHE'S A LADY – Decca, Parrot
She's a Lady/Do What You Gotta Do/In Dreams/Nothing Rhymed/Till I Can't Take it Anymore/Resurrection Shuffle/Puppet Man/It's up to the Woman/Ebb Tide/One-Night-Only Love Maker/You're My World.
LIVE AT CAESARS PALACE – Decca, Parrot
Dance of Love/Cabaret/Soul Man/I Who Have Nothing/Delilah/Bridge Over Troubled Water/My Way/God Bless the Children/Resurrection Shuffle/She's a Lady/Till/hit medley: I'll Never Fall in Love Again, Daughter of Darkness, Love Me Tonight, It's Not Unusual/Hi-heel Sneakers/rock and roll medley: Johnny B Goode, Bony Moronie, Long Tall Sally.

1972
CLOSE UP – Decca, Parrot
Witch Queen of New Orleans/Tired of Being Alone/Woman You Took My Life/If/The Young New Mexican Puppeteer/All I Ever Need is You/You've Got a Friend/Time to Get It Together/I Won't Be Sorry to See Suzanne Again/Kiss an Angel Good Morning.

1973
BODY AND SOUL OF TOM JONES – Decca, Parrot
Running Bear/Ain't No Sunshine When She's Gone/I Don't Want To Be Right/Since I Loved You Last/Lean on Me/Letter to Lucille/Today I Started Loving You Again/I'll Share My World with You/I Still Love You Enough/Ballad of Billie Joe.

1974
SOMETHIN' 'BOUT YOU BABY I LIKE – Decca, Parrot
Somethin' 'Bout You Baby I Like/You Make Me Smile/Till I Get It Right/Raining in My Heart/It Never Hurts To Be Nice to Somebody/Run, Cleo, Run/Make Believe World/Which Way Home/Sing for the Good Times/Right Place Wrong Time.

1975
MEMORIES DON'T LEAVE LIKE PEOPLE DO – Decca, Parrot
Memories Don't Leave Like People Do/I Got Your Number/The Pain of Love/My Helping Hand/City Life/Lusty Lady/We Got Love/Son of a Fisherman/You Inspire Me/Us.

1977
SAY YOU'LL STAY UNTIL TOMORROW – EMI, Epic (USA)
Say You'll Stay Until Tomorrow/One Man Woman, One Woman Man/Anniversary Song/When It's Just You and Me/Papa/Take Me Tonight/At Every End There's a Beginning/Come to Me/We Had It All/Have You Ever Been Lonely.
WHAT A NIGHT – EMI, Epic (USA)
What a Night/We Don't Live Here/No One Gave Me Love/Day to Day Affair/If This is Love/I Wrote This Song/That's Where I Belong/Easy to Love/The Heart/Ramblin' Man.

1979
RESCUE ME – MCA (USA)[+]
Rescue Me/Never Had a Lady Before/Somebody Out There Will/Dancing Endlessly/Dark Storms on the Horizon/What Becomes of the Broken Hearted/Once You Hit the Road/Flashback/Don't Cry for Me, Argentina.

1981
DARLIN' – Polygram/Mercury+
Darlin'/But I Do/Lady Lay Down/No Guarantee/What in the World's Come Over You?/One Night/A Daughter's Question/I Don't Want to Know You That Well/Dime Queen of Nevada/The Things That Matter Most to Me/Come Home, Rhondda Boy.

1982
COUNTRY – Polygram/Mercury+
I Don't Wanna Be Alone Tonight/A Woman's Touch/If I Ever Had to Say Goodbye to You/We're Wasting Our Time/Somebody's Cryin'/Marie/My Last Goodbye/Touch Me (I'll Be Your Fool Once More)/We Could Be the Closest of Friends/It'll Be Me.

1983
DON'T LET OUR DREAMS DIE YOUNG – Polygram/Mercury+
You've Got a Right/The One I Sing My Love Songs To/This Ain't Tennessee and She Ain't You/I've Been Rained on Too/You Are No Angel/Don't Let Our Dreams Die Young/This Time/That Old Piano/Loving Arms of Tennessee/You Lay a Whole Lot of Love on Me.

1984
LOVE IS ON THE RADIO – Polygram/Mercury+
My Kind of Girl/All the Love is on the Radio/That Runaway Woman Mine/Give Her All the Roses/Bad Love/A Picture of You/The Moonlight Hours/Still a Friend of Mine/Only a Heart Knows/I'm an Old Rock and Roller.

1985
TENDER LOVING CARE – Polygram/Mercury+
Not Another Heart Song/That's All That Matters/It's Four in the Morning/Dallas Darling/Tender Loving Care/I Can Help/A Million Times a Day/Love Burned a Hole in the Night/Still Enough of Us/Hold Me to It.

1989
AT THIS MOMENT – Jive
Kiss/What You Been Missing/Move Closer/After Tears/Who's Gonna Take You Home Tonight/(I Can't Get No) Satisfaction/I'm Counting on You/At This Moment/Touch My Heart/Till the End of Time.
    Released in USA as MOVE CLOSER.

1991
CARRYING A TORCH – Dover Records*
Carrying a Torch/Some Peace of Mind/Strange Boat/I'm Not Feeling It Anymore/Do I Ever Cross Your Mind/Fool for Rock 'n' Roll/Only in America/Couldn't Say Goodbye/Killer on the Sheets/Give Me a Chance/Zip It Up/It Must Be You/Old Flame Blue.

1994
THE LEAD AND HOW TO SWING IT – Interscope/ZTT
If I Only Knew/A Girl Like You/I Wanna Get Back with You/Situation/Something for Your Head/Fly Away/Love is on Our Side/I Don't Think So/Lift Me Up/Show Me/I'm Ready/Changes.

1999
RELOAD – Gut Records*
Burning Down the House – The Cardigans/*Mama Told Me Not to Come* – Stereophonics/*Are You Gonna Go My Way* – Robbie Williams/*All Mine* – Divine Comedy/*Sunny Afternoon* – Space/*I'm Left, You're Right, She's Gone* – James Dean Bradfield/*Sexbomb* – Mousse T/*You Need Love Like I Do* – Heather Small/*Looking Out My Window* – James Taylor Quartet/*Sometimes We Cry* – Van Morrison/*Lust For Life* – Pretenders/*Little Green Bag* – Barenaked Ladies/*Ain't That a Lot of Love* – Simply Red/*She Drives Me Crazy* – Zucchero/*Never Tear Us Apart* – Natalie Imbruglia/*Baby, It's Cold Outside* – Cerys from Catatonia/*Motherless Child* – Portishead.

* Not released in USA
⁺ Not released in UK

EXTENDED PLAYS

Very much a sixties phenomenon, *Record Retailer* published a separate EP chart from March 1960 to November 1967. Some of the tracks appeared on US albums.

1965

TOM JONES ON STAGE (with the Squires)
Bama Bama Bama Loo/I Can't Stop Loving You/Lucille/Little By Little.
WHAT A PARTY
What a Party/Any Day Now/Promise Her Anything/It Ain't Gonna Be That Way.

SINGLES

Tom has released dozens of singles over the years on a variety of labels. This is as complete a resource as I can muster, with the British label and year shown. Chart placings are Top 75 in the UK and Top 100 in the USA.

		UK	USA
Chills and Fever	(Decca 1964)	–	–
It's Not Unusual	(Decca 1965)	I	10
Once Upon a Time	(Decca 1965)	32	–
With These Hands	(Decca 1965)	13	27
What's New Pussycat?	(Decca 1965)	11	3
Thunderball	(Decca 1965)	35	25
Little Lonely One	(Columbia 1965)	–	42
Lonely Joe	(Columbia 1965)	–	–
Stop Breaking My Heart	(Decca 1966)	–	–
Promise Her Anything	(Parrot 1966)	–	74
Not Responsible	(Parrot 1966)	–	58
Once There Was a Time	(Decca 1966)	18	–
This and That	(Decca 1966)	44	–
Green Green Grass of Home	(Decca 1966)	I	11
Detroit City	(Decca 1967)	8	27
Funny Familiar Forgotten Feelings	(Decca 1967)	7	49
I'll Never Fall in Love Again	(Decca 1967)	2	6*
Sixteen Tons	(Parrot 1967)	–	68
I'm Coming Home	(Decca 1967)	2	57
Delilah	(Decca 1968)	2	15

Help Yourself	(Decca 1968)	5	35
A Minute of Your Time	(Decca 1968)	14	48
Love Me Tonight	(Decca 1969)	9	13
Without Love	(Decca 1969)	10	5
Daughter of Darkness	(Decca 1970)	5	13
I Who Have Nothing	(Decca 1970)	16	14
She's a Lady	(Decca 1971)	13	2
My Way	(Decca 1971)	–	–
Puppet Man	(Decca 1971)	47	26
Resurrection Shuffle	(Parrot 1971)	–	38
Till	(Decca 1971)	2	41
The Young New Mexican Puppeteer	(Decca 1972)	6	80
Golden Days	(Decca 1973)	–	–
Letter to Lucille	(Decca 1973)	31	60
Today I Started Loving You Again	(Decca 1973)	–	–
La La La	(London 1973)	–	–
Pledging My Love	(Decca 1973)	–	–
Somethin' 'Bout You Baby I Like	(Decca 1974)	36	–
Ain't No Love	(Decca 1975)	–	–
I Got Your Number	(Decca 1975)	–	–
Memories Don't Leave Like People Do	(Decca 1975)	–	–
Baby As You Turn Away	(MAM 1976)	–	–
Say You'll Stay Until Tomorrow	(EMI 1976)	40	15
No One Gave Me Love	(EMI 1977)	–	–
Have You Ever Been Lonely	(EMI 1977)	–	–
Do You Take This Man	(EMI 1979)	–	–
What a Night	(Epic 1979)	–	–
Sonny Boy	(London 1981)	–	–
But I Do	(Polydor 1981)	–	–
Come Home Rhondda Boy	(Polydor 1981)	–	–
Darlin'	(Polygram 1981)	–	–
One Night With You	(Polygram 1981)	–	–
Touch Me	(Polygram 1982)	–	–
A Woman's Touch	(Polygram 1982)	–	–
Here Is Where the Heart Is	(Polygram 1983)	–	–
I've Been Rained on Too	(Polygram 1983)	–	–
Give Her All the Roses	(Polygram 1984)	–	–
All the Love is on the Radio	(Polygram 1984)	–	–
Tender Loving Care	(Polygram 1985)	–	–

Four in the Morning	(Polygram 1985)	–	–
A Boy From Nowhere	(Epic/CBS 1987)	2	–
It's Not Unusual (reissue)	(Decca 1987)	17	–
Born To Be Me	(Epic/CBS 1987)	61	–
Kiss	(Polygram 1988)	5	31
Move Closer	(Jive/RCA 1989)	49	–
Couldn't Say Goodbye	(Dover 1991)	51	–
Carrying a Torch	(Dover 1991)	57	–
I'm Not Feeling It Anymore	(Dover 1991)	–	–
All You Need is Love	(Childline 1993)	19	–
If I Only Knew	(ZTT 1994)	11	–
I Wanna Get Back with You	(ZTT 1995)	–	–
You Can Leave Your Hat On Movie – The Full Monty	(RCA 1997)	–	–
Burning Down the House (with the Cardigans)	(Gut 1999)	7	–
Baby, It's Cold Outside (with Cerys Matthews)	(Gut 1999)	14	–
Mama Told Me Not to Come (with Stereophonics)	(Gut 2000)	–	–
Sexbomb+ (with Mousse T)	(Gut 2000)	–	–

* *I'll Never Fall in Love Again* was a US Top 10 hit on its second release in 1969.

+ *Sexbomb* was a Europe-wide hit in January 2000 but was not released in the UK until later in the year.

INDEX